A LIVING TRADITION

KINGSWOOD BOOKS
Rex D. Matthews, Director
Candler School of Theology, Emory University

EDITORIAL ADVISORY BOARD

Ted Campbell
Perkins School of Theology

Joel B. Green
Fuller Theological Seminary

Richard P. Heitzenrater
Duke Divinity School

Henry Knight III
Saint Paul School of Theology

Mary Elizabeth Mullino Moore
Boston University School of Theology

Sam Powell
Point Loma Nazarene University

F. Douglas Powe Jr.
Wesley Theological Seminary

Karen B. Westerfield Tucker
Boston University School of Theology

Sondra Wheeler
Wesley Theological Seminary

M. Kathryn Armistead, ex officio
Abingdon Press

Neil Alexander, ex officio
Abingdon Press

A LIVING TRADITION

CRITICAL RECOVERY AND RECONSTRUCTION

OF WESLEYAN HERITAGE

EDITED BY

MARY ELIZABETH MULLINO MOORE

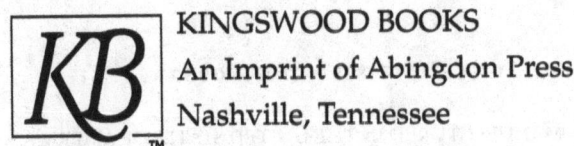

KINGSWOOD BOOKS
An Imprint of Abingdon Press
Nashville, Tennessee

A LIVING TRADITION:
CRITICAL RECOVERY AND RECONSTRUCTION OF WESLEYAN HERITAGE

Copyright © 2013 by Abingdon Press

All rights reserved.

No part of this work may be reproduced or transmitted in any form or by any means, electronic or mechanical, including photocopying and recording, or by any information storage or retrieval system, except as may be expressly permitted by the 1976 Copyright Act or in writing from the publisher. Requests for permission should be addressed to Permissions, The United Methodist Publishing House, P.O. Box 801, 201 Eighth Avenue South, Nashville, TN 37202-0801 or permissions@umpublishing.org.

This book is printed on acid-free paper.

Library of Congress Cataloging-in-Publication Data

A living tradition : critical recovery and reconstruction of Wesleyan heritage / edited by Mary Elizabeth Mullino Moore.
   pages cm
   ISBN 978-1-4267-7751-6 (pbk., binding: soft back : alk. paper) 1. Methodist Church—History. I. Moore, Mary Elizabeth, 1945- editor of compilation.
   BX8231.L58 2013
   287—dc23

2013026750

All scripture quotations unless noted otherwise are taken from the New Revised Standard Version of the Bible, copyright 1989, Division of Christian Education of the National Council of the Churches of Christ in the United States of America. Used by permission. All rights reserved.

All scripture marked KJV is from the King James or Authorized Version of the Bible. Rights in the Authorized Version are vested in the Crown. Reproduced by permission of the Crown's patentee, Cambridge University Press.

All scripture marked WEB is from the World English Bible.

This project uses the SBL Greek font and SBL Hebrew font, which are available from the Society of Biblical Literature at www.sbl-site.org.

13 14 15 16 17 18 19 20 21 22—10 9 8 7 6 5 4 3 2 1

MANUFACTURED IN THE UNITED STATES OF AMERICA

Contents

CONTRIBUTORS vii

PREFACE xi

CHAPTER 1: ENGAGING THE PAST—ENGAGING THE FUTURE 1
   MARY ELIZABETH MULLINO MOORE

CHAPTER 2: THE WESLEYAN TRADITION AND THE MYTHS WE LOVE . . 13
   RICHARD P. HEITZENRATER

CHAPTER 3: AFRICAN AMERICAN METHODISTS AND UNITED
METHODISM: A PECULIAR RELATIONSHIP OR A STRANGE AFFAIR? . . . 45
   WILLIAM B. MCCLAIN

CHAPTER 4: SUSANNA ANNESLEY WESLEY: A WOMAN OF
SPIRIT AND SPIRITUALITY 65
   W. STEPHEN GUNTER

CHAPTER 5: HOSPITALITY AS A LIVING WESLEYAN TRADITION 85
   AMY G. ODEN

CHAPTER 6: RECONSIDERING SIN: WOMEN AND THE
UNWITTING WISDOM OF JOHN WESLEY 103
    DIANE LECLERC

CHAPTER 7: A HERITAGE RECLAIMED: JOHN WESLEY
ON HOLISTIC HEALTH AND HEALING 127
    RANDY L. MADDOX

CHAPTER 8: HOLY HEART, HOLY LIFE, HOLY WORK:
WORK, VOCATION, AND CALLING IN THE WESLEYAN TRADITION 155
    REBEKAH L. MILES

CHAPTER 9: RECOVERING *LOS DESAPARECIDOS* 183
    ELAINE A. ROBINSON

CHAPTER 10: PROPHETIC GRACE: A WESLEYAN HERITAGE
OF REPAIRING THE WORLD 203
    MARY ELIZABETH MULLINO MOORE

NOTES 225

CONTRIBUTORS

W. Stephen Gunter is Associate Dean for Methodist Studies and Research Professor of Evangelism and Methodist Studies, Duke Divinity School. Previously he was the Bishop Arthur J. Moore Associate Professor of Evangelism in Candler School of Theology, Emory University. He is author or co-author of *Resurrection Knowledge: Recovering the Gospel for a Postmodern Church*, *The Limits of Love Divine*, *The Quotable Mr. Wesley*, and *John Wesley and the Netherlands*. He is also co-editor of *Wesley and the Quadrilateral: Renewing the Conversation* and *Considering the Great Commission: Evangelism and Mission in the Wesleyan Spirit*.

Richard P. Heitzenrater is William Kellon Quick Professor Emeritus of Church History and Wesley Studies Duke Divinity School. He is General Editor of the *Bicentennial Edition of the Works of John Wesley*, which includes his work in the seven volumes of *Journals and Diaries*. Known for cracking the code of John Wesley's diaries, his publications include *The Elusive Mr. Wesley*, *Wesley and the People Called Methodists*, and *Mirror and Memory*.

Diane Leclerc is Professor of Historical Theology, Northwest Nazarene University. Her books include *Singleness of Heart: Gender, Sin and Holiness in Historical Perspective*; *I am Not Ashamed: Sermons by Wesleyan-Holiness Women*; and *Discovering Christian Holiness: The Heart of Wesleyan-Holiness Theology*. She has also published numerous chapters and journal articles in areas including Wesley studies, Holiness theology, and religious women's history. She has been President of the Wesleyan Theological Society and is a member of the Wesleyan-Holiness Women Clergy Society. Leclerc lives with her husband and son in Boise.

Contributors

William B. McClain is the Mary Elizabeth McGehee Joyce Professor of Preaching, Wesley Theological Seminary. An active Civil Rights leader in Alabama, he is the recent author of *Beyond the Burning Bus: The Civil Rights Revolution in a Southern Town*. He has also written extensively on the history of Methodist traditions and on worship, including *Black People in the Methodist Church: Whither Thou Goest?* and *Come Sunday: The Liturgy of Zion*, and he co-edited *Heritage and Hope: The African American Presence in United Methodism*.

Randy L. Maddox is William Kellon Quick Professor of Wesleyan and Methodist Studies, Duke Divinity School. He is author of *Responsible Grace: John Wesley's Practical Theology*, a contributor to *Wesley and the Quadrilateral*, and editor of *Aldersgate Reconsidered* and *Rethinking Wesley's Theology for Contemporary Methodism*. He is the Institute Secretary of the Oxford Institute of Methodist Theological Studies and Associate General Editor of the Wesley Works Editorial Project.

Rebekah L. Miles is Professor of Ethics and Practical Theology, Perkins School of Theology, Southern Methodist University. Her books include *When the One You Love Is Gone*, *The Pastor as Moral Guide*, and *The Bonds of Freedom: Feminist Theology and Christian Realism*. Miles is co-editor of *Wesley and the Quadrilateral: Renewing the Conversation*. She has also written many articles on Wesleyan theology and ethics, clergy ethics, cloning and genetic ethics, work, and other topics.

Mary Elizabeth Mullino Moore is Dean and Professor of Theology and Education, Boston University School of Theology, having recently been Professor of Religion and Education and Director of Women in Theology and Ministry at Candler School of Theology, Emory University. She has contributed to many anthologies on theology and ecclesial practice in the Wesleyan traditions. Her books include *Teaching as a Sacramental Act*; *Teaching from the Heart: Theology and Educational Method*; *Ministering with the Earth*; and *Covenant and Call*, plus the co-edited *Children, Youth, and Spirituality in a Troubling World*.

Amy G. Oden is Professor of Early Church History and Spirituality, Saint Paul School of Theology at Oklahoma City University. Prior to that, she was Dean of Academic Affairs and Professor of the History of Christianity, Wesley Theological Seminary. Her publications include *In Her Words: Women's Writings in the History of Christian Thought*, *And You Welcomed Me: Sourcebook on Hospitality in Early Christianity*, *God's Welcome: Hospitality for a Gospel-Hungry World*, and contributions to the *Wesley Study Bible*.

Elaine A. Robinson is Academic Dean, Saint Paul School of Theology at Oklahoma City University, where she is also Professor of Methodist Studies and Christian Theology. She is author of *Race and Theology, Godbearing: Evangelism Reconceived,* and *These Three: The Theological Virtues of Faith, Hope, and Love.* She is also co-editor of *Considering the Great Commission: Evangelism and Mission in the Wesleyan Spirit.*

Preface

A Living Tradition is a curiously Wesleyan book, both in the title and in the making. The title suggests a tradition that continually responds to movements of God and the world. It suggests a heritage that roots itself in many soils and responds to each soil uniquely, while bearing strong continuities from the red clays of one region to the brown sands and volcanic ash of others. The title also suggests a community of people who, over time, seek to know the Holy and themselves more deeply, correct their misconceptions, act more faithfully, and repent and reform their brazen injustices and unintended wrongs.

The book itself began as a celebration of the bicentennial of John Wesley's birth. Interestingly, the exact date of Wesley's birth in June 1703 is contested, revealing the first challenge: *to recover Wesleyan traditions critically*. This challenge is unearthed throughout the book as an invitation to ponder little-known, distorted, and under-interpreted traditions. After the bicentennial event at Candler School of Theology in 2003, the book was expanded to include more dimensions of the Wesleyan tradition, though we immediately faced a second challenge: *to include sufficient diversity in one book to recover and reconstruct traditions in a range of historical moments and cultural contexts*. We chose to focus on the Western Hemisphere and mostly on the United States, recognizing the need for a larger project to trace historical recovery and reconstructions more globally and from even more points of view.

The book that has emerged represents a span of the Methodist family with contributions from diverse Methodist theological traditions (United Methodist, Nazarene, and Argentine traditions), diverse areas of scholarship (historical, theological, ethical, and practical theological), and a diverse range of issues. Issues span from hospitality to racism, from recovering John Wesley's medical concerns to discovering historical fallacies, from uncovering prophetic traditions in Wesley to discovering elements of colonialism and struggles for justice. What is revealed in this span, itself limited, is that Wesleyan theological traditions are multiple, but whole. They are held together by similarities and vivid debates regarding beliefs and values, and they are flexible, like a tree transplanted into many soils.

Wesleyan traditions are also communal. The authors of this book have been together in diverse venues, and their conversations in person and in print are larger than what appears here. Indeed, the impetus for the original book arose from Candler School of Theology, Emory University, and I thank the former Dean Russell Richey for his ingenuity and energy in initiating the project. The Wesleyan community is seemingly an itinerant one, however, even today. Two of the Candler faculty who participated in the project from the beginning, including myself, are now serving in other United Methodist theological schools; other contributors have similarly moved in recent years. The conversation is thus not geographically centered, but it continues to honor the living tradition, even as conversation partners move.

I add one last personal word: sorrow for delays in the final production of this manuscript, caused by personal circumstances combined with other circumstances beyond my control. Having been involved in five years of intensive family care, I delayed my own final work on this book and am deeply regretful. Without justifying my flaws, I do recognize that the situation reveals one more insight into the Wesleyan tradition—a continual engagement of tradition in relation to the vicissitudes of earthly life, combined with a determination to bring seeds to full flower. Perhaps, I should have set the project aside or passed it to someone else, but my passion for it was palpable, and I hope that the reader will experience similar passion in the reading.

The authors collectively appreciate the communities that have nourished and challenged us, as well as Russell Richey, who mentored the early phases of the book, and Rex Matthews, who mentored the book into its final form. Thanks also to people who read parts of the manuscript and made editorial suggestions or tracked down missing references, including Erin Maddox McPhee, Josey Bridges Snyder, and Amanda Sawyer. The collective authors are grateful to the many communities and people who made this book possible, and we hope the book contributes to deeper understanding of the Wesleyan tradition as alive and moving. Our larger hope is that the "people called Methodist" will accept the challenge to rediscover, reclaim, re-question, and reconstruct that tradition so it will contribute ever more strongly to ecumenical theological discourse and to life on this planet.

CHAPTER ONE

ENGAGING THE PAST—ENGAGING THE FUTURE

Mary Elizabeth Mullino Moore

The first four decades of the twenty-first century mark many anniversaries for the Wesleyan movement, posing a critical question. Where does the Wesleyan legacy point its inheritors today, especially as we near the end of the movement's third century? The quadricentennial of John Wesley's birth in 1703 and Charles Wesley's in 1707 were significant, but they did not mark the birth of a movement. In one sense, it was already born in its historical and cultural antecedents; in another sense, it was not born in its unique Wesleyan way until many years later. John Wesley dated the origins with the founding of the Holy Club in 1729, and another significant marker is John Wesley's Aldersgate experience (to be celebrated again in 2038). Anniversaries invite attention to the shared historical roots and identity of people called Methodist. More profoundly, they invite close examination of the Wesleyan-Methodist legacy—its theological substance and its historical trajectory. One aspect of that legacy—Wesleyan ways of doing theology—has been highlighted in recent years but never fully engaged by a community of scholars working together from diverse fields of expertise and diverse concerns for the future. The present volume gives opportunity to *engage in critical recovery and reconstruction of the Wesleyan theological legacy in relation to theological concepts and Christian practices in the present world and with intention to point directions for the future.*

The authors are a community of scholars who engage the Wesleyan legacy with critical scholarship and urgent questions from the contexts in which people now live, particularly questions regarding social holiness and Christian practices. To that end, the authors focus on historical figures (John Wesley, Susanna Wesley, Harry Hoosier, and Richard Allen), historical developments (such as the ways in which African Americans appropriated Methodism), and theological themes (such as holistic healing, work and vocation, and prophetic grace). The purpose is not to provide a comprehensive historical and theological coverage of the tradition, but to *exemplify approaches to historical recovery and reconstruction that follow appropriately the mentorship of John Wesley and the living tradition that has emerged from his witness*. What marks this volume as unique and urgent is its focus on recovery and re-visioning. It is not a straightforwardly historical study of the Wesleys or of Methodism.[1] It is, rather, a record and analysis of the *living* quality of the Wesleyan tradition and the ways in which that tradition now points to the future.

In this book, we consider the fruits and challenges of Wesleyan-Methodist scholarship as we near the close of the third century, pausing to reflect on where we are and where we are going. The goals of this first chapter are (1) to explore the significance of critical retrieval and reconstruction for theology, and (2) to identify promises and challenges in a praxeological approach to Wesleyan studies. As to the first, the volume is clearly historical and is continuous with recent scholarship in Methodist theological studies, though with unique accents. As to the second, the explicitly praxeological character of this book has been less fully developed in Methodist studies heretofore, though with some stunning examples in a similar genre.[2] To extend this dimension of Wesleyan scholarship, the authors focus attention on human action and the theological logic thereof. They draw critically upon John Wesley and other leaders of the past as mentors for theological activity (*how* we do theology); they engage with issues critical to people at the present moment of time; and they project futures for Wesleyan scholarship and Christian life. The book is thus historical, theological, contextual, and practical—an effort to embody John Wesley's practical divinity.

SIGNIFICANCE OF CRITICAL RETRIEVAL AND RECONSTRUCTION

The very process of passing on a heritage, or sharing the stories of John and Charles Wesley and the "people called Methodist," is an act of re-telling, re-interpreting, and re-shaping. The heritage is amplified and reshaped as people live within it, as larger cultural movements shape it and are shaped by it, and as scholars and adherents actively structure and restructure the historical memories. Inevitably, periods of intense remembering raise questions about historical fact and neglected or distorted traditions. The act of remembering also raises issues regarding the interpretation, coherence, practices, and adequacy (or inadequacy) of a tradition.

The process of remembering, with its attendant values of critical retrieval and reconstruction, is shared by most (if not all) religious and cultural traditions of the human family. People rehearse the past for many reasons, and the reasons have been studied through the lenses of diverse disciplines and religious traditions. The essays in this volume reveal passions that motivate and inform historical remembering in the broader religious literature and in Wesleyan studies. Five purposes for remembering are particularly evident in recent work, and this book engages and extends these purposes in distinctive ways.

Define a Unique Tradition

One purpose for remembering is to *define or develop the uniqueness of a community's particular tradition in the encounter with other cultures*. This dynamic is exemplified in the tradition-defining and tradition-forming processes among Jews after the conquests of Alexander the Great released powerful currents of Hellenization in the eastern Mediterranean region.[3] Similar efforts to define identity emerge throughout history, particularly in chaotic cultural contexts. Anthropologists argue that communities often act reflexively to establish a definitive culture as an effort to counteract the fragmentation of cultures.[4]

Such processes of self-definition can be seen as major accents in some chapters of this volume; the accent is present to some extent in every chapter. Consider Amy Oden's writing on hospitality in the Wesleyan tradition. Oden identifies the virtue and values of hospitality within the Wesleyan tradition, continuing her studies of hospitality in early Christianity. In so doing, she establishes a defining perspective on the heritage, which can then be claimed and expanded by inheritors of that tradition. Given the present urgency for the human family to engage more adequately with immigrant peoples on all continents, and to engage more respectfully with strangers in a highly mobile world, Oden's recovery of hospitality in Wesleyan traditions reveals a way to define the tradition in relation to its past and, simultaneously, in relation to challenges of the present world. This provides a way for Wesleyan peoples to identify themselves as people of hospitality and to find clues for their present self-reflection and public action.

Other authors in this volume have similarly stressed Wesleyan themes as central to Wesleyan identity today. Accents include the theme of evangelistic fervor and social inclusiveness in the chapter by William McClain; the theme of holy work and vocation in the chapter by Rebekah Miles; and the theme of prophetic grace in my chapter. One sees similar efforts in recent Wesleyan scholarship, in which authors seek to define the tradition with historical thoroughness and conceptual coherence in relation to an identifying mark. One such work is Theodore Runyon's description of Wesley's theology in relation to creation and New Creation, a work that has been amplified by others.[5] Other efforts focus on love, as in Albert Outler, Stephen Gunter, and the collection of Bryan Stone and Thomas

Oord.⁶ Still others emphasize the priority of attending to and valuing the lives of people living in poverty—an accent of Richard Heitzenrater, José Míguez Bonino, Joerg Rieger, John Vincent, Harold Recinos, and many others.⁷ These are all efforts to name distinctive, identity-forming emphases in the Wesleyan traditions, informed by historical remembering.

Rediscover and Reclaim Religious Beliefs, Values, and Practices

A second purpose of historical remembering is to *rediscover and reclaim religious beliefs, values, and practices* in a rapidly changing world. The discovery process can be seen in explorations of particular aspects of the past or in the retrieval of historical resources for contemporary practice. It often takes the form of intellectual discovery or rediscovery, as in the retrieval and analysis of underplayed aspects of the sixteenth-century Lutheran tradition.⁸ The discovery process also includes the study of newly emerging forms of ancient traditions, as exemplified in a recent study of Sufism in its encounters with global Muslim cultures.⁹ Further, the discovery process is generating research and publications on the salutary effects of traditional religious practices, such as recent studies of Buddhist compassion meditation in the treatment of depression and other neuroendocrinological problems.¹⁰ Finally, an increasingly popular form of discovery is the expanding effort to provide popular, salutary access to religious values and practices, whether from Buddhist, Celtic, Benedictine, or other traditions.¹¹

The effort to rediscover and reclaim is evident in this volume. Randy Maddox, for example, highlights Wesley's attention to physical healing as a distinctive accent for recovery. Maddox describes Wesley's approach as having theological integrity, biological wisdom, and ministerial importance. Drawing on *Primitive Physick* and other works, he argues that John Wesley valued healing and health as a gift from God and viewed acts of healing as a compassionate response to human hurt. Further, Maddox uncovers social dimensions of poor health and healing in Wesley, like the role of poverty in obstructing healthy life practices and accessibility to healthcare. Maddox argues that these Wesleyan accents need to be recovered during an era when healthcare needs are crying for more attention by Christian communities.

Other chapters in this volume similarly accent rediscovery and reclaiming of the Wesleyan tradition. Richard Heitzenrater urges a rediscovery that is more accurate and more accountable to the historical evidence, counteracting false tales and popular misconceptions. Stephen Gunter urges rediscovery of proto-feminist strains in the tradition, and Rebekah Miles accents Wesley's penetrating perspectives on work and vocation. Miles makes a case that the Wesleyan tradition illumines the role of work in human life and advocates holistic life patterns. She argues that

Wesley's own work habits are a poor model, but "the larger pattern of his life, particularly his reflections on work, vocation, and calling," provide a more nuanced model. Miles explicates this larger, more nuanced view and points to its implications for Christian practice today. Thus, she engages in critical rediscovery and robust reclaiming.

The goal of rediscovery has dominated the field of Wesleyan studies in recent years. The efforts are not hagiographic, to be sure. They are attempts to recover a more accurate, critical, and illuminating picture of John and Charles Wesley and the global Wesleyan movement, with its multiple institutional forms. The goal of rediscovery and reclaiming is found in such works as Richard Heitzenrater and Reginald Ward on John Wesley's diaries; Randy Maddox on Wesley's practical theology; Ted Jennings, José Míguez Bonino, Joerg Rieger, John Vincent, Pamela Couture, Douglas Meeks, and Heitzenrater on Wesley and the poor; Russell Richey, William Lawrence, Tom Frank, and Mary Elizabeth Moore on ecclesiology and ministry; Grant Shockley, Bobby McClain, and William Graveley on Methodism, slavery, and race; Melvin Dieter, Donald Dayton, and Kenneth Rowe on accents of holy living in the Wesleys and in Holiness traditions; Rosemary Skinner Keller, Paul Chilcote, and Diane Leclerc on women in Methodist traditions; Rob Weber, Elaine Robinson, Henry Knight, F. Douglas Powe, and John Sungschul Hong on Wesley and evangelism; Manfred Marquardt and Ted Weber on Wesleyan ethics and political order; and Greg Clapper, Paul Chilcote, and Sondra Matthaei on spiritual experience and formation in Wesleyan heritage. This list is a small sample; indeed, a large portion of recent Wesleyan scholarship focuses on rediscovery and reclaiming as a major purpose.[12] Naming a few works reveals the breadth of recent research aimed toward re-appropriating Wesleyan traditions.

Critique and Reconstruct Religious Beliefs, Values, and Practices

A complementary purpose of historical remembering is to *critique and reconstruct religious beliefs, values, and practices*. Many authors seek to do both reclaiming and critique in relation to one another; however, many works emphasize one or the other. The purpose of critique and reconstruction is represented by classic liberation theology, beginning with the early works of James Cone, Rosemary Radford Ruether, José Míguez Bonino, Delores Williams, Hyun Kyung Chung, and Mercy Amba Oduyoye, to name a few.[13] This literature has expanded exponentially in the past four decades. Even with the growing emphasis on liberation and the radical transformation of traditions, however, the purposes of critique and reform have played a lesser role in Wesleyan studies until more recently. The minimal attention to these purposes may be attributed to the demographics of people engaged in Wesleyan studies or the lack of public awareness of the tradition as an influence in theology and public practice beyond the Methodist and Wesleyan churches. Perhaps, also, the Wesleyan rediscovery and reclaiming work has not yet been fully done and is a necessary precursor to the more critical, reformative work. Whatever the reasons, this work is ripe for present attention and is well represented in this volume.

Most chapters in this volume have elements of critique and reform, but I will highlight two here. Bobby McClain raises a critical question to the tradition as he rehearses the history of African American peoples in Methodist communions in the United States. He asks what was the original appeal and why have so many African Americans stayed in a tradition that was oppressive to them, and especially why have so many stayed in what is now The United Methodist Church. McClain argues that the evangelistic fervor and anti-slavery stance of early Methodists in the United States drew many African Americans, slaves and free. Since that time, the road has been filled with overwhelming challenges, but the persistent presence and witness of African Americans is itself a powerful legacy, as are the critiques they have raised. Their legacy points to the urgency of inclusiveness in the contemporary church.

Diane Leclerc has similarly seen in the Methodist tradition threads to celebrate and threads to critique and reform. She finds Wesley's theology of sin, and his interactions with women, to be more complex than most interpreters have recognized. Close investigation reveals a persistent and lingering misogyny. Leclerc chooses to adopt the stance of "strategic essentialism" to critique Wesley's misogynistic view of women's sin as "inordinate affection." She finds Wesley's view of sin to be more nuanced than often recognized, but inadequate to address the fullness of women's and men's lives. Thus, she concludes with an argument that feminist theology is still needed to probe, critique, and reform Wesleyan hamartiology.

These two essays are joined in this volume by chapters by Elaine Robinson on *los desaparecidos* ("the disappeared") in Latin America and Mary Elizabeth Moore on prophetic grace. Together with the larger critical and liberatory literature in theology, these several chapters represent a newly emerging movement in Wesleyan studies. While such efforts have not been dominant heretofore, they have not been absent. One example of such effort is the collection by Joerg Rieger and John J. Vincent, entitled *Methodist and Radical: Rejuvenating a Tradition*.[14] The authors represented in that book are themselves people who have written many other essays and books that point to radicality in the Methodist movement and failures in the theologies and practices of the movement to live fully into its own prophetic heritage. Further, some of the liberation theologians who address theology more generally, such as James Cone, José Míguez Bonino, and Mercy Amba Oduyoye, are themselves part of the Methodist family. The purpose of critique and reconstruction is part of the tradition itself and, increasingly, part of research in Methodist or Wesleyan studies.

Celebrate a Tradition's Persistence and Growth over Time

A fourth purpose for historical remembering is to *reveal the persistence and diachronic movements of a tradition over time*. One finds studies of these diachronic movements in many religious traditions, such as those focused on Judaism.[15] One also finds such research in Wesleyan theological studies, especially in reviews of particular periods or regions.[16] Other research on historical trajectories focuses on particular aspects of the tradition, such as evangelism, women leaders, music, or global collaborations.[17] In all of these cases, the literature generally reveals the fullness and nuances of the focal theme, such as Methodism in Latin America or the Baltic States. It often fills gaps in earlier literature or attends to understudied aspects of the tradition, such as the study of women or of Charles Wesley and Methodist musical traditions.

Study the Complex Interactions of Traditions with Living Communities

One last purpose of historical remembering is to *study interactions between historical traditions and living communities*. This purpose is always implicit because scholars bring their own communal formation and issues to their research, often in the form of prejudgments or questions, whether or not they acknowledge and examine them. Some researchers are explicit about the purpose of studying interactions between traditions and living communities, and much recent work in religious and theological studies explores the interactions of history, culture, and local communities. These studies not only explicate differences across Christian communities and traditions, but they also reveal how the Christian faith has been transmitted and kept vital over centuries of time and miles of geographic distance. Orlando Espin states the case boldly: "Without 'traditioning'—the transmission of Christianity across generations and across cultural boundaries—there would not be a Christian religion in the twenty-first century."[18] One approach to the study of traditioning processes has been to research the complex ways in which a particular tradition embeds itself in a particular community, as in studies of traditions of Our Lady of Guadalupe embedded in communities of Mexico and New Mexico.[19] Another approach has been to bring the beliefs and practices of local communities into dialogue with the beliefs and practices of a larger movement or denomination.[20]

The interactive approach to Wesleyan studies has largely been limited to biographical, autobiographical, and regional studies, though one recent book studied United Methodist congregations as they wrestled to decide whether or not to become reconciling congregations.[21] In this work, the five congregational studies revealed complexities of living communities through ethnographic observation and analysis. The authors worked together to bring these studies into dialogue with Wesleyan traditions and the unique traditions of each congregation, revealing the interplay among unique congregations and the overarching Wesleyan values.

The clearest exemplar of such interactive study in the present volume is Elaine Robinson's chapter. Robinson explores the unique experience of Argentinean Methodists in relation to the larger Methodist movement, beginning with the reality of *los desaparecidos* across Latin America, "the disappeared," whose lives were wiped away by oppressive regimes. Robinson invokes this reality as a metaphor to probe the dynamics between Methodism in the United States (especially The United Methodist Church) and Methodism in other countries, focusing particularly on the Methodist Church in Argentina. She describes her work as "recovering *los desaparecidos* within the Methodist family itself." This effort involves her in postcolonial analysis and proposals for reconstituting ideas and practices of the center and periphery. This is clearly a critical and reformative chapter, at the same time that it is a study of the complex interaction of tradition in dominant cultures with tradition and religious life in colonized cultures.

I have identified five purposes for historical remembering, each of which is represented in this book. Whatever the purposes, however, the historical process in religious communities is a continual one of remembering and reshaping history to fit the present moment. Heritage is reshaped as people live in it, adding the textures of their complex lives into the ever-enlarging, ever-changing tapestry. This is why critical retrieval and reconstruction are significant for research and for the lives of religious peoples; they reveal dense patterns of religious life in which beliefs, values, and practices are intricately woven. The processes of retrieval and reconstruction are both generative and challenging. They are generative when they instill meaning, virtue, and hope in a people. They are challenging when researchers and people of faith face the unending, interlocking processes that do not stand still long enough to be studied and described with any finality.

CHALLENGE OF A PRAXEOLOGICAL APPROACH TO WESLEYAN STUDIES

Wesleyan studies are, as we have seen, an exercise in historical remembering for multiple purposes. Some of these purposes have been developed more fully in the past than others. The present book amplifies previous work and builds on all five purposes named here; however, it places a stronger accent on critique and reconstruction and on interactions with living communities than most previous work in Methodist studies. The present work introduces one further accent that stretches the genre of Wesleyan studies, namely its praxeological approach. The generative Wesleyan research of recent years has created a need for more robust reflection on praxeological questions. *A Living Tradition* seeks to take up this challenge. The authors are explicit about how research in the Wesleyan traditions can include a study of praxeology (science of human action) and can generate proposals for future action. In this way, as stated at the outset, the book is in the tradition of John Wesley's "practical divinity," which Randy Maddox identifies as a Wesleyan practical theology.[22]

The authors of this collection have included three elements in their analyses: reflection on Wesleyan practices, past and present; analysis of those practices with the unique disciplinary methods of each author (historical, theological, ethical, or practical theological); and projection of new directions for the practice of scholarship and Christian life in Wesleyan traditions. This praxeological approach bears much promise, but it is also challenging. I identify three particular challenges here: the humanness of John Wesley and other Methodist forebears, the enormity of critical issues in the present world, and the daunting task of projecting future action.

Challenge of Discovering, Selecting, and Critiquing Theological Mentors

One challenge is to look to John Wesley and other leaders of the Methodist movement as theological mentors, evaluated with critical and reconstructive eyes. This is really a large nest of challenges. One challenge in the nest is to discern the actual history of these figures, an issue that Richard Heitzenrater approaches directly in this volume. A second challenge is to identify the multitude of theological mentors upon whom we might draw, a challenge taken up by Bobby McClain as he identifies Richard Allen, Harry Hoosier, and others as mentors to whom people might turn today. Stephen Gunter similarly points to Susanna Wesley as a potential mentor. A third challenge is to focus on *how* these mentors of the past did theology and ministry and not just on what conclusions they offered. Fourth, modern peoples are challenged to engage critically with these figures, seeking to discern what in their lives and teaching are directly or indirectly informative for theology and practice today and what needs to be discarded or radically transformed.

A mentor is not simply someone to be imitated, but a person with whom to be in conversation and from whom to seek guidance. Mentoring is generally understood as a process by which people pass on knowledge, support, and guidance through informal communication and interpersonal relationship.[23] In the case of historical figures, such as John and Charles Wesley and other Methodist forebears, a mentor might be seen as a person whose unique wisdom or experience provides exemplification (with strengths and foibles), questions, and insights to ponder in the present age. The form of mentoring invited by this book is for readers to engage the lives and practices of historical figures as a guide to their own practices of theology and Christian life. By focusing on the life practices of these figures, we have reversed the common practice of placing forebears' beliefs and values in the foreground, and their contextual origins and actions in the background. In this book, the contextual origins and actions move to the foreground.

The present book, like most others of the last two decades, is not a hagiography of John Wesley or anyone else; however, many of the authors find the lives and teachings of certain Methodist leaders to be instructive for Christian living in the present world. As noted above, Rebekah Miles argues that John Wesley was not an ideal model of good work because he himself worked without ceasing and allowed his personal relationships to suffer. On the other hand, she finds in Wesley a theological mentor on work and vocation because his thinking and writing were more profound than his lifestyle.

Challenge of Facing Critical Issues of the Present World

A second nest of challenges is to engage Wesleyan studies in dialogue with critical issues in the present world. These may vary considerably, but the issues addressed in this book include intellectual, physical, personal, socio-political, and ecclesial ones. Richard Heitzenrater raises the intellectual issue of honesty in scholarship and historical memory. Randy Maddox raises issues of physical and psychological health in relation to Christian faith and ministerial practice. Stephen Gunter and Diane Leclerc raise issues of gender equity and gendered critique in theological, ecclesial, and ethical practice. Rebekah Miles analyzes the pressing issues of work and vocation, while Amy Oden addresses the personal and ecclesial issues of hospitality. Bobby McClain and Elaine Robinson address ecclesial and socio-political issues as they relate to one another. Both analyze social oppression within the church and larger society, recognizing that oppression in one reinforces oppression in the other. For McClain, these issues are largely racial; for Robinson, they are grounded in neocolonial power relations between North and South America. Finally, I raise issues of injustice in my chapter, focusing on theological understandings of prophecy and grace, and recognizing in the Wesleyan tradition an unnamed and largely unacknowledged accent on "prophetic grace."

Challenge of Proposing Futures in Scholarship and Christian Life

The third nest of challenges is to propose future directions for scholarship and Christian life. These challenges flow from the study of Methodist forebears and communities in this volume and the diverse forms of historical, theological, and social analysis employed. Each author approaches history in a distinctive way, corresponding with what Elizabeth Tonkin describes as the various ways by which the past enters into memory and "helps to structure it."[24] Tonkin explains that people "try to shape our futures in the light of past experience—or what we understand to have been past experience."[25] The dynamic process of historical retelling can thus take many forms—reinforcing the status quo, revising historical accounts, reshaping the present moment, or even inspiring revolution in worldviews, ethical values, or social structures.

The chapters of this book suggest significant ways of responding to the Wesleyan heritage. My proposal is to place prophetic grace at the center of Wesleyan theological reflection, thus infusing the identity and ethical action of Methodist communities with that spirit. I suggest that the biblical prophetic tradition has a sharp edge that is present but easily missed in John Wesley's words, while Wesleyan tradition has a communal emphasis that is easily missed in popular biblical interpretation. A dialogue between the two can foster a robust, communally grounded emphasis on grace infused with prophecy, and prophecy infused with grace.

Each chapter similarly offers proposals for practice. Heitzenrater advocates for intellectual honesty and meticulous care in historical scholarship, naming three important criteria for Wesleyan theological practice: historical integrity, ideological congruence, and contemporary relevance. McClain urges for honest analysis of racial injustice in the Methodist tradition, combined with renewed acts of racial justice and inclusiveness in contemporary Methodist communities. Gunter calls attention to the gendered dynamics of the Methodist movement and invites modern people to celebrate the early proto-feminist strands in their tradition. Oden makes a case for a robust practice of hospitality in the contemporary church—hospitality rooted in deep understanding of the personal and social dimensions of Wesleyan and biblical traditions. Leclerc urges a critical reading of the gendered Methodist tradition, the gendered interpretations thereof, and the ways by which a careful reading of John Wesley can be used to critique and reform the gender-denigrating dynamics in contemporary theology and church practice. Maddox proposes that people of faith learn from the gestures of John Wesley to become actively engaged in healing practices, rigorous in their social analysis of illness and health, and advocates for healthcare. Miles advocates for understanding work in relation to vocation, encouraging an approach to daily living that includes meaningful work, a full-bodied sense of vocation, and Sabbath time. Robinson advocates a restructuring and revaluing of churches in North and South America, particularly The United Methodist Church as it becomes increasingly global, with the attendant trends toward neocolonialism.

I have only touched upon the proposals that these several authors give for the future of Wesleyan scholarship and Christian life. The pages of this volume will unfold with depth and nuance as you read. As you turn the pages, the shared authorial hope is that readers will be inspired to engage in critical retrieval and reconstruction in their own distinctive theological work and in their daily life practices and public witness. The Wesleyan tradition is rich with possibilities for ever-deeper understanding and more faithful and fruitful action. We hope this book helps those possibilities become reality.

CHAPTER TWO

THE WESLEYAN TRADITION AND THE MYTHS WE LOVE

Richard P. Heitzenrater

First, let me tell the beginning of a story—a story well known to most Methodists and to many others. Most of this story will be recognizable, presenting images that are universally present in the minds and hearts of those who are familiar with John Wesley. But you should be aware from the beginning that not one sentence in this account is completely and undeniably true on the basis of historical evidence.[1]

THE LEGEND

Once upon a time . . .
Samuel Wesley, Anglican priest, was happily married to Susanna Annesley, twenty-fifth child of a dissenting preacher.[2] Their family of nineteen children made for a rather full dinner table in the parsonage at Epworth.[3] In 1703, a son was born whom they named John Benjamin Wesley, for two of his previously deceased siblings.[4] When John was six, he was miraculously preserved from a fire that destroyed their home.[5] Upon discovering that John had been rescued, Susanna knelt down with him in the front yard and gave thanks to God for saving him "as a brand plucked from the fire."[6] Her conviction that he was providentially preserved led to his self-image as one designated for a special destiny and mission.[7] She met with him every Thursday evening at 8:00 for prayers and Bible reading.[8] Trained in the classics, learned in several languages, and sophisticated in theology, Susanna was well prepared for teaching her own children and for conducting Sunday evening services for two or three hundred people packed into her kitchen while Samuel was out of town.[9]

After attending Charterhouse School in London, John became a student at Christ Church College at Oxford.[10] While John was in Wroot one summer helping his father as curate, his brother Charles started the Holy Club at Oxford.[11] When John returned to Oxford, he took over the leadership of the club, which then met regularly in his rooms at Lincoln College where he was a fellow.[12] *One of the people who met regularly with them was a student of Pembroke College, George Whitefield.*[13] *The members of the Holy Club thought that people could earn their salvation by doing good works, so they visited the prisons and helped the poor.*[14] *They were all of like mind on matters of theology and mission, following John's ideas and leadership.*[15]

The story goes on and on. Although not one sentence in this account is fully accurate and verifiable by historical evidence, much of the story has the ring of authenticity because most of the comments have been repeated so often. The story is *not true*, but it is *traditional*. Another account, all historically accurate, could be presented that would sound rather unfamiliar and untraditional. That account might include a few parts of the Wesley story that represent more recent scholarship but do not have widespread popular circulation. Therefore, they do not have the same kind of familiar ring or implicit authenticity; yet they are historically verifiable. Many of these newer statements form significant parts of a true story but are not yet a part of the traditional view of Wesley and early Methodism.

Why should we be concerned about how Wesley is portrayed or how early Methodism is described? Do the pictures of those people and events from nearly three centuries ago have any actual relevance to our present situation? My assumption is yes, at least to some degree. How we understand our roots has a great influence on how we understand ourselves, and an adequate view of our heritage is an important prerequisite to faithful living as Wesleyan Christians in the present.

Why do so many elements of the questionable or unverifiable account persist as parts of the traditional story? One would suspect that a vital tradition would depend upon both the *careful transmission* of the heritage over the years and the *suitable appropriation* of it in the present. How do these legendary parts of the tradition get started? Why do they persist as "true"? In what ways do many popular aspects of the continuing Wesleyan tradition present difficulties? Do they present a threat to the integrity of the ongoing tradition? And how does one cope with the legends that persist in our heritage?[16]

At the center of the traditional accounts of the rise of Methodism is the larger-than-life-size image of John Wesley, the founder of the movement and the hero of the story. He of course considered himself the most qualified person to chronicle the development of the Methodist revival in his day, as he once told his readers: "As no other person can be so well acquainted with Methodism, so called, as I am, I judge it my duty to leave behind me, for the information of all candid men, as clear an account of it as I can."[17] He claimed to present the "bare relation of a series of naked facts," vacant of bias.[18]

Yet in the process of telling his story, he tended to exaggerate reality, to collapse timelines, to simplify matters, to stretch the truth, to introduce ambiguity, and frequently to ignore facts in order to make points that he thought were important. The problems that he thus began to create, while telling the story of the Wesleyan movement to his liking, were perpetuated, multiplied, and magnified by successive generations of Methodists, who had an exciting story to tell and enthusiastically used many methods to convey that story. When combined with a practiced anti-intellectualism in matters of religion, a developed anti-historicism in matters of faith, and an easy credulity in matters related to saints and heroes, the story of Wesley and early Methodism all too readily slips into the realm of myth and legend.

Factors That Created the Legend

Wesley became a legendary figure in his own day. Whether intentional or not, he actually originated and lent support to some of the larger-than-life stories by his own attempts to portray Methodism in a good light.

Stretching the Truth: Distortions by Wesley

Modern readers often have difficulty recognizing Wesley's own weaknesses as a historian or biographer by modern standards of scholarship. Wesley tended to manipulate the facts to suit particular purposes. He exaggerated or embroidered events or results to his advantage. He could be free with chronology, collapsing, stretching, or switching dates to create a better story. In short, he was not trying to write accurate, objective history.

Manipulation of the Facts

In many of his autobiographical stories, Wesley was trying to make a point that was more important than maintaining faithfulness to the facts. For example, his sermon "On Redeeming the Time" was intended to point out how one might waste less time and use that time for useful religious purposes. A personal illustration in the sermon recounted an incident at Oxford when he realized how much time he wasted by not sleeping soundly through the night or rising promptly in the morning. Wesley therefore bought an alarm clock that assisted him to rise an hour earlier on four successive mornings. He thus moved back his awakening time by four hours and reclaimed that time for devotion and study, time that he had previously wasted. This anecdote makes for a very good illustration of his point. Actually, as recorded in his diary and financial accounts at the time of the events, this development occurred over a six-month span of time, which does not produce as forceful a sermon illustration as the four-day story. The main point is true, in a way, but the facts are manipulated to strengthen the story.

Wesley exhibits this same tendency to telescope time in other developments as well. His accounts of the "three rises of Methodism"—the origins of Wesleyan societies at Oxford, Savannah, and London (Fetter Lane)—are likewise telescoped or simplified chronologically. In each of those stories, he portrays himself as being a more central figure in the story than is warranted by accounts from other participants. Nearly every activity incorporated into the group of Oxford Methodists, for instance, was suggested by one of the other members. The religious society in Savannah had already begun under the auspices of the previous priest and his parish clerk. The founding of the Fetter Lane society in London was primarily the work of the Moravians, James Hutton and Peter Boehler, and the rules that Wesley lists as being in force at the beginning actually took several months to develop (during which time he was in Germany). The stories in his published journals should be seen in the light of their purpose, being more a Methodist apologetic or propaganda tool than a careful piece of history.

Wesley also tended at times to manipulate facts in order to support his own position of power within the Wesleyan movement. His successive stories over the years, telling of the origin of Methodism, shifts the number of persons involved and the date of origin depending upon the desired impact of the story. In his earliest account, written in 1732, he recounts the number as four in November 1729.[19] This number becomes fuzzy in 1742, when he refers to "three or four."[20] By 1749, his account of early Methodism focuses on "two young clergymen," himself and his brother Charles, the others having faded into the background.[21] Later, the beginnings of the story come down to one person—himself, a solitary pilgrim starting out in 1725 without companions on the voyage toward holiness (until one more joined with him in 1729, and two more at the end of that year).[22] By that time, he was in a power struggle with Charles over certain features of Methodism, such as the use of lay preachers, disagreeing over the necessary prerequisites for those preachers, the impropriety of lay preachers administering the sacraments, and the question of whether such preachers should be ordained. Charles used his allies both inside and outside of the Wesleyan world to force his brother to acquiesce to his view on these points. In this process, each brother tried to support his position of power within the movement by claiming priority in the origins.[23]

Wesley also tried at times to make a political or theological point against his opponents by stretching historical truth. When John described those first Methodists some years later, he often pointed to the unity and continuity of the early stages of the movement by asserting that all the Oxford Methodists were of a single mind. He sounds a bit like Irenaeus talking about a unified Christendom, using Paul's words as both prescriptive and descriptive: "There is one Lord, one faith, one baptism."[24] Wesley seemed less intent on historical description than on instilling the image of an earlier unified approach as the model for a later period. In fact, the letters and diaries of the Oxford group reveal a variety of positions and a tendency toward controversy, so much so that one of the rules Wesley gave them was to refrain from debating when they met. Perhaps the controversies of the later days made the differences of the earlier days pale in comparison. In any case, the description is far from accurate and can easily be misleading.

Ambiguity

In addition to intentional or inadvertent manipulation of facts to embellish certain stories, Wesley's accounts of some events at times lack clarity and create ambiguity. He at times identifies the location or timing of an event or development in a confusing way, often unwittingly. For example, Wesley's own journal, in October 1771, states that he preached at South Leigh where, forty-six years earlier, he had preached his "first sermon." This comment creates two problems. First, the ambiguity of the phrase "first sermon" might lead one to think that he meant his first occasion of preaching, whereas he is actually referring to preaching the first sermon that he ever wrote. Second, his memory was off by two years: he does not point out (or perhaps remember) that, by the time he preached that sermon at South Leigh in 1727, he had preached it eight times in the previous two years.[25] Notwithstanding those facts, a brass plaque on the pulpit of the church at South Leigh commemorates the preaching there of Wesley's first sermon the Sunday after he was ordained in 1725, a longheld tradition, unconfirmed in any contemporary documents but often repeated in Wesleyan biographies.

Wesley's autobiographical reflections also contain a note of ambiguity at other important junctures. While recounting the major events leading up to his experiences of assurance at Aldersgate, he tells of a point when the light flowed in so mightily upon him that "everything appeared in a new view."[26] This crucial moment of insight occurred upon his reading of William Law's *Practical Treatise upon Christian Perfection* and his *Serious Call to a Devout and Holy Life*. In the flow of the story, this epiphany occurred between 1725 and 1730, but he specifies no particular time for this important development. The two books were published in 1726 and 1729, respectively. So it is very hard to say precisely when this important step took place in Wesley's spiritual development—quite a contrast to the precision of his account of the event on May 24, 1738, which he says began at "about a quarter before nine."[27]

For those who like to pinpoint Aldersgate as the watershed experience in his life, Wesley makes other self-reflective statements that cast some ambiguity on the situation. For instance, in the months after Aldersgate, he includes in his journal several introspective notes that indicate his doubts about his spiritual condition, in effect saying that he wondered if he was yet a Christian. In April 1739, he introduces the story of the beginning of his field-preaching in Bristol by a reference to "this new period in my life." Then in the following years, his retrospective comments upon the important "change" that took place during this period is variously calculated from 1737 to 1739, which could include any number of important developments and fails to pinpoint any particular one.

Similar ambiguity arises from his 1781 story of the "second rise of Methodism"[28] in Georgia, which he describes in terms of founding a religious society in Savannah that met in addition to the regular services of the church. He describes that development as the beginning of Methodism in the colony, having occurred in April 1736. He at least leaves that impression by saying, "I now advised the serious part of the congregation to form themselves into a sort of little society." What Wesley actually describes as having started at that time is a group that developed in February 1737, when it started meeting in his home on Sunday afternoons. In fact, he was not even in Savannah during most of April 1736. The first Methodist group in Georgia actually began in Frederica in June 1736 and is described as such in his journal for that period.[29] The ambiguity caused by these different accounts leads to two different views of the time and place of Methodist origins in America.[30]

These instances of chronological or geographical ambiguity are relatively minor, however, compared with the theological ambiguity caused by some of Wesley's comments. For instance, while he generally holds the position that faith is the only requirement on our part for our salvation (*sola fide*), he claims, in his crucial sermon on "The Scripture Way of Salvation" (1765), that good works are "in *some sense*" necessary for salvation. By this statement, he not only antagonizes the Calvinists, who think any such statement reflects the dangerous position of "works righteousness," but he also confuses his own followers. He further explains that such works are indeed necessary but not in the same sense (only *conditionally*) or the same degree (only *remotely*) as faith, which is both *immediately* and *proximately* necessary. This ambiguous sophistry does not solve the mystery for many readers, who often ignore Wesley's attempt to modify a hard and fast fideism and thus miss one of the important theological nuances of his mature theology. The tradition persists in portraying Wesley's position on "justification by faith alone" with no qualifications. By ignoring the subtleties of "The Scripture Way" sermon, people miss the fact that Wesley also argued strongly for the necessity of good works before justification (as "fruits meet for repentance"). This important point gets lost in the truncated picture of his theology, and such oversimplifications distort the richness of his mature theological position on the "way of salvation."

Misstatement

Sometimes Wesley distorted the truth simply by getting it wrong. Just as he assigned the wrong date to his preaching at South Leigh and the wrong date to his forming a society in Georgia, so also he occasionally misdates or implies a misleading time span for other events. His journal contains several such errors, which may be the result of hasty editorial preparation or more complicated causes. For instance, in the middle of May 1743, John's journal says that Charles Wesley set out for the southwest and Cornwall, whereas Charles's journal says that he headed for the north and Newcastle.[31] In the journal for April 1762, he includes an obituary for William Grimshaw that begins, "It was at this time that Mr. Grimshaw fell asleep." Grimshaw actually died in April of the following year.[32] A similar misdating occurs in an entry for February 14, 1772, which notes that he began publishing an edition of his *Works*—a project that he actually began twelve months earlier.[33]

These mistakes by Wesley, while frustrating to the reader, are relatively inconsequential in the larger picture. However, these mistakes challenge one of the basic myths of Methodism: that everything Wesley said was true. At times, Wesley will claim that he has never changed his mind on a particular matter, when anyone who has access to his works can see where he said something quite different at an earlier or later time. Occasionally, his critics noted this tendency to express quite different points of view. One commentator in 1739 pointed out that John Wesley had promoted faith "contradistinguished" from good works in the preface to his hymnal, whereas the previous year, John Wesley (could it be the same person? he asks) pointed out that one must have faith "inclusive of all good works" in order to attain salvation.[34] Some of these instances can be explained as Wesley's nuancing and shifting of emphasis; however, in many cases, he simply changes his mind, often without acknowledging it. The result is that people today can argue over a theological issue, all quoting Wesley, but from different parts of his works.

Changes of Mind

In spite of his claim of consistency and desire for continuity on many issues, Wesley changed his mind rather substantially over the years. In some instances, the reader might not notice. For example, in his post-Aldersgate Moravian mode, he claimed that he had earlier tried to earn his salvation by doing good works while at Oxford. His later accounts might be read in such a way as to suggest that he drifted in and out of Christianity: he was a Christian at Oxford in 1727; questioned his status in Georgia in 1736; became a real Christian at Aldersgate in 1738; claimed he did not measure up as a Christian in 1739; questioned the necessity of assurance in 1747; felt like he had never properly "believed" in 1766;

and cried out to his brother, "Let me again be an Oxford Methodist," in 1772. These personal shifts in self-perception on Wesley's part, while a normal part of most people's spiritual pilgrimage, are often overlooked by readers, perhaps to avoid the interpretive challenge in assessing Wesley's spiritual heroism.

In some cases, such as his doctrine of the witness of the Spirit, Wesley's changes are minor qualifications that readers can handle when he includes two sermons from different decades in his collected sermons. In other cases, different theological positions result from redefinitions or refinements of main concepts such as "sin," which affects basic doctrines, such as Christian perfection. At times, Wesley defends himself as consistent even though he has in fact changed his mind, and one wonders whether he simply hopes that people will not notice the change. On occasion, he does admit a change of position, such as the matter of assurance, and admits that the Methodist preachers were wrong when they first preached the absolute necessity of experiencing assurance.[35]

Many people are more familiar with the "middle" Wesley (1738–1760) because of the British tradition of emphasizing his "standard" sermons, all of which come from publications during that period. The significant sermons of the 1760s (some of his best) and the *Arminian Magazine* sermons of the 1770s and 1780s are often overlooked, and the mature Wesleyan theology of that later period frequently is lost to the current theological discussion. Of note in this context are Wesley's qualifications of his earlier ideas on the nature and necessity of assurance of salvation, the role of good works in relation to justification by faith, and the definition of sin in the context of Christian perfection. To fasten upon Wesley's views on these issues during the twenty years after Aldersgate is to miss the development of his mature theology as expressed in his work during the last thirty years of his life, during which time he produced more than half of his published sermons.

When the mature Wesley produced his first collected *Works* during 1771 to 1774, he made corrections to his journal that have a tremendous impact on his spiritual autobiography in the 1730s. While he reprinted the text as it had always appeared in several previous printings, he added an errata sheet in the new edition, which not only corrected typographical and grammatical errors, but also qualified some of the most quoted Wesley comments. For instance, the well-known comment from his closing observations in the first journal (which appear to be made on his way back from Georgia) was probably written post-Aldersgate (1740), when he published the extract under Moravian influence: "I who went to America to convert others, was never myself converted to God." In his *Works*, Wesley qualifies this earlier comment: "I am not sure of this." He also qualifies the insinuation that in 1737 he had no faith in Christ, saying, "I had even then the faith of a *servant*, though not that of a *son*." And although he had earlier implied that he was "'a child of wrath,' an heir of hell," he later strongly denies this assertion with the comment, "I believe not" (meaning, I now think that was not the case).[36]

These comments by the mature Wesley destroy the common myth that Aldersgate was his only conversion, which marked the beginning of his having any faith in Christ; however, these comments have been ignored or unnoticed by most biographers and commentators on Wesley's spiritual development.[37] One can place part of the blame on Wesley, who for some reason or other did not bother to change the basic text of these accounts, leaving these major changes in perspective to entries in an errata sheet that is often separated from the volume for which it was intended. Wesley's earlier version—that he was finally converted at Aldersgate where he discovered faith in Christ—betrays the Moravian perspective under which he labored at the time. This is the view repeated in most popular accounts of Wesley as though he never had a second thought about the matter.

Another implicit myth concerning Wesley is that his views can be reduced to a series of declarative statements on various subjects, theological and otherwise, as though he never changed his mind. Again, Wesley is partly to blame for this inaccurate view. In later life, Wesley often claimed that he had preached the same doctrines, such as Christian perfection, consistently from the beginning. Such claims about what he taught or did not teach can often be disproved or qualified simply by looking through the corpus of his works. In his *Plain Account of Christian Perfection* (1777), he quotes his "Thoughts on Christian Perfection" (1759), in which he claims that *"sinless perfection"* is a phrase he never uses; yet earlier in the same work, he quotes his sermon on "Christian Perfection" (1741), in which he asserts that "a Christian is so far perfect as not to commit sin."[38]

The result of the implicit myth of consistency is that people make simplistic claims that Wesley held this or that view, stated in an uncritical declarative proposition. On many issues, however, Wesley's changing views negate such simplistic claims. For instance, Wesley's view of the nature of the Christian, vis-à-vis faith and sin, takes a number of interesting turns during his lifetime, which are often overlooked by people who rely upon a single writing of Wesley, usually a sermon in the 1740s or 1750s, and ignore later qualifications of that view. The main point of his early sermon on "The Almost Christian" (1741), which implies that the almost Christian is not a Christian at all, is turned on its head in his later sermon, "On Sin in Believers" (1763).[39] Similarly, his early view that being a Christian is more than doing good, avoiding evil, and using the means of grace[40] is strongly qualified in many of his later writings, in which Peter's phrase in Acts 10:35 takes on new life: "He that feareth him [God] and worketh righteousness is accepted with him."[41]

In these many ways, Wesley himself provides the basis for many of the myths that persist concerning early Methodism. That he himself contributed to the creation of the Wesley legend is not unusual—such is the case with many leaders who have become famous in their own day. That modern Methodists would not recognize the legends as such is another issue. Whether ascribed to uncritical admiration, trust in authority, good intentions, naive credulity, or unhistorical persuasion, these myths have been perpetuated for generations and have grown in number over the years. Our attempt to recover and practice a vital tradition entails a critical and reconstructive approach to many of these legends, even when Wesley is their source.

STRETCHING THE TRUTH: DISTORTIONS BY WESLEY'S BIOGRAPHERS

Myths that derive from Wesley's own distortions represent only part of the problem that confronts us in the present day. Biographers and historians down through the generations have often become complicit in the perpetuation of old myths and the creation of new legends surrounding the Wesleyan heritage.

Uncritical Selectivity and Biased Information

Sometimes the post-Wesley biographical story fits the biographer's bias more than the facts. The accounts written by Wesley's early biographers often lack critical selectivity and do not have the benefit of chronological distance. They accept Wesley's view of events if they happen to fit the author's bias, even though Wesley himself is an uncritical historian of the movement.

In addition, writers often increase the confusion by the addition of wrong information or one-sided views. One example of the former is Jonathan Crowther's contention that Wesley's parents named him for two deceased siblings, John and Benjamin, which Robert Moore later fit into his psychological theories.[42] John Hampson provides an example of the latter. Also an early biographer, he had been excluded from the Legal Hundred (the official "Conference" that inherited Wesley's leadership of the connection) and indulged his resentments in his accounts of Wesley's political management of Methodism.[43] Thomas Coke and Henry Moore's early biography also portrayed Wesley as dictatorial in order to support their view of the importance of the conference.[44] On the other hand, John Whitehead, who was a part-time local preacher and antagonist of Coke and Moore, critiqued Wesley's apparent favoritism for the full-time lay preachers who were members of the conference.[45] Luke Tyerman's opposition to the High-Church Oxford Movement in the nineteenth century led him to criticize anything in Wesley (especially the early Wesley) that seemed unevangelical.[46]

Uncritical Repetition: Creation of "Twice-told Tales"

The second way events and ideas become distorted in the stories about Wesley and Methodism, as well as fixed in the minds of successive generations, is in their unexamined repetition. If stories from our past are repeated often enough, they become twice-told tales and gain credibility with the retelling. Not examined carefully to begin with, much less in the repetition, the stories over time are simply *assumed to be true*, though in fact they are merely authoritative-sounding misinformation. And these days, the greatest source of creative and repeated misinformation, the Internet, is a treasure trove of material about Wesley that is simply not true.[47] But this is only a latter-day exponential explosion by digital means of the twice-told tale process that has been going on for centuries.

This latter-day misinformation that is continually replicated in biographies and histories can be illustrated by a number of examples that fall into typical categories.

Talents

Some stories about the Wesleys fall into the "could be true, should be true, therefore must be true" category. John is frequently the object of the language myth. Many people assume that he was fluent in a number of biblical languages and a cartful of modern languages, such as Spanish, Italian, French, and German. This assumption is based on his having published brief grammars in French, Greek, and Hebrew languages, plus a few brief references in his works.[48] But there is little evidence that his fluency extended much beyond the biblical languages.[49]

Practices

Many times, Wesley is given credit (though he himself does not claim it) for being the originator of an idea or practice that has actually been used previously by others. Wesley's pattern of self-examination, while seeming to be unique to a person unfamiliar with the history of Christian thought, is identical in many ways to the practices of both Ignatius Loyola and many of the English Pietists such as Robert Nelson.[50] Or conversely, he is portrayed as copying an idea from some group when he actually had used it himself before he had any contact with that group. The idea that Wesley learned the use of casting lots and the formation of bands from the Moravians is an example—he used both practices in Oxford many months before he ever met a Moravian.

Sayings

Many quotations, bon mots, or apothegms attributed to Wesley simply sound like something he might have said or written, rather than being something he actually expressed. The most common misattribution, perhaps, which has been passed down through Methodism for generations, is the "Wesley Grace," which starts, "Be present at our table, Lord, be here and everywhere adored." From there, the wording branches into several variations, depending on who is quoting it. But none of the versions has Wesley as its source, even though it is printed on replicas of the "Wesley teapot," on napkins used in Methodist churches, on bookmarks, and on many other knickknacks. The poem is, in fact, the creation of John Cennick, one of Wesley's early preachers, and, even if used by Wesley, it certainly did not originate with him.

Many other sayings sound like they could be Wesley's but in fact are not. Such is the case with the set of injunctions known as "Wesley's Rule": "Do all the good you can, by all the means you can, in all the ways you can, in all the places you can, at all the times you can, to all the people you can, as long as ever you can."[51] Another such saying is "In essentials unity, in non-essentials liberty, in all things charity."[52] Further, there are several sayings falsely attributed to Wesley on the Internet, such as, "I set myself on fire and people come for miles to see me burn."[53]

Stories, sayings, and ideas gain credibility if they are repeated often enough and convincingly enough, especially if by supposedly reliable people or acknowledged experts (not necessarily in this particular field) who themselves have become convinced of the truth of an idea or event. Quite often, their conviction derives from their own perspectives, which are grounded in later institutional or theological developments.

"INVENTED TRADITIONS": STORIES MADE UP BY SUCCESSIVE GENERATIONS

In addition to stretching the truth, another common distortion is the creation of "invented traditions,"[54] which are superimposed on the original events, furthering the inaccurate revision of those events. Although some of these views arise from outside critics and some from inside critics, many inventions arise from inadequate, selective, or incomplete use of sources by well-intended persons.

Proof-texting and Partial Truths

Many traditions develop from a partial reading of the Wesleyan corpus, lifting an idea from one place, taking it at face value (often out of context), and assuming that it represents a universal truth about early

Methodist history, whereas authors are typically thereby supporting their own biases or positions.

Incomplete, Faulty, or Unreliable Information Resulting in Biased Interpretation

The flawed idea that Charles Wesley was the "first Methodist" is one such myth, based on a 1780s letter and ignoring other Wesley writings from earlier and later periods that allege otherwise.[55] The interpretation of John Wesley as supporting homosexuality because he defended Thomas Blair, accused of sodomy,[56] does not take into account a letter from John Clayton to John Wesley from that same period, which sheds light on the Methodists' view of the case: the Wesleyans supported the accused prisoner Blair only after they became convinced of his innocence.[57]

One of the common recent myths of Methodism is that Wesleyan hymns in the eighteenth century were often set to drinking songs and bar tunes. This notion probably comes from a misunderstanding of the musical concept of bar tunes[58] and the misapplication of the concept of "secular" tunes (e.g., music by Handel, Purcell, and other popular musicians of the day, which they occasionally used) as being drinking songs. In any case, the story is often repeated, without any explanation or evidence.[59]

Another modern myth is that Wesley saw conference meetings as a means of grace. The probable source of this misconception is Wesley's list of "instituted means of grace"[60] in the "Large" *Minutes*, in which the fifth item (after prayer, the Lord's Supper, scripture, and fasting) is "Christian conference."[61] But this phrase does not refer to meetings of preachers or anyone else—Wesley is referring to what we would call "religious conversation."[62]

Partial Information Selected to Support Contemporary Views

Many subsequent interpretive portrayals of Wesley also present new images that at times catch the imagination of the public and, even though they are equally "invented," become part of the traditional lore of Methodism. The idea that Wesley was an evangelical preacher opposed to the formality of Anglican worship comes from the pen of Luke Tyerman, who in the late nineteenth century was trying to define evangelical Methodism as opposite the High-Church Anglicanism of the Oxford Movement in his day.[63] Never mind the fact that Wesley encouraged people to attend the services of the Church throughout his lifetime and, when he provided a printed book of worship for the American Methodists, he virtually copied the service of the Church of England.

Many people who try to show how forward-looking Wesley was point to his encouragement of women in leadership positions in the Methodist societies. This observation, however, often slips into the easy assertion that Wesley allowed or even encouraged women preachers, in spite of Wesley's firm assertion, "The Methodists do not allow of women preachers."[64] Granted, there is a fine distinction to be made between "women preachers," which would assume that they played the same role as the male lay preachers, and Wesley's encouragement of selected women to speak to the societies, so long as they didn't call their activity "preaching" or the occasion a "preaching service." But these distinctions get lost in the myth of the women preachers, who then make Wesley look very modern and tolerant in an area where he was perhaps pushing the envelope but not willing to challenge fully the deep-seated prejudice of his church against women preachers.[65]

Stories Misheard or Misunderstood

The origins of many myths about Wesley do not rest in the hands of an author or a speaker but in the minds of a reader or listener. Misheard or misrepeated stories occasionally account for rather preposterous views of Wesley. One modern example is the report to her congregation given recently by a lay delegate to the Florida Annual Conference, who said that a guest speaker at the conference had explained the origins of Methodist small group meetings.[66] It seems, according to her story, that Wesley was a very fit person who exercised vigorously and regularly. He played tennis six days every week—every day except Thursday. On that day, he stayed at home and on that day every week his wife physically beat him. In order to escape his whippings, he organized a small group that met on Thursdays, thus giving him an excuse to get out of the house and save his skin. This was the beginning of the Methodist small groups.

Although Wesley as a young man did play tennis at Oxford, there is no way that the speaker in Florida, an expert on early Methodist class meetings, could have told that story seriously. How it evolved into that fabrication in the mind of the lay delegate is anyone's guess. Nevertheless, her report was reinforced by a printed handout that she gave to members of the congregation, and no doubt the story will gain increasing circulation among credulous Floridian Methodists. It may even begin to show up in sermons and seminary term papers.

Bias of Opponents and Critics

In addition to proof-texting and partial truths by people within the movement, critics (generally outside the movement) have also painted a faulty picture of Wesley by misconstruing the evidence, whether through bias, ignorance, or oversight. The attacks that Wesley faced in his own day were often vicious, based on half-truths and conscious distortion of the facts, as one might expect. The many folk remedies that Wesley proposed in *Primitive Physick*, for instance, even though they have helped people overcome medical infirmities for centuries, provided not only contemporary physicians but also the pseudo-sophisticated skeptics a source of jest for generations.[67] The Methodists presented an easy target for both jest and suspicion, as some of their practices seemed by many people to be fanatical religious exercises. Critics easily conjoined their late-night meetings with the terminology of "Love Feast" and pictured suspicious midnight conventicles as sexual orgies, with virgins being debauched on the altars of the preaching houses.[68]

The less-than-subtle sexual innuendo of such a picture is not far removed from some present-day claims that Wesley broke up married couples because he demanded love and deference from his followers, the majority of whom were women.[69] Henry Abelove has claimed, for instance, that most early preachers in eighteenth-century England were gay, as they referred to each other as "dear brother," stayed under the same roofs, and occasionally kissed each other.[70] This shows ignorance of the literary conventions and cultural practices of the day. These pictures, built on half-truths by outside critics, do not usually persist among reasonable people but are ever-present grist for the mills of anyone who cares to make Methodism an object of scorn in any age. The irony is that the same type of twisting the truth that outside critics have used to cast aspersions on Methodism can at times be seen unwittingly used among the faithful in more recent days.[71]

Biases of Friends and Supporters

The portraits drawn by defenders of Methodism can also be biased. In trying to stand by their leader and friend, many of Wesley's lieutenants were inclined to paint a picture that had an unrealistic aura of heavenly sanctity, as in accounts of Wesley's death. Some eulogies surpassed the audacious hagiographic etching that portrayed Wesley being carried bodily by angels "into Abraham's bosom."[72] The account of the two weeks leading up to Wesley's death, written by his friend and housekeeper Elizabeth Ritchie, portrays the "art of dying" at its saintly best, just as Wesley would have hoped.[73] This glorification of the actual event became fixed in the Methodist consciousness by a nineteenth-century painting of Wesley's deathbed scene. Claxton's painting creates an iconic disjunction between the ideal and the real—it not only portrays Wesley with an unreal heavenly white aura but also includes in the room everyone who visited him during the last two weeks—more people than actually would have fit in the small room.

One pervasive myth of the post-Wesleyan era, perpetuated by friends for generations, is the idea that all, or nearly all, of Wesley's ideas originated with him—that his theology unfurls *ex nihilo*. This myth is not often stated as such, but it lies behind much of what has been said about Wesley during the last two hundred years. Wesley thus gets credit for originating many theological ideas that he in fact learned from previous thinkers, such ideas as prevenient grace, assurance, constant communion, sanctification, catholic spirit, Christian perfection, the analogy of faith, the second blessing, the primacy of Scripture, and a number of other ideas.[74] Each of these concepts has a fairly long history that Wesley himself knew and adapted within his own perspective and experience. The list of credits in this regard would include most of the major thinkers in the history of Christian thought, from the Early Church Fathers to the eighteenth-century Pietists. To see Wesley as creating *ex nihilo* every major doctrine in Methodism is perhaps one of the most pervasive and yet perverse myths of our doctrinal heritage

An outgrowth of this approach, which generally idealizes Wesley's thought, is the more recent invented tradition of the so-called "Wesleyan quadrilateral," a way of defining guidelines for theological reflection that was never formulated as such by Wesley and is not unique to Methodism.[75] Most Christians for centuries have used some combination of their understanding of Scripture, tradition, reason, and experience to guide their critical and constructive thinking.

Larger-Than-Life-Size Images

Wesley was a legend in his own day, as we have seen above, and within the Wesleyan denominations, the larger-than-life image of their founder has continued to expand. Many of the myths of Methodism have grown as Wesley's followers have continued to enhance his image by looking at him through a magnifying glass—not a glass that allows for more careful examination, but one that enlarges and projects his image into nearly superhuman proportions. Even the more recent portraits, such as the one by Salisbury in the 1920s, make him look much larger than the five foot three inches that he was. There are several myths that simply build on this tendency to magnify the image of the founder.

Myths of image and importance. Wesley was a significant religious leader, and the message that he preached had a powerful impact on the lives of many people. However, the myth that Wesley was a powerful preacher arose when the reputation and content of his preaching was transferred to an inflated view of his preaching style. One would expect a revival preacher of Wesley's impact to be a dynamic preacher with dramatic gestures and a powerful voice. Thus, many people are surprised to discover that such traits, easily attributable to George Whitefield, do not apply to Wesley.[76] His message, not the manner of his saying it, contained the power.

Some of the synthetic conclusions about Wesley's impact take on the aura of grandiose significance that raises the eyebrows of the faithful followers and the skeptical scholars alike. Such is the case with the "Halévy thesis," the idea broached in the late nineteenth century that (to give its popular rendition) Wesley's steadfast loyalty to the crown combined with his sympathy for (and support from) the lower classes saved England from the horrors of a French-like revolution. Such a conclusion is easier to declare than to support, and the exact nature and probability of such a claim has been controversial since it was first proposed.[77]

Wesley became a phenomenon in his own day. The fact that he lived to be nearly eighty-eight years old was not terribly remarkable in the eighteenth century, but few people were as energetic as he was at that age.[78] Even though he had several bouts with serious illness during his lifetime, and at times felt that the end was near, he seems to have assumed an aura of healthy old age in his frequent birthday reflections recorded in his *Journal*.[79]

Myths of numbers. In a related matter, Wesley's own accounts of his preaching to large crowds in the open air, field preaching, leave the impression that there were huge crowds in attendance. But the obvious question of whether he could be heard by thirty-two thousand people in the open air leads to the question of whether that many people were actually there to hear him.[80] A quick visit to that site, still present in rural Cornwall, leaves one wondering where that many people would have stood.[81] One also wonders if there were that many people who lived within a reachable distance from the location. Only a slightly more realistic set of assumptions results in a dramatic difference in the estimated attendance. A simple recalculation, based on a circle rather than a square, and considering three persons per square yard (which is still crowded), results in a total of fifteen thousand, less than half the Wesleyan calculation. The logistics of managing such a crowd, given even the smaller figure, never seem to make their way into the stories about these events. The practice of overestimating numbers at public gatherings has become so prevalent that even though similar exaggerations in historical accounts often strain the boundaries of verisimilitude, the stories are repeated as though they were indeed fact.[82]

The often-repeated story that Methodism spread "like wildfire" after 1738 leaves the impression that the membership of the movement was in keeping with the huge numbers reported at the field preaching after 1739. However, the actual figures indicate that at Wesley's death, after more than fifty years of revival, there were fewer than seventy-five thousand members in England, which means an average increase of fewer than fifteen hundred members per year and a total far below 1 percent of the total population—a picture hardly in keeping with the popular image.

The myths of numbers also touch other areas, such as the number of "hymns" that Charles Wesley wrote. The discussion usually focuses on a range of numbers from about six thousand to something more like nine thousand. These numbers, however, relate to the number of *poems* that Charles wrote, not the number of poems that were sung as *hymns* (in our terminology) or ever set to music—a number that would be in the low hundreds, not in the thousands.[83]

Myths of persecution and protection. Some anecdotes and details gain certain validity simply because they support and illustrate a known Wesleyan viewpoint and therefore are *assumed* to be *original* or old. Especially in his early days, Wesley felt that it would be difficult to be a "true" Christian without experiencing persecution, and some stories that illustrate this view have developed, though without historical documentation. One account tells of Wesley riding along on his horse one day when he was suddenly aware that he had not been persecuted for some time. Fearing for his state as a true Christian, he dismounted and fell on his knees in the ditch alongside the road. A farmer in the adjoining field recognized the despised Methodist preacher and heaved a rock at him as he prayed. The rock caught Wesley's attention as it grazed his head, upon which he realized the import of his prayer being answered, remounted his horse, and went on his way, rejoicing and praising God for such a clear sign of assurance.

Likewise, Wesley's stories of preservation in the midst of persecution are often not just unverified but even challenged by other accounts. John's story of his surviving the violence at Wednesbury in October 1743, preserved by his "guardian angel" from bodily injury and damage to the clothes (minor damage to the flaps on his jacket pockets), is challenged by his brother Charles's comments the following day that his clothes were in tatters and that his escape from a clubbing was probably more due to "his lowness of stature" than any protection from a guardian angel.[84]

Myths of kindness and friendliness. Another set of questionable stories is built around a picture of Wesley the jovial companion and congenial friend. One account, which remains questionable for lack of evidence, tells of Wesley entertaining his close friends in the evening through pleasant conversation and good stories. There is no verification of this in any easily accessible accounts of the private Mr. Wesley. A similar story, portraying a similarly attractive view but without corroboration, tells of Wesley coming early before preaching services in City Road Chapel in order to give rides to children in his rather nicely appointed carriage. These stories present the sort of image that we would like to think might be true and, although not common, they continue to circulate in the repertoire of unauthenticated stories.

Smaller-Than-Life-Size Images

A few of the invented traditions within the Wesleyan heritage entail the conscious diminution of one person's image in order to enhance another's. Three examples will suffice to illustrate this type of legend.

The mythical Charles. In order to emphasize the importance of Charles Wesley (which consequently diminishes the role of John Wesley), Frederick Gill tries to fasten upon Charles the moniker, "the First Methodist."[85] His rationale is based on a comment made by the younger Wesley brother in a letter to Dr. Samuel Chandler, who was embarking for America in 1785, shortly after John's ordination of Thomas Coke as an American bishop.[86] This statement of priority, based on Charles's claim to have started the movement at Oxford, essentially takes Charles's side in a political dispute between the two brothers, exhibits credulity in following Charles's intentionally revisionist account of the early history of the Methodists, and overlooks several crucial facts that are evident from contemporary documents: that John had earlier exercised all the practices that Charles later adopted at Oxford, that no "group" as such was started by Charles before John returned to Oxford in 1729 to begin Methodism, and that Charles's claim to priority came in the midst of a power struggle with John within the movement. By claiming to have started the movement, Charles was playing a political hand to gain support within Methodism for his positions that challenged several of John's ideas about lay preachers, ordination, and implicit separation from the Church. To accept Charles's claim of priority would depend, for instance, upon defining Oxford Methodism as consisting of two students studying together and going to church on Sunday, hardly a distinctive definition. The effect of Gill's claim, fixed in many minds by the title of his book, is to downgrade the significance of John in the origins of the Methodist movement in ways that are unhistorical and unwittingly artificial.

Likewise, Charles's image is enhanced beyond realistic proportions by the reputation ascribed to him as a hymn-writer. First, it should be recognized that Charles wrote no music—he was not a composer (though many people assume that he was). Second, of the large number of poems that he wrote, many of which were called "sacred poems," relatively few were ever put to music and sung as hymns.[87] Third, Charles is never listed as a literary figure among the great poets of the age.[88] His works are seldom included in anthologies of English poetry, and even John recognized that much of his work was hastily produced. Fourth, most of the hymn publications of the Wesleys were edited by John Wesley, though Charles chafed at some of John's omissions or revisions to his lyrics and published a few items independently.[89] Fifth, the whole Wesley family had a poetic gift—both Samuels, father and son, published collections of poetry, at least one of the sisters was a published poet, and John published poems and hymns from his own pen before Charles ever did. Such comments are not made to diminish the fine work of Charles, but simply to put it in a wider and more realistic perspective.

The mythical Susanna. Susanna Wesley needs no artificial enhancement for her important role in the story of Methodism. Nevertheless, authors in the past have perhaps inadvertently raised her to new heights by downgrading others, such as her husband, Samuel. Elsie Harrison, in her biography of John Wesley, portrays Samuel as a numbskull who could not manage his parish, his finances, his family, or even the rescue of his son John from the rectory fire in 1709.[90] Her negative rhetoric in regard to Samuel has attached itself indelibly to his image and pervades the current literature on the Epworth household, in spite of his significant role in his children's developing spiritual and theological perspective.

Harrison does not simply rely on the consequences of this approach to enhance Susanna's image, however. She manages to include nearly every hypothetical story about Susanna's influence, verifiable or not[91]—from the claim that she knew several foreign languages (untrue) to the claim that she met with John for an hour every Thursday evening (unverifiable), to the assertion that she designated John as "a brand plucked from the burning" in the yard of the burned-out rectory (unsupported). Susanna is important enough in the story without magnifying her image with unwarranted claims.

These questionable traditions, whether they were told by the Wesleys themselves, enlarged by their biographers and critics, or begun and perpetuated by friends, foes, and competitors in successive generations, have been passed on for centuries to eager and credulous congregations of listeners. That rather persistent process raises the question of why people who in general tend to be grounded in rationality and skeptical of inflated or deflated images still soak up unlikely stories about religious predecessors as though they were the gospel truth.

TRANSMISSION AND RECEPTION

The transmission of myths through repetition from generation to generation represents only part of the problem of these images becoming fixed in the imagination. The tradition is not only passed on but, if it is to persist, must also be received.[92] Considering the question of how a tradition is formed and shaped over the years is essential for Christian communities within the Wesleyan heritage as well as for ecumenical engagement with that heritage.

Assumptions for the Acceptance of Myths

The willing acceptance of less-than-adequate stories within a tradition as though they were historical, meaningful, or even true can result from a number of misleading assumptions.

Reliability

People usually do not have the time, opportunity, or inclination to check all information presented to them. Many people assume the reliability of virtually any printed source. In some cases, the ability to check the historical sources is long since passed—the people and their documents are sometimes either missing or beyond the reach of most people. We are left to determine the veracity of stories on the basis of some sort of inherent reliability. In most cases, we simply trust the storytellers, based on reputation or familiarity, and assume their pure motives and proper judgments of the information they pass along. In many cases, people think the stories have the ring of truth, and it is easier to accept them as reliable than to verify them.

Authority

A second assumption is trust of authorities. As we saw above, the Wesleys themselves were the authors of many legends about themselves, often unintentionally. In their own day and subsequently, friends of the Wesleys and the movement assumed that the Wesleys' statements were authoritative and true, meaning factual. In many cases, however, the Wesleys' truth did not entail historicity. Nevertheless, modern readers still tend to take the written record literally, based on the source, which often results in the credulous acceptance of non-factual material from seemingly authoritative sources.

Plausibility

Contemporary interpreters also make assumptions based on a story's verisimilitude to reality, especially if the account bears a close relationship to our understanding of history and reality. In some cases, the familiar sound of the story, either through repetition of the story itself or its similarity to other well-known stories, results in the tacit reception of the material as true.

Desirability

In some cases, we go a step further and believe traditions to be true because we *want* them to be true—it *should* be true, even if it might be questionable on some other grounds. Even if we suspect that Wesley did not do or say a certain thing, we sometimes think that it could be true because we wish he would have said or done it. We do not necessarily recognize these accounts to be myths or legends, but see them simply as part of our perception of the right ordering of the universe.

Preferability

Some perplexing questions persist in the midst of these quandaries: Why do some people seemingly *prefer* myths rather than the facts? Why do the legends often seem more attractive than the history? What role does "truth" have in all this? At times, the natural inclination toward hagiographic and iconographic associations with the saints of old interferes with truer pictures of what happened. For centuries, Christians loved to read or hear the *Acta Sanctorum* or Foxe's *Book of Martyrs*—lives of the saints and heroes of the faith. We are attracted to the virtue and virtuosity of religious leaders like Wesley—their stories provide a model or goal, if not an alter ego. Thus, we sometimes *believe* more about Wesley than we *know* about him.

SORTING OUT TRUTH:
THE QUESTION OF HISTORICAL VERACITY

To distinguish between "traditional" and "historical," or between "myth" and "truth," is perhaps an unfortunate approach, especially if we are trying to discern "a living tradition." As has often been acknowledged, myths are often about truths. Traditions are often grounded in history. Many of the favorite stories about Methodism, though not accurate or fully verifiable, might be seen as true to some extent and perhaps more meaningful than some of the verifiable facts of Methodist history. In fact, most of the stories as we know them are true, in one way or another.

The question is, just how much correlation should there be between tradition and history? Between myth and fact? Between the stories we repeat and the history we know? One would hope for, and expect, some correlation between history and tradition. Nevertheless, it seems at times that the relationship between memorable tradition and accurate history is often a matter of inverse proportion—the more accurate, the less memorable.

In conversation one day in his office next door to mine, Grant Wacker asserted that quite often "the importance of an historical assertion is inversely proportional to its verifiability." He went on to explain that the claim "slavery caused the Civil War" is a meaningful assertion that cannot be fully proved, and, although the claim that "my house has 423 shingles" can be easily proved or disproved, it does not mean much (unless, of course, it's raining).[93] Similarly, to say, as Elie Halévy did, that Wesley helped prevent a revolution from occurring in England might be a meaningful though unverifiable concept, while to say that Wesley's hair as a young man was reddish brown might be verifiable but has little importance. To say that a tradition is truly historical (i.e., historically true) does not necessarily imply that it is important. At the same time, is it possible to say that a tradition can be truly important (or significantly true) if it is not historically verifiable?

An example or two might draw out this question more particularly. Does it make any difference whether Wesley ever said or wrote the "ecumenical motto": "In essentials, unity; in non-essentials, liberty; in all things, charity"?[94] If we think this perspective is an important part of our tradition, does it matter if we attribute it incorrectly to Wesley? It sounds very much like part of Wesley's view of "catholic spirit," but even that principle has been truncated and twisted by many people to the point of incredibility, when compared with what Wesley actually said.[95]

Another example is the characterization of Wesley as a powerful revival preacher. Never mind that one observer said that, if he had not occasionally raised his hand to turn the page of his sermon manuscript, one would have thought him to be a "speaking marble statue"; yet, people often think of him as a fiery preacher in the mold of George Whitefield.[96] Does it matter that his gestures were actually quite minimal and his voice moderate? Does it matter that the power emanating from the content of his sermons was not matched by the manner of its presentation?[97] What do we discover about Wesley's revival influence when we consider this contrast between his method and his message?

Lack of correlation between history and tradition may result in a lack of credibility, which can spread far beyond any particular instance of myth or legend. If part of an amalgam of traditions is shown to be patently false, totally without historical basis, then the rest of the package might easily be seen as suspect, regardless of whether the suspect portion was significant. If someone has been making up some things, he or she might have made up other things.

SORTING OUT TRUTH: THE QUESTION OF SIGNIFICANCE

In light of this discussion, historical veracity is an important part of any critical practice of a tradition. But that is not the whole picture. We are also left with the task of discriminating between elements of the tradition that might be less significant and other aspects of the heritage that have important consequences for our understanding of what it means to be "Wesleyan" in the past, present, and future.

One must take seriously the fact that, at various times within Methodism, large segments of the denomination have based their understanding of the Wesleyan tradition on less-than-complete or accurate information and have determined the question of significance in the short view rather than the long. Many myths and invented traditions within Methodism tell us more about the present than the past and better describe those who have crafted those images and those who have perpetuated those myths than the people and events from the past that are their supposed focus. The days of Methodist triumphalism in the nineteenth century, based on a self-perception of success that was grounded more in short-term than in long-term memory, had many positive results, in spite of having little knowledge of or concern for Wesley. But Wesley is never too far below the surface of Methodist programs at any point, and attempts to recapture and reassert a Wesleyan perspective are often to be found waiting in the wings.

Desiderata for an Appropriate Understanding of Tradition

To fulfill this task adequately, the first necessity is to discern an accurate picture of the original events. Finding an authoritative source of the Methodist movement who has recorded events objectively and without some kind of bias is difficult. There has never been a need to embellish the facts within Methodist history in order to make the story more exciting—the actual story of the early Wesleyan movement is remarkable enough, without any superfluous distortions or additions. But, given the historiographic situation, the observer must exercise care in order that the past might speak to the present with authenticity. Three characteristics of the story should persist in order for the tradition to have appropriate current applicability: historical integrity, ideological congruence, and contemporary relevance.[98]

Historical Integrity

Stories without any historical basis should not be repeated from generation to generation just because they sound good or have always been told. The process of distortion began very early. As Wesley himself noted in the opening paragraph of his *Short History of Methodism* (1765), "It is not easy to reckon up the various accounts which have been given of the people called Methodists; very many of them are as far remote from truth as that given by the good gentleman in Ireland: 'Methodists! Ay, they are the people who place all religion in wearing long beards.' " With the passing of time, the stories about the Methodists took on additional baggage, and the legends surrounding John Wesley expanded. His image became more remarkable but less personal, more heroic but less believable, more saintly but less relevant to many people.[99] Accuracy does matter; intellectual honesty does matter; verisimilitude to reality does matter.

Ideological Congruence

The appropriation of basic theological principles by later generations should exhibit a continuity of concerns and core ideals over the generations. The variety of ways the Wesleyan principles have been applied is evident in the fragmentation of the heritage into many different denominations. The nineteenth century witnessed many groups in America that took a part of the Wesleyan message and made it the whole. Arguments over the nature of Wesley's views and how they should be applied resulted in the formation of several denominations, all of which thought that they represented the "true Wesleyan" position for their day. Ideas do matter; truth does matter; spirituality does matter.

Contemporary Relevance

Finally, the contemporary application of these principles should represent a congruence of relevance that is proportional to the original principles and practices within the tradition. In some cases, the tendency to disregard Wesleyan views in favor of more recent ideas or practices was considered by some to represent a very Wesleyan approach to pragmatic and contemporary relevance. Credibility does matter; propriety does matter; relevance does matter.

Our task, to be faithful to our Wesleyan tradition, includes understanding the principles and practices of our heritage as being grounded in its origins and development, not as disembodied ideals or activities, but as actual ways in which God has interacted with people who were struggling to experience God's power and presence in the midst of their search for truth, strength, comfort, and meaning. Our stories as a people of God moving into the future should be characterized by integrity, continuity, and propriety.

THE TRADITION AND THE FUTURE

Just as critical reception of the tradition is important to the integrity and vitality of any heritage, so also careful transmission of the tradition is an important part of faithful practice within a group with a significant past. Does it make any difference that many church night dinners are accompanied by the use of napkins adorned with the "Wesley Grace," even though it is not by Wesley? Or that bulletins or newsletter articles occasionally include "Wesley's Rule," which is not really by Wesley? Or that the home pages of many church websites have sayings attributed to Wesley, such as "Set yourself on fire for God and people will come for miles to watch you burn," which does not even resemble an authentic Wesleyan saying? Does such misuse of Wesley really do any harm? Do most of the myths of Methodism simply present a playground for revisionist historians who are finicky about accuracy?

If the question is asked that way, the implication is that no one's health will be threatened, no one's salvation will be jeopardized, and no one's life will be disrupted by the repetition of many of these somewhat innocuous myths. True. But the same is true if we say that no personal or national disaster will occur if we say that George Washington chopped down a cherry tree, or that Jimmy Carter invented the Second Law of Thermodynamics, or that Dwight Eisenhower said, "It was like *déjà vu* all over again."

If anyone is interested in truth anymore, or institutional integrity, or historical accuracy, then every attempt should be made to check on the veracity of traditional stories, sayings, and practices. Many of the myths of Methodism are known to be such by a host of knowledgeable people, and the repetition of such bits of misinformation might bring into question the integrity, if not intelligence, of the person or institution that repeats such nonsense. If a preacher uses a quotation that he or she misattributes to Wesley, who is to say that other parts of the sermon are not equally fallacious? If a book or article cites mythical material as though it were factual, what is to keep the reader from wondering if the whole work might not be questioned? If an account of Wesley's life sounds more like hero worship than biography, who is to say that the details can be trusted or that the interpretation is at all reliable?

There are also, besides the more or less "harmless" myths, some elements of misinformation about Wesley and early Methodism in common circulation that are actually misleading in more important ways. When a world mission program cites Wesley as an early supporter of Methodist foreign missions, based on a misunderstanding and a misquote ("The World is My Parish"), then the whole denomination looks inept if not devious. If Wesley is portrayed in larger-than-life proportions, singularly creative and without error or flaw, then people have difficulty relating to him as a human being and the expectations for Methodist practice can be put beyond reach for most of us. If the picture of early Methodism is painted without the turmoil and inconsistencies that accompany missional development, then the current imperfections of the institution seem to be magnified by comparison.

For these reasons and many others, the people called Methodists would be well served by preachers, teachers, authors, and other leaders who made the effort to verify historical elements of the tradition that are often cited to support current positions or to propose new programs. The maintenance of historical accuracy, ideological veracity, institutional integrity, and missional relevance is not too much to ask within a major global denomination that attempts to remain faithful to its heritage.

And for those parts of the story that, when examined closely, are found to be less than relevant or attractive today, there are other options besides simply tossing aside that bit of the tradition (which should be understood as a real option). We should point out that some of our historical past, though clearly accurate, need not be passed on a part of the living tradition. Wesley himself exhibited many quirks of his day, in terms of cultural biases, personal interests, and dated viewpoints. Wesley believed in witchcraft; he had an obsessive-compulsive personality; he was incapable (for whatever reason) of having a lasting intimate relationship with a woman; he had no trust in political democracy; and he thought all Catholics were traitors to his country.

The questions of what we choose to appropriate and why we pass it on within the living Wesleyan tradition (as a set of stories, practices, beliefs, institutions) present us with a large set of issues. All of these issues raise the basic question of how we can be faithful to our heritage as we transform a tradition that is grounded in the eighteenth century to meet the needs of the present and the future. The task entails an attempt not only to understand the original context within which the tradition developed, but also to distill the intentions and principles that provided the impetus and direction for the movement. Having understood that point, we must still try to figure out how to translate the positive elements of the tradition into the present in ways that are appropriate and meaningful in the present context and that will be relevant to the needs of the future. We must also realize that there are negative, time-bound elements of the tradition that cannot and should not be transmitted into the present in their previous form. A note of honesty on those matters can make any explicit consideration of the ongoing Wesleyan tradition not only a teaching opportunity but also a more credible and appropriate framework for understanding the present and future.

Appropriating Misused Stories and Quotations

Some myths of Methodism that result from an inadequate long-term memory can be corrected by recapturing their intended sense within the original context and reapplying them appropriately in today's world. For instance, to use Wesley's phrase "I look upon all the world as my parish" (to quote it correctly) as a support for a world missions program is totally inappropriate—out of keeping with the original intent. Wesley was not talking about global missions—in fact, he opposed Thomas Coke's attempts to start a missionary society in the 1780s. Wesley did not think that the Methodists had enough resources to handle the needs within the British Isles, much less broaden their work out into other parts of the world. To make Wesley the unwitting supporter of world missions, by quoting (or misquoting) this phrase, then, is something akin to false advertising or misrepresentation.

However, if we look at what Wesley was actually trying to say, the application of his idea might be just as exciting today. He was giving a rationale for field-preaching—preaching outside the comfort of a church building, generally within the boundaries of some other priest's parish (not good etiquette, even today). The technicalities of his rationale included the facts that his Oxford ordination was not to any particular parish but to the whole country, and that, in fact, he had no specific parish assignment. His vocation was to preach across parish boundaries, to break down the parochial barriers that prevented the gospel from being heard in many parts of Great Britain. He was arguing for *innovative ministry* that breaks down some of the institutional barriers that limit the work of God in the world. That principle, applied in our own day, can result in many exciting forms of ministry that look beyond the traditional forms and allow for the presence and power of God to enter new arenas in new ways. That can be just as exciting as world missions and even more broadly applied across the life of the church.

The same can be said of many stories or ideas that have been compartmentalized in ways that are not necessarily appropriate to either their Wesleyan origins or the most adequate appropriation today. Viewing Wesley's Aldersgate experience very narrowly as a singular moment of conversion that was a watershed moment in his life can result in giving exaggerated significance to this event and lead to a nineteenth-century misunderstanding of the Wesleyan way of salvation—by assuming that he held the idea of "once saved, always saved," which is certainly not true (the reality of backsliding can more than cancel any such experience), or by assuming that his major stress was on justification by faith, which is certainly not true (since he focused primarily on the need for holy living, or sanctification). An appropriate application of the Aldersgate story would be to show how it was an important, key step in Wesley's spiritual pilgrimage—that it emphasized in his own experience the centrality of the **assurance of faith** through the witness of the Holy Spirit—that we can know that we are children of God, that we can experience the presence and power of God in our lives in very real and meaningful moments. As Methodists, we can live in hope and expectation of our own lives being marked by such experiences on our spiritual journeys toward the reign of God in our lives and in the world.

Some other inaccurate elements of the Wesley story might still be put to use in the ongoing tradition. For instance, contrary to the common assumption, Wesley did not say (or write), "In essentials unity, in nonessentials liberty, in all things charity." That originated with an obscure sixteenth-century Dutch theologian and was quoted by English dissenters who were concerned about the toleration of smaller nonconformist groups by the larger established Church. Although the phrase can be found in works that Wesley read, it apparently was never used or repeated by Wesley himself. Nonetheless, the sentiment expressed therein does coincide rather well with Wesley's views on the relationships between religious groups or denominations as found in his sermon on "Catholic Spirit." So that to use this "ecumenical motto" as an indication of the spirit of toleration that was *in accord with* the Wesleyan spirit would certainly be appropriate, without ascribing it to Wesley himself.

This same task of understanding and re-appropriating the myths in our day can also be exercised in a wide array of other instances within the Methodist story. Our attempts should focus on authentic exercise of our heritage in the present context, with propriety and integrity. In some cases, however, a simple correction of misinterpretations will not accomplish the task, because at times more radical treatment is necessary.

Ignoring/Re-evaluating Time-bound Views

The consideration of outdated perspectives sometimes goes beyond the need for a more accurate interpretation or a new application in the future. In some cases, the views and sayings of Wesley himself present nearly insurmountable challenges. Even in these cases, however, contextual readers can discover insights that allow them to see beyond the particular claims of Wesley toward his larger concerns.

Witchcraft

Wesley believed in witchcraft, a sincerely held view that would, however, make most post-Salem witch trial folks shudder. In his mind, he had good reasons for holding this view. The Old Testament speaks of witches; thus, to challenge their reality would be to diminish the veracity of the Bible. Like haunted houses and ghosts (in which he also believed), witchcraft spoke to the reality of the supernatural—a view that directly challenged the "watchmaker" theology of the Deists.[100]

This view results from the fact that Wesley held to the traditional views of biblical inspiration and infallibility that were also prevalent in the eighteenth century, even though he accepted the rudimentary attempts at biblical criticism that were available in his day, such as the work of Johannes Bengal. Thus, the same Wesley who allowed women a greater role in his movement than was prevalent in the established Church of his day could figure out a way to agree with St. Paul that women should be silent in church.[101] And while Wesley opened his arms wide to faithful brothers and sisters in an irenic "Letter to a Roman Catholic," he commented in his notes on a passage of Revelation that every pope since Gregory VII was Antichrist.[102]

The core idea, from our perspective, is that Wesley took seriously the Scriptures as the revealed Word of God and felt that a belief in supernatural reality was an important part of understanding the divine-human relationship in the universe. Although he was, as we all are, constricted by the cultural biases and norms of his place and time, he looked at his times with an eye toward seeing and understanding the workings of God in the world. He would no doubt understand the biblical sciences today, just as the physical, nuclear, and other sciences, to be a useful result of God's blessing humankind with intelligence and reason, so as to enable a better understanding of God's revelation, God's people, and God's universe.

Circulation of Blood

Wesley's sermon "The Image of God" betrays a view of human physiology that we would consider primitive, and he applies it in such a way that, while making a conventional theological point and prefiguring some modern thinking, is implausible as a scientific theory. He uses William Hervey's recent discovery of circulation to describe what happens to Adam as a result of eating the forbidden fruit: a substance in the fruit caused the blood to coagulate and attach itself to the inside walls of the vessels, causing the smaller capillaries to clog up, eventually shutting off the circulation of the blood in the body and causing death.[103] Now, while this sounds suspiciously like arterial sclerosis, that is not what Wesley is actually talking about. He is talking about spiritual and physical death being the result of original sin.

Although this particular application of scientific theory to explain theological concepts is fraught with problems, one can say that Wesley was open to the possibility that science could help us understand the reality of the universe in ways that were previously impossible, a point well made by Randy Maddox in this volume. Wesley does not always recognize the limits of science for his purposes, but his interest in and openness to new scientific ventures is an important part of the Wesleyan tradition.

Providence and Natural Disasters

Wesley had a very lively sense of divine providence. His use of "casting lots" and "bibliomancy" was based on his firm belief that God was speaking to him (guiding the process) by what choice was picked in the lot or which Bible verse he randomly opened. He would go so far as to say that the death of his sister's child may have been providential, in that she now had more time for spiritual disciplines (which she had earlier explained were difficult because of the demands of child-rearing). Such views are hardly in vogue today, seeming to make God into an arbiter of indifferent things and even a cause of evil.

Wesley's views on the Lisbon earthquake fall into the latter category. The natural disaster befell the Portuguese in 1755, according to Wesley, because of their sinful ways (we can perhaps also see some blatant anti-Catholic bias in his view).[104] A close parallel appeared recently when a Korean pastor claimed that the tsunami tragedy of 2005 was the result of God wreaking his vengeance on sinners who knew not Christ (as a large majority of the victims was Muslim).

Wesley's understanding of providence and theodicy (theory of God and evil) does not coincide with most modern views more than two centuries later. Nevertheless, the time-bound nature of those views, which were very prevalent in his day, should not distract us from noticing that they derived from his very persistent view, contrary to the Deists, of God's active presence in human events and the effects of human actions on creation. He considered Scripture to be, above all, an account of God's activity in human affairs, and he would say that his own day was a continuation of that scriptural truth. Wesley, more than most people then or now, had a lively sense of the presence of God in the world about him and in his own daily activities. The "exercise of the presence of God" was his recommendation to his people, based on his constant recognition that "God is with us," one of the foundational assumptions of his theology.[105]

Focusing On and Adapting the Significant

Most of the traditions about Wesley do not present the problems of antiquarian revisionism addressed in this chapter. A large proportion of the tradition is accurate, appropriate, and historical. A persistent, perhaps larger problem through much of Methodism's history has been a simple ignorance of and an ignoring of the Wesleyan tradition as a vibrant reality that has roots in the past, relevance for the present, and some exciting possibilities for the future. Millions of lives have been transformed by God through contact with the Wesleyan heritage. Thousands of Wesleyans have served humanity in the offices of president, prime minister, prince, senator, representative, governor, speaker of the house, general, judge, pastor, doctor, teacher, lawyer, and countless other positions of authority and responsibility around the world during the last two and a half centuries. One would like to think that the fulfillment of their duties benefited from a vibrant grasp of the life and thought of Wesley and other early Methodists—the forebears' perception of theology, ethics, health, justice, catholic spirit, discipline, spirituality, education, hard work, and love.

Many of Wesley's ideas find their way into various lists of "Wesleyan distinctives," such as those noted in the United Methodist Book of Discipline.[106] But above all, Wesley seemed to stress those ideals that were common to all Christians. While many people today try very hard to be good Wesleyans, Wesley himself was not that interested in creating clones of himself. Wesley would have everyone press forward in God's grace, that is, with the assistance of the presence and power of God, "toward having the mind of Christ and walking as he walked."[107] The measure of authenticity—of historicity, of verisimilitude, of propriety, of desirability—of the Wesleyan tradition is, in part, whether it continues to promote faithfulness in the journey toward that goal.

Most myths of Methodism do not negatively affect the main principles of the Wesleyan heritage that continue to form the core of the ongoing tradition. Some of these central claims are that God is active in creation and human history, that the main source and criterion of divine revelation is the living and written Word in Christ and Scripture, that God's presence and power can transform persons and institutions through the work of the Holy Spirit, and that love of God and neighbor are the heart of the Christian faith. The list goes on, but my central point is that these parts of the Wesleyan story will determine whether Methodism survives, not only with the form but also with the power of religion. While it might be useful to rid the ongoing heritage of false stories, misquotes, invented traditions, and faulty interpretations, the key to the future of the tradition as a lively force assisting the reign of God in the world is not whether a few myths persist. The key is whether, as Wesley said, Methodists hold fast to the "doctrine, spirit, and discipline with which they first set out."[108]

CHAPTER THREE

AFRICAN AMERICAN METHODISTS AND UNITED METHODISM: A PECULIAR RELATIONSHIP OR A STRANGE AFFAIR?

William B. McClain

The continued presence of African Americans in Methodism in the twenty-first century, and particularly in The United Methodist Church, more than three hundred years since the birth of John Wesley, is still a great anomaly. How could African Americans remain in a church with its checkered career in matters of faith and practice, its acts of courage and cowardice in matters of race and justice, and its schisms and mergers as a Christian Protestant denominational body? What does their staying reveal about Christian faith, and how does it point to the future? Whereas other authors in this volume approach history in order to make corrections (as Richard Heitzenrater) or to retrieve little-known elements (as Randy Maddox and Amy Oden), my intention is to explore this anomaly in the Wesleyan movement and to draw wisdom from the African American peoples within it.

In another place and time, I have said that "African American Methodists are both a remnant of hope and a reminder of the ideal for *their* church to match its practice with its proclamation."[1] In a later writing, I concluded: "This hope was probably based more on pride than reason, more on eager expectation rather than anything reality suggested, but it was nevertheless a hope, a faith, a gossamer anticipation that sometime, somewhere, somehow, their presence in the church would cease to be the great anomaly that it was."[2] Now, I raise the question whether this is a genuine relationship, peculiar though it may be, or simply a sentimental affair that has lasted because neither could (or dared to) get rid of the other.

From the earliest days of the advent of Methodism—with its peculiar and promising proclamation of prevenient grace—to the present, the descendants of Africa in the United States have embraced Christianity as preached by the Methodists. The "magnolia missions," class meetings, societies, and camp meetings all worked together. Slaves heard about a grace in one called Jesus Christ, who included them in the work of salvation. These disinherited ones said, "Yes!" to the invitation offered them by circuit riders, accepting that they had been accepted through God's amazing grace in Jesus Christ and the scandal of the cross of Calvary. It was for them, as the writer of the Gospel of John put it, "grace upon grace" (John 1:16).

African Americans with common Wesleyan roots (African Methodist Episcopal, Christian Methodist Episcopal, African Methodist Episcopal Zion, and others) are now being invited to dialogue with United Methodists about unity and cooperation and, perhaps somewhere down the road (in the dreams of some of us), merger. At the same time, African Americans in these denominations are raising critical and important questions. They are not doing so in the same way or for the same reasons that they used to slam and shame and chide "those Black people who are in the 'White' church." They question now in a different and perhaps more serious and hopefully more objective way, and certainly for different reasons. A brief review of Methodism and its encounter with the American descendants of Africa may help to put even more sharply their questions and the reasons for their questions and to offer a clearer perspective on the question I raised at the beginning of this discussion.

FIERCE FIDELITY OF AFRICANS TO METHODISM

On an unusually warm Sunday morning in April 1787, the history of Methodism in this country would change forever. The descendants of Africa had enthusiastically embraced Methodism with its mostly British leaders preaching the gospel as understood by that branch of Christianity; however, they were to enter an almost soap opera saga, which would extend throughout the rest of American history. On that warm Sunday morning in April, Richard Allen, Absalom Jones, and a small group of African Americans walked out of St. George's Methodist Episcopal Church in Philadelphia. The exact details of the precipitating incident are not completely clear. Apparently, members of the group were asked to leave their places of prayer while on their knees around the altar and to return to the racially segregated balcony (or some such segregated section) that had recently been created as a place for African Americans to sit in church. Jones, Allen, and others indicated that, if they were allowed to finish their prayers, they would not only leave the altar but would also leave the church and not bother the Methodist Episcopal members anymore. Some left. *But some stayed.*

As humiliating and painful as the departure proved to be for those who left, Allen was candid and clear in his commitment: "As for me, I could never be anything but a Methodist . . . and I am thankful that ever I heard a Methodist preacher."[3] Allen, of course, would go on to establish and become the first bishop of the African Methodist Episcopal Church (A.M.E.), and Absalom Jones would be the first African American Episcopal rector in America.

In 1791, Richard Allen's fellow members of the Free African Society—a mutual-aid "self-improvement" association that he had helped organize in November 1787—asked him to form them into an Episcopal Church. Allen acknowledged the honor but politely and definitely declined. He repeated his earlier words: "As for me, I could never be anything else but a Methodist . . . and I am thankful that ever I heard a Methodist preacher." Allen, a Delaware ex-slave, had been converted under Methodist preaching, was later licensed to preach, and had traveled the various Methodist circuits in Delaware, Maryland, and New Jersey with Richard Whatcoat, Irie Ellis, and Peter Morratte. He enthusiastically engaged in these preaching missions to spread the simple gospel of grace by which Methodism was so clearly and closely identified, and which he had so personally experienced.

Allen undoubtedly moved many by sharing the details of his own dramatic conversion, and he exhorted others to seek what he had himself found, albeit lost and found:

> I was awakened and brought to see myself, poor, wretched and undone, and without the mercy of God must be lost. Shortly after, I obtained mercy through the blood of Christ, *and was constrained to exhort my old companions to seek the Lord.* I went rejoicing for several days and was happy in the Lord, in conversing with many old, experienced Christians. I was brought under doubts, and was tempted to believe I was deceived, and was constrained to seek the Lord afresh. I went with my head bowed down for many days. My sins were a heavy burden. I was tempted to believe there was no mercy for me. I cried to the Lord both night and day. One night I thought hell would be my portion. I cried unto Him who delighteth to hear the prayers of a poor sinner, and all of a sudden my dungeon shook, my chains flew off, and, glory to God, I cried. My soul was filled. I cried enough for me the Saviour died. Now my confidence was strengthened that the Lord, for Christ's sake, had heard my prayers and pardoned all my sins.[4]

Given this experience, one is not surprised at Allen's response to the Free African Society when they sought to become Episcopalians and to make him their pastor:

> I cannot be anything else but a Methodist, as I was born and awakened under them ... for the plain and simple gospel suits best for any people; for the unlearned can understand, and the learned are sure to understand; and the reason that the Methodist is so successful in the awakening and conversion of the colored people, the plain doctrine and having a good discipline.[5]

Even though Allen refused to form the Free African Society into an Episcopal church, the Society proceeded to vote to become Episcopalians and to use the building that Allen and Jones had secured subscriptions to build as "The African Church," albeit with the clear intention of remaining within the Methodist relation. When The Methodist Episcopal Church rebuffed Allen by refusing to supply a minister, he proceeded to move an old blacksmith shop to a lot he owned and to renovate it as a place of worship—a *Methodist* place of worship, of course. Allen, in recounting the situation later and explaining his view about the offer, added: "*I was confident there was no religious sect or denomination that would suit the capacity of the colored people as well as the Methodists, for the plain and simple gospel suits best for any people*"[6] (emphasis added).

Richard Allen's staunch loyalty to Methodism, and his tenacious commitment to the particular and peculiar Wesleyan understanding and expression of Christian faith, is but one dramatic example of the fierce fidelity and extraordinary bond that has characterized so many millions of African Americans in their devotion to the Methodist Church from its inception. Although Allen left the Methodist Episcopal Church to found an African Church, the new church was thoroughly Methodist in its doctrine, polity, theology, hymnody, worship, and practice. And, if one would visit it or study its history and present circumstance, *it still is*. Some would argue that the AMEs are far more Wesleyan than most of the other descendants of John and Charles Wesley.

Other African Americans who departed at later times were to follow Allen's pattern and practice. Consider some historical examples. James Varick and Peter Williams from John Street Church in New York formed the basic structures of the African Methodist Episcopal Zion Church (A.M.E.Z.) in 1796, just a few years after the formation of the A.M.E. Church. In 1866, other Black Methodists petitioned the General Conference of the Methodist Episcopal Church South in New Orleans to form a Colored Methodist Episcopal Church (C.M.E.). The latter church was formed in 1870 in Jackson, Tennessee, and changed its name to The Christian Methodist Episcopal Church (still CME) in 1954.[7]

AFRICAN AMERICAN PRESENCE AND METHODIST FAITH

What can be said of the presence of Africans in the founding of the Christian Church when it was born on Pentecost (Acts 2) can also be said of Africans and the founding of Methodism in this country. They have been a part of the Methodist Church in the United States from its very beginning. In fact, the two Antiguan women whom Wesley baptized at Bristol in 1758—elsewhere I called them the "Holy Nameless Two"—can be credited with being the first Methodists in North America.[8] These two were so moved by the simple gospel of grace preached by John Wesley that they went home and converted their master, Nathaniel H. Gilbert. They then returned to Antigua to establish the first Methodist Chapel in the Western hemisphere, in the West Indies.

When Methodism spread to the United States, Annie Sweitzer was present with Robert Strawbridge at Sam's Creek in Frederick County, Maryland, part of the first meeting of the first Methodist society in colonial America. Two years later, Black Bettye was present as one of the five people in New York when Philip Embury held the first Methodist service at Barbara Heck's house. Several Black subscribers were on the roster of membership, paying their part when the John Street Church built its first meeting house in 1768. In addition to Bettye, several African servants, including Margaret and Rachel, were on the list of contributors to the building of John Street Chapel.[9]

"Black Harry" Hoosier, Horseman for the Lord: Methodism's Hall of Fame Candidate

Richard Allen and Harry Hoosier were at Lovely Lane in Baltimore, Maryland, when the Christmas Conference was convened in 1784 to organize The Methodist Episcopal Church. They were there as lay preachers, as were many others. In fact, "Black Harry," as he was familiarly known and called by his associates, had gone up and down the East Coast as a "horseman for the Lord," traveling with Coke and Asbury to spread news of the impending, organizing Christmas Conference.

Harry Hoosier, born a slave near Fayetteville, North Carolina, around 1750, heard the eminent British Methodist preacher, Francis Asbury, preach, and he was converted. He was soon licensed to preach. Although he could neither read nor write, he refused to allow Richard Allen to teach him. He reportedly told Allen: "I sing by faith, pray by faith, and do everything by faith; without faith in Jesus Christ, I can do nothing."[10]

Those who were quite literate, as well as the scholars and journalists of his day, testified to Harry Hoosier's utterly amazing eloquence and ability and to what his professed faith apparently enabled him to do. Abel Stevens, in his first volume of *History of the Methodist Church*, quotes one of those learned observers' commendation of Hoosier's "preaching abilities, complete command of his voice, aptness in language, and free delivery, as to Scripture and doctrinal truth."[11] Dr. Benjamin Rush—a noted physician of Philadelphia, one of the signers of the Declaration of Independence, and a leading abolitionist and friend of African Methodists—heard Hoosier preach and made this comment about him: "Making allowances for his illiteracy, he was the greatest orator in America."[12] Bishop Thomas Coke paid perhaps the highest tribute of all to Hoosier: "I really believe he is one of the best Preachers in the world, there is such an amazing power attends his preaching, though he cannot read; and he is one of the humblest creatures I ever saw."[13] Clearly, Matthew Simpson Davage was correct when he said, "Any story of the beginning of Methodism in America which does not give a prominent place to Harry Hoosier, familiarly called 'Black Harry,' is inadequate.... Surely he deserves a place in Methodism's Hall of Fame."[14]

The Staunch Loyalty of African American Methodists

By the time the Civil War split this nation into northern and southern fragments, with the church divided into corresponding regional parts, there were over two hundred thousand African Americans who claimed fierce loyalty and utter devotion to The Methodist Episcopal Church, South. That number was reduced to a little more than seventy-eight thousand in 1866, owing to the number of Black Americans who defected to "African" churches as the Union Army opened up new territories in which northern African Methodist evangelists could crusade and urge Black Methodists to join the independent churches as a badge of their freedom.

Even in the face of contradictory realities, however, African Americans remained in The Methodist Episcopal Church, both North and South, and probably all would have said, as Richard Allen had said seventy-five years earlier: "As for me, I could never be anything else but a Methodist.... And I am thankful that ever I heard a Methodist preacher."[15] They were a part of that group whose descendants are now the African American constituency of The United Methodist Church, the heirs of Harry Hoosier and the makers of Zoar. They are the loyalists and the remnant that became "a church-within-a-church." About these people, the question is whether they have been part of a genuine relationship or a mere affair.

My colleague at Vanderbilt University, church historian Lewis Baldwin, has made the point many times that of the several Black preachers active in the early Methodist movement—Richard Allen, Daniel Coker, Henry Evans, Absalom Jones, Christopher Rush, Abraham Thompson, James Varick, Harry Hoosier—all except Absalom Jones remained Methodist in some form.[16] These were people who traveled the circuits, preached at Methodist meetings, and provided spiritual leadership for their people. In their experiences of denominational structures, hospitality, as Amy Oden writes in this volume, was often absent, but African American Methodists were staunchly loyal nevertheless.

WHAT WAS THE APPEAL OF METHODISM TO AFRICAN AMERICANS?

The question is still in order after all this time: Why were these African Americans drawn to Methodism in the first place? What was the appeal of this nascent communion? Why did this relationship begin? Commonly accepted explanations are (1) the Methodist tradition's evangelistic appeal and (2) the church's attitude toward slavery. The opposition to slavery was reflected officially and forcefully in the Christmas Conference of 1784, which formed The Methodist Episcopal Church in America.[17]

There is little question that the simple gospel, as preached by Methodist itinerants, appealed to slaves as it did to poor white farmers, coal mine workers, and others who were the outcasts and déclassé masses. Great numbers flocked to hear the good news, and they expressed their feelings with cries, screams, shouts, tears, prostrations, physical convulsions, and other physical and emotional responses, sometimes even fainting and falling insensibly. John Thompson, born as a slave in Maryland in 1812, draws the clear distinction between this revivalist preaching and the more ritualistic and staid approach of the established church:

> My mistress and her family were all Episcopalians. The nearest church was five miles from our plantation, and there was no Methodist church nearer than ten miles. So we went to the Episcopal Church, but always came home as we went, for the preaching was above our comprehension, so that we could understand but little that was said. But soon the Methodist religion was brought among us, and preached in a manner so plain that the wayfaring man, though a fool, could not err therein. This new doctrine produced great consternation among the slaveholders. It was something which they could not understand. It brought glad tidings to the poor bondsman; it bound up the broken-hearted; it opened the prison doors to them that were bound, and let the captive go free. As soon as it got among the slaves, it spread from plantation to plantation, until it reached ours, where there were but few who did not experience religion.[18]

As Donald Mathews has pointed out in his careful writing and research, "Methodist ideology was also a collage of sound, symbol, and act. It was style and mood evinced in oral communication."[19] Some people who observed it and opposed its expression called it noise. One such man in New Bern, North Carolina (1807), made his feelings especially clear, but also pictured the scene of this *communitas*, which he condemned and called "farcical:"

> About a week past there was a Methodist conference in this place which lasted 7 or 8 days & nights with very little intermission, during which *there was a large concourse of people of various colors, classes & such*, assembled for various purposes. Confusion, shouting, praying, singing, laughing, talking, amorous engagements, falling down, kicking, squealing and a thousand other ludicrous things prevailed most of the time and frequently of nights, all at once—In short, it was the most detestable *farcical* scene that ever I beheld.[20]

The initial strong stance the Methodists took against slavery is well known. The fact that the church compromised its principled position is even better known and has had more serious consequences. My late colleague at Wesley Theological Seminary, Clarence Goen, called it *Broken Churches, Broken Nation* in a book that has not received the reading it deserves.[21] The church initially was ardent in its anti-slavery posture, and that hardly escaped the African slaves' attention. It hardly escapes our minds now, however, that the nation was able to come back together long before the church found a way to be reunited. Even then, the reunion was made at a very expensive price to the church's African American Methodist constituency: a demeaning and insulting, racially constituted, segregated Central Jurisdiction.

Perhaps the clearest evidence of how the slaves felt about Methodists and their stance on slavery is seen in an account of the Gabriel Prosser slave revolt in Virginia. Prosser was convinced on religious grounds—perhaps due to the influence of evangelical Methodists—that slavery should be overturned and that he had been chosen by God to be a deliverer of his people. Thus, he planned a rebellion. His plan was to destroy Henrico County and to establish a new Black kingdom in Virginia, killing whites and looting the treasury at Richmond, taking all necessary arms and artillery. In Gabriel's testimony, we find a serious student of the Bible, twenty-five years old, with unusual physical strength and impressive mental capacities. His revolt was well planned, and Gabriel said he had ten thousand men ready to go into battle. The plot failed, however, because of logistical problems, frightened and fearful slave informers, and a serious storm. Gabriel, along with several other slaves, was hanged. But central to our point here was Gabriel's instruction concerning the two groups of Christians he believed to be on God's side against the evil and un-Christian practice of slavery: "All Methodists and Quakers were to be spared."[22] How Gabriel and his army were to distinguish who were the white Methodists and Quakers, I have no earthly idea, but that is surely beside the point.

The point is that Gabriel clearly knew of the Methodist stance against slavery. Some would maintain that it was through the itinerant Methodist ministers who went back and forth from circuit to circuit that information was transmitted to the insurgents. The central point here is that the Methodists were known for their strong position against slavery, even though the church would later compromise that stance. The slaves had been won over by this principle of justice and encouraged by the church's original opposition to slavery. John Wesley had expressed it in 1743 in the original *General Rules*, and the Christmas Conference of 1784 had adopted a strong position against the institution of slavery.

Such early Methodist preachers as Francis Asbury, Freeborn Garrettson, Thomas Rankin, Ezekiel Cooper and Thomas Coke were inspired by the moral claims of John Wesley against slavery. They took rather seriously Wesley's mandate and answer to the question of what could be expected of Methodists: "to reform the nation, and especially the church, and spread scriptural holiness throughout the land."[23] These circuit riders were evangelically enthusiastic in their commitment to preach the theology of free grace, available to all, and to defend the principle of freedom from slavery in spite of social and economic pressures. Lewis Baldwin cites an important grievance of Francis Asbury, who, in one of his journal entries, complained that Methodists often had serious problems gaining access to minister to slaves because "their masters are afraid of the influence of our principles."[24]

At first, it was the English-born Methodist preachers such as Asbury, Rankin, and Coke who led the vigorous anti-slavery struggle, but then preachers who were born on American soil came along and took up the charge against slavery. For example, on the Delmarva Peninsula, the Methodist preacher Joseph Everett not only preached against slavery, but also refused to eat with slaveholders until they freed their slaves. In a study of Methodism in that region, William H. Williams, a history professor at the University of Delaware at Georgetown, has discovered the following:

> In 1797, an Episcopal rector in Talbot County [Maryland] observed that the Methodist preachers "relish the manumitting subject as highly as the Quaker preachers and spread the evil far and wide." In Somerset County, in 1801, a circuit rider told his congregation to assume that "the clouds of vengeance are collecting over the heads of the inhabitants of this country for their cruelty to the poor distressed Africans."[25]

We can see from this discussion that the Wesleyans' rejection of slavery was well documented and had much to do with the appeal of Methodism to African Americans.

In addition to the Wesleyan evangelical appeal and attitudes toward slavery (factors named above), I think that three other factors can be added: (3) the Wesleyan style of preaching and worship, which appealed to the slaves; (4) the slaves' ability to serve as lay preachers and exercise influence among blacks and whites, despite restrictions on their movement and limited opportunities for leadership; and (5) Methodism's adaptability to fit the slaves' unique situations so they could make faith their own. I will not amplify these factors further in this chapter, as I have discussed them in earlier writings, and at considerable length in my book, *Black People in the Methodist Church: Whither Thou Goest?*

Is There a Romance between African Americans and Methodism?

Our question at the moment is not why African Americans *came* into the Methodist Church, but why they have *stayed* in it, especially in The United Methodist Church and its antecedents with the checkered history of dealing with issues of race and justice. Why would a people continue to be part of a church that compromised its principles on slavery to the developing American culture and to a strange economic system that incorporated manifest destiny? Why did they remain when, in a pernicious plan concocted at Kansas City in 1939 (a plan worthy of Machiavelli), they were officially segregated into a separate "church within a church" for the first time in their almost 175-year history of association with Methodism? The 1939 reunification of The Methodist Episcopal Churches, North and South, and The Methodist Protestant Church was not a reunification for African Americans; it was rather the institutionalization of segregation through the establishment of a separate jurisdiction for African Americans, the Central Jurisdiction.

Why did African Americans endure the demeaning institutional machinery set in motion to effect this humiliating "church-within-a-church" contrivance? Why have African Americans remained Methodists when the church they love so often puts convention above conscience, is often more concerned about unity than uniqueness, and is more willing to conform than to create? Why have they remained faithful to a church when what they perceived as a genuinely decorous romance has so often been made into a sordid affair—unrequited and contemptible? What have African Americans contributed to this romance and to this church-as-church, whose history is so filled with missed opportunities to be uniquely Christian and to be a world church in the United States? The church's failures in one period have too often negated its success in another. What does this suggest for United Methodism's future in the twenty-first century, especially after we closed the twentieth century that began with

Methodism's correct, if dubiously based, claim to be the largest and "most American Church"? What can this history and these claims possibly mean now and for the future?

First, we need to say that The United Methodist Church is not alone in the problems it currently faces. The facts are well documented that the predominantly white, connectional Protestant Christian bodies in the Western world are in the same predicament.[26] They all face aging and declining memberships and a loss of enthusiasm about their unique claims and identities. They listen to straying, struggling, and competing apologists. They hear calls for a more interiorized and privatized form of religion with an attending self-fulfillment ethic, and they receive conflicting and confusing messages about what salvation means—salvation *from* what and *to* what. As they produce fewer zealous youth, their very existence is threatened by lessened loyalty and support from those who have been their mainstay and by a decline in those who are their natural heirs.

Present Methodism: Perils of the Past, Hope for the Future

Part of the positive uniqueness for Methodism and the promise for its future may lie in the very perils of its past and its present. Its hope for vision and fulfillment may be inherent in the solutions found to one of *its most pressing present problems—its perspective on and its practice of inclusiveness.* I do not merely offer this as alliterative poetry, but as a solid prophetic reality. Methodism is still, by grace, the most multicultural church in the nation: pluralistic, democratic, and with the means to effect change within its particular and diverse theological, historical, homiletical, liturgical, and ecclesial tradition. It also has the human resources to forge a new and creative history. But does the church have the will to face the dilemma? The desire to find a will is the challenge with which the late Bishop James S. Thomas, the highly respected and beloved Black general superintendent, closed the bicentennial United Methodist General Conference on May 12, 1984, at 12:32 a.m. He prayed passionately: "Lead us now to make new history."[27]

If the church is to move in this direction, it will need to drink fresh water from old clean springs. It will also need to purify those streams from the left and the right, for those streams have been polluted and poisoned by a non-yielding, intolerant, contemporary, right-wing fundamentalism. In an intolerant mode, the church at present focuses on nonessential issues of faith with efforts to dominate and control the symbols of legitimacy, while offering non-dialogical, iron-clad theological absolutes. While fundamentalism is usually associated with conservatives, liberals and even progressives can be fundamentalists, too: being guilty of focusing on non-essentials, attempting to dominate and control the symbols of legitimacy, and so on. But what threatens the future of the multicultural church and impedes its efforts at being the church of "open hearts, open minds, and open doors" is a fundamentalism linked to a very conservative political and free market ideology in which the political ideology is interpreted to be synonymous with the Gospel of Jesus Christ. People do not lack understanding of the moral and spiritual imperatives of the biblical tradition so much as they are willing to trivialize the Gospel.

The sad and startling fact of so many of our mainline churches is not so much that we have abandoned the Gospel, but rather that we have trivialized the Gospel. The ethical and spiritual demands of the Gospel have been transformed into an inoffensive prudential morality. The grammar of grace has become the language of the marketplace. It is even with great difficulty that people with such attitudes are able to admit with the Apostle Paul that "we see through a glass darkly," for they are certain of who Jesus is and what he has done, and what love accomplished in him and continues to accomplish in his name. Yet, Love is resurrected at Easter and is alive and available to all. Such love lives and is shown abroad when the church reaches to take the hands of those who are reaching for tomorrow—whatever color those hands may be.

WHY HAVE AFRICAN AMERICANS REMAINED IN THE METHODIST CHURCH?

Reviewing the theological debate is revealing, but it is not the primary consideration of this chapter. To be the totally inclusive community that Methodism espouses—in obedience to its Lord—and to be the church that African Americans have so long dreamed of, hoped for, worked for, and constantly called the church back to, we must be aware of the impediments.

To be biblically centered is one thing. To be fundamentalist is quite another. African American Methodists have not historically viewed Scripture as fundamentalists do. Rather, they have seen the Bible as the story of divine redemption of the natural and human realms, a story of God's constant overture to reclaim the straying and lost creation, and God's willingness to get *to* us by getting *with* us. It is not a textbook for science, the chest of rigid moral codes upon which we can structure a society, nor is it the repository of proof-texts, but it is the story of human experiences with God with which people can identify. One need only look at the African American spirituals to see this epitomized. Spirituals also reveal the quintessential roles that hermeneutics, reading strategies, and imagination play in appropriating Scripture.

I think one can safely say that, theologically, most African American Methodists have not closely identified with the liberal left or the conservative right, but certainly they have never identified with the literalists and fundamentalists. If a label could be placed on them at all, it would probably be that of *evangelical essentialists*. That is to say, they have separated out of the faith that which is essential and substantial from that which is accidental and peripheral. They have dwelt with and accented that which is at the center, or essential, in the faith, and not what is at the edges and boundaries. For them, Jesus, the liberating Word—the one who brings freedom and justice, the one who identifies with the poor and disinherited, the one who gives perspective on facts and makes them truth—is essential. For them, Jesus himself is always the necessary and sufficient Word. That Word made flesh in Jesus the Christ, who became "grace upon grace," was the necessary and sufficient Word in the past, as it is now and shall forever be for all time. Trusting in this Word is at the center of why African Americans have remained in churches of the Methodist family, even in The United Methodist Church, whose record in race relations is so checkered with both good and destruction.

To Affirm and Live Out a Belief in the Gospel They Heard

We can say, first of all, that African Americans have stayed because they believe that God is for real in Jesus Christ as revealed both in Scripture and in their experience. They believe the gospel of grace, the glad tidings of Jesus—of love, redemption, and release—that they heard from the Methodist preacher. For them, this was not merely an enticement to increase numbers or to make them more serviceable, obedient, and subservient to earthly masters. It was instead the grand and royal invitation of the Word of God to come and accept their God-offered place as valuable creatures, created by a loving God who has made them "a little lower than the angels" or "a little less than God" (Ps. 8:5, KJV and NRSV, respectively). Their dignity, worth, freedom, and identity were bestowed upon them at birth and could be claimed through the complete transaction of God through Christ at Calvary. That was at once humbling and gratifying, freeing and joy producing, but also obliging and disciplining. More than anything, it was, for certain, good news of "de kingdom coming."[28]

Further, African Americans understood that the action of the gospel of grace broke down every barrier that distinguished or divided those who recognize and receive that grace. Those first Black women at Bristol believed it. Annie Sweitzer at Sam's Creek believed it. Bettye at the John Street society believed it. Harry Hoosier believed it, sang it, prayed it, and eloquently preached it. He proclaimed grace with faith, power, and passion from the flowering hills of North Carolina to the teeming northeastern shores of the Atlantic in Massachusetts. Millions of African Americans were part of early Methodist meetings, and they continue coming to Methodist churches, offering their fierce loyalty to the church because they have heard the love of God there. They still believe the promise that God's love, manifest in a crucified and risen Lord, welcomes, pardons, cleanses, and relieves. Many today, and many thousands who have gone before, bear witness to their own experience that those whom Christ frees are free, indeed! In words heard in churches and chapels from one coast to the other, they speak their faith: "The world didn't give it to me, and the world can't take it away."[29]

To Claim Their Own History and Heritage

Second, African Americans have remained in the Methodist family, including The United Methodist Church, because they feel the church is as much theirs as anyone else's. The history of John Wesley and African Americans began in South Carolina in 1737 when Wesley sought to instruct Africans in the Christian faith. These were the people he met when he crossed over from Savannah to the colony of South Carolina. These Wesleyan encounters with African Americans pre-date the first Methodist Society meeting in Frederick County, Maryland, by almost thirty years. As indicated earlier, when that society was formed with Robert Strawbridge at Sam's Creek in 1764, Annie Sweitzer ("Aunt Annie," who was a slave of the Sweitzer family) was entered as a charter member. That was true of Bettye, an African, at the John Street Society in New York in 1776, when they first met at Barbara Heck's house. By 1789, seventy of the 360 members of the New York group of Methodists were African Americans. The African Americans, slaves and free, who joined the movement not only participated in the services, gave to the building funds, and attended and led the class meetings; these new African American Methodists also preached and evangelized. Slaves, ex-slaves, free people, and indentured servants preached and converted wherever and whenever possible.

Henry Evans, a free African American and an early preacher, established Methodism in Fayetteville, North Carolina, and served that mixed church until he died. Bishop Capers points out that Evans "was confessedly the father of the Methodist Church, white and black, in Fayetteville, and the best preacher of his time in that quarter."[30] He sustained beatings for preaching to Whites until they defended him and urged him to stay and serve them. In his last sermon and his farewell to his congregation, the old man appeared from his quarters. Capers, who had come as his replacement, told the story in reverent detail:

> The little door between his humble shed and the chancel where I stood was opened, and the dying man entered for a last farewell to his people. He was almost too feeble to stand at all, but supporting himself by the railing of the chancel, he said: "I have come to say my last word to you. It is this: None but Christ. Three times I have had my life in jeopardy for preaching the Gospel

to you. Three times I have broken the ice on the edge of the water and swam across the Cape Fear to preach the Gospel to you. And now, if in my last hour I could trust to that or to anything else but to Christ crucified, for my salvation, all should be lost and my soul perish forever."[31]

With such faith and passion, Capers, along with so many millions of African Americans, witnessed to their bonding to Christ and The Methodist Episcopal Church.

Grant Shockley, a beloved scholar of Methodism and United Methodist leader and seminary president, pointed out that "the thousands of Black converts who accepted Christianity as their religion and Methodism as their denomination represented one of the largest non-white accessions to the Christian church in North America."[32] These African American Methodists claimed the Methodist Church as their church, and they refused to be "defined out" of Methodism on racial grounds. It is their church. Its failures as well as its achievements are part of their history as well. The choice to stay was as much an exercise of freedom as the choice to leave. For those African Americans who have stayed, the choice to stay has been the more viable option of their freedom. This is their church, their spiritual home. They will witness where they are. And they have chosen to stay and weather the enticements and embarrassing criticisms, insults, humiliation, taunts, and jibes from other African Americans—sometimes from those well-meaning brothers and sisters, the African and colored Methodists who chose to depart. They are prepared to defend, define, and stand on their history and their relationships. This may require reform and renewal. It may require organizing for causes and establishing caucuses, but Black United Methodists say they are in the church to stay. The church's history and heritage, its doctrine and didactics, its hymnody and humanity, its struggles and accomplishments, its challenges and opportunities are also theirs. They represent part of the long history and relationship between African Americans and Methodism. And they intend to help God to answer their revered African American Bishop Thomas's prayer: "Lord, Lead us now to make new history!"

Nevertheless, the question was, and still is: When will the rest of the church, including Methodist historians and scholars of the universities and seminaries, accept and claim that these realities of the past represent a *common history*, a shared history? When will they stop writing and speaking of the history of Methodism without including all Methodists in that history? Other ethnic people in the rainbow of Methodism are asking the same question.[33] Our required United Methodist history textbooks will and should look and read differently when we respond.

To Be a Missional Presence

Third, African Americans have remained in the Methodist family and United Methodist Church because they have felt their presence is required for the mission of the church. Their understanding of the Bible and the meaning of Christian community is that God's church is made up of people from every nation and station, just as it was at Pentecost. Witnessing to this understanding, African American United Methodists initiated and joined with other ethnic-minority theologians (Asians, Hispanic-Latinos, and Native Americans) and a few invited Euro-Americans for two quadrennia in the Roundtable of Ethnic Theologians. This community issued its report in a publication entitled *Out of Every Tribe and Nation*.[34]

These ethnic theologians met over time in their diverse native settings: a sweat lodge in Arizona, a place in San Antonio accompanied by mariachis, a Korean church in Chicago with a pan-Asian ambience and Korean-tradition prayers, and Black St. Helena Island in South Carolina at the Gullah Penn Center with the beat of ancient spirituals and the moss hanging from the live oak and Palmetto trees in the background. For African Americans and others to leave The United Methodist Church would deprive Methodism of its authenticity as the Church of Jesus Christ where people of God of every tribe and nation, every hue and language, from the East and from the West, occidental and oriental, gather together around the Word and Sacraments. To leave would mean an empty seat at the roundtable. To leave would deprive the church of the peculiar voices of many peoples, all of whom are vitally needed in the conversation interpreting God's grace. It would deprive the church of these diverse witnesses to what God is doing in the world—their reading of the "signs of the times," which they see through their eyes and experience in their hearts and souls. Would that such a group of ethnic theologians could resolve to continue meeting, and perhaps expand to other religious groups who search for wholeness and peace, who dare call God's name. The decided wisdom of the Roundtable was that such voices must be heard from every tribe and nation.

Even in the decades during which African American United Methodists have existed in separate congregations, they have been both a protest and a testimony that nothing—segregation, racism, mistreatment, discrimination, a central jurisdiction, or anything else—can dissuade them from what Shockley describes as "their bonding to Christ and the church through Wesleyan, as well as Episcopal, Methodism." Shockley elaborates on this determination: "This attitude was not a fleeting one or limited to that [any] generation. It has persisted since the late 1700s to the present."[35] The people have believed that the redeemed of the Lord ought to say so by joining with others who are being saved for the upbuilding of the church, and as a sign of the presence of God's reign and the coming of God's beloved community. The presence of African Americans is necessary so that "all flesh shall see it together" (Isa. 40:5 KJV). African Americans believe that part of their mission and ability is to help the church keep its priorities in sight, remembering what is essential for the church to be the church, lest it allow itself to forge an unholy and unhealthy union with the culture and betray its Lord.

To Be the Primordial Conscience of Methodism

Fourth, African Americans have remained to be the conscience of Methodism, and of United Methodism in particular. From the very beginning, African Americans have believed that the church would somehow rise above the accidents of race, the ephemeral nature of station, and the changing and shifting political ideologies of the nation, and would finally *be* the church. When that has not been the case, as has happened so often in American Methodism's more than two and a half centuries, African Americans have raised again and again the cry: "Let the church be the church!"

We hear that cry from Richard Allen and those who left The Methodist Episcopal Church with him in Philadelphia. We hear that cry as the Methodist Episcopal Church split into North and South over the issue of slavery. We hear that cry in Kansas City (1939) when the white members of the church *stood* to celebrate the victory of an ultimate compromise to segregation with a central jurisdiction (which gave structural unity but maintained segregation) while Black members of that general conference *sat* and wept. We hear that cry now as The United Methodist Church hedges and hesitates to practice its own principled policy of inclusiveness and a truly open itinerancy. If this is the reality, and it is, where do we expect the church to deal with the issue of the physically challenged? I was almost prepared to surrender my orders again when I heard about a blind colleague being rendered "unappointable." This man is a fine preacher and one to whom I would have given high marks in my preaching classes! The cry for true inclusiveness is stuck in the throats of the rainbow-colored Methodists who gather in their local churches each Sunday morning at eleven o'clock, still the most segregated hour of the week. The churches are more segregated than the jobs where people work, the schools where they study, or the sports and entertainment events where they participate during the week.

African American United Methodists have seen many changes take place as a result of their persistent prodding and pushing the church. Their presence in the church has indelibly influenced every decade and development of the church's life in the United States, as well as its ability to effect change in the larger society. Consider some of the visible influences: Black bishops elected to serve the whole church; Black superintendents appointed to administer districts that include all United Methodists in their region (a move that eventually led to the appointment of female superintendents as well); Black executives of national boards and agencies; Black staff of annual conferences (though many such appointments have been made to avoid appointing well-qualified African Americans to majority-white membership churches); a few African American pastors serving predominantly white local churches; and a hymnal that includes many songs from African American tradition, now sung in churches all over the nation and world. All of these examples bespeak relationship for African Americans: a sense of belonging and claiming The United Methodist Church as their own, and a history of loving accountability, conscience, justice, prophetic imagination, and responsible grace. Such are values of evangelical essentialists, whose mission is to focus on what is central and essential and not on the trivial and unnecessary, to witness in word and deed to the saving power of grace through Jesus Christ, to love and serve those whom Jesus loved and served, to the end that kingdoms of this world may become kingdoms of our Lord and our Christ. In so doing, we keep so busy serving our Jesus that we enact the words of the ancient African American spiritual that we sang in my home church in Gadsden, Alabama, Sweet Home United Methodist: "Ain't got time to die."

> When we're serving the poor . . . we're serving our Jesus;
> When we're feeding the hungry . . . we're serving our Jesus;
> When we're seeking justice . . . we're serving our Jesus;
> When we visit the sick . . . we're serving our Jesus;
> When we visit the jails . . . we're serving our Jesus;
> Lord, we keep so busy, serving our Jesus, we ain't got time to die.
>
> So, get out of our way . . . get out of our way,
> If we don't serve him, the rocks will cry out:
> "Glory and Honor! Glory and Honor!" Ain't got time to die.

WHAT ABOUT A FUTURE?

Where does this discussion point for the future? Can we now see reflected in local United Methodist churches all of the hues of the "people called Methodists" who reside in our towns and cities? Can we truthfully speak of the church as having "open hearts, open minds, open doors"? Are we a church where Jesus Christ is Lord and every human creature is affirmed (whatever his or her color, place of origin, sexual orientation, age, or native language), as special in God's creation?

These questions take particular focus at the communion table. Who is at the Lord's Table? With whom do we eat? Whom are we *willing* to welcome to the table to join us in communion? Do we have some people who thought they had a seat, but actually have to continue looking to the future? Perhaps some people have to sing again, as my grandmother used to sing so sweetly and joyfully and hopefully: "I'm gonna sit at the welcome table, one of these days."[36] My grandmother would add, as if she were certain that this was not going to happen soon, that the reality of this welcome table was beyond this place of wrath and tears. It had to do with being seated at the eschatological feast in glory, where the streets are paved with gold and every meal is like my grandmother's prepared Sunday's dinner: "I'm gonna tell God how you treated me, one of these days" (the last phrase sometimes changed to "when I get home").

As United Methodists, can we reach out to the *separated* African Americans who call themselves *Methodists*, too? Can we restructure The United Methodist Church, alter its attitudes and practices, and say, "Please come back! We are ready to *be* the church!" Will we? Can we? Do we have room at the table? Will those separated African Americans—those who still claim Wesleyan roots with John and Charles and Susanna Wesley as their essential ecclesial ancestors—find "fruits of repentance" after an emotional, agonizing, and soul-baring confession of racism and bigotry at the 2000 General Conference (UMC), and in many annual conferences across the United States after that? Will the "fruit inspectors" find the fruits and have anything good to report? Can this church—so Wesleyan, so American, so willing to change organizational structures, so willing to move furniture around—be willing to truly be the church, no matter what the culture does?

If we cannot, then, what word do we have for other African Americans or for the many other persons who people our cities, populate our towns, and live in our rural communities, who are un-churched and languish in doubt, despair, disorder, and un-freedom? What hope can we offer for reconciliation—for being a restored people, a redeemed world, the beloved community? What word do we have for the brothers and sisters who have no faith, no confidence, and no interest in the church or the Christ it represents? That is the challenge to all of Methodism as we try to be the church in this new millennium. That reaching out, restoring, reclaiming, and proclaiming may be the real future of Methodism in the United States. The growth, the survival, and even the very *raison d'être* of *United Methodism* (certainly a misnomer!) and of the Methodist family may well depend upon it.

CHAPTER FOUR

SUSANNA ANNESLEY WESLEY: A WOMAN OF SPIRIT AND SPIRITUALITY

W. Stephen Gunter

Discussion of a living Wesleyan tradition requires attention to the woman who shaped the Wesley children so profoundly, and hence shaped the Wesleyan traditions—their mother, Susanna Annesley Wesley. What is especially important in Susanna's life is the living tradition that she inherited from the Annesley family, and the daring way she lived her life within the seventeenth- and eighteenth-century English context. Within her context and sphere of influence, Susanna was clearly a woman of spirit and spirituality, leaving a spiritual legacy that continues to enliven Wesleyan traditions today.

The purpose of this chapter is to reflect on Susanna Wesley as a woman who could not keep silent about her faith. In particular, her ability to connect faith and reason, a gift of her Puritan heritage, was a gift to her children. She was thus a major shaper of Wesleyan theology in its later forms. In this chapter, we first consider Susanna Wesley as a woman of her time and beyond her time, exploring how women in her context were limited, but were pushing social and educational boundaries. In that world, Susanna Wesley distinguished herself as an "able divine," drawing from her intellectual world and exploring the relations of truth and faith. One can see proto-feminist strands in her spirited life, suggestive of work for the future of a living tradition.

SUSANNA: WOMAN OF HER TIME—WOMAN BEYOND HER TIME

Susanna Annesley Wesley—why would one use the modern convention of retaining the maiden name in conjunction with the married name to identify the spouse of an obscure eighteenth-century Anglican parish priest who was the mother of at least nineteen children? This gives rise to the related question of why the modern convention of double last names has become fashionable in segments of the Anglo-Saxon world. The answer is partly a matter of identity; a person does not lose his or her birth identity simply because he or she marries. A woman brings to marriage the uniqueness of her personage, and this singularity is recognized as fundamental to the newly formed identity. While in the Victorian Era in which Susanna lived wives were expected to be subsumed under the identity of their husbands, some women of that period, and every period before and since, had personal strength that was impossible to subordinate. Susanna Wesley was a woman of both an indomitable spirit and spirituality, so it would be less than appropriate in our age of equal rights to identify her other than as Susanna Annesley Wesley.

The shape and substance of Susanna's identity as a woman were formed initially within the Annesley family, and only later in the Wesley family into which she married. Susanna was the remarkable daughter of Dr. Samuel Annesley, the apple of his eye and the youngest of twenty-four or twenty-five children. The Rev. Dr. Manton, who baptized her, could not remember for sure if she was the twenty-fourth or twenty-fifth; yet Susanna came to be both distinctive and memorable. She was a woman who dared to defy customary patterns of subordination and, even more strongly, to seek intellectual knowledge and engage in intellectual exchange in ways that were quite unconventional for women in her day. I am willing to press this even further in the case of Susanna—the wife of an Anglican parish priest whose diaries show that she not only read, but noted and questioned, the likes of John Locke and the bishops of her chosen church. I say "chosen church" because she decided in late 1681 or early 1682 "not being full thirteen" to declare membership in the Anglican Church even though her father, the Rev. Samuel Annesley, was a well-known London Nonconformist minister before, during, and after the Cromwellian era.[1] Annesley had gained part of his notoriety during his first pastorate, when he antagonized the Royalists in a sermon before the House of Commons.

When a teenager who is barely through puberty changes ecclesial loyalties, especially in a day when these loyalties evoke sharp responses, one might imagine a paradigmatic strong-willed child. Whatever the reasons, the young Susanna was declaring her own identity. Would any recent feminist ask for more? And yet there is more. When Susanna's tenth child, John, was studying for his ordination at Christ Church, Oxford, she mentored him by sending suggestions for further reading. When this failed, she admonished him directly for the shortcomings in his theology and epistemology. We see in these exchanges a woman with more than a simplistic piety. Susanna's theological convictions had been sharpened like flint against steel by her interactions with the theological and philosophical lights of her age. Susanna Annesley Wesley might well be identified as an "early feminist," or a precursor thereto, a woman of spirit and spirituality.

Women Bending the Status Quo

People need to be viewed within their contexts if they are to be properly understood; this is a fundamental assumption of social-historical analysis. One way to engage in contextual analysis in a biographical study is to view your subject as one among her contemporaries. The women listed below, Susanna's contemporaries, were significant in their day for their intellectual endeavors, most specifically their published literature. Learning about these contemporaries and near-contemporaries of Susanna Annesley Wesley is important for our gaining some level of objectivity with regard to Susanna's singularity. Any estimation of Susanna's stature must be set amid that of other women of accomplishment in the same era. Thus, I offer an alphabetical listing of such women in the eighteenth century:[2]

1. **Mary Astell** (1666–1731) was a religious polemicist who gained public respect with *Letters Concerning the Love of God* (1695).[3] This was her correspondence with the philosopher and theologian John Norris of Bremerton, whose thought also influenced John Wesley.[4] Astell's example as an independent intellectual influenced Mary Chudleigh (below); the Anglo-Saxon specialist Elizabeth Elstob; and Lady Mary Wortley Montagu, founder of the "Bluestocking Circle," a gathering of women who thrived on intellectual discourse among themselves.
2. **Elizabeth Carter** (1717–1806) was a scholar, poet, translator, and essayist who was also a member of the Bluestocking Circle. She is best known for her translation of Epictetus' writings, which was the standard English version for over a century.
3. **Hester Mulso Chapone** (1717–1806) was a poet and essayist who was a friend of Elizabeth Carter and Elizabeth Montagu and a member of Richardson's circle. Her best-known work is *Letters on the Improvement of the Mind*, but she also published *Miscellanies in Prose and Verse* (1773).[5]
4. **Lady Mary Chudleigh** (1657–1710) was a poet and essayist and admirer of Mary Astell. She is best known for her poem published in 1700, "The Ladies' Defence: or, The Bride Woman's Counsellor Answer'd."[6] This is her response to a sermon preached in 1699

by the Reverend John Sprint, who had argued that wives owed absolute obedience to their husbands.
5. **Anne Dutton** (1692–1765) was a Methodist and prolific religious writer whose best-known correspondence was with John Wesley and focused on the topic of salvation and election.
6. **Catherine Macaulay Graham** (1731–91) was a Whig historian, best known for her *History of England from the Accession of James I to that of the Brunswick Line*.[7] Hers was the first history of the Civil War written by a woman and a republican. She wrote in the last year of her life a reply to (Member of Parliament) Edmund Burke's *Reflections on the Revolution in France*.
7. **Eliza Haygood** (1693–1756) was a novelist and periodical writer whose early seduction narratives were later surpassed in transgressing social respectability by *The Female Spectator* (1744–46).[8] Haygood also wrote *The History of Miss Betsy Thoughtless* (1751).[9]
8. **Hannah More** (1745–1833) was a teacher turned professional writer and also a member of the Bluestocking Circle. She taught many other women as well.
9. **Mary Robinson** (1758–1800) learned under Hannah More, and she became a novelist who combined sentimental morality with an Enlightenment concern for justice and social values.
10. **Elizabeth Singer Rowe** (1674–1737) was a poet and Dissenting writer on moral and religious subjects. She was often cited in the late eighteenth century as an example of the virtuous literary woman.

All of these women are part of the English social fabric into which a story about Susanna Annesley Wesley must be woven. Recognizing the complexity of this social feminine fabric may prevent students of Susanna Wesley from assuming that her strong personality and passion for learning were anomalous for her era. On the other hand, the social complexity of that era also included conventional social constructs by which women were often idealized as paragons of virtue without distinct identities. This phenomenon is reflected in a January 1794 obituary of one "Mrs. Barclay, wife of Mr. Robert Barclay," whose full name was not given alongside her husband's in her obituary:

> To those who enjoyed the happiness of an intercourse with the numerous and well-ordered family over which she presided, with equal eloquence and decorum, it cannot be necessary to describe the excellencies which distinguished her character as a wife, a mother, a mistress, and a friend, amiable, affectionate, upright, and humane. . . . Her mind was early imbued with sentiments that regarded the serious and important duties of life . . . [the] education of her children, twelve of whom survive her . . . duties which were

marked with acts of tenderness and benevolence . . . [leaving behind an] afflicted husband! to whom the deceased was endeared by every consideration that a constant attachment, and a continued scene of domestic felicity can suggest.[10]

Once the glow of the star-studded halo has filled our eyes with the glare, we realize that we know everything and at the same time nothing about this woman's uniqueness. Mrs. Barclay's life could not have been all velvet and cream.

Vivien Jones places this obituary in an analytical light by introducing a metaphoric comparison between the obituary and a tract from Edmund Burke published in 1757.[11] The critical words for comparison are from a section on "How far the idea of BEAUTY may be applied to the qualities of MIND":

> Those virtues which cause admiration, and are of the sublimer kind, produce terror rather than love. Such as fortitude, justice, wisdom, and the like. Never was any man amiable by force of these qualities. Those which engage our hearts, which impress us with a sense of loveliness, are the softer virtues: easiness of temper, compassion, kindness and liberality; though certainly those latter are of less immediate and momentous concern to society, and of less dignity. But it is for that reason they are so amiable. The great virtues turn principally on dangers, punishments, and troubles, and are exercised rather in preventing the worst mischiefs, than in dispensing favours. . . . The subordinate [virtues] are therefore more lovely, though inferior in dignity.[12]

Burke's view of the "female virtues" is strikingly reminiscent of those reflected in the Barclay obituary. Mrs. Barclay conforms to the paradigm in Burke's *Enquiry*, an influential work on aesthetic theory even into the twentieth century. To be sure, Burke was not writing overtly about women, but the reigning cultural assumptions about difference between the sexes are no less apparent here than they are in the last public words over the departed spirit of Mrs. Barclay. Vivien Jones concludes that Burke's "categorization of mental attributes in terms of a comparison between the 'softer virtues' and those of the 'sublimer kind' depends on a distinction between 'feminine' and 'masculine' qualities."[13] Feminine softness is opposed to masculine strength; feminine amiability is set against masculine dignity; and feminine nurture is not as desirable as masculine authority. As we now know, all of these principles were assumed in eighteenth-century England to be a naturalistic part of the gendered order. The assumption was that two identity-giving gender identities exist, as do two accompanying sets of virtues, also identity giving. While modern people know that this view is ideology and not actuality, we are not yet entirely beyond the stereotypes that inform these distinctions. The temptation to succumb to gender stereotypes must be especially avoided when people in the twenty-first century seek to understand a woman who lived in the eighteenth.

Part of the difficulty in writing about an eighteenth-century woman, especially when one is committed to a significant use of her personal writings, is the knowledge that women of that era lived in culturally defined and confining categories of womanhood. Within those constructs, women had to negotiate their way and they often suffered. But here too, one must not lapse into uncritical rhetoric. In the latter part of the twentieth century, a more sophisticated reading of the eighteenth-century "conduct metaphors" emerged. Formerly seen as demeaning, they are now viewed in a more complex light. Students of this period now argue that the dominant ideal of femininity, with its emphasis on morality and feeling (the softer virtues), emerged as a powerful factor in shaping what came to be called the "middle class" in the eighteenth century. The emergence of the middle class was likened to the feminization of culture.[14]

If a man of culture and refinement wanted to win the hand of his love, the rules increasingly changed in the course of the century. Increasingly, the eighteenth-century man had to win the woman's hand in marriage through a display of refined sensibility that complemented the woman's, a reflection of the changing reality that the softer virtues were in subtle but discernible ways becoming tacit masculine values. More forthrightly, one can say that virtue was being recognized as truly virtuous. The stereotype of who does or does not act in certain ways was beginning to lose its undeserved universality, and women who had the spirit to challenge the inherited status quo were emerging as change agents, especially in the realm of intellectual discourse and the consequent rise in expectations for women's education.

Women and Education

Susanna Wesley is well known for her emphasis on education—that which she received and that which she made sure her children received. Her parents educated her at a level that was well above average for the latter part of the seventeenth century. The more typical pattern for girls' education can be seen in a tract by Francois de Fénélon, which was widely read in England in its translated form for more than a century. His *Treatise*,[15] under the heading "On the Importance of the Education of Daughters," opens with a promising admonition: "The Education of Girls is, in general, exceedingly neglected: custom, and maternal caprice, often appear to have the entire regulation of it." From this promising refrain, we should not assume that this oft-read and cited essay represented the beginning of a cultural reformation. The lead sentence of the following paragraph is the more representative cultural view:

It is true, that we should be on our guard not to make them ridiculously learned. Women, in general, possess weaker but more inquisitive minds than men; hence it follows that their pursuits should be of a quiet and sober turn. They are not formed to govern the state, to make war, or to enter into the church; so that they may well dispense with any profound knowledge relating to politics, military tactics, philosophy, and theology. The greater part of the mechanical arts are also improper for them: they are made for moderate exercise; their bodies as well as mind are less strong and energetic than those of men; but to compensate for their defects, nature has bestowed on them a spirit of industry, united with propriety of behaviour, and an economy which renders them at once the ornament and comfort of home.

Although the remainder of Fénélon's essay is not as comprehensively condescending, he never recovers from the diminutive cast of this paragraph's assertions.

These comments are similar to the sentiments of King James I. When someone suggested that his daughter Elizabeth should receive instruction in Latin, he responded, "To make women learned and foxes tame had the same effect; to make them more cunning."[16] Fortunately, Elizabeth (1596–1662) educated herself far above the expectations of her father. It is clear, however, that a woman educated to the standards of Fénélon and James I would never in this life bear the testimony of Vicesimus Knox's fictional correspondent, also the daughter of a minister, who represented the ideals of striving women:

I am the only daughter of a clergyman, who, on the death of my mother ... when I was about three, concentrated his affections in me, and thought he could not display his love more effectually than in giving me a good education.... As soon as I could read, I was initiated in Lilly's Grammar, and, before I was eight years old, could repeat every rule ... I was taught indeed all kinds of needle-work; but two hours every day were invariably set apart for my improvement in Latin.... My father was so well pleased with my proficiency ... that he resolved ... to open to my view the spacious fields of Grecian literature. The Greek Grammar I mastered with great ease ... I was enabled to drink at the fountain-head, while others were obliged to content themselves with the distant and polluted stream.... The French and Italian languages became easy after my acquaintance with the Latin, and my father was of opinion that they are indispensably necessary... After having laid a foundation in the languages, which I believe is seldom done with success but at an early age, my father allowed me to feast without control on the productions of my own country.... All the classical poets, from Shakespeare to Pope, were my study and delight. History, which my father always recommended as peculiarly suited to adorn the female mind, was a favourite pursuit.... Yet, notwithstanding my improvements, ... I find myself received in the world with less cordiality than I had reason to expect.

> My own sex stand too much in awe of me to bear me any affection. . . . I am avoided by gentlemen who are ambitious of the company of other ladies. . . . Though they think me extremely clever, . . . they cannot reconcile the ideas of female attractions and the knowledge of the Greek.[17]

From these two extracts, we may draw at least two tentative conclusions. On the one hand, even people who were not inclined to educate girls to become "ridiculously learned" women recognized that it was not good for society to neglect the education of girls. If a girl's parents ever expected her to fare well as a middle-class woman, she needed some education. On the other hand, a highly educated girl might well face the plight of spinsterhood, which was highly undesirable in that social world. On the latter point, consider the fate of an intelligent woman from a home of moderate means who did not marry well, or marry at all:

> Few are the modes of earning a subsistence, and those very humiliating. Perhaps to be an humble companion to some rich old cousin, or what is worse still, to live with strangers . . . above the servants, yet considered by them a spy, and ever reminded of [your own] inferiority when in conversation with superiors . . . If what I have written should be read by parents, who are now going on in thoughtless extravagance, and anxious only that their daughter may be genteelly educated, let them consider to what sorrows they expose them; for I have not over-coloured the picture.[18]

When we picture Susanna Wesley within the educational trajectory of the eighteenth century, she seems to fit within the social structures. Well educated, she defies the categorization of Fénélon that a woman is by nature "not formed . . . to enter the church . . . or [gain] any profound knowledge relating to . . . philosophy, and theology." On the other hand, despite the high pedestal on which previous biographers have placed Susanna, we have no evidence that she knew much Greek and was among the most learned of her society. She was physically attractive and educated enough to marry young and reasonably well, but not so intellectually cultured as to destroy the structures of societal expectations. As one reads her correspondence and diaries, one sees traces of her kicking against societal controls on women of strong spirit and high acumen, but there are no indications that she would be willing to support other women's public efforts to tear them down.

Susanna also seemed to be astute as regards the importance of education for girls, and her daughters in particular. If we envision the plight of an eighteenth-century daughter left in penury, we see the potentially desperate plight of a widow who outlives her husband by twenty years, unless she is fortunate to have children who can take her in. Within this context, we need to picture Susanna's care for the education of her daughters. She embodied much of what was expressed by a more forthright author about girl children, Catherine Macaulay Graham:

> The moderns, in the education of their children, have too much followed the stiff and prudish manners of ancient days, in separating the male and female children of a family . . . [following] the absurd notion that the education of females should be of an opposite kind to that of males. . . . Be no longer niggards, then, O ye parents, in bestowing on your offspring, every blessing which nature and fortune renders them possible of enjoying! Confine not the education of your daughters to what is regarded as the ornamental parts of it, nor deny the graces to sons. . . . Let your children be brought up together; let their . . . studies be the same; let them enjoy in the constant presence of those who are over them, all that freedom which innocence renders harmless, and in which Nature rejoices. By the uninterrupted intercourse which you will establish, both sexes will find that friendship may be enjoyed between them without passion . . . [thereby] your sons will look for something more solid in women, than a mere outside; and no longer be the dupes to the meanest [least intelligent], the weakest, and the most profligate of the [opposite] sex.[19]

While Susanna was not explicitly defying the gendered structures of education in her day, she implicitly defied the structures by providing an extensive education for her daughters while doing all within her power to assure university for Samuel Jr., John, and Charles Wesley.

What we now consider good education for children was slowly evolving in the early modern English context.[20] King Henry VIII in the sixteenth century founded 50 schools, followed by Queen Mary's 19, and then Queen Elizabeth I, who outpaced others in the House of Stuart by establishing 138 schools. The great majority of these were located in towns and villages and, although they were legally open to both boys and girls, most girls were still tutored at home—as was Susanna and as were her daughters in the eighteenth century. While ALL boys were required to study Latin, only the very brightest girls were even considered to study the *lingua franca* of intellectual discourse. Generally speaking, only wealthy citizens trained their daughters in Latin and modern languages, and this was an inconsistent practice. If there is an early trailblazer to be named in opening educational doors to women, the honor might well go to Bathsua Reginald Makin. She penned and published "An Essay to Revive the Ancient Education of Gentlewomen" (London, 1673). This essay, a challenge to Parliament and local politicians to provide education for young girls, went unheeded; but Bathsua, recognized as one of the most learned women of her day, was employed by Charles I as tutor to Princess Elizabeth (namesake of Queen Elizabeth), who achieved a wide reputation for brilliance in languages, specifically tutored by Makin in Greek, Latin, Hebrew, French, Italian, and Spanish, as well as mathematics.[21]

In spite of these movements and exceptions, academies were not established for women until the eighteenth century. Even then, the classics were ignored in favor of curricula designed more to produce good wives than to develop leaders of society. British universities were not opened to women until the late nineteenth century. Oxford University did not grant degrees to women until 1920, and Cambridge held out until 1948. Such was the educational travail of women in English society.

By the time of Susanna Wesley's birth on January 20, 1669, there was little emphasis in England on the education of daughters, even those born to established London ministers of some reputation. Unfortunately, no information on the exact nature of Susanna's education has survived. We may assume that she attended a school for Nonconformists' children in London, but this would be pure assumption. More likely is the scenario that she took advantage of the tutors retained for the education of her male siblings, and that her curious mind took full advantage of the library and learned atmosphere of the manse in which she was raised. The sale catalogue for Rev. Samuel Annesley's library contains nearly eight hundred volumes, mainly works of divinity, but also such authors as Hobbes, Locke, Boyle, and Malebranche.[22]

However she acquired it, the education of Susanna is evident in the content and sustained logic of her writings. She read widely, especially in theological literature, and her considerable education infuses her "Educational, Catechetical, and Controversial Writings."[23] From her collected writings, we can determine that she read prodigiously. Judging from the authors she quotes, alludes to, or struggles with, she had a primary interest in what John Wesley later called "practical divinity." She read Anglican divines such as the English Bishops Pearson and Beveridge, Dean William Sherlock, Doctors John Norris and Richard Lucas, the Scot Episcopalian Henry Scougal, the Irish Bishop Jeremy Taylor, and the rector-poet of Bemerton, George Herbert. Reflecting a measure of theological inclusiveness, she also read at least two works of Catholic spirituality, Thomas à Kempis's *Imitation of Christ* and Lorenzo Scupoli's *Spiritual Combat*. Further, she recommended to her sons the work of the prolific Puritan Richard Baxter, her father's old friend, and she knew the work of the Nonjuror William Law. She accepted some aspects of the not quite orthodox Anglican Samuel Clarke, and she held in high esteem Pascal's *Pensées*, now considered to be a spiritual classic of this period. In addition, Susanna was intrigued by John Locke's writings, especially his *Essay Concerning Human Understanding*, and she pondered how Locke's empiricism could serve practical divinity. Sustained reflection on Susanna's intellectual inheritance and repertoire is needed in future biographies, but the following analysis reveals something of the acumen and influence of this remarkable woman.

SUSANNA: ABLE DIVINE

The background on Susanna's education points to her as an able divine, a person who communicates in words and actions a depth of theological understanding. The critical edition of Mrs. Wesley's known writing includes her personal diaries, letters, theological tracts, and spiritual musings. This edition makes it possible to look beyond hagiographic interpretations of Susanna.[24] The early nineteenth-century account by the Methodist Adam Clarke recounts Susanna's roles as wife, mother of a large family, Christian, spouse, and friend. Recognizing the formative role she had for John and Charles Wesley, he exudes: "If it were not unusual to apply such an epithet to a woman, I would not hesitate to say she was an able divine!" In exuberant words typical of early Methodist piety, Clarke says of Susanna, "Many daughters have done virtuously but SUSANNA WESLEY has excelled them all." (Cf. Prov. 31:29)[25]

Clark's hagiography notwithstanding, *able divine* and *good woman* are not bad places to begin an overview of Susanna Wesley. If "able divine" reflects a depth of theological understanding, and if "good woman" connotes excellent accomplishments and righteous personhood, these two descriptors may not be far from our intended mark of appreciating this singularly important woman in the history of Methodism. As Charles Wallace has aptly noted, we may no longer regard her as "St. Susanna, mother of St. John, but [we] might justly discover her to be a competent, practical theologian-educator and a complex and extraordinary woman in her own historical context."[26]

Susanna's Intellectual World: The Age of Reason

To understand Susanna Wesley as an able divine, we turn to the intellectual world into which Susanna Wesley was born and educated and in which she raised her family. For this we must go back at least to 1660. Susanna was born January 20, 1669. It is accurate to say that a great portion of Christian believers in the world in which she was reared did not assume any discontinuity between revelation and faith: faith in revelation was compatible with confidence in reason.[27] England had just emerged from the extremes of the Cromwell era; thus, the comprehensive appeal to reason was strengthened by forceful reactions against the fanaticism, or appeals to religious experience, made by radical Puritans, which were described by others as "enthusiasm." What England sought at this time were critical, closely reasoned statements of the faith, like those of Bishop John Pearson's *Exposition of the Creed*, 1659. Indeed, Susanna quoted Pearson and penned theological corrections to Pearson in her diary. John Wesley began requiring his preachers to read Pearson as early as 1749. He would write in a May 11, 1764 letter to C. Glascott of Jesus College, Oxford: "In order to be well acquainted with the doctrines of Christianity, you need but one book, (besides the Bible,)—Bishop Pearson on the Creed."[28]

Cambridge Platonists like William Stillingfleet, later Bishop of Worcester, were convinced, and convinced many others, that the witness of reason was sufficient to prove even the efficiency of our moral freedom and our certainty of a future life. Revelation was accepted rather than disputed, but the usual practice was to construct a reasonable pattern of belief, and then prove that revelation corresponded to that construction. The Latitudinarian move, in the interest of clarity, was to remove profundity from theological assertion. The simplicity with which they defined the rules of reason, together with their interest in practical problems, persuaded them that essential beliefs were few and simple. A strong ethical emphasis was characteristic of all the Latitudinarians, and their consequent stress on moral duty led Anglicanism down the path of moralism, against which Susanna found it also necessary to react. John Wesley would later follow a pattern of reaction similar to that of his mother.

John Locke towers over this period of intellectual history, and his shadow stretches far into the eighteenth century. Along with Isaac Newton, Locke shaped a new frame of reference that affected religious thought profoundly. Sometimes he referred to theological matters in passing, but at other times he gave theology his concentrated attention. Whatever the span of attention or level of intensity, Locke never minimized the importance of belief. In *An Essay Concerning Human Understanding* (1690), his argument moved progressively toward the singular conclusion that God exists, which he argued through reason: this is "the most obvious truth that reason discovers"; "its evidence . . . is equal to mathematical certainty." For Locke, belief was the consequence of rational proof. The Lockean assumption, and that of the entire age, was that reason could resolve difficulties and banish mysteries, for the evidence of reason runs through all things. It is not difficult to imagine how this conviction about pervasive reason, combined with the simplicity and push for clarity among Cambridge Platonists and Latitudinarians, would result in the deism typified in John Toland's *Christianity Not Mysterious* (1696).

When we enter the eighteenth century, the intellectual stream of the Latitudinarians is continued by Dr. Samuel Clarke's Boyle Lectures, *A Demonstration of the Being and Attributes of God* (1705). Clarke convinced his contemporaries that his account of the created and moral order was itself a miracle of lucid and reasonable exposition. In a universe of order and beauty, humanity was freed from all dark, foreboding fears; if the galaxies of heaven were fashioned for our delight, how great must be our native dignity. Pope, with his genius for giving memorable form to popular convictions, perfectly expressed the outlook of his age: "Know then thyself, presume not God to scan, / The proper study of mankind is man."[29]

John Locke's *The Reasonableness of Christianity* epitomizes the basic conviction of the age, and it is this conviction with regard to utter reasonableness that revealed the Achilles heel of the resultant deism. Consider the work of Matthew Tindal, a fellow of All Souls, Oxford. Tindal's *Christianity as Old as the Creation* (1730) asserted that God's work is perfect, thus it reveals God perfectly. His logic was simple: if creation needed to be supplemented in order to be understood, it would be imperfect; because it is perfect, nothing can be added to it without casting aspersions on God's original handiwork or God's intended purpose. The assumption here reveals the division between deists and historic Christianity. Tindal, and deistic moralists in general, had little sense of history, and they oversimplified the problem of human existence. They assumed in their perfectly created, rational world that human beings were capable of grasping this perfect religion of rationality.

At the risk of oversimplification, I point to the split in Toland's two-pronged assertion that Christianity contained nothing that was either above reason or contrary to it. Christian apologists conceded the second part of this assertion, but not the first, for there were many things that one would never know unless God chose to reveal them. Apologists agreed that revealed truths were congruous with reason if pursued patiently and faithfully; however, our human limitations might blind us to these truths were it not for God's graciousness to us. Such views of reason marked Susanna Wesley's world and her own patterns of thinking.

Susanna Wesley's Concept of Truth and Faith

If Susanna Wesley is to be properly understood, she must be seen as a woman of her times, an age characterized by the supremacy of reason. She must be seen as a woman who had the ability and acumen, though not the public privilege, to differentiate between assertions that were generically religious and those distinctively Christian. In her diary entries, we encounter Susanna making theological distinctions that would later become hallmarks of John Wesley's theology. Perhaps the most foundational was her theological definition of the distinctive Christian word *faith*. In the development of John Wesley's theology, we may discern three distinct definitions of faith: **fides**, faith defined as mental assent to propositional truth; secondly, **fiducia**, faith defined as a trusting confidence in God; and finally, faith as direct spiritual experience of God and the divine realm. John's early emphases were more focused on the rational, however. In a letter dated July 29, 1725, he wrote to his mother:

> Faith is a species of belief, and belief is defined, an assent to a proposition upon rational grounds. Without rational grounds there is therefore no belief, and consequently no faith. . . . I call faith an assent upon rational grounds because I hold divine testimony to be the most reason-able of all evidence whatsoever. Faith must necessarily at length be resolved into reason.[30]

In this definition, we see the young Oxford don working predominantly with the rationalist definition at his disposal, one in which reason defines and confines the definition of faith.

What is clear in his mother's response is that she had more theological sophistication than her Oxford son. Her prompt reply on August 18 was a lesson in both logic and theology:

> You are somewhat mistaken in your notion of faith. All faith is assent, but not all assent is faith. Some truths are self-evident, and we assent to them because they are so. Others, after a regular and formal process of reason, by way of deduction from some self-evident principle, gain our assent; and this is not properly faith but science. Some again we assent to, not because they are self-evident, or because we have attained the knowledge of them in a regular method, by a chain of arguments, but because they have been revealed to us, either by God or man, and these are the proper objects of faith.
>
> The true measure of faith is the authority of the revealer, the weight of which holds proportion with our conviction of [God's] ability and integrity. Divine faith is an assent to whatever God hath revealed to us, because he hath revealed it.[31]

Susanna clinched her point by referring her son to Bishop Pearson's comments on "I Believe" in his *Exposition on the Creed*. She made essentially the same point in a letter on November 10, 1725, responding to another letter from John (now lost to us) in which he had insisted that "faith must necessarily at length be resolved into reason." Drawing again on Bishop Pearson, she referred to "Pearson's definition of divine or saving faith" in her response to John:

> Though the same thing may be an object of faith as revealed, and an object of reason as deducible from rational principles, yet **I insist upon it** that the virtue of faith, by which through the merits of our Redeemer we are saved, is an assent to the truth of whatever God hath been pleased to reveal, because he hath revealed it, and not because we understand it.[32]

Wesley, convinced by his mother's theological sense, became convinced that his original formulation was at best a mere rationalism. He had earlier borrowed his definition from Richard Fiddes' *Body of Divinity* (1718) but, writing to Susanna on November 22, 1725, he conceded:

Fiddes' definition of faith I perceived on reflection [and we might add, listening to his mother theologian] to trespass against the first law of defining, as not being adequate to the thing defined.... An assent grounded both on testimony and reason takes in science as well as faith, which is on all hands allowed to be distinct from it. I am therefore at length come over to your opinion, that saving faith (including practice) is an assent to whatever God has revealed because he has revealed it, and not because the truth of it is evinced by reason.[33]

Susanna had evidently been providing John with a reading list, for she wrote, "I can't recollect what book I recommended to you, but I highly approve your care to search into the grounds and reasons of our most holy religion, which you may do if your intention be pure, and yet retain the integrity of faith." The net result of her efforts was that the "mother of Wesleyan theology" succeeded in moving John Wesley a decisive step away from the rationalism of the era with regard to propositions and faith, and she also shaped him with regard to his other two definitions of faith, the fiduciary and the experiential. Foundational to John Wesley's mature doctrine of Christians' assurance of salvation, Susanna had helped him connect the concepts of a sure abiding trust in the efficacy of Christ with the experiential nature of that assurance.

When one reads through her diaries, the range of her theological reading is striking—Puritans, Continental Catholics, and all stripes of Anglicans. We are only beginning to understand how much this woman moved against the grain of her times in subtle but persistent ways. The theological amalgam that she composed was not only a solvent against "the patriarchal biases then prevailing,"[34] but her theology of spirituality (combining conscience, reason, and experience) was foundational to what we would later identify as Wesleyan theology.

In her diary, near the section in which she described her resolution to meet at least once per day with each child, and twice on Sunday with her children as a group, for the purpose of their spiritual admonition, Susanna offered a series of quotations from Bishop William Beveridge. Drawing from his *Holiness the Great Design of the Gospel Dispensation*, she described an intrinsic connection between knowledge about God and knowledge of God—what we know with our head and what we know with our heart:

> But the knowledge of God which is the first act of godliness and that whereupon all the rest are grounded . . . consisteth principally in a due sense of God upon the heart; what that is I must confess myself unable to express so as that anyone should apprehend it, but they that have it. But only in general we may call it an experimental knowledge whereby a man hath the sense or experience of those perfections upon his own heart, which he knows and

believes to be in God, whereby his thoughts and conceptions are so strangely enlarged, that he seems to apprehend him that is altogether incomprehensible, so that he is no longer able to endure himself, but is forced to cry out with Job in the same case, "By reason of God's highness I cannot endure." Job 31:23.[35]

Although she presented these citations from Beveridge *approvingly*, she also corrected him when she deemed it necessary. The corrections were mostly along the same lines in which she later corrected her son, namely the tendency to ascribe too much to the supremacy of reason. She substituted for a generally religious sense of reason a more distinctly Christian dialectic of faith with reason. She called this section of her diary "I Cannot Altogether Acquiesce." Seeing Susanna Wesley as an able divine, we can now look afresh at a well-known story about her role in the Wesley manse—an occasion when she could not bring herself to "altogether acquiesce," even when she was required by her minister-husband to cease and desist.

Susanna: A Feminist before Feminism?

In the winter of 1711–12, the Reverend Samuel Wesley Sr. attended the Church of England's governing convocation in London, a meeting that lasted several weeks, sometimes more than two months. During his absence, Susanna paid special attention to the spiritual nourishment of her children through their individual meetings; she also gave special attention to the time of family prayers each Sunday evening. The practice involved reading prayers and a homily, as well as discussing topics of a devotional nature. A neighboring family asked to be included in the family prayers, and word spread through the community. Susanna was evidently so effective as a teacher and "preacher" that the family soon grew into a neighborhood gathering. From there it evolved into a Sunday night church service in the manse, which some evidently decided was better than the morning services under the curate, Rev. Inman, whom Samuel, Sr., had hired to substitute for him. Large numbers stopped attending in the morning, and eventually more than two hundred came to the manse on Sunday evening, according to Susanna's letter (cited below). When Inman, obviously insulted, related the state of affairs to Samuel, Sr., in London, Samuel wrote his wife with instructions that she cease the gatherings and desist from preaching. Samuel built his admonition around a threefold rationale, as recorded in Susanna's reply:[36]

> I heartily thank you for dealing so plainly and faithfully with me in a matter of no common [insignificant] concern. The main of your objections against our Sunday evening meetings are, first, that it will look particular; secondly,

my sex; and lastly, your being at present in a public station and character. To all which I shall answer briefly.

The word "particular," in eighteenth-century context, referred to a private meeting that was not legal according to the Conventical Act, which restricted private meetings, and was not approved by the Church. "Particular" also meant "more than usual," or unusual, thus drawing attention to itself. Although Samuel's apparent usage may have focused on the political definition, Susanna seized on the latter meaning:

> As to its looking particular, I grant it does; and so does almost everything that is serious, or that may any way advance the glory of God or the salvation of souls, if it be performed out of [the confines of] a pulpit, or in the way of common conversation; because in our corrupt age the utmost care and diligence have been used to banish all discourse of God or spiritual concerns out of society, as if religion were never to appear out of the closet, and we were to be ashamed of nothing so much as of professing ourselves to be Christian.

With regard to Susanna's being a woman and wife of a minister, she still dared to defy the convention of her day that forbade women ministers. She did not seek to overturn the positions of ecclesial bodies; however, she challenged the logic of those positions by insisting that she had been doing what was needful for the soul care of those under her maternal wing:

> To your second, I reply that as I *am* a woman, so I am also mistress of a large family. And though the superior charge of the souls contained in it lies upon you as head of the family as their minister, yet in your absence I cannot but look upon every soul you leave under my care as a talent committed to me under a trust by the great Lord of all the families of heaven and earth. And if I am unfaithful to him or to you in neglecting to improve these talents, how shall I answer unto [God], when he shall command me to render an account of my stewardship?

Susanna gave some detail about the Sunday evening prayers of her family, which had grown in scale by happenstance and word of mouth. Actually, an account of Danish missionaries on her husband's desk, translated and published by the Society for the Propagation of the Gospel in London, had inspired her fervency to discuss her faith:

> For several days I could think or speak of little else. At last it came into my mind, though I am not a man nor a minister of the gospel, and so cannot be employed in such a worthy employment as they [the missionaries] were; yet if my heart were sincerely devoted to God, and if I were inspired with a true zeal for [God's] glory and did really desire the salvation of souls, I might do

something more than I do. I thought I might live in a more exemplary manner in some things; I might pray more for the people and speak with more warmth to those with whom I have an opportunity of conversing.... With those few neighbors who then came to me I discoursed more freely and affectionately than before. I chose the best and most awakening sermons we had, and I spent more time with them in such exercises. Since this our company has increased every night, for I dare deny none that asks admittance. Last Sunday I believe we had above two hundred, and yet many went away for want of room.

But I never durst positively presume to hope that God would make use of me as an instrument in doing good; the farthest I ever durst go was, "It may be: who can tell? With God all things are possible." [See Mark 10:27.]

Susanna Wesley then quoted from the poem "The Priesthood," by George Herbert, extracting verses from two stanzas:

Only, since God doth often make
Of lowly matter, for high uses meet,
I throw me at His feet;
There will lie until my Maker seek
For some mean stuff whereon to show His skill;
Then is my time.
And thus I rested without passing any reflection on myself or forming any judgment about the success or event of this undertaking.

With regard to Samuel's third concern, his being of a public station, Susanna said that she was willing to leave this concern to be answered by his own judgment. She posted her letter after composing it on February 6, and she received an immediate reply dated the 16th. Her next letter to her husband, dated February 25, began by explaining why she did not sit down and respond the moment his letter arrived. She wrote that she was not moved by his fear that parishioners disapproved of her ministry: "There is not that I can hear more than three or four that is against our meeting, of which Inman is the chief, for no other reason, as I suppose, but that he thinks the sermons I read better than his own." She then added:

Some families which very seldom came to church now go constantly. One person that has not been there this seven year is now prevailed on to go with the rest. I need not tell you the consequences if you determine to put an end to our meeting. You may easily foresee what prejudices it may raise in the minds of these people against Inman especially, who had so little wit as to speak publicly against it. 'Tis true I can now keep them to the church, but if 'tis laid aside, I doubt they'll ever go to hear him more, at least those [200+] that come from the lower end of the town. Whereas, if this be continued till your return (which now will not be long), it may please God by that time so to change their hearts that they may love and delight in his public worship so as never to neglect it more.

And then, as if this perspective were not adequate, she added:

> If you do after all think fit to dissolve this assembly, do not tell me any more that you desire me to do it, for that will not satisfy my conscience; but send me your positive command in such full and express terms as may absolve me from all guilt and punishment for neglecting this opportunity of doing good to souls, when you and I shall appear before the great and awful tribunal of our Lord Jesus Christ.

Are you surprised when I tell you that this is the last word we have in print between this Sunday night woman minister and the rector of Epworth parish regarding her extraordinary ministry?!

CONCLUSION

Susanna Wesley was a woman of her age, but she was clearly a precursor of later women (Methodist and otherwise) who could not keep silent when they sensed a gospel vocation. Might we say that she was a reticent feminist before feminism? Hardly a woman or man who came to the Wesley manse on the Sunday nights of 1711–12 could even read a homily; yet Susanna could read the sermon with great benefit to the hearers. She could also analyze the creeds and the expositions on the creeds with her incisive critique. While theologians of her day remained largely captive to the rationalistic assumptions of the era, Susanna Wesley conceptualized a connection between faith and reason that few mainstream Anglicans recognized. She did not do this *de novo*, having learned much from Puritans like Richard Baxter, but her synthesis of multiple definitions of faith was clearly her own. She passed this first version of Wesleyan theology to the Epworth parishioners, as well as to her children.

We have looked at only two theological areas in which Susanna's influence on John Wesley was decisive; there are several more. We have also witnessed her preaching the gospel against the grain of conventional wisdom. When John Wesley became "more vile" and preached in the fields, and when, under his leadership, Methodist revival leaders asserted themselves in ways contrary to ecclesial convention, they emulated Susanna Wesley, whether consciously or unconsciously. Susanna was perhaps less radical than the bluestocking women, who were feminists of a different order. She was, however, a woman of unusual acumen and determination. In her day and in her chosen way, she delivered faith to her children and to the people of the Epworth parish. She was Susanna Annesley Wesley—*a woman of spirit and spirituality.*

In light of Susanna Wesley's witness, we can draw several conclusions for the future of Methodist practice and the practice of Wesleyan studies. As to Methodist practice, we are challenged to question and push social boundaries when faith demands it. We are challenged especially to trespass gender boundaries, boundaries between domestic and public spheres, and intellectual boundaries between faith and reason. In Wesleyan studies, we are challenged to explore more fully the life of Susanna Annesley Wesley, raising sharp questions about hagiographic claims and seeking to make a more honest and nuanced appraisal of her significant contributions to Wesleyan theology and practice, especially as regards the relation between reason and faith. If Methodist communities and scholars of the Methodist tradition took up these challenges, the living tradition itself would be imbued and renewed with spirit and spirituality.

CHAPTER FIVE

HOSPITALITY AS A LIVING WESLEYAN TRADITION

Amy G. Oden

"Tradition is the living faith of the dead. Traditional*ism* is the dead faith of the living."[1] At its best, faithful living of the tradition is a dangerous and difficult task. With an eye to the past and an eye to the future, it is hard to see the ground on which one currently steps. We understand our Christian traditions only when we observe the forms by which they were and are concretely lived. To understand our historical traditions of worship, we look at practices. Where did Christians worship? How did they gather? What did they do in gathered worship? Their lived practices are windows into deeper theological claims and traditions. We know, however, not to confuse forms of Christian practice with the traditions they embody. Forms of Christian practice change over time, as new days require new expressions to keep faith alive. Too often, Christian people have been seduced into thinking that the forms must be preserved statically in order to preserve tradition. This sort of idolatry, mistaking the form for the faith it expresses, pulls us into traditional*ism*. Tradition cannot be reduced to the forms themselves; it is, rather, the living faith that the forms express, a faith deeper and truer than any particular expression of it.

Hospitality is a Christian tradition that runs deep and wide. Just as early Christian practices embody hospitality, many early Methodist practices express hospitality. My interest here is to explore hospitality as a lens through which to examine some practices of the early Methodist movement in England and its subsequent expressions in America. These practices can be seen as fresh forms of the hospitality tradition, which extends from early Christian practices. Three theological themes come into focus here: (1) God's welcome, through strangers, into the divine life; (2) our welcoming others, though strangers, to participate in the way of salvation; and (3) the recognition of the stranger as Christ. The next section of this essay will lay foundations for the tradition and practices of hospitality in early Christianity. The following section will then explore some early Methodist practices through the lens of hospitality, with attention to points of continuity with early Christian practices. Finally, hospitality as an expression of the living faith of early Christians and early Methodists offers insights for our current Wesleyan communities. The living faith to which Wesleyan practices of hospitality give testimony is powerful, pointing always to God's inviting love, the gratitude out of which we invite others to God's love, and the new eyes of recognition God bestows, which allow us not only to see ourselves and the stranger, but also to see and know Jesus. How might we recover hospitality as a living Wesleyan tradition for our own day? What insights might be brought to bear through such a lens?

HOSPITALITY IN THE EARLY CHRISTIAN WORLD[2]

The Christian tradition has much to say about hospitality. The New Testament church believed the practice of hospitality was central to Christian life. Throughout early Christianity, the faithful told stories about hospitality, preached about it, practiced and praised it. Most important, early Christians found in the tradition of hospitality a theological vocabulary of welcome, gratitude, and recognition: God's *welcome* into the divine life, *gratitude* for God's inviting love, and *recognition* of Christ in the stranger. They sought tangible practices that embodied this good news.

What Is Hospitality?[3]

At the very least, hospitality is welcoming of the stranger (*hospes*).[4] While hospitality can include acts of welcoming family and friends, its meaning within the Christian biblical and historical traditions has focused on receiving the stranger and extending one's resources to them. In the ancient world, hospitality was required for one's friends and family. For Christians, hospitality applied particularly to vulnerable populations, identified primarily as the alien, the sojourner, the sick, the poor, the orphan, and the widow. Stranger status can be based on economic as well as social factors, but it almost always entails vulnerability.

On the face of it, hospitality begins with basic physical needs of food and shelter, most powerfully symbolized in table fellowship—sharing food and drink at a common table. Sharing food together offers more to participants than just the nourishment they need to live. Eating together is symbolic of partaking of life itself.[5] Jesus' own table fellowship with sinners and socially marginalized people witnesses to the central place of hospitality in the reign of God.

In addition to food, hospitality might also entail meeting other physical needs, such as a foot washing or bath, medical treatment, shelter, clothing, supplies for one's journey, and even care of animals. Jesus' final meal with the disciples (Matthew 26:17-30; Luke 22:14-28; Mark 14:12-25) illustrates several of the material features of hospitality, namely, washing feet, a servant host, food, and drink.

Hospitality includes social as well as physical needs, so while food and drink are central, welcome may also require a recasting of social relations. Including the stranger in one's circle of friends or business associates expresses hospitality. Sponsoring an outsider, welcoming a servant, or mentoring an apprentice can be an act of social hospitality. Acts of inclusion and respect, however small, can powerfully reframe social relations and engender welcome.

Finally, hospitality encompasses spiritual needs. In early Christian texts about hospitality, prayer is an acknowledgment of the common dependence of both host and guest on God for everything. Prayers of healing and safe travel are frequent, as are prayers of gratitude. Sometimes hospitality means including the stranger in worship, Eucharist, or other liturgical acts.

While we may look at hospitable practices of early Christians and see them as good deeds, hospitality was not simply a matter of private virtue. It was embedded in community and a sign of God's presence in that community; thus, it embodied a biblical ethic. Both the Old and New Testaments identify a duty of hospitality (e.g., Gen. 18:4, 19:7f; Judg. 19:20; Matt. 10:40f; Rom. 12:13). Abraham in particular is identified as embodying hospitality when he receives strangers under the oaks of Mamre (Gen. 18:1-15), the benefits of which extend far beyond himself. Through "entertaining angels unawares," the creation of God's people begins with the promise of a child and the subsequent birth of Isaac to Abraham and Sarah. The New Testament continues this theme through frequent references to the breaking of the bread, which symbolizes the presence of sacred community.[6] While texts usually focus on a particular host and a particular guest, hospitality almost always involves a larger communal context that orients and undergirds it.

Early Christians grasped the insight that hospitality begins with recognizing that we are all strangers. The stranger status at the heart of Christian identity has biblical roots as well as cultural and political ones. Remembering that "we were strangers in Egypt" is central to Christian identity because it is central to the salvation history told in the Hebrew Bible.[7] God saved God's people from their alien, slave status in Egypt. In delivering them, God reminded them of who they truly are: God's own chosen people far from home. Salvation history reinforces a central aspect of Jewish and Christian identity as an alien, foreigner enslaved in a strange land, or sojourner wandering in a foreign desert.

As a feature of Christian life, hospitality is more than a singular act of welcome; it is a way of life. As such, it is grounded in the knowledge that, although one is a stranger, one has been received into the divine life and so, out of gratitude, receives strangers. Thus, the one who is welcomed by God becomes a host to others. For early Christians, hospitality as an orientation of life also entailed a recognition of Christ in the stranger. The hospitable one looks for God's good news in the other, confident that it is there if one has eyes to see and ears to hear.[8] Hospitality springs from knowing oneself as a stranger received by God, and then seeking to recognize Christ in strangers. Early Christians teach us that such a way of life calls for readiness, repentance, and risk.[9]

Hospitality as a Moral Category

The word *hospitality* has lost its moral punch over recent centuries. It has largely been reduced to refreshments at meetings or magazine covers of gracious living.[10] The moral landscape in which it resides has all but faded into the background. Yet, this moral and spiritual landscape is what early Christian voices can help us recover.[11]

Hospitality is characterized by a particular moral stance in the world that can best be described as readiness. Early Christian voices tell us repeatedly that, whether we are guest or host, we must be ready—ready to welcome, ready to enter another's world, ready to be vulnerable. This readiness is expectant. It may be akin to moral nerve. It exudes trust, not in the idea that one will succeed in some measurable way, but that participation in hospitality is participation in the life of God. Such readiness takes courage, gratitude, and radical openness. This moral orientation to life relinquishes to God both the practice of hospitality and its consequences. Because we are ready to receive Christ as the stranger, we can release expectations about what will happen as a result of hospitality. Our readiness is to know Jesus, not to produce a particular outcome. Further, the radical openness that accompanies readiness is an openness that also leads to repentance.

Repentance in the New Testament connotes turning from one path to another. For those who participate in hospitality, a "decentering of perspective" occurs.[12] In the experience of hospitality, both the host and the guest encounter something new—approaching the edge of the unfamiliar and crossing it. Hospitality shifts the frame of reference from self to other to relationship. This shift invariably leads to repentance, for one sees the degree to which one's own view has become the only view. The sense one has of being at home, and of familiarity with the way things are, is shaken by reframing one's reference to the other and one's relationships. One cannot be at home in quite the same way after such a shift. When we realize how we have inflated our own frame of reference and imposed it on all of reality, we know we have committed the sin of idolatry by taking our particular part and making it the whole.

The turn to idolatry is developed with penetrating fullness in Diane Leclerc's chapter. She sees idolatry as the center of John Wesley's understanding of sin. Her interpretation inspires readers to seek alternatives to idolatry—a move enhanced by early hospitality traditions. The decentering and reframing that accompany hospitality are the very movements that the New Testament calls *metanoia*, or "turning," which is usually translated as "repentance." This turning occurs not only in the interior landscape of the individual, but also in the exterior landscape of the community. As communities become more hospitable, they experience a decentering of perspective and become more aware of structural inequalities that exist in and around them. These experiences lead them to repent.[13]

One wonders whether, without these injunctions to reach out to the vulnerable, early Christians would have offered hospitality to other groups. Welcoming vulnerable populations entailed risk in the ancient world and continues to do so in the present one. By extending to others, one might be exposed to illness, injury, theft, or disgrace when little reward could be expected and danger was likely. Early Christians were not naïve about this reality. The risk that accompanies hospitality is precisely the circumstance that makes a population vulnerable. It was not the call to good works that moved early Christians to practice hospitality, though that must surely have played a part. Rather, it was the location of hospitality within a larger spiritual economy—God's *welcome* into the divine life, *gratitude* for having been received into the household of God, and *recognition* of Christ in the stranger. These faith commitments moved early Christians to practice hospitality.

WESLEY AND WELCOMING THE STRANGER

The lens of hospitality can offer an important perspective on John Wesley's articulation of the way of salvation and on some practices of early Methodism. Both reveal familiar themes from the tradition of hospitality in early Christianity: the proclamation of God's welcome, our grateful response by welcoming others, and the gift of recognizing the stranger as Christ.

God Welcomes Us

Wesley's notion of prevenient grace proclaims God's invitation, God's welcome to all into the divine life, even before we have accepted the invitation. Wesley insists throughout his writings that God initiates relationship with us. God seeks us and invites us, offering relationship unceasingly. The entire process of salvation, for Wesley, is predicated on God's inviting love. In his "Plain Account of Genuine Christianity," Wesley's treatise is given over to describing the life of a "genuine Christian," infused by God's initiating love:

> He is peculiarly and inexpressibly happy in the clearest and fullest conviction: "This all-powerful, all-wise, all-gracious Being, this Governor of all, loves *me*. This lover of my soul is always with me, is never absent; no, not for a moment. And I love him: there is none in heaven but thee, none on earth that I desire beside thee [cf. Ps. 73:25]! And he has given me to resemble himself; he has stamped his image on my heart."[14]

God's act of reconciling us to God's self is an act of hospitality. God reaches out and welcomes us first. All we are and all we have are gifts from God, the Host of the universe. We are guests here, residing in creation through divine invitation to share in the divine life. Thus, each of us is a stranger who becomes the guest, indeed even the child of God.

In Gratitude We Welcome Others

Gratitude at being received into God's life calls us to welcome others. For Wesley, this welcome was expressed in a profound identification with the helplessness of the stranger. The Methodist Societies themselves became welcoming places for the economically marginalized.[15] Wesley called upon Methodists to receive the poor into fellowship, to make bonds that not only reached out to the poor, but also drew them into the community. Wesley argued that Methodists should welcome the poor in the way God has welcomed us:

> If you cannot relieve, do not grieve the poor. Give them soft words if nothing else; abstain from either sour looks or harsh words. Let them be glad to come, even though they should go empty away. Put yourself in the place of every poor man, and deal with him just as you would God would deal with you.[16]

Identifying human hospitality to the stranger with God's hospitality to each of us is a key claim of early Christian hospitality and of Wesleyan practice. Wesley implies his awareness of this claim as he appeals to the way each of his listeners desires to be welcomed by God. God's initiating welcome brings each of us, as strangers, into the household of grace.

The many ministries of the early Methodist societies in caring for the sick, the poor, orphans, the imprisoned, the hungry, and the stranger embody forms that express gratitude to God by welcoming others. The many schools, training houses, and infirmaries that sprang up mid-eighteenth century were ministries of hospitality among early Methodists. Education programs for children and adults alike invited those who had long stood outside the walls of learning to enter as welcomed guests who could belong and share in the benefits of education. This welcome brought strangers into new relationship and offered them a new home in the scheme of things.

Randy Maddox's chapter in this volume on holistic health and healing sets these ministries of healing and education within Wesley's insistence on a *"truly holistic salvation."* Maddox shows that God's welcome of salvation is, for Wesley, much more than forgiveness: "participation in God's present saving work involved nurturing not only our souls but our bodies, and addressing both of these dimensions in our outreach to others."

In the latter decades of the eighteenth century, Methodism took on a particularly focused ministry of hospitality in the Strangers' Friend Society. Tim MacQuiban has chronicled this movement and its significance for British Methodism.[17] A lay Methodist, John Gardiner, founded the Strangers' Friend Society in 1785.[18] Gardiner was a member of the London Methodist Society, so, perhaps not surprisingly, John Wesley was one of the charity's first subscribers. The aim was to render assistance to the "destitute sick poor, without distinction of sect or country, at their own habitations."[19] The Strangers' Friend Society was devoted to extending hospitality to those who did not have food or lodging, or who needed a connection to get a foothold on a job. Notably, these Methodists did not screen strangers as worthy of welcome on the grounds of religious belief or affiliation ("without distinction of sect or country"). This mark of risky hospitality reflects grateful Christians who knew that they too were strangers, welcomed by God.

In the last two decades of the eighteenth century, other such societies emerged across the country. In a letter to Adam Clark dated February 9, 1791, John Wesley said briefly in passing: "You have done right in setting up the Strangers' [Friend] Society. It is an excellent institution."[20] Extant in the Methodist archives is the "Cash Book of Manchester Branch of the Strangers' Friend Society, 1791–92." It details the receipt of funds from donors and the disbursement of those funds by "visitors" to the poor.[21] Another book chronicles individual cases of strangers: "The Report of the Strangers' Friend Society (Instituted in the Year 1786) for the purposes of visiting and relieving the sick and distressed strangers and other poor at their respective habitations, For the Year, ending the 29th February, 1804; and a list of the subscribers."[22] The Society was made up largely of Methodists, though others participated as well.

A review of the Strangers' Friend Society reveals many examples of hospitality. One case reported is that of Mary Ann Reilly:

> a native of Ireland, on her journey to London, to receive some Prize-money, due to her deceased husband, was detained by a severe fit of sickness, in a

house in Temple-street, in this City;—application being made to the Society, she was attended and properly relieved, until she recovered sufficiently to pursue her intended journey; she was found in absolute want of every necessary.[23]

Another case reported:

William Dyer, a native of Shepton-Mallet, was visited by the recommendation of a Subscriber. He labored under an asthmatic complaint, and with much difficulty was enabled to gain a few shillings per week, to help support his wife and four children; his complaint being increased, his family stood in need of additional assistance, and during this period, his wife was thrown into premature labor, through a fright, occasioned by some sudden alarm. . . . [T]he visitors provided them with necessary assistance, and through the Good Providence of God, they were restored to health, and the capacity of providing some means of subsistence.[24]

Finally, a particularly pathetic case dramatizes the vulnerability and tangible needs of those to whom the Strangers' Friend Society ministered:

Mary Mais, a native of St. George's, near this city, was found in a state truly deplorable:— Her husband had been in the employ of several Tradesmen as a Tyler and Plaisterer and in an unfortunate moment involved himself and innocent family in ruin, by a deviation from the paths of rectitude: he paid the full price of his fault, by suffering the penalty inflicted by the laws of his country; —his wife with one child and very forward with another, was left to struggle with the very severe circumstances of her case; she had, previous to her marriage, lived as an upper servant with some of the first families about the City, with much credit, and was now reduced to the lowest distress; she subsisted on the pittance produced by the sale of her apparel, until that source was exhausted; she was then cast on the humanity of a person with whom she lodged, and to whom she already owed arrears of rent; the critical day of labor arrived, without any provision, medical or otherwise; with the assistance of a soldier's wife in the neighborhood, she was delivered of a living child: —Her distress at length was made known to the Strangers' Friend Society, who visited her; she appeared in the extremest state of poverty, emaciation, and despondency; the ability of the Institution was never more acceptable to an object of their notice, nor to their own feelings, than in this case, her gratitude for their aid was unbounded, and the hope of relief afforded by their means contributed to effect her recovery.[25]

This account attests to the hospitable practice of reaching out to a stranger and also to the strong feeling of identification and sympathy that Mary's situation provoked in those extending hospitality, as well as the gratitude that marked Mary's recovery. The Strangers' Friend Society illustrates the three-fold dynamic we see in early Christian hospitality: (1) we all are strangers who have been welcomed into God's own life as sons and daughters; (2) in gratitude, we welcome strangers, the "least of these"; and (3) with eyes to see, we recognize that, when we welcome "the least," we welcome Christ and are pulled ever deeper into the divine life, the life of sanctification.

Recognizing the Stranger as Christ

John Wesley had a keen sense of the suffering of those who were strangers in society—those on the outside of the economic system looking in, those dehumanized in a class system that rendered their most basic human needs invisible, those who were strangers to the grace of the gospel.[26] In his sermon "Scripture Way of Salvation," Wesley describes the practices of the sanctified life, "such as feeding the hungry, clothing the naked, entertaining the stranger, visiting those that are in prison, or sick, or variously afflicted."[27] His writings comment frequently on the sea of human misery arising from human failure to address the needs of "the least of these," who represent Christ himself. Wesley often turns to the following list from Matthew 25 when identifying the concrete acts in which Christians engage in the sanctified life:

> "Lord, when was it that we saw you hungry and gave you food, or thirsty and gave you something to drink? And when was it that we saw you a stranger and welcomed you, or naked and gave you clothing? And when was it that we saw you sick or in prison and visited you?" And the king will answer them, "Truly I tell you, just as you did it to one of the least of these who are members of my family, you did it to me."[28]

It is no surprise, then, that Wesley appeals to the imperatives of Matthew 25, just as early Christians did, to authorize practices of hospitality.

Wesley also connects the Matthew 25 teachings with the Sermon on the Mount, as in his sermon "Upon Our Lord's Sermon on the Mount (VI)":

> And, first, with regard to works of mercy. "Take heed," saith he, "that ye do not your alms before men, to be seen of them. Otherwise ye have no reward of your Father which is in heaven." "That ye do not your alms"—although this only is named, yet is every work of charity included, everything which we give, or speak, or do, whereby our neighbour may be profited, whereby another man may receive any advantage, either in his body or soul. The feeding the hungry, the clothing the naked, the entertaining or assisting the stranger, the visiting those that are sick or in prison, the comforting the afflicted, the instructing the ignorant, the reproving the wicked, the exhorting and encouraging the well-doer; and if there be any other work of mercy, it is equally included in this direction.[29]

In tying this familiar list of commands from Matthew 25 to the Sermon on the Mount, Wesley expands the notion of charity to include all works of mercy. While he does not explicitly identify the "least of these" with Christ in this sermon, he does make the connection in another sermon on the beatitudes:

> But in the full extent of the word a "peacemaker" is one that . . . being filled with the love of God and of all mankind cannot confine the expressions of it to his own family, or friends, or acquaintance, or party; or to those of his own opinions; no, nor those who are partakers of like precious faith; but steps over all these narrow bounds that he may do good to every man; that he may some way or other, manifest his love to neighbours and strangers, friends and enemies . . . that when his Lord cometh He may say, "Well done, good and faithful servant!"

Wesley immediately goes on acknowledge that in all these acts, Christ is welcomed:

> He doth good, to the uttermost of his power, even to the bodies of all men. He rejoices to "deal his bread to the hungry," and to "cover the naked with a garment." Is any a stranger? He takes him in, and relieves him according to his necessities. Are any sick or in prison? He visits them, and administers such help as they stand most in need of. And all this he does, not as unto man, but remembering him that hath said, 'Inasmuch as ye have done it unto one of the least of these my brethren, ye have done it unto me.'[30]

Wesley appropriates the passage from Matthew 25 to identify the "least of these" with Christ and calls for his listeners to practice hospitality. Recognizing the stranger as Jesus brings one full circle. God first welcomes us. We, in turn, welcome others. In so doing, we are brought back into full communion with Christ.

Tetney, a small village near the east coast of England, had a Methodist Society with extraordinary giving practices. When Wesley visited the Tetney Society, he asked how such a small group of modest means could accomplish this. The exchange that Wesley reported reveals that these early Methodists recognized a connection between giving "all we have to God" and entertaining strangers:

> I observed, one gave eightpence, often tenpence a week; another thirteen, fifteen or eighteenpence; another, sometimes one, sometimes two shillings. I asked Micah Ellmoor, the Leader . . . "How is this? Are you the richest society in England?" He answered, "I suppose not. But as we are all single persons we have agreed together to give ourselves, and *all we have*, to God. And we do it gladly, whereby we are able to entertain all the strangers that

from time to time come to Tetney, who often have no food to eat, or any friend to give them a lodging."[31]

Their giving was grounded in gratitude, knowing that all they had came from God; thus, "we have agreed together to give ourselves, and all we have, to God." For the society at Tetney, giving to strangers was giving to God. They could recognize Christ in the "least of these."

Wesley and those in the movement continue the explicit connection between giving to the poor and giving to Christ at many points. In his sermon "The Good Steward," Wesley stated:

> In what manner didst thou employ that comprehensive talent, money? ... first supplying thy own reasonable wants, together with those of thy family; then restoring the remainder to me, through the poor, whom I had appointed to receive it; looking upon thyself as only one of that number of poor whose wants were to be supplied out of that part of my substance which I had placed in thy hands for this purpose ... ? Wast thou accordingly a general benefactor to mankind? Feeding the hungry, clothing the naked, comforting the sick, assisting the stranger, relieving the afflicted according to their various necessities?[32]

Wesley posed the question reminiscent of the king in Matthew 25, identifying giving to the poor with giving to God, "restoring the remainder to me, through the poor."

Early Methodist practices stand in continuity with early Christian practices in expressing the notion that hospitality extended to a stranger is hospitality extended to Christ.[33] On first glance, the poor at the gate or the stranger at the door may seem to be just that, the supplicant wanting something. The stranger may seem suspicious or even dangerous. The very presence of the stranger can be disorienting.[34] However, if we look a little closer, we will see our initial reading of the situation is wrong. The apparent stranger is not simply the poor, the stranger, the widow, or the sick person who knocks, but Christ himself. For those with eyes to see, hospitality offered to another is always hospitality offered to Christ. In receiving others, we receive Christ. In rejecting them, we reject Christ.[35]

Early Christians and early Methodists both claimed that, when strangers are welcomed, Christ is recognized and we are able to participate more deeply in God's household of grace. These three themes—God welcomes us, we welcome others, and we recognize Christ in them—accompany the practices of hospitality in early Methodism. These themes give us some insight into the understanding early Methodists had of what they were doing and their reasons for doing it. Early Methodists experienced a profound awakening to God's love, which, shed abroad in their hearts, compelled them to extend that love to others. As the Wesleyan movement proceeded into its second century, the theme of God's welcome, particularly to the least of these, continued.

NINETEENTH-CENTURY DEVELOPMENTS: GOD'S HOUSEHOLD OF GRACE

This image of household as the central locus for expressing the gracious hospitality of God was carried into the nineteenth century as Methodism responded to the desperate hunger for gospel hospitality in urban centers of the United States. Sarah Sloan Kruetziger has shown that the settlement movement among nineteenth-century US Methodists began as evangelistic outreach. Women, in particular, championed urban missions as an expression of the gospel command in Matthew 25 to feed the hungry, welcome the stranger, care for the sick, and clothe the poor.[36] The Women's Home Missionary Society of the Methodist Episcopal Church, as well as the many women's home missionary groups that emerged at this time, understood their ministries as providing more than the social services that secular institutions were also beginning to offer. Women's home missions proclaimed the transforming power of God's "Mother love," employing the language and imagery of the domestic sphere to bring gospel hospitality to the gritty suffering in the cities.

In 1819, in New York City, "a number of females met at the Wesleyan Seminary" to organize a women's mission auxiliary. By mid-century, their Wesleyan vision under the leadership of Phoebe Palmer had produced the earliest city mission in America, which had "raised money for a building, appointed a paid missionary, and provided the volunteer energy to conduct church services, Sunday schools, and a nursery for working women."[37] Their Five Points Mission produced an impressive record of public baths, shelter, clothes and food, a medical clinic, and even a reading room for the uplift of the workers. These efforts reflected similar developments in other cities, led by Methodist women determined to extend gospel hospitality through personal engagement with strangers and outsiders.[38]

Hallmarks of these urban missionary efforts were two central commitments. The first was a commitment for missionaries to live with and among the urban poor and destitute to whom they ministered. A common pattern involved several women moving into a neighborhood together to set up shop with a common base of operations for offering a variety of ministries. The second key commitment of women's home missions was visiting. Phoebe Palmer and others called upon women to be hands-on in visiting the poor and sick in their homes and neighborhoods, creating communities rather than simply dispensing goods and services.[39] One can hear in these two commitments expressions of prophetic grace that Mary Elizabeth Moore calls for Wesleyans today to reclaim and recover. The rise of the deaconess movement and ministry reflects the influence and effectiveness of these women, practicing prophetic grace in home missions through the end of the nineteenth century and into the early decades of the twentieth.[40]

The ministry of the "visitor" (one who visits the sick and poor in their homes), in both home missions in America and in the Strangers' Friend Society in England, parallels early Christian practices of hospitality. Among early Christian texts that describe this practice, we find instructions to Christian visitors who extend hospitality to the sick and the poor.[41] In particular, such visitors are advised not to talk too much and not to give offense: "We should not do anything with partiality or for the shaming of others, but love the poor as the servants of God, and especially visit them."[42] Often, hospitality requires going out to meet others where they are, being willing to enter the world of the other.

The urban mission movement of the nineteenth century stands in continuity with the practices of hospitality among early Methodists and goes further. Whereas early Methodists extended hospitality to the poor, the urban mission movement practiced hospitality by living *with* the poor. Among home missionaries, hospitality takes a much more holistic form, as these women sought ways to address the systemic causes of poverty. The vision of hospitality expands, so that welcoming the stranger requires Christians to examine the social forces that create strangers.

INSIGHTS FOR WESLEYANS TODAY

Early Christian and early Wesleyan practices of hospitality offer rich resources for Wesleyan communities today. I want to focus on two. First, this tradition of hospitality reminds us of our missional identity as Wesleyans. We are a people who know we have been welcomed into God's life, who welcome the stranger through radical practices of hospitality, and who meet Christ on the way. As Wesleyans, our mission is to embody this good news through personal and social holiness. We can reclaim and recover this missional identity through practices of hospitality.

A second resource for Wesleyans today that we can glean from this discussion of hospitality is both conceptual and practical. It is a framework for understanding and articulating the Christian life, a simplified *ordo salutis* of sorts that can be an effective tool for evangelism in today's world. Welcome, gratitude, and recognition are familiar activities and categories of relationships in which all humans engage. The conceptual framework of hospitality claims that God welcomes us (justification), in grateful response we welcome others, and in so doing we come to know Jesus more truly (sanctification). This framework of welcome, gratitude, and recognition is tethered to everyday experiences. When we articulate the good news through this vocabulary, we are not reciting an exotic code or "churchspeak" that those outside the church must decipher in order to come into God's life. Words and phrases such as "in God's will," "saved," and even "good news," as well as the citation of Scripture, may reflect precious words that we hold dear. To unchurched people, however, this is an insider language that places them clearly outside. More troubling, the insider language of Christians can leave the impression that God is removed from everyday life and can be reached only through special words or rituals. Gospel hospitality does not call us away from our own lives and into some netherworld in order to walk with God. Rather, it calls us more deeply into the very lives we are living, in order to see how God is already at work and welcoming us into closer relationship and recognition. While this vocabulary of welcome, gratitude, and recognition may not carry the full weight of the gospel, it is a particularly good starting place for evangelism, as it has powerful corollaries that resonate in everyday experience.

Welcome

When non-believers encounter Christians, the good news we offer first and foremost is God's amazing grace, the gift of salvation. Too often, non-believers encounter the Christian life as being focused almost wholly on judgment, or on getting things right, or on *being* right. These are not particularly inviting messages, nor are they the crux of the good news. In fact, folks can encounter the rhetoric of superiority all around them in society, not just among Christians. Simply to proclaim to non-believers that we, as Christians, have a monopoly on the truth and are always right puts us in the same league as political candidates, TV advertisements, and football teams. The heart of the gospel is not what we *have* or what we *know*. The good news is that God welcomes each of us into God's arms regardless of who we are or what we have done; God invites us, again and again, into abundant life; God's offer of forgiveness, mercy, and grace has no expiration date but is the saving activity of God in all things. This is a message of welcome one does not hear in the daily barrage of expectations to look, earn, wear, or be certain ways in order to be welcome. The language of God's welcome must be our first step toward those encountering Christianity. As with human development, we welcome a spiritual infant into our lives, taking care that it has what it needs, unconcerned in the beginning with whether it will ultimately measure up to the family's expectations. The Christian family has important claims to make on the lives of the faithful, but those are subsequent, not first, steps.

Welcome as a form of proclamation means Wesleyans must take care not to set conditions in order for people to enter the church to see what the good news is all about. We cannot send the message that one must look a certain way, have a certain level of income, or meet any other condition of any kind. There is no belief test one must pass in order to hear the Gospel of Jesus Christ. We must take care because conditional expectations can take many forms: You are welcome here if you speak our language. You are welcome here if you fit in with our class of people. You are welcome here if you have a car to get here. You are welcome here if you can walk up the steps. You are welcome here if you agree with us. These are dangerous and tempting conditions, subverting grace rather than proclaiming it, as Mary Elizabeth Moore points out in her chapter on prophetic grace. Matthew 25 does not command Christians to welcome the stranger only under certain conditions. There are important and hard issues for discussion with those committed to following Christ. But with regard to those who are newly investigating Christian faith, or returning after some absence, we are called to welcome them to the Gospel with no condition. God has offered the good news to all, and we cannot parse it out only to those we deem worthy.

Gratitude

The language of gratitude has taken on some currency in American culture of late. Popular spirituality has pointed to gratitude as a key posture for healthy living, but secular sources have not cornered the market on gratitude. It is a central tenet of most religious traditions. This shared territory gives non-believers some familiar handholds as they hear the Christian story. God welcomes us. We are grateful. These simple, powerful truths are the ground of the good news. Gratitude is one of the deepest human experiences we have. Life's most precious blessings are sheer gifts: our families, the forgiveness of a loved one, or the discovery of one's true vocation. When we stand in gratitude, we are powerless, for the gift is not of our own making, and we are also empowered by the awe and utter amazement we experience in the presence of the gift. For those outside Christianity, gratitude is a doorway into the Christian life that provides continuity with the ways God has always been at work in their lives. When Christians cultivate the practices of gratitude, they give witness to God's love and create doorways for others to enter the faith.

Recognition

The practice of recognition is pervasive in Jesus' teaching as he calls his followers to "have eyes to see and ears to hear." Recognition is more than just seeing. Recognition is seeing deeply, seeing beyond what appears to be. When God recognizes us as God's children, rather than as strangers, God sees beyond our appearances. When we recognize strangers as Jesus, we too see beyond appearances. When a harried young mother scolds her child in the grocery checkout line, she wants to be seen as the loving, committed mother she is. When an unemployed man shows up for an interview, he wants to be seen as the capable, employable man he is. Recall here Rebekah Miles's description in chapter eight of contemporary American views of work. We all know the pain of not being seen for who we truly are, of being misunderstood. Recognition sees beyond what appears, to what truly is. This powerful language speaks to our deepest longings to be seen and known.

The Christian tradition of hospitality claims that recognition is rooted in the *imago Dei*, which each person, regardless of appearances, bears.[43] Early Christians sought encounters with the poor, sick, foreigner, and traveler in order to recognize the deeper reality of the image of God in them. The Strangers' Friend Society of early Methodism and the later urban missions required Methodists physically to go to and be present with the strangers, in order to see them fully and recognize the breadth and depth of their lives.

Wesleyan communities today can heed Jesus' frequent call "Look! See! The Kingdom of God is near!" through the framework of hospitable practices that cultivate deep seeing. Unfortunately, it is all too easy to ignore the visitor, or to render invisible the stranger by simply not looking at him or her. We can avoid seeing the poor simply by never driving through hurting neighborhoods. We can avoid seeing the vulnerable by never going to the hospice, nursing home, or immigration office. Hospitality calls us to see, to physically look at, the "other," even if the experience threatens or challenges us. The kind of recognition that is central to hospitality often requires us to leave the walls of our church in order to see. If we are willing to see, then God can bless us with recognition, the recognition that this stranger is a gift from God and bears God's image.

Beyond physical sight, the kind of deep seeing that hospitality invokes takes time and patience. To recognize the presence of Christ in another may not happen quickly. It often requires our getting to know them, taking time to look beyond their clothes, employment, language, manners, or needs. We may need to listen to a person's life story to fully appreciate Christ's presence there. We may have to work together or pray together before we begin to *recognize* another. We may also have to modify our idea of what Jesus looks like in order to recognize Christ in another. In addition to time and patience, this deep seeing also requires prayer asking for the gift of sight to see Christ in another. Embedded in all these acts of recognition is the proclamation that God has already been at work in the other's life, however new the person may be to Christian community.

Hospitality offers Wesleyans today a framework of welcome, gratitude, and recognition to reach out to those who have not heard the good news of God's saving love. We stand in the tradition of early Christians and early Methodists who also employed welcome, gratitude, and recognition to the stranger and the "least of these."

Hospitality, Justification, and Sanctification

The third resource the tradition of hospitality can provide for Wesleyans today is a way to hold together both for ourselves and for those exploring the faith our claim that what God has done for us (justification) and what God is doing in us (sanctification) are integral parts of one whole experience of salvation. As Wesleyans, we witness to the truth that God has reconciled us through Jesus Christ into divine life (justification) and calls us ever deeper into holiness of life in God (sanctification). The theological framework of hospitality described here includes both of these movements as well. God's welcome justifies us, redeeming and restoring us to relationship with God in the Triune life. God's love in us sanctifies us, enabling us to welcome others into closer relationship with Christ Jesus through the stranger. Through hospitality, Wesleyans can participate on the ground in God's work of justification and sanctification.

Of course, like other "churchspeak" words, "justification" and "sanctification" can be obstacles for those new to faith. To be sure, I am not arguing that we jettison these faithful and important ways of talking about salvation, or water down theological language. The language of welcome, gratitude, and recognition cannot exhaust the language of justification and sanctification. Rather, the vocabulary of hospitality offers some contemporary paths to walk with folks as they discover what God has done and is doing in our lives—"God's love shed abroad in our hearts."

These insights from historical practices of hospitality are merely starting places for Wesleyans today, not ending places. Gospel hospitality holds promise as a living Wesleyan tradition. If we can successfully avoid the temptation to trivialize or sentimentalize hospitality in contemporary Christian culture, we can proclaim a gospel hospitality that the world is hungry to hear: the power of God's welcome, the risky gratefulness of our welcoming others, and the transforming grace of coming to know Jesus in the stranger. All good welcomes are starting places.

CHAPTER SIX

RECONSIDERING SIN: WOMEN AND THE UNWITTING WISDOM OF JOHN WESLEY

Diane Leclerc
for Virginia Burrus[1]

The Augustinian understanding of the essence of original sin as pride has dominated the theological trajectory of Western Christianity. Augustine's hamartiology, however, not only neglects Eastern Christianity (to which Wesley is so indebted); it also neglects insights that arise when "women's experience" is given credence as a theological source. Catherine Keller succinctly articulates feminist concerns with an Augustinian construct: "Feminist theology has shown . . . that the traditional definitions of sin as pride, arrogance, self-interest and other forms of exaggerated self-esteem *miss the mark* in the case of women, who in this culture suffer from too little self-esteem, indeed too little self."[2]

In an article first printed in 1960, Valerie Saiving (Goldstein) embraced the difficult task of critiquing the Augustinian definition:

> The temptations of woman *as woman* are not the same as the temptations of man as man, and the specifically feminine forms of sin—"feminine" not because they are confined to women or because women are incapable of sinning in other ways but because they are outgrowths of the basic feminine character structure—have a quality which can never be encompassed by such terms as "pride" and "will-to-power." They are better suggested by such terms as triviality, distractibility, and diffuseness; lack of an organizing center or focus; dependence on others for one's own self definition . . . in short, underdevelopment or negation of the self.[3]

A slightly later thinker, Judith Plaskow, defines a woman's sin as "the failure to take responsibility for self-actualization."[4] Despite this definition, a new hesitation can also be seen in Plaskow's work: a hesitancy to "blame the victim." This hesitation finds its full expression in the work of other feminists, such as Mary Daly.[5] Feminists since Daly have tended to see original sin as patriarchy or sexism itself;[6] there is yet a need for articulating a theology of sin with attention to women's lives and agency. Marjorie Hewitt Suchocki adds to a working definition:

> [F]eminist scholars see the sin of pride as describing the sins of the powerful who refuse to recognize the rightful boundaries of others, and the sin of hiding as the refusal of the responsibility to become a self that is so often the plight of [many] who are not in positions of power. In the process, they effectively show that [a] one-sided treatment of sin through the notion of pride demonstrates the bias of . . . culture and gender, and therefore the particularity rather than universality of [this] description of sin.[7]

However new such insights appear in light of the dominant Augustinian theological tradition, they are not without precedent. Given the weight of "heritage," not only for theology, but also for a feminism that seeks therein not so much legitimacy as a sense of texture or depth, it has seemed to me worthwhile—perhaps even urgent—to pursue historical precursors in other historical texts for the feminist critique of the more traditional doctrine(s) of sin.[8]

The task of providing historical foundations for Saiving's alternative, gendered doctrine of sin, however, is influenced by ongoing debates. First, while Saiving's insights productively disrupt the theologically orthodox position, to speak of a basic feminine character structure is no longer orthodox among more recent feminist theorists. Indeed, such a purportedly essentialist construction has become a rather heretical view.[9] The philosophical underpinnings of Saiving's theory have increasingly been called into question over the course of the last forty years. Even those who want to maintain the strategic value of naming a female essence for the purpose of addressing a situation do so from a very different place.[10] That different place is where difference, not essence, is the new and dominant charter.[11] Meta-narratives have been replaced by microresistances.[12] The category of "femaleness" has become tenuous. The characteristic distinctions between men and women are now seen as culturally constructed, and thus malleable. Some theorists are now questioning even the casual differentiation between sex (as a biological reality) and gender (as a social construct); sex itself has been identified as a cultural construction.[13]

If gender can no longer be defined with certainty, if the differences and diversity among women are now the points of emphasis, and if there is nothing that is essentially female, then many are asking, where is the commonality that once fueled the political fires of the feminist movement?[14] Does feminism itself stand at the cliff of a theoretical paradox that elicits political despondency? Is it at the brink of linguistic non-existence? Can there be such a thing as a postmodern, post-structuralist, anti-essentialist feminism?[15] Feminism seems to be looking for a "courage to be" in the face of such anxiety over ontology.[16]

If feminism has most recently been defined as anti-essentialist (to overgeneralize), then is not feminist theology also at risk of becoming oxymoronic if all speech about essences—and even speech about truth—is strongly rejected in the post-structuralist scheme? If theology, in its traditional sense, aims at articulating foundational, essential truth(s), and the "winner of the feminist theory contest"[17] rejects such a paradigm, can feminist theology still be done? More specifically to the argument here, what is the fate of theological anthropology as a specific field of study? According to the terms introduced by Saiving and Plaskow, a truly comprehensive theology requires an acknowledgment of "woman" as a theological question and theological source (despite obfuscation of this reality by centuries of theologians). Indeed, feminist theology originally arose to demand that this reality be recognized by its male counterparts.

It would be an ironic twist of events if post-feminist theology, where the category "woman" is contested, and traditional theology, where "woman" is not taken seriously, were to become unknowing cohorts—both speechless about and apathetic toward "woman" as a theological category. It is apropos to apply Susan Bordo's words to the field of theology: "Most of our institutions have barely begun to absorb the message of modernist social criticism; surely it is too soon to let them off the hook via postmodern heterogeneity and instability."[18] Surely the work of *feminist* theology is not complete.[19] Nor is the historical analysis of Wesley from a feminist perspective.

Strategic essentialism has been advocated by many as a means of negotiating the tension between feminism and post-structuralism. The following pages will draw upon strategic essentialism as a means to negotiate the theological implications of Wesley's relationships with women, as a type of *via media* between the extremes of abandoning "woman" as a relevant theological category and inscribing that category with the mark of stagnant universality.

WESLEY AS FEMINIST OR MISOGYNIST?

With the intentions of strategic essentialism, I thus explore whether John Wesley might be classified as a feminist with strong advocacy for the values and rights of women or as a misogynist with a tendency to denigrate the being, rights, and leadership of women.

Wesley the "Feminist"

Paul Chilcote and Kent Brown are among those scholars who have provided primary evidence of John Wesley's very strong advocacy of women.[20] Such evidence is highly credible. Compared to Churchmen of his era, John Wesley stands out as an exception to the rule. The women of early British Methodism were afforded ecclesiastical opportunities rare to women in the eighteenth century.[21] Wesley himself made exceptions to rules that prevented women from preaching; he believed that God would use extraordinary means to accomplish extraordinary ends in extraordinary times.[22] Finally, he even made preaching by women an "official" position of Methodism (as we see in the case of Sarah Mallet, the first such sanctioned female preacher).[23] While formal institutional power remained with the male preachers, whom Wesley himself placed and moved at will, his class leaders—often women—served, for all practical purposes, as the veritable pastors of Wesley's "congregations," since the male circuit preachers were rarely present.[24]

These pastoral roles of women do reveal Wesley's more feminist impulses. He also deeply valued his more reciprocal friendships with women, counting them his true equals. Women such as Sarah Ryan, Mary (Bosanquet) Fletcher, and Sarah Crosby acted the part of Wesley's confidants; they were clearly part of his inner circle.[25] "To his female correspondents . . . he writes with peculiar effluence of thought and frankness of communication. He, in fact, unbosoms himself, on every topic which occurs to him, as to kindred spirits, in whose sympathies he confided, and from whose re-communication he hoped for additional light."[26] He wrote and visited them as often as he could. As they apparently were to him, Wesley remained loyal to his women friends over the decades. When Mary Fletcher lost her husband,[27] Wesley wrote, "should not you now consider me as your first human friend?"[28] He invested even more in the relationship for the remainder of his life.

Sarah Ryan was converted out of a life of ill repute, and Wesley took a pastoral interest in her spiritual progress. However, he also soon found himself depending on her for emotional support; she was often the bearer of his burdens. This alarmed some of Wesley's colleagues. Still, in 1758 he comments:

> The conversing with you, either by speaking or writing, is an unspeakable blessing to me. I cannot think of you without thinking of God. Others often lead me to Him; but it is, as it were, going round about: you bring me straight into His presence. Therefore, whoever warns me against trusting you, I cannot refrain, as I am clearly convinced He calls me to it.[29]

Another important relationship was with Sarah Crosby, a prominent female preacher. Wesley seems to have placed himself under her spiritual direction, and there are several examples of Crosby's "plain dealing" with him. The Leytonstone society was apparently disposed to criticize Wesley's own spiritual experience. Crosby wrote a letter in which she outlined their complaints. Wesley responded that they knew nothing about his personal experience and thus had no basis for their harsh dealings with him; he added, however, that Crosby *had* been given access to his inner life, and she therefore had more right to judge him:

> My Dear Sister,—Last night I received yours, and was in some doubt whether to write again or no; and if I did, whether to write with reserve or without. At length I resolved upon the latter, and that for two reasons: 1) because I love *you*; 2) because I love myself. And if so, I ought to write and write freely; for your letters do me good. . . . I take well all that you say; and I love you the more, the more free you are. That is another total mistake, that I dislike any one for plain dealing. And of all persons living Sarah Crosby has least room to say so.[30]

In a comment reminiscent of Jerome, when speaking of his male co-laborers, Wesley said, "I have none like-minded."[31] In a select few women in his life, he found kindred spirits. These brief examples show that Wesley not only allowed women to serve in places of leadership within his movement, but he also considered his intimate friendships with women invaluable.

Wesley the Misogynist

Can a case be made for recognizing misogynism in Wesley?[32] Evidence for a grade of theoretical misogynism can be found in Wesley's *Explanatory Notes upon the New Testament*. Most of Wesley's notes about women further display equivocalness in Wesley's exegesis. Three will serve as exemplary; first, Acts 17:4:

> Our freethinkers pique themselves upon observing that women are more religious than men; and this, in compliment both to religion and good manners, they impute to the weakness of their understandings. And, indeed, as far as nature can go in imitating religion by performing outward acts of it, this picture of religion may make a fairer show in women than in men, both by reason of their more tender passions, and their modesty, which will make those actions appear to more advantage. But in the case of true religion, which always implies taking up the cross, especially in time of persecution, women lie naturally under a great disadvantage, as having less courage than men. So that their embracing the gospel was a stronger evidence of the power of Him whose strength is perfected in weakness, as a stronger assistance of the Holy Spirit was needful for them to overcome their natural fearfulness.[33]

When commenting on Paul's infamous passage that "women [are to] be silent in the churches" (1 Cor. 14:34), Wesley writes, "*be in subjection*—To the man whose proper office it is to lead and to instruct the congregation." However, he also writes, "*Let your women be silent in the churches*—Unless they are under an extraordinary impulse of the Spirit."[34] The first section of 1 Peter 3 deals with the subjection of wives to their husbands. Here, Wesley advises men to "*Dwell with the woman according to knowledge*—Knowing they are weak." Yet again he clarifies, "Yet do not despise them for this, but *give them honour*—Both in heart, in word, and in action; as those who are called to be *joint-heirs of . . . eternal life*."[35] In accordance with this type of exegesis, Wesley writes to one of his female preachers, "Be subject to no creature, only so far as love constrains. By this sweetest and strongest tie you are now subject to, dear Sally, Your affectionate friend and brother."[36] While Wesley maintained the typical (and misogynist) interpretive conclusions of his day regarding women, a certain degree of ambivalence nudged his exegesis in novel directions.

Was Wesley a "practical misogynist"? If this case is to be made, it is most readily supported by examining Wesley's romantic relationships. The Sophy Hopkey affair, the Grace Murray debacle, and the Mary Vazeille marital disaster are the parts of Wesley's biography that provide the most embarrassment for his devotees, even today: "Generations of biographers have rehearsed the curious facts of these relationships and responded with varying degrees of scholarly distress and rationalization about the spectacle of Wesley's odd judgment and behavior regarding affairs of the heart."[37] Although accounts of these relationships are surprisingly detailed, there is no *conclusive* interpretation regarding Wesley's romantic failures, only historical accounts and educated guesses, often taking the form of biased hagiography.

The Sophy Hopkey affair took place during Wesley's mission to Georgia (1735–37). The result was a sudden departure from America, for fear of his life. Wesley contemplated marriage but was vague and indirect about his intentions. Apparently, he was torn between an informal vow of celibacy (influenced by the strong authority that "primitive" Christianity had over Wesley at the time) and "the fire in his bosom" that he tried to resist. Hopkey wearied of the ambivalence and pressured Wesley to make a decision. He resorted to drawing lots between "marry" and "think of it no more." The lot fell on the latter. Despite this definitive moment, however, Wesley still insisted that Sophy make no important steps without consulting him. In the end, Hopkey married a Mr. Williamson without such consultation. While Wesley would certainly plead innocence about any connection, by all appearances it seems that he sought retaliation through the pastoral office. (He refused to give her the sacrament of Holy Communion.) Her angry family brought Wesley up on charges before the magistrate, and thereupon Wesley decided to make his exit back to London.

His romantic involvement with Grace Murray, some twelve years later, reveals striking parallels, particularly regarding Wesley's fatal vagueness. Wesley was quite in love. He seemingly had every intention of marrying Grace and, by all evidence, officially proposed.[38] However, he must have conveyed some indeterminate sentiments, for Grace also accepted a proposal from one of Wesley's preachers, John Bennet. According to Henry Rack, "It was the story of Sophy Hopkey and Williamson all over again."[39] Both women clearly felt the rejection implicit in Wesley's ambivalence.

There is quite a bit of evidence to suggest that the proposal by Bennet was actually instigated by Charles, John Wesley's brother. Charles apparently believed that Grace, Wesley's housekeeper, was from too low a station and that this would cause scandal among the Methodists. To prevent his brother's mistake, Charles secretly took Grace away and performed the marriage between her and John Bennet. Wesley progressed from this thwarted love affair into a "disastrous" marriage. This time, John Wesley guarded himself against any outside interference or from brotherly advice. Mary (Molly) Vazeille became his wife in a private ceremony in mid-February 1751, while Charles "fell into one of his depressions," completely "thunderstruck."[40] Charles was again most anxious about the effect of the marriage on the growth and reputation of Methodism. Despite John's attempts to maneuver past brotherly intervention, he ultimately suffered from this decision. In the estimation of some early interpreters, he had married one of the "three bad wives" of history.[41]

Just before the marriage, Wesley wrote in his journal: "For many years I remained single, because I believed I could be more useful in a single than in a married state. . . . I now as fully believe that in my present circumstances I might be more useful in a married state."[42] There is some speculation that these "present circumstances" might have been continuing rumors about the nature of the relationships he and the women of Methodism actually shared.[43] A marriage might put such rumors to rest. Some credence can also be given to the theory that he was concerned about his health and looking for a "nurse" who could always be at his side.[44] Of course, there is the common assumption that Wesley was on the "rebound."[45] It is also quite possible that Wesley had struggled through all the internal issues when he decided to marry Grace Murray and now saw marriage as the logical conclusion of all his reasoning. All of these theories reveal that it is not at all conclusive that Wesley married Mrs. Vazeille because he loved her.

In Wesley's early letters to Molly we see a degree of positive affection,[46] but symptoms of tension can be detected from early in the relationship. John Wesley's letters paint Mrs. Wesley as intensely jealous of the time his ministry stole from her. Only a month after his marriage, Wesley articulated a principle for which he was already well known among his preachers: "I cannot understand how a Methodist preacher can answer it to God to preach one sermon or travel one day less in a married than in a single state. In this respect surely, 'it remaineth that they who have wives be as though they had none.'"[47] Wesley did not alter his own traveling, but rather carried on his preaching and administrating exactly as he had while single. For a short time, Mrs. Wesley attempted to travel with him, but she quickly gave it up.

Mrs. Wesley was also jealous of Wesley's relationships with other women and could not understand the immensity of his correspondence with them. She apparently asked him to stop writing, but he refused. There is even some evidence that the women themselves slowed their correspondence out of respect for the situation; however, Wesley's determination to defy Molly's jealousy intensified. Instead of being attentive to his wife's wishes, he instead made the fateful mistake of telling her that she was free to open any of his letters. Although Wesley believed this would prove his innocence, it did everything but.[48] Sarah Ryan was the biggest threat in Mrs. Wesley's mind, for she had been converted out of a rather scandalous lifestyle.[49] Although there is no evidence that Wesley was ever guilty of sexual misconduct, he was certainly unsympathetic to his wife's sentiments. Some evidence for the legitimacy of Mrs. Wesley's anger can be seen in the following quotation from a letter to Sarah Ryan:

> My Dear Sister—Last Friday, after many severe words, my wife left me, vowing she would see me no more. As I had wrote to you the same morning, I began to reason with myself, till I almost doubted whether I had done well in writing or whether I ought to write to you at all. After prayer that doubt was taken away.[50]

Nearly a year later, he wrote the following to Mrs. Wesley directly:

> Dear Molly—I was much concerned, the night before I left London, at your unkind and unjust accusation. You accused *me* of unkindness, cruelty, and what not. And why so? Because I insist on choosing my own company! because I insist upon conversing, by speaking or writing, with those I (not you) judge proper! For more than seven years this has been a bone of contention between you and me. And it is so still. For I will not, I cannot, I dare not give it up. "But when *you* will rage and fret and call me names." I am sorry for it. But I cannot help it. I do and must insist that I have a right to choose my own company.[51]

Another year passed before Wesley wrote his infamous letter to Mrs. Wesley, in which he outlined (in ten points) what he disliked about her and what he demanded her to change.⁵² Although Mrs. Wesley came and went from the relationship repeatedly, in the end she exited for good. In October 1778 (seven years after she had left for the last time), Wesley felt compelled to sum up his position by asserting that the wrong she had done to him could not be undone and by bidding her farewell.⁵³ When Mrs. Wesley died in 1781, he was not informed until several days afterwards.

Although earlier hagiographers of Wesley paint Molly Vazeille as having a very bad temper, a rebellious nature, and some degree of insanity, more recent assessments of the relationship rightly criticize Wesley's part in the disaster. "John was not without blame," Edwards argues. "At no time, and emphatically not when he married at forty-eight years, could he give to any woman that attention that was her due. Never would he consent to compromise in the interests of their mutual happiness."⁵⁴ Samuel Rogal agrees that the failure of the marriage was very much related to "Wesley's character and ideals. . . . Wesley had, too early in his life, wed himself to social and religious reform, and it appears doubtful he would have been willing to spare any significant amount of time from his grand commitment to devote himself to a partner, a home, or a family."⁵⁵ Kenneth Collins, after analyzing Wesley's letters and journal, concludes, "[M]arriage is presented as a trap, a snare, which prevents one from following the will of God in its highest sense."⁵⁶ Collins insightfully adds, "Indeed in a real sense, Wesley was already married before February, 1751, but not to Grace Murray as Baker suggests. Rather, John Wesley was already married to the Lord."⁵⁷ Whether Wesley's inability to invest himself in romantic relationships was due to this type of religious devotion or due to his failure to resolve an oedipal conflict,⁵⁸ what is clear is that, in his treatment of Hopkey, Murray, and Vazeille, Wesley can rightly be accused of "practical misogyny" in his more domestic relationships with women.

In Wesley, one can see a theology that contains *both* misogynist and feminist aspects; he can affirm a woman's "spiritual equality" while avowing her natural weakness.⁵⁹ Likewise, ambivalence can be seen in his actual dealings with women. Wesley was a confusing, indirect, and sometimes cruel lover, especially when spurned, and an undoubtedly patriarchal husband. Yet, Wesley also held certain friendships with women as the most important relationships of his life. He counted these women as his peers; depended on them for wisdom, guidance, and strength; and saw them as equal partners in ministry.

The evidence presented above regarding John Wesley's relationships with women, and his theories on women, have caused some scholars to take up one cause or the other, to argue for Wesley's feminism or for Wesley's misogyny. My intention here is not to resolve this issue. Rather, my aim is to propose that, regardless of the apparent complexity of feminist and misogynist themes, John Wesley clearly advocates for a desexualized, or de-gendered, *theory of subjectivity* and consequently offers a liberated space subsequently occupied by many Methodist women. What Wesley is advocating is misogynist in that he all but rejects women as sexual or maternal in his practical advice.[60] Yet, his advice had a liberating effect on many of these women. Similar to more ancient Christian history, Wesley advises a practical celibacy. In doing so, Wesley offers Methodist women a means to the same personal power and liberated space as was offered to women ascetics in centuries before. I propose that this space is *not* created through Wesley's feminism, but rather precisely through a *rhetorical* misogynism that surfaces around traditional female roles.

A Recurring Theme: "Singleness of Heart"

Wesley's "misogynism" can be gleaned from a recurring theme in his letters to women:[61] he often, in a variety of ways, counsels women against the dangers of domesticity. As was the case for the ascetic women of the late fourth century, many women of early Methodism took Wesley's "misogynistic" advice and put it to good use. Once again, we see a particular historical moment that evidences how excesses of misogyny can be "reclaimed" to create a "radical new" option.[62]

In 1743, John Wesley penned "Thoughts on Marriage and a Single Life," which was redrafted as "Thoughts on a Single Life" in 1765.[63] Here, Wesley exhorts anyone "called" to the single life to "use all the advantages you enjoy."[64] After listing many such advantages, he writes:

> Above all, you are at liberty from the greatest of all entanglements, the loving one creature above all others. It is possible to do this without sin, without any impeachment of our love to God. But how inconceivably difficult! to give God our whole heart, while a creature has so large a share of it! How much more easily may we do this, when the heart is, tenderly indeed, but equally attached to more than one; or, at least, without any great inequality! What angelic wisdom does it require to give enough of our affection, and not too much, to so near a relation![65]

When Wesley writes a final redraft near the end of his life ("A Thought upon Marriage," 1785[66]) and speaks of "those youthful yearnings for happiness with a woman, [he] now interpreted them as a substitute for waning love of God."[67] Plainly, Wesley's own experience with marriage did not convince him of its potentially positive influence on spirituality. Despite his attempts to reason himself out of his predilection for celibacy,[68] his views on marriage remained generally negative throughout his life. This, no doubt, influenced his advice to anyone else who might consider matrimony. Yet, there is an observable difference between the responses he gave to men and women. Despite his wariness of men's "unholy desires" and his belief that his male preachers should behave as if they had no wives, Wesley was not particularly inclined to discourage men from marrying. Rather, he only advised them to make good choices so that their ministry would not be hindered.⁶⁹ His letters to women show that they were an entirely different case. If a woman marries, only in very rare exceptions could she remain as useful to God. Thus, the domestic life is painted as a great temptation, even an "unnecessary" evil to be resisted.

Marrying Women

Jane Hilton sought Wesley's advice about marrying William Barton in 1766. Wesley responded by saying, "See that you stand fast in the liberty wherewith Christ has made you free. You need never more be entangled with . . . desire of any creature. Christ is yours! . . . O be all His, and admit no rival into your heart!"⁷⁰ Three years later, she did in fact marry him, and Wesley was compelled to write, "Both of you have now more need than ever continually to watch and pray that you enter not into temptation. There will be great danger of so cleaving to each other as to forget God, or of being so taken up with a creature as to abate your hunger and thirst after righteousness."⁷¹ Marriage, according to Wesley, threatens spiritual "singleness of heart." When one of Wesley's woman preachers,⁷² Jane Bisson, married Mr. Cock, Wesley inquired: "I shall be glad to know how you have found your soul since you altered your condition. You must needs (sic) have abundantly more care now than you had in a single life. And are you able still, among all these cares, to attend upon the Lord without distraction?"⁷³

A few months after Ms. Bisson's wedding, he admitted, "When I heard of your marriage it gave me pain. I was afraid least you should have suffered loss."⁷⁴ The following year, Wesley remained focused on his apprehension. "I cannot but say that it was some concern to me when I first heard that you was married; because I was afraid that you would be less useful than you might have been in a single life."⁷⁵ A few months later, he repeated himself. "When I first heard of your marriage, I was afraid of two things: the one was, that it would hurt your soul; the other, that it would prevent your usefulness—at least, that you would not be useful in so high a degree as otherwise you might be."⁷⁶ Wesley still could not let the issue drop; another year passed and his reminiscence continued:

> When I saw the wonderful manner wherein He had dealt with you from your early years . . . I thought He was preparing you for a large sphere of action. Surely you was not then designed to be shut up in a little cottage and fully taken up with domestic cares! I was in hopes of seeing all the graces which He had given you employed in far other things. However, although I cannot deny that you are now acting in a lower sphere than was originally designed for you, yet I trust you still enjoy communion with God.⁷⁷

Unfortunately, we have no evidence of Bisson's response to this repetitious and invasive chiding. For Wesley, the domestic life is of an unquestionably lower spiritual station. We see this theme maintained and abstracted in a letter to another woman preacher,[78] Penelope Newman, about her marriage: "Only the danger will be lest, when you have more opportunity, you should have less desire of doing good. This is the case of many pious persons when they marry, and I do not wonder at it. I should rather wonder it is not the case of all."[79]

Single Women

Not only did Wesley counsel women who had married to stay as active in Christian service as possible (while resigning himself to the fact that they would be bound by other priorities), he also advised single women to recognize their great advantages. In a note preceding a letter to Peggy Dale, John Telford explains that Peggy and her sister Molly had devoted themselves to the single life, but that "Molly fell away—into matrimony. Peggy, who had been firmer, felt her sister's defection, with perhaps an undercurrent of regret that she had been so firm, since she was now left alone."[80] Wesley responded to the situation by writing the following:

> The hearing from my dear Peggy at this critical time gives me a particular satisfaction. I wanted to know how you bore such a trial, a wound in the tenderest part. You have now a first proof that the God whom you serve is able to deliver you in every trial. You feel, and yet conquer. We conquer all when we say, "Not as I will, but as Thou wilt." I hope you are delivered not only from *repining* with regard to her, but from *reasoning* with regard to yourself. You still see the more excellent way and are sensible to the advantages you enjoy. I allow *some* single women have fewer advantages for eternity than they might have in a married state. But, blessed be God, you have all the advantages which one can well conceive.[81] (emphases his)

Wesley's gaze once again turns to the "tenderest part," and his advice to a single woman is to resign hope for a married life and to recognize God's apparent will for her singleness and consequent "deliverance." To Elizabeth Ritchie, who only felt free to marry after Wesley had died, Wesley writes, "I am glad you were enabled to withstand that plausible temptation which few young women have power to resist, particularly when you had to encounter the persuasion of those you esteemed and loved."[82] He continues elsewhere, "Surely it is your wisdom to stand fast even in the outward liberty wherewith Christ has made you free. You are now happily disengaged from caring for the things of this world, and need only care for the things of the Lord."[83] In a letter to Martha Chapman in 1784, Wesley repeats his theme again: "It was well for you that God did not suffer you to find rest in any creature. He had better things in store for you."[84]

Wesley's intimate friendship with Ann Bolton began when Bolton considered a proposal of marriage and sought the advice of the leader of her movement; the theme of her singleness runs throughout their twenty-three-year correspondence. In response to Bolton's inquiry, Wesley wrote, "The best and most desirable thing of all is that you should live and die wholly devoted to God, waiting upon Him without distraction, serving Him without carefulness."[85] Bolton did not marry. Two years later, Wesley reiterated the wisdom of her decision:

> The Lord has done great things for you already: He has preserved you even in the dangerous season . . . from ten thousand snares to which a young woman of a pleasing form and behaviour and not an ill temper would naturally be exposed, and to which your own heart would surely have yielded had you not been preserved by His gracious power. . . . He has made you more than conqueror, even a gainer thereby.[86]

Through subsequent years, he repeatedly asked her, "Is your heart whole with Him, free from idols";[87] "Do you find constant power over the old enemy, inordinate affection";[88] "Are you never hindered by any person?"[89] Then, in 1774, another offer of marriage came. Wesley replied:

> Let me not hurt my dear friend if upon such an occasion I speak with all plainness. You are now highly favoured. I trust God has made you a partaker of His great salvation. He has given you a good understanding improved by experience and free conversation with many of His dearest children. He has placed you as a city set upon an hill in a situation wherein you have full exercise for all your talents. . . . And is it a little thing that would induce my sister, my friend to quit such a situation as this? If, indeed, you could enlarge the sphere of your action; if you could be more extensively useful; or if you could have a closer union than you ever had yet with a person of very eminent grace and understanding . . . [and] I would add, "And one that will furnish you with full liberty of action that you may exercise your every grace," . . . I should instantly acknowledge the call of God and say, "Go, and the Lord be with thee!" But I can see nothing of this in your present case. All dark, I fear; evil is before you.[90]

Wesley's concern is for an "enlarged sphere" and "full liberty." In other words, Wesley denigrated the traditional feminine roles once again, under the rubric of entire devotion to God. Bolton took Wesley's advice and again broke this second engagement. Perhaps in response to a direct question from Bolton regarding the intentions of his repeated advice to stay single, Wesley felt impelled to relay the following information: "I have often examined *myself* (to speak without any reserve) with respect to *you*, and I find 'no fever's heat, no fluttering spirits dance,' but a steady rational affection, 'calm as the warmth of life.' "[91]

Several years later, Wesley again found cause to reflect on the wisdom of Bolton's decision to stay single. Apparently, Bolton was second-guessing such a resolution. Wesley writes:

> My Dear Sister,—You know how nearly I am concerned in whatever relates to *you*. My regard for you has been invariable ever since you was with me in London. I then set you down for my inalienable friend, and such I trust you will always be, until the union of our spirits will be complete where our bodies part no more.... God has lately delivered you out of imminent danger.... And now, instead of praising God for your great deliverance, you are [set] against Him, as [if] it were no deliverance at all! You are fretting and grieving yourself because the snare is broken, because your soul is taken out of the net! But must not this grieve the Holy Spirit of God? What deep unthankfulness! And it is well if here be not a little inordinate affection lying at the bottom of all.... My Nancy, arise and shake yourself from the dust! You have acted wisely and faithfully.[92]

In the previous letter, Wesley set up his need to scold Bolton by invoking her sentiments toward their long-term intimacy. However, despite his rhetoric regarding the wisdom of her decision, Wesley must have wrestled with his own conscience over his part in this decision. He penned the following three years later:

> Some years since, one of our preachers said, "Mr. W. has hindered me from marrying *once*, but I am resolved he shall not hinder me again." He was as good as his word. Without asking my advice he married a woman of a thousand, who exercised him well while he lived and sent him to paradise before his time. I do not know that this is your case. But I tell *you* whatever rises in my mind. I only want you to attain a *full reward*.[93]

This was Wesley's last mention of Bolton's singleness. Of note, Ann Bolton married a year after Wesley's death.

Parents and Children

Wesley's understanding of domestic temptation extended beyond marriage, to family life in general; the demands of parents and children on an individual's spirituality also received his attention. To a Mrs. Woodhouse he writes, "[God] has permitted that difference which prevents your finding comfort even in a near relation, that you may seek it with a free and disengaged heart in Him who will never deceive your hope."[94] Miss Ellen Gretton wrote to Wesley and explained that, if she stayed in Methodism, her father would take away her means of income. In response, Wesley did not hesitate to proclaim adamantly that her loyalty belonged to God and to her Methodist "religious friends."[95] Not only was there no mention of a daughterly responsibility to honor or obey her parents, there was also no practical advice regarding how she would support herself. Wesley's only concern was the "sustenance" of her complete devotion. Hester Ann Rogers, one of the most beloved and remembered Methodist women, faced similar struggles. While reviewing her biography, Chilcote comments, "Her wholehearted involvement with the Methodists led to harsh persecution and ostracism from family and friends."[96] For this, she was praised.

Wesley's requirement of "Christian resignation,"[97] or emotional detachment, also extended to a woman's children. A long letter to Jane (Hilton) Barton, in which Wesley expounded upon the nature of temptation, concludes with his remarking that "you have the temptations which you had not [before]. You have little children, you have worldly care."[98] Several years later, he again writes of her children:

> Every proof you have had of God's care over you is a reason for trusting Him with your children. He will take care of them, whether you are alive or dead; so that you have no need to be careful in this matter. You have only by prayer and supplication to make your requests known to God; and whenever He sees it will be best for you, He will deliver you out of your captivity.[99]

This statement near the end of Wesley's life parallels one written years earlier. In 1749, in a letter to his own sister, he says quite matter-of-factly:

> I believe the death of your children is a great instance of the goodness of God towards you. You have often mentioned to me how much of your time they took up. Now that time is restored to you, and you have nothing to do but serve our Lord without carefulness and without distraction, till you are sanctified body, soul, and spirit.[100]

Martha Wesley Hall had lost nine out of ten children in infancy. Her husband also left her after twenty years of marriage, which seemed to have pleased Wesley for similar reasons.

Idolatry

Wesley's preference for keeping "his" women single,[101] and his concern that parents and children not dissuade a woman's spiritual commitment, received further theological definition in terms of idolatry. Wesley's primary concern was that those under his spiritual direction were *single in heart*.[102] Interestingly, Wesley did not use the more typically coupled opposite, "double-mindedness," in conjunction with this theological tenet. Rather, he repetitiously chose to use an alternative phraseology: "keep yourself from idols." This is especially evident in the 1770s and 1780s, when Wesley was reaching his mature theological convictions.[103]

One young woman wrote to Wesley about a particular conflict in her band; Wesley, in turn, determined that she had been far too affected by the participants in the situation. "O beware of setting up any idol in your heart!"[104] In a later letter, he extended his advice. "As your mind is tender and easily moved, you may readily fall into inordinate affection; if you do, that will quickly darken your soul."[105] To yet another young woman, Ann Taylor, he penned:

> Your real temptation will be, especially while you are young, to seek happiness in some creature. It is well if you are not entangled already—if you do not already begin to think, "Oh, how happy I should be if I were to spend my life with this or that person." Vain thought! Happiness is not in man; no, nor in any creature under heaven.... No. When you begin to know God as *your* God, then, and not before, you begin to be happy.... [Therefore,] by almighty grace keep yourself from idols.[106]

Sarah Mallet was the preacher who received Wesley's official recommendation, despite the fact that her call was quite unconventional.[107] Still, Wesley recognized that she was receiving a great deal of acclaim and popularity, and he became anxious on her behalf. Rather than fearing an increasing haughtiness in her, his anxiety was focused elsewhere. "Above all beware of inordinate affection! Those who *profit* by you will be apt to love you more than enough; and will not this naturally lead you into the same temptation? Nay, Sally, is not this the case already? Is your heart filled wholly with God? Is it clear of idols?"[108]

Very near the end of his life, Wesley was asked an odd question, one that he apparently answered only after serious thought:

> Since I had the pleasure of seeing you I have been thinking much on what you said concerning your loving others too much. In one sense this cannot be; you cannot have too much benevolence for the whole human race: but in another sense you may; you may grieve too much for the distresses of others, even so much as to make you incapable of giving them relief which otherwise you should give them. So I know one that, when he sees any one in pain, directly faints away. It is something like this which you mean by feeling too much for others? You can give me two or three instances of it, and then I shall be better able to judge.[109]

As this quotation shows, Wesley's own perception of emotional dependency was limited. Yet, an alternative to the Augustinian definition of sin as *pride* is present in aspects of Wesley's own (gender) theory and practical relationships with women. Because most interpreters have failed to recognize such an alternative and its implications for theological anthropology, especially a Wesleyan theory of subjectivity, a review of scholarship around Wesley's doctrine of sin will be helpful to the present study.

A SINFUL ALTERNATIVE: WESLEY'S HAMARTIOLOGY RECONSIDERED

To explore Wesley's view of sin and its linkage with pride requires a revisiting of conventional interpretations and reconsideration of those interpretations in light of a fuller analysis of evidence. How and why is pride named as a sin, and in what relation to original sin?

Conventional Interpretations

"That Wesley regarded human nature as corrupt is too well known to need proof."[110] Wesley himself writes, "If, therefore, we take away this foundation, that man is by nature foolish and sinful ... the Christian system falls apart at once."[111] According to Wesley, the doctrine of original sin must never be rejected nor neglected as the condition of humanity or as a reality of human experience. This much, at least, is clear. Yet, as Robert Chiles has argued, the scholarly assessments of John Wesley's doctrine of original sin differ.[112] At first glance, this may appear surprising; Wesley did in fact write a lengthy and detailed treatise on the theme, *The Doctrine of Original Sin*. Yet, despite its appearing to be a clear and comprehensive treatment of the subject (covering historical, sociological, existential, and Scriptural evidence for the doctrine), its rhetorical style—which counters the treatise of his "heretical" opponent almost point by point—distracts from its systematic value. Further, it raises the possibility of varied restatements of its less prominent themes. As a consequence, people have offered multiple and diverse interpretations of the significance of Wesley's doctrine of sin, specifically his view of the consequences of original sin—that is, the extent of human depravity.

Even with the variations, however, I have found many interpretations surprisingly similar when it comes to the *content*, or essence, of original sin. Although people use various maneuvers to distance Wesley's *overall* doctrine from a more Augustinian, Reformed, or Calvinistic position, the traditional Western definition of the content of sin—pride or self-will—is imposed on Wesley without much scholarly comment. An alternative interpretation needs to be considered—one that is particularly well supported by Wesley's practical works and by his more formal theological treatises. As John Tyson puts it, "The fall of humanity ... turned them into ... practical idolaters who traded the love of God for the love of the world since they affixed to creation the loyalties they justly owed to the Creator."[113]

Craig Alan Blaising offers one of three comprehensive treatments of John Wesley's doctrine of original sin. After giving a lengthy review of the Calvin-Arminius debate and its effects upon the English theological scene (particularly upon English Puritanism), Blaising provides an analysis of Wesley's construction of original sin "from his explicit statements on the subject."[114] He goes on to correlate this hamartiology with Wesley's doctrine of grace.[115] The chapter that actually covers Wesley's doctrine of original sin has a specific aim: "to demonstrate that in the content Wesley gave to original sin, he did not differ at all from the Augustinian and Reformation tradition."[116]

In a subsection entitled "The Nature of the Primal Sin," Blaising quotes Wesley directly:

> Here sin began, namely, unbelief. "The woman was deceived," says the Apostle. She believed a lie: she gave more credit to the word of the devil than to the word of God. And unbelief brought forth actual sin. "When the woman saw that the tree was good for food, and pleasant to the eyes, and to be desired to make one wise, she took of the fruit and did eat," and so completed her sin. But "the man," as the Apostle observes, "was not deceived." How then came he to join in the transgression? "She gave unto her husband, and he did eat." He sinned with his eyes open. He rebelled against his Creator, as is highly probable, "Not by stronger reason moved, but fondly overcome with female charms." And if this was the case there is no absurdity in the assertion of a great man that "Adam sinned in his heart before he sinned outwardly, before he ate of the forbidden fruit"; namely by inward idolatry, by loving the creature more than the Creator.[117]

Blaising then offers his own analysis of the content of original sin, primarily based on this quotation. He begins by saying that Wesley closely follows the Augustinian tradition:[118] "Unbelief . . . leads to pride, then to self will, then foolish desires, then the outward act of sin."[119] In one sense, Blaising is correct. Augustine offers an interpretation of Adam's sin of *idolatry* in book 14 of *The City of God*.[120] However, Blaising, like Augustine—and *unlike* my reading of Wesley (see below)—interprets Adam's "idolatry" as self-love. Blaising writes, "It was a gradual displacement of the love for God, the Creator, which was the essence of original righteousness, with love for *self* ('inward idolatry'), the creature, which is the essence of original sin."[121] Blaising's error comes from over-interpreting the adjective "inward" to mean idolatry of self. An alternative interpretation sees "inward" as a contrast to outward sin; Wesley himself elucidates that "Adam sinned in his heart before he sinned outwardly."[122] Blaising ignores Wesley's own clarification of what he means by "inward idolatry," namely, "loving the creature more than the Creator."[123] For Wesley, the "creature" is not Adam (self), but Eve (the other).

Barry Bryant offers a very similar reading to Blaising, but only after steps in another direction. After reiterating part of the same quotation from Wesley given above, Bryant offers the following comment: "If Adam had been persuaded it was certainly not on rational grounds, but by feminine charms in an appeal to the senses. Through his action he exemplified the human propensity to worship creature rather than Creator."[124] Bryant even turns to Wesley's "A Thought upon Marriage" for further illumination, observing: "[Wesley] warned that seeking happiness in a wife was no different from idolatry. Then, quoting himself, from 'On the Fall of Man' (1783), he remarked, 'Is it not, in effect, loving the creature more than the Creator?' Adam's fall could also be a Methodist preacher's fall by putting wife and family before the circuit."[125] Yet, when Bryant offers his only statement of original sin's content, he simply states that "the meanest forms . . . are pride and self-will."[126]

The third and final comprehensive treatment of John Wesley's doctrine of sin is given by Seung-An Im. His work is set in the broader context of his interpretation of Wesley's theological anthropology, as compared with and contrasted to the anthropologies of Gregory of Nyssa and Augustine. Im also recognizes the theme of "inward idolatry." He writes, "The primary cause of the Fall, [Wesley] said, was in the disposition of Adam, that is, his external act of eating the forbidden fruit proceeded from his inward disposition against God, by loving the creature above the Creator."[127] Like Blaising, Im interprets "inward idolatry" as pride. Unlike Blaising, Im does not infer pride from this text alone. Im goes on to list and review several passages (primarily from Wesley's sermons) that explicitly deal with pride. According to Im, Wesley's statements in such passages are clear and precise: pride is clearly emphasized as the root of sin. Im's conclusions, much like Blaising's and Bryant's, seem to be founded on a preference for viewing Wesley's doctrine of original sin as Augustinian in orientation.[128]

This tendency of scholars to place Wesley's hamartiology in the Augustinian stream has been questioned by Leon Hynson.[129] Hynson argues that Wesley's emphasis on the "privation" inherent in original sin, rather than on human depravity, shifts Wesley's definition away from Augustine's and strongly seals Wesley's alliance with Arminius on the issue of sin.[130] Hynson is also attracted to Mildred Bangs Wynkoop's "relational" interpretation of Wesley and sees relational theology as a means that "avoids the Augustinian and Reformed associations of original sin with the body and sensuality."[131] Yet, Hynson, like Blaising, Bryant, and Im, is primarily interested in the *effects* of original sin, *not* its content. In other words, major (and even minor[132]) treatments of Wesley's doctrine of original sin focus on the issue of human depravity and God's compensating grace, and *not* on how sin first manifests itself, not on its root or essential nature.

Randy Maddox sharpens the discussion of Wesley's hamartiology by underscoring the influence of a more Eastern view of sin on Wesley—specifically, the East's tendency to explicate sin as "disease." Maddox argues that Wesley's theology of sin must be interpreted as containing both Eastern and Western elements; (the West's) judicial language is mixed with metaphors of disease in Wesley's comprehensive hamartiology.[133] Yet, Maddox's primary concern is also on the effects of sin and depravity on Adam's posterity, not on sin's essence or content.

In summary, the primary focus of Wesley's interpreters has not challenged them to question the presence of an Augustinian definition of original sin's content, although some have questioned an Augustinian paradigm that affirms total depravity, offering various explications of Wesley's doctrine of prevenient grace. To question total depravity without also examining the validity of Augustinian pride is, in my estimation, to offer an unbalanced treatment of Wesley's hamartiology.

Wesley's strong belief in a doctrine of original sin cannot be questioned. As he states, "If we take away this foundation . . . the Christian system falls apart at once."[134] I am not suggesting an interpretation of Wesley that sees him as rejecting Augustine's insistence on this doctrine. Nor am I suggesting that he spurns Augustine's conclusions completely when formulating his own doctrine of sin, even in his definition of original sin's essence. Wesley uses the word "pride" frequently. Yet, pride is only one of Wesley's hamartiological terms; in my reading of Wesley, pride is certainly not the only, or even the primary, definition of original sin. Although Wesley's letters have been my primary source for discerning an alternative hamartiology, a brief review of other works by Wesley is appropriate.

A Reconsideration

In a survey of John Wesley's employment of the word "pride" in his journals,[135] I found *no* instance of its use in conjunction with the doctrine of original sin. When it does appear, it surfaces in a list of sins with no explicit or implicit dominance.[136] The same can be said of many of Wesley's sermons.[137] In "Justification By Faith," Wesley lists pride with "anger" and "love of the world" as evidence of humanity's fallenness.[138] Wesley did prefer "pride" when he described Satan's fall.[139] In "Deceitfulness of the Human Heart," he explicitly articulates,

> See how this [wickedness] was first planted in heaven itself, by Lucifer, "Son of the morning"—till then undoubtedly "one of the first, if not the first archangel." "Thou saidst, I will sit upon the side of the north." See self-will, the first-born of Satan! "I will be like the Most High." See pride, the twin sister of self-will. Here was the true origin of evil. Hence came the inexhaustible

flood of evils upon the lower world. When Satan had once transfused his own self-will and pride into the parents of mankind, *together with a new species of sin—love of the world, the loving the creature above the Creator.*[140]

While pride and self-will were present in Satan's Fall, Wesley adds to pride his oft-used definition of *idolatry* when speaking of the human fall.

Randy Maddox demonstrates that Wesley often relied on Augustine's interpretation of 1 John 2:16 by repeating Augustine's phraseology, "the desire of the flesh, the desires of the eye, and the pride of life."[141] As Maddox shows, these refer to *actual* sins that result from human depravity. Wesley needed to go further to find "the source of such actual sins," to find the nature of "inbeing sin."[142]

To clarify his thoughts on Christian perfection (what it does and does not mean), Wesley wrote, among other sermons, "Repentance of Believers." Here, Wesley spoke of "inbeing sin" or the "sin that remains":

> For it is seldom long before he who imagined all sin was gone feels there is still *pride* in his heart. He is convinced, both that in many respects he has thought of himself more highly than he ought to think, and that he has taken to himself the praise of something he had received, and gloried in it as though he had not received it. And yet he knows he is in the favour of God. He cannot and ought not to "cast away his confidence."[143]

Wesley clearly specifies pride here as a "remaining" sin; he also identifies self-will as a remaining sin. Wesley goes on to offer a somewhat surprising classification of these two sins. "Now self-will, as well as pride, is a species of idolatry; and both are directly contrary to the love of God."[144] Wesley continues, "The same observation may be made concerning the *love of the world*.... He may feel the assaults of *inordinate affection*, yea, a strong propensity to 'love the creature more than the Creator'—whether it be a child, a parent, an husband or wife, or 'the friend that is as his own soul.' "[145] Once again, pride is portrayed as a sin among many and, in this case, "a species of idolatry."

Wesley offered a similar interpretation of pride in his most direct sermon on the topic, "Original Sin." Here, idolatry is unmistakably classified as the primary definition of original sin, with "pride," "self-will," and "love of the world" listed under it.[146] Wesley says, "All pride is idolatry,"[147] as is "love of the world." In other words, there are two forms of original sin, both originating from idolatry: inordinate love of self (pride) and inordinate love of others, here listed as "love of the world." Wesley further explains this phrase: "What is more natural to us than to seek happiness in the creature instead of the Creator?"[148] Wesley also wrote a sermon entitled "Spiritual Idolatry," which he penned nearer to the end of his life. It will be helpful to quote one passage at length:

> Undoubtedly it is the will of God that we should all love one another. It is his will that we should love our relations and our Christian brethren with a peculiar love; and those in particular whom he has made particularly profitable to our souls. These we are commanded to "love fervently"—yet still "with a pure heart." But is not this "impossible with man"? To retain the strength and tenderness of affection, and yet without any stain to the soul, with unspotted purity? I do not mean only unspotted by lust. I know this is possible. I know a person may have an unutterable affection for another without any desire of this kind. But is it without idolatry? Is it not loving the creature more than the Creator? Is it not putting a man or woman in the place of God? Giving them your heart? Let this be carefully considered, even by those whom God has joined together—by husbands and wives, parents and children. It cannot be denied that these ought to love one another tenderly: they are commanded so to do. But they are neither commanded nor permitted to love one another idolatrously! Yet how common is this! How frequently is a husband, a wife, a child, put in the place of God! How many that are accounted good Christians fix their affections on each other so as to leave no place for God! They seek their happiness in the creature, not in the Creator. One may truly say to the other, I view thee, lord and end of my desires. That is, "I desire nothing more but thee! Thou art the thing that I long for! All my desire is unto thee, and unto the remembrance of thy name." Now, if this is not flat idolatry, I cannot tell what is![149]

The evidence given above shows that Wesley's journals and sermons concur with the opinions expressed in Wesley's letters to women on the topic of idolatry. While Wesley did not hesitate to use the word pride (i.e., idolatry of self), he gave equal attention to relational idolatry. Such evidence thus challenges the assumption that Wesley's understanding of the essence of original sin simply mimics Augustinian pride.

In Wesley's correspondence with the women of early Methodism, he often expressed the depth of his concern, his outright fear that they would succumb to the temptation of inordinate affection. One can see, however, that his concern may have been a projection of himself onto them. For example, Wesley says (to Sarah Crosby), "I find scarce any temptation from any *thing* in the world. My danger is from *persons*. 'Oh for an heart to praise my God, an heart from sin set free!'"[150] In fact, years earlier, another of Wesley's inner circle, Sarah Ryan, dared to write the following: "You are apt to worship God in His children. I mean you *cleave* too much to those whom you believe to be dear to God. You do not let the help you receive from them raise your heart to God Himself, that, while you love for His sake, you may be free from them, finding Jesus *nearest* to your heart."[151] Some of Wesley's letters do show that his relationships with women (both romantic and platonic) were clearly a danger to his own ideal of "singleness of heart."

Perhaps the irony of all ironies is that Wesley himself could have provided many women with the very temptation he most feared on their behalf. The type of intimacy he demanded from many of them could have been disastrous to their own spirituality. Yet, the majority of "his" women "transcended" this temptation to depend excessively on Wesley and "transcended" their station, embracing a type of power rare for women of the eighteenth century. Wesley's feminism worked. The women of early Methodism could be seen as those who "transcended" even their gendered scripts. Wesley's repeated charge to submit *only* to God and not to any creature allowed many women to defy convention and centuries of suppression. Put simply: Methodist women preached. Their single devotion to God freed them to do so.

THE PRACTICAL APPLICATION OF WESLEY'S SIN(FUL) ALTERNATIVE

Many women of early British Methodism performed responsibilities usually connotative of more traditionally male roles. Women of John Wesley's movement led class meetings, carried on pastoral functions, traveled itinerantly, and preached. These religious duties offered women a spiritual "transcendence" as well as the opportunity to transcend the established *social* roles for women of eighteenth-century England. Such an opportunity was afforded to these women because of an underlying theological anthropology. Despite John Wesley's rather obsessive speculations on the female body, and despite his blatantly androcentric behavior (especially in his romantic relationships), which often demanded he be included in females' private spaces, he *did* hold to an overarching optimistic theology that gave women equal spiritual status and overcame any "natural" essentialisms. John Wesley's strong concept of prevenient and redemptive grace even restored women's "original freedom" and allowed them to strive for a more transcendent existence in a spiritual context that approximated a new Eden. Wesley's theology strongly supports (and arguably advances) the spiritual equality of women, while diminishing, if not eliminating, any essential difference between genders. Particularly in his later works, and specifically in his explication of the first chapters of Genesis (as he interprets women's subjugation as a direct result of the Fall),[152] Wesley advocated the "restoration of the social equality of women as one aspect of the Christian healing of the damage of the Fall."[153] His rather sanguine social vision is based on a theology that is fervently optimistic about the impact of grace on original sin.

As we have seen, the practicalities of such "equal opportunity" were most often directed toward women who fit John Wesley's preferred status, being single of heart. This stands as evidence for a rather misogynistic rejection of women's images and functions that are associated with the maternal body. "Most of the women with whom Wesley corresponded were either single, widowed, or separated from their husbands."[154] For Wesley, "singleness of heart" often found its fullest realization in those who were single in life. As I have suggested, "relational idolatry" was, in John Wesley's estimation, the foe of religious devotion for women, for it often entangled them in matter(s) unspiritual and, thus, "trivial."[155] Because of the great difficulty of resisting the temptation to "seek the Creator in the (bodily) creature," Wesley often advised "his" women to avoid the entanglements of marriage, childrearing, and domesticity. He encouraged them to find their greater calling, their "praxis," in serving God alone.

I am suggesting that the type of liberating space occupied by women in early Methodism was deeply intertwined with Wesley's *theology* of sin, not just with his egalitarian social vision. His theology gives support for the suggestions of early feminist hamartiologies. For those of us who still need a strategic essentialism in order to counter lingering misogynism in the Church, Wesley's misogynistic view of women's sin can, ironically, help to undergird a feminist theology that still has reason to exist.

CHAPTER SEVEN

A HERITAGE RECLAIMED: JOHN WESLEY ON HOLISTIC HEALTH AND HEALING

Randy L. Maddox
for Paul M. Basset[1]

John Wesley's ecclesial descendants have long evidenced some ambivalence about honoring their founder. From the beginning, there was a natural tendency toward hagiography, epitomized by most of the biographies published through the nineteenth century, with their triumphalist panegyrics about "Wesley the Dynamic Evangelist," "Wesley the Tireless Church Founder," "Wesley the Pious Christian," and so on. However, this praise has almost always been mixed with some uneasiness about making Wesley's precedent the standard for later Methodism. Among Methodists in North America, this uneasiness was spawned by Wesley's rebuttal of their charges of the injustice of British colonial rule. After his death, as Methodists on both sides of the Atlantic pulled away from the Anglican context that shaped Wesley's theological activity, there was growing embarrassment about his lack of fit with the model of a "theologian" assumed by their new peers and competitors.[2] Thus began a diminishing of Wesley's significance for later Methodist theology that was accentuated by the spread of Enlightenment optimism. The impact of these forces can be illustrated by Randolph Sinks Foster, a Methodist Episcopal bishop and former professor of theology at Drew Theological Seminary, who began a multivolume series of *Studies in Theology* in 1891 (the centennial of Wesley's death!) with the claim that "We know more today than our fathers a hundred years ago. We have truer beliefs than they had." It is little wonder that Foster seldom interacts with Wesley in his series![3]

The twentieth century witnessed a growing professionalization of Wesley studies that was reflected in biographical works that brought to their investigation increasing knowledge of Wesley's context and greater realism about his contribution. While some popular legends still abound in lay circles, current historical scholarship is rarely accused of hagiography. Meanwhile, interest in Wesley's relevance for current theological issues has grown among his descendants in recent decades, as they have questioned the privileging of present knowledge over all past beliefs and practices. As David Ford has felicitously put it, this enlightenment about the Enlightenment has created a situation in which "we are free in a new way to recognize what is of value in premodernity, modernity, and postmodernity."[4]

Ford's description suggests that we in the traditions descended from Wesley's ministry would do well to spend some time probing anew the life and writings of our founder, to see what of value can be recognized. As a sample of what this probing might reveal, I offer here a test case: a consideration of John Wesley's emphasis on holistic health and healing.

WESLEY'S SERIOUS INTEREST IN HEALTH AND HEALING

I chose this test case precisely because Wesley's emphasis on health and healing is not one of those aspects of his story that has been consistently recalled and celebrated by his heirs. Few in Wesleyan traditions today are aware that Wesley published a collection of advice for preserving health and treating diseases called *Primitive Physick*, even though it went through twenty-three editions in Wesley's lifetime—more than anything else that he published—and stayed in print (and use!) continuously into the 1880s. Moreover, those who are aware of this collection, and have glanced at a few of his prescriptions for ailments (see the samples in Appendix A), tend to dismiss it in bemusement. This is true even of many scholars. For example, a recent book on Wesley's ethics describes *Primitive Physick* as "a collection of folklore prescriptions for various ailments . . . [revealing] his reliance on testimony and a sometime credulity in belief in what the folk tradition contained," while a new historical study of Wesley characterizes the work as "a strange mix of old wives' tales and recent insights."[5] Such evaluations, and the larger neglect of this dimension of Wesley's work, are called into question when one begins to recognize the seriousness of his interest in health and healing.

Lifelong Study of Medical Works

In considering Wesley's interest in health and healing, it is helpful to recall that study of basic medicine had become part of the training of Anglican clergy candidates in the seventeenth century, since it was common—at least in smaller villages—for priests to offer medical care as part of their overall ministry.[6] This helps explain why so many clergy in this period who left parish settings took up medicine as an alternative career. A relevant case in point is Wesley's great-grandfather Bartholomew Wes(t)ley, who consulted from time to time as a physician while rector of Charmouth in Dorset, and turned to this career for his full livelihood when his refusal to sign the Act of Uniformity in the early 1660s led to his ejection from his pastoral charge.

Following in this tradition, we know from the diary that Wesley began at Oxford, and from other sources we know of several medical treatises by Robert Boyle and others that he purchased or read between 1724 and 1732.[7] To take another snapshot, diary entries for 1736, when Wesley was serving as a missionary priest in Georgia, show continued reading of medical texts, including one by John Tennent listing medicinal herbs that were available on that continent.[8] This reading continued more sporadically throughout Wesley's life and included consultation of the *Philosophical Transactions* of the Royal Society and the *Medical Transactions* of the Royal College of Physicians. My working list of all the medical works that Wesley cites or mentions reading over the span of his life stands at nearly one hundred items.

Publication of Health and Healing Advice

It is also important to recognize that this reading stands behind Wesley's publication of works offering medical advice. In particular, the *Primitive Physick* was based on much more than "folklore" and "old wives' tales." Wesley's own most detailed account traces its origins back to remedies he transcribed from the books of Robert Boyle and John Tennent, along with "a few more from books or conversation."[9] In preparation for publishing a critical edition of Wesley's medical writings, James Donat has been seeking to identify these various literary sources of Wesley's prescriptions in *Primitive Physick*. So far, he has traced nearly a third of the remedies back to texts of medical advice, including texts by such other authors as Hermann Boerhaave, Kenelm Digby, Thomas Dover, John Huxham, Richard Mead, Lazarus Riverius, Thomas Short, Thomas Sydenham, and Thomas Willis.[10]

The fact that Wesley drew heavily on his reading of medical works for the original text and later updates of *Primitive Physick* suggests that, far from being a tangential or idiosyncratic concern, publication of this resource should be seen as parallel to Wesley's fifty-volume *Christian Library*. In both cases, he distilled the fruits of his broad reading for the benefit of his Methodist people and a larger public. Because his ministry was larger than a single parish, Wesley dispensed the spiritual and medical guidance expected of his priestly office in printed form.

Just as Wesley published more than the *Christian Library* offering spiritual guidance, his efforts in medical guidance reached beyond the *Primitive Physick*. He published several other works related to maintaining or restoring health, including *A Letter to a Friend Concerning Tea* (1748); *The Desideratum, or Electricity Made Plain and Useful* (1760); *Thoughts on the Sin of Onan, chiefly extracted from [Tissot]* (1767); *Advices with Respect to Health, extracted from [Tissot]* (1769); "Extract from [William] Cadogan on the Gout" (in vol. 26 of his *Works*, 1774); and *An Estimate of the Manners of Present Times* (1782).[11]

Holistic Understanding of Salvation: Healing for Body and Soul

While Wesley's practice of offering medical advice was in keeping with a traditional role of clergy, his life spanned the period when the newly organized Royal College of Physicians in London was seeking to professionalize the practice of medicine by restricting the ranks of those certified to offer treatment. These efforts classed clergy with barber-surgeons, apothecaries, and various "quacks" as groups to be inhibited from further practice of medicine.[12] Like many in the other groups, Wesley resisted the suggestion being made that he refrain from offering medical care and advice, leaving it to those now certified by the College.[13] Unlike most of these others, Wesley's motive for resisting was not to protect a source of income. His resistance was grounded instead in his understanding of the holistic salvation his movement was called to spread.

One of Wesley's deepest theological convictions was that the mediocrity of moral life and the ineffectiveness in social impact of Christians in eighteenth-century England could be traced to an inadequate understanding of salvation assumed broadly in the church. The root of this inadequacy, and the core of Wesley's alternative understanding, can be seen in his own most pointed definition of salvation: "By salvation I mean, not barely (according to the vulgar notion) deliverance from hell, or going to heaven, but a present deliverance from sin, a restoration of the soul to its primitive health . . . the renewal of our souls after the image of God in righteousness and true holiness, in justice, mercy, and truth."[14]

The notion that Wesley was rejecting here reduces salvation solely to forgiveness of our guilt as sinners, which frees us from future condemnation. Wesley consistently encouraged his followers and his broader contemporaries to seek the benefits of *truly holistic salvation*, where God's forgiveness of our sins is interwoven with God's gracious healing of the damages that sin has wrought in our lives.[15] The scope of the healing that Wesley invited all to expect is captured well in pastoral letters like his reminder to Alexander Knox: "It will be a double blessing if you give yourself up to the Great Physician, that He may heal soul and body together. And unquestionably this is His design. He wants to give you ... both inward and outward health."[16]

While most Christians shared the conviction that God would provide full healing of body and soul at the resurrection, Wesley's emphasis on the degree to which both dimensions of this divine healing can be experienced *in the present* is less common. On the spiritual side, this became clear in his debates with the Calvinist branch of the Wesleyan revival, which—reflecting a characteristic stress of the Augustinian strand of Western Christianity—insisted that we can hope for only limited transformation of our fallen spiritual nature in this life.[17] The assumption that we should expect only limited expression in this life of God's promised salvation of our bodies was more widespread, but it is notable that resistance to suggestions of clergy including medical care as part of their ministry in the English church during the reign of James I (1603–25) also came from the most Calvinist voices in the church. These objectors urged that labor for the souls of their parishioners, by preaching and counseling, should fill the full time of the pastor. In contrast, the more Arminian "High Church" voices, which gained in strength after 1625, elevated a model where, in addition to reverent leadership in defined times of regular worship, clergy were expected to spend a significant part of their time in good works—like medical care—among the needy in their parish.[18]

Wesley's ancestors, on both the paternal and maternal sides, were among those who objected to the reinstatement of the Act of Uniformity governing Anglican worship in 1662 and eventually formed dissenting congregations. While most of these dissenters were moderate to strong Calvinists, they tended to be more willing than their predecessors to make some room for offering medical care in their understanding of the pastoral task. We have already noted how this is reflected in the case of Wesley's paternal great-grandfather. The library of Samuel Annesley, Wesley's maternal grandfather, also suggests this broader understanding of the pastoral office, in that it contained nearly twenty volumes of medical reference works.[19]

Wesley's strong commitment to this more holistic conception of the pastoral office is evident in his instructions to his lay assistants about their ministry among the Methodist people. As they visited the various societies, Wesley charged them to leave behind books that could provide ongoing guidance, highlighting most often two works that should be in every house: (1) his excerpt of Thomas à Kempis's *The Imitation of Christ*, which Wesley valued as a guide to spiritual health; and (2) *Primitive Physick*, which Wesley had prepared as a guide to physical health.[20] Moreover, on analogy with his own training, when one compares lists of the readings that Wesley recommended for all lay persons to the list that he assigned to those who assisted in pastoring the movement, the one notable addition to the latter list is the study of medical works.²¹ Wesley clearly intended for the assistants to be capable of dispensing personal advice along with the books.²²

This expectation of participation in God's ministry to body and soul was not limited to the itinerant lay assistants in early Methodism. As in many other areas of the movement, Wesley developed a layered structure that included a role for local lay women and men in day-to-day ministry. In this case, the office was the "visitor of the sick," lay leaders who were expected to visit sick members in their area three times a week, to inquire into the state of their souls and their bodies, and to offer or procure advice for them in both regards.²³ As all of this reflects, while he allowed that it will be complete only in our resurrected state, Wesley resisted the tendency to minimize the physical dimension of God's healing work in the present world. He longed for Christians to see that participation in God's present saving work involves nurturing not only our souls but also our bodies, and addressing both of these dimensions in our outreach to others.²⁴

WESLEY'S HOLISTIC APPROACH TO HEALTH AND HEALING

Just as Wesley's commitment to care for the body was grounded in his conviction of the holistic nature of salvation, careful consideration reveals a concern for holistic balance in his emphases about how to care for the body. The goal of this section is to sketch the broad outlines of this balance, clarifying Wesley's emphases within the assumptions and debates of his time. An initial sense of some of the dimensions to be sketched can be gained from instructions that Wesley sent to Samuel Bradburn, one of his assistants, in 1788 when Bradburn was caring for John's brother Charles, who was in declining health:

> With regard to my brother, I advise you: (1) Whether he will or no, carry Dr. Whitehead to him. (2) If he cannot go out, and yet must have exercise or die, persuade him to use [the wooden horse] twice or thrice a day, and procure one for him. (3) I earnestly advise him to be electrified.²⁵

Valued Both Professional and Traditional Medical Treatment

The first thing to notice in these instructions is the insistence on Charles consulting a physician. This makes clear that Wesley's opposition to the attempt of the London College of Physicians to restrict who could offer medical care did not lead him to pose traditional and self-help methods in polar relationship to professional medical treatment. Even in

Primitive Physick, which was devoted to providing self-help advice, there are instances where Wesley makes clear that the best advice is to consult a good—and honest!—physician.[26]

Wesley speaks respectfully of several physicians over the years, and he said particularly positive things about John Whitehead, his personal physician in later years.[27] Indeed, in the context of praising Whitehead, Wesley reminded readers of his *Journal* of the exhortation in Sir. 38:1-2, "Honor the Physician, for God hath appointed him."[28] Yet Wesley was also convinced that many physicians unnecessarily protracted the cure of patients' bodies in order to derive the maximum fee, which is why he stressed finding an *honest* physician.[29]

Affirmed Both Divine and Medical Healing

There is an even broader implication evident in Wesley's instructions for Charles to be checked by a physician: John's rejection of sole reliance upon seeking divine healing. There was some debate in Wesley's setting over whether Christians should seek medical treatment or rely on divine healing. A longstanding strand of Christian tradition viewed specific cases of pain, disease, and death as part of God's plan for the person affected. The corollary of this assumption was that the proper response to these events was submission to God's will, though there was room within this submission to request divine healing. In some cases, the use of "natural" remedies that God had provided in herbs, roots, and the like was also allowed, but there was generally suspicion of specially concocted remedies. With the emergence of "scientific" medicine in the seventeenth century, this earlier suspicion was called into question. Indeed, in some circles there developed the opposite deistic tendency to provide purely secular accounts of the origin of disease and to commend solely medical forms of healing, viewing appeals for miraculous healing as superstitious. Most eighteenth-century British Christians sought a median between the traditional view and this polar option.[30]

John Wesley shared this mediating conviction. On the one hand, he was convinced of the possibility of miraculous healing, often highlighting apparent instances in his publications—in part as a rebuttal of deism.[31] On the other hand, he refused to pose prayer for divine healing as a preferred alternative to use of traditional or professional medical treatments. On analogy with his basic "co-operant" model of God's work in salvation, Wesley's characteristic advice for treating physical ailments was "as God is the sovereign disposer of all things . . . I earnestly advise every one, together with all [their] other medicines, to use the medicine of medicines—prayer."[32] There is no polarizing of divine and medical means of healing in this advice![33]

But what about the treatment of mental or emotional ailments? Puritan thought through the seventeenth century generally considered all such disorders to be rooted in spiritual causes and prescribed for their cure repentance, faith, and prayers for deliverance. As the eighteenth century unfolded, many physicians began to explain mental afflictions instead in secular terms and to focus on medical treatments. While some Anglicans embraced this change, others reacted with vigorous defenses of the traditional account. A few scholars have pointed to Wesley as exemplifying this reactionary stance on the cause and cure of mental and emotional disorders.[34]

In assessing this claim, it is important to remember the dynamics of the early Methodist revival. From the beginning of the revival, it was common for those who were not sympathetic to equate Methodist emotionalism with lunacy, and to seek medical treatment for family members who had been brought under conviction by Methodist preaching.[35] Understandably, Wesley's immediate response was to defend the emotional displays as genuine expressions of religious conviction, and to argue that the only therapy that could heal those under conviction was the pardoning touch of the Great Physician.[36] But in the ensuing debate, he was soon allowing that at least a few cases of emotional display might be signs of the "natural distemper of madness" rather than the grief of religious conviction, with the clear recognition that the former would require more than simply a sense of God's reconciling love for their cure.[37] This proved to be more than a passing concession.

In fact, a growing openness to natural dimensions of many emotional disorders can be traced in Wesley's thought, making it difficult to equate his mature position with the traditional Puritan stance. Consider, in particular, the severe disorders known in his day as "lunacy" or "raving madness." Wesley's *Journal* account of the early years of the revival presents several instances of such afflictions solely in terms of demonic causation—and divine deliverance.[38] After reading a book by George Cheyne in 1742, which argued that true lunacy and madness are due to natural causes and require natural cures, Wesley's *Journal* comments began to reflect more nuance.[39] Soon thereafter, he assessed a case of raving madness to be attributable simply to a fever.[40] He also began to record instances where prayer for deliverance was not sufficient for curing lunacy/madness.[41] Conversely, while he was initially sarcastic about the value of confining anyone in "Bedlam" (i.e., Bethlehem Hospital), the first public asylum in London, he came to believe that institutional care of lunatics could be beneficial, particularly at Saint Luke's Hospital, which William Battie established in 1751 with an emphasis on providing medical treatments for mental illnesses.[42] In this light, it should be no surprise that, from its appearance in 1747, the *Primitive Physick* included suggested natural cures for lunacy (see Appendix A). While Wesley continued to remind readers in his later years that some physicians considered many cases of lunacy to be diabolical in origin,[43] on balance it appears that he came to consider most clear cases of insanity to be natural in origin, and assumed that—in addition to prayer—they should be treated by either professional or traditional medical means.[44]

Appreciated the Interconnection of Physical and Emotional/Spiritual Health

The influence of George Cheyne upon Wesley's approach to health and healing was broader than just sparking awareness of the natural dimensions of serious mental disorders. Cheyne's writings played a major role in nurturing Wesley's mature emphasis on the broad interconnection of physical health with emotional and spiritual health. Recognition of the importance of this connection had been central to Cheyne's own journey. He started his career seeking to provide a type of "Newtonian revolution" in medicine—to explain health and disease solely in mechanical terms of the movement of fluids through the various bodily canals. After a physical and spiritual crisis (in 1705), his work shifted to stress more clearly the integrity of the human spirit and the impact of the intimate interaction between body and spirit upon health.[45]

In 1724, Cheyne published a summary of his new approach in *An Essay of Health and Long Life*. The book offered a series of recommendations for diet, exercise, living conditions, and the like, which Cheyne contended were ideally suited for helping British citizens to preserve health. As noted earlier, Wesley read the *Essay* shortly after its publication.[46] The passing years convinced Wesley of the wisdom of Cheyne's advice, so much so that, when he published *Primitive Physick* in 1747, Wesley chose to conclude the preface with an abstract of Cheyne's recommendations in *Essay* (see Appendix B). We will explore the range of this appropriated advice later; the relevant point here is Cheyne's specific emphasis on the influence of emotions upon physical health.

Emotional/Spiritual Dimensions of Physical Health

Cheyne devoted Chapter VI of his *Essay* to the "passions," the current umbrella term for emotional states that arise naturally in response to events and agents external to the self—such as joy, grief, fear, and love. Wesley's abstract of Cheyne's summary captures well his main points:

1. The passions have a greater influence on health than most people are aware of.
2. Violent and sudden passions dispose to, or actually throw people into, acute diseases.

3. Slow and lasting passions, such as grief and hopeless love, bring on chronical diseases.
4. Till the passion which caused the disease is calmed, medicine is applied in vain.
5. The love of God, as it is the sovereign remedy of all miseries, so in particular it effectually prevents all the bodily disorders the passions introduce, by keeping the passions themselves within due bounds. And by the unspeakable joy, and perfect calm, serenity, and tranquility it gives the mind, it becomes the most powerful of all the means of health and long life.[47]

One sees in this summary not only the stress that passions affect physical health but also Cheyne's refusal to reduce the passions to mere epiphenomena of physical states, reflected in his insistence that inordinate passions cannot be cured by medicine alone. Turning this around, Cheyne equally avoided a construal of the passions as mere psychological dynamics, assuming instead the integrity of their spiritual dimension; thus, his model of proper care for the passions, and thereby for physical health, included attention to one's spiritual life.

There is no better evidence that Wesley appropriated the conviction of the need for such a holistic approach to physical healing than the following sharp comment in his journal:

> Reflecting today on the case of a poor woman who had a continual pain in her stomach, I could not but remark the inexcusable negligence of most physicians in cases of this nature. They prescribe drug upon drug, without knowing a jot of the matter concerning the root of the disorder. And without knowing this they cannot cure, though they can murder the patient. Whence came this woman's pain? (Which she would never have told, had she never been questioned about it.) From fretting from the death of her son. And what availed medicines while that fretting continued? Why then do not all physicians consider how far bodily disorders are caused or influenced by the mind? And in those cases which are utterly out of their sphere, call in the assistance of a minister—as ministers, when they find the mind disordered by the body, call in the assistance of a physician?[48]

Physical Dimensions of Emotional/Spiritual Health

This pointed 1759 comment also introduces an emphasis on balance in Wesley's holistic approach to health and healing. It mentions the need not only for physicians to consider possible spiritual dimensions of physical health but also for ministers to consider physical dimensions in the cause and cure of mental or spiritual disorders. Wesley did not derive this balancing note from Cheyne's *Essay of Health*. In this early work, Cheyne limited consideration of the emotional dimension of human life to the passions, and he approached the passions not as disorders that need to be cured, but as essential mental faculties that need to be regulated. Most importantly, he insisted that this regulation "is the business, not of physick, but of virtue and religion."[49] The fact that Wesley omitted this line in his abstract of Cheyne for the *Primitive Physick* may reflect his awareness that Cheyne subsequently came to emphasize the contribution of physick to certain forms of emotional well-being.

The early eighteenth century witnessed a growing interest among physicians in England in a set of disorders that they termed "nervous diseases," which spanned the range from mild "lowness of spirits" to hysteria. In the years following publication of *Essay*, Cheyne devoted attention to these disorders, and in 1733 he published *The English Malady; or, a Treatise of Nervous Diseases of all Kinds*.[50] His focus in this book shifted from the "passions" as mental faculties to the "nerves" as the point of connection between the body and the mind or spirit. His main emphasis was that these disorders should be traced not to spiritual causes, like sorcery or demonic possession, but to physical causes—specifically, they result from defective connection between body and spirit when the nerves are clogged or atrophying. The corollary was that Cheyne assigned treatment of nervous diseases to physick rather than religion (i.e., the inverse of his stance on the passions). His own prescription for treating nervous disorders included some medicines but placed primary emphasis on diet and exercise.

Wesley appears to have read this Cheyne volume as well shortly after it was released, and to have placed a copy in the library of his school at Kingswood.[51] But he did not fully embrace Cheyne's one-sided assessment of the cause and cure of nervous diseases. His own, more balanced, assessment can be best summarized by a set of "Thoughts on Nervous Disorders" that Wesley published in the *Arminian Magazine* in 1786:

> When physicians meet with disorders which they do not understand, they commonly term them *nervous*; a word that . . . is a good cover for learned ignorance. But these are often no natural disorder of the body, but the hand of God upon the soul, being a dull consciousness of the want of God. . . . It is no wonder that those who are strangers to religion should not know what to make of this; and that, consequently, all their prescriptions should be useless, seeing they quite mistake the case. But undoubtedly there are nervous disorders which are purely natural. . . . One cause is the use of spiritous liquors. . . . Another more extensive cause is use of tea; particularly where it is taken either in large quantities, or strong, or without cream or sugar. . . . But the principle causes are, as Dr. Cadogan justly observes, indolence, intemperance, and irregular passions.[52]

The first thing to note in these reflections is Wesley's continuing objection to accounting for all instances of emotional dis-ease in purely natural terms. While he had come to accept the physical dimension of serious cases, he remained convinced that many of the milder instances were authentic responses to spiritual realities. As he put it ten years earlier: "We know there are such things as nervous disorders. But we know likewise that what is commonly called *nervous lowness* is a secret reproof from God, a kind of consciousness that we are not ... as God would have us to be, we are unhinged from our proper centre."[53] Because the cause of such disorders was not purely natural, Wesley insisted that medical treatment alone would not be sufficient to restore well-being in these cases. Their healing also requires the touch of the Great Physician.[54]

But it is also crucial to note Wesley's mature recognition that there *are* physical causes or contributors to many instances of emotional or spiritual dis-ease. This was a particularly important concession in light of his emphasis on a sense of assurance and joy as characteristic of authentic Christian responsiveness to God's grace. While Wesley never backed away from this standard as the ideal, he came to stress as well in pastoral sermons the potential impact of physical realities on our spiritual or emotional state. In particular, he reminded his followers that spiritual heaviness should not always be attributed to spiritual causes; it often reflects instead the impact of bodily disorders, acute diseases, calamities, poverty, and the like.[55]

The creative tension between these two tendencies is reflected in the balance of Wesley's advice about dealing with nervous disorders.[56] He was ever ready to affirm the value of prayer. But he was also quick to caution against the assumption that prayer alone will cure every type of nervous disorder. As he once put it, "Faith does not overturn the course of nature. Natural causes still produce natural effects. Faith no more hinders the *sinking of the Spirits* (as it is called) in a hysteric illness than the rising of the pulse in a fever."[57] Thus we must address physical factors as well in seeking emotional and spiritual health. Like Cadogan and Cheyne, Wesley's main emphasis in this regard was on proper diet, sufficient exercise, and appropriate rest, though he also advised electrifying (see Appendix A, #502)—a topic to which we shall return.

Emphasized Preventive Care/Promoting Well-Being: The "Cool Regimen"

This emphasis on diet, exercise, and rest needs to be appreciated in its historical context. Through the nineteenth and twentieth centuries, medical care in the North Atlantic context came to be equated largely with surgical interventions and administered medications. Against this backdrop, the recent emphasis on diet and exercise for promoting wellness, which could appear to be a modern insight, is better seen as a recovered balance. From early medieval times, Western approaches to health care reflected a distinction between (1) administering therapies to the sick and (2) counseling people how to live in accordance with nature by proper diet and exercise, both to restore health and to retain it. The first concern was typically associated with the term "medicine," while the second was more commonly associated with "physic[k]" through the early modern period. These concerns were often the focus of different practitioners and frequently posed against one another as alternatives. But at their best, they were seen as complementary.[58] The dramatic explosion in new knowledge and skills related to "medicine" in the past two centuries tended for some time to eclipse the concern for "physick." The recent emphasis on wellness and preventive medicine is a recovery from this eclipse.

Eighteenth-century Britain bears the marks of a transition stage in these developments. While those most involved in promoting "scientific medicine" emphasized mainly surgical and chemical therapies, popular health-advice manuals continued to devote significant attention to lifestyle advice for promoting health—the writings of Cheyne are a prime example. This made it natural for Wesley to include an abstract of Cheyne's advice for retaining health in the preface to his collection of medical therapies. At the same time, his title for the collection shows that the traditional distinction between "medicine" and "physick" was breaking down. Perhaps because the term medicine was increasingly displacing physick, Wesley chose to label his collection of *primitive* therapies a book of *physick*.[59]

His apparent failure to appreciate the traditional distinctive meaning of physick should not suggest a lack of appreciation for the full range of the traditional concern of physick. A long tradition assigned to physick the six "non-naturals" in Galenic medicine. These were items that, while not constitutive parts of our bodily nature, have a profound impact upon bodily health—namely (1) air, (2) food and drink, (3) motion and rest, (4) sleeping and waking, (5) retentions and evacuations, and (6) the passions of the soul.[60] A quick check of Wesley's abstract of Cheyne's *Essay of Health* (Appendix B) will confirm that each of these items is addressed.[61]

What might be less clear is that there is a distinctive eighteenth-century British stamp to the advice given on various items. This approach came to be known as the "cool regimen" and gained near consensus status in eighteenth-century British health advice manuals. The basic assumption of this regimen was that the key to promoting health was to harden the body by exercise and moderate diet, and to bring it into harmony with its environment. Because the environment in England was cool, this meant that it was important to get plenty of fresh cool air, drink plenty of cool water, take cold baths, favor cool vegetables in one's diet, and so on.[62]

A brief survey of Wesley's health advice can demonstrate his embrace of this "cool regimen."[63]

Proper Diet, Stressing "Cool" Vegetables and Water

The longest section of Cheyne's advice in *Essay of Health* focused on issues of diet (Appendix B, §II). The overall tone of his advice is a call for temperance, avoiding in particular overly spicy dishes and excessive consumption of meat, and favoring the drinking of water. In essence, as Cheyne admitted later, he was advising his patients and readers—most of whom were from the upper class—to eat the diet and embrace the lifestyle of the middle to lower-middle classes. In repeating Cheyne's advice Wesley likely served to reinforce the wisdom of this diet among these lower classes.[64]

Cheyne actually held up as ideal a vegetarian diet, as well as total abstinence from alcohol. Wesley committed himself to this ideal diet on two different occasions, though in each case he returned to moderate consumption of meat and wine after a couple of years.[65] His own advice to readers in later years echoed Cheyne's less idealistic goal of temperance, even now protesting suggestions of abstinence from wine.[66] But he clearly understood this moderate approach to remain within the guidelines of a "soft, cool, open diet."[67]

Regular Exercise, Particularly in the Fresh Air

The second longest section of Cheyne's advice in *Essay of Health* focused on exercise (Appendix B, §IV). His basic theme was that a due degree of regular exercise is indispensably necessary to health and long life. He also suggested that the value of exercise is enhanced when it is done outdoors in the fresh air.[68] The same points emerge frequently in Wesley's advice to his followers. Consider a few examples:

> Exercise, especially as the spring comes on, will be of greater service to your health than an hundred medicines.[69]
>
> Not that any one particular kind of exercise is necessary for all persons. Indeed Dr. Cheyne supposes the natural exercise of walking, where the strength suffices, to be preferable to any other. But it should be used every day, not less than an hour before dinner, or after supper. Where the strength will not admit of this, the want of it may be supplied by riding two hours at least on horseback every day before dinner or supper. If neither of these can be borne, the end of both may be answered by riding in a carriage. . . . Those who cannot afford this, may use a chamber-horse, which will suit every constitution.[70]
>
> Every day of your life take at least an hour's exercise, between breakfast and dinner. If you will, take another hour before supper, or before you sleep. If you can, take it in the open air; otherwise, in the house. If you cannot ride or walk abroad, use within a dumb-bell or a wooden horse. If you have not

strength to do this for an hour at a time, do it at twice or thrice. Let nothing hinder you. Your life is at stake. Make everything yield to this.[71]

These quotations leave no doubt as to the importance Wesley placed on exercise. They may raise some questions about the types of exercise commended. The first point to note is that Cheyne was not the only one to favor walking. When Wesley was leaving home for school, his father had also distilled advice about health into one maxim: "Fail not, on any account whatever, to walk an hour every day."[72] Moving to a second point, riding was broadly recommended in Wesley's day, even referred to as "Dr. Horse," due to the belief that the bouncing action helped to clear the lungs, improve circulation, and raise a healthy sweat.[73] The potential loss of this benefit in bad weather, or because of advancing age, is what led to the development of an aerobic alternative that could be used indoors—what Wesley refers to as a "wooden horse" or "chamber horse." Actually, a "wooden horse" was the inexpensive version, "a double plank nine or ten feet long, properly placed upon two tressels."[74] The "chamber horse" was a permanent piece of furniture, a chair with high arms on both sides and a seat that would rise on springs, allowing the person to bounce up and down. Wesley attributed this design to Bishop George Berkeley.[75] He purchased one for his London house in his later years, and as he neared death he encouraged his niece Sarah to borrow it and use it at least a half-hour daily.[76] This was also, of course, the equipment that John charged Samuel Bradburn to procure for Charles Wesley, Sarah's father, when he was in declining health. The other exercise equipment Wesley mentions is a "dumb-bell." This was not the set of weights we think of today, but a form of upper-body aerobic exercise developed in the seventeenth century. A rope was run into the attic of a house, where it wrapped around a cylinder with weights attached. As one pulled down on the rope, unwrapping it and spinning the cylinder, the weights gave the cylinder sufficient momentum to wrap the rope back up in the opposite direction (like a yo-yo), ready to be pulled down again.[77]

Appropriate Rest and Sleep

When Cheyne makes a point of suggesting a standard of seven to eight hours of sleep a night (Appendix B, §III), it is important to see that his concern was that people may be sleeping *too much*, not too little. This reveals again that the lower classes were not his main audience. They are the ones least likely to have the luxury of sleeping late! But there are persons in every economic class who withdraw from life in depression, often lingering in bed, and these can be seen as the ultimate focus of Cheyne's concern.

Wesley makes this connection explicit in his own health advice about sleep. He actually set a standard shorter than Cheyne, and explained it by direct reference to depression:

> I would allow between six and seven hours [of sleep], at an average, to a healthy man; or an hour more, between seven and eight hours, to an unhealthy man. And I do not remember that in threescore years I have known either man or woman who laid longer in bed than this, (whether they slept or no), but in some years they complained of lowness of spirits. The plain reason of which seems to be, while we sleep all the springs of nature are unbent. And if we sleep longer than is sufficient, they are relaxed more than is sufficient, and of course grow weaker and weaker.[78]

In a related sermon, he charged that sleeping too much was not only the chief cause of all nervous diseases but also the chief cause for the recent increase in nervous disorders in Britain.[79]

Cold-bathing and Cleanliness

One other theme worth highlighting in Cheyne's advice in *Essay of Health* is his call for greater cleanliness and his specific advocacy of cold-bathing (Appendix B, §I.3, §IV.5, §IV.10). In both of these areas, Wesley not only echoed, but amplified his mentor. Wesley's emphasis on cleanliness is legendary, drawing the attention of all who study the topic. Indeed, he is often credited with inventing the proverb "cleanliness is next to godliness."[80] While he definitely did not invent this rabbinical proverb, he did cite it often to his people as he exhorted them to seek diligently to be clean in their person, clothing, and housing.[81] The health benefits of this advice are clear today, though it must be admitted that Wesley was concerned in these instances as much, if not more, with the public perception of Methodists.

By contrast, Wesley's emphasis on cold-bathing was primarily for the assumed health benefits, with any sanitary effect or contribution to tidiness being an incidental extra. While Cheyne focused such health benefits in terms of hardening and acclimating the person, Wesley became convinced that cold-bathing could not only cure several disorders, it could also inhibit many hereditary diseases.[82] Because he believed these benefits were underappreciated, he included cold-bathing as a suggested remedy for many specific disorders in *Primitive Physick* and appended to the collection a list of the various disorders supposedly cured or prevented.[83] His major source for this list was a book by two physicians, John Floyer and Edward Baynard.[84] But his appropriation has been credited, much more than their book, with the popularity of cold-water therapy by the end of the eighteenth century.[85]

Favored God's "Natural" Cures over Emerging "Chemical" Medicines

Wesley's interest in cold-bathing straddled the line between preventive regimen and prescribed therapy for healing specific disorders. When one begins to focus on the collection of prescribed remedies in *Primitive Physick*, the characteristic that stands out most is his strong preference for simple, natural remedies. By one count, Wesley refers to 225 distinct treatments in his prescriptions, of which 184 are made from plants, 17 are derived from animals, and 24 are minerals.[86] While one could quibble about the details of this count, Wesley makes clear in his preface that he is giving preference to plants and roots over all "chemical, or exotic, or compound medicine."[87] In this preference, he was swimming against the stream of emerging professional medicine, as well as the current practice of many apothecaries.[88]

But he was not swimming alone. For example, on the preference of simple medicines over compound, Wesley cited the authority of Hermann Boerhaave.[89] He could as easily have cited Robert Boyle, for in his early Oxford years he read Boyle's discourse touting the advantages of simple medicines.[90] The reasons Boyle offers in this discourse are largely "scientific," stressing how use of simple medicines makes it easier for medical observers to determine which ones have the desired effect or undesired side effect. But he also mentions that they are easier to procure and use. This final benefit is what most motivated Boyle to publish his collection of simple remedies, in hopes of improving self-care among the poor.[91] Wesley appropriated several of Boyle's simple remedies for *Primitive Physick* because he shared the same concern. As he explained in a 1755 postscript to the original Preface, his aim in making his collection was "to set down cheap, safe, and easy medicines; easy to be known, easy to be procured, and easy to be applied by plain, unlettered men."[92]

If this explains Wesley's preference for simple medicines, what was his objection to exotic cures—which are often simple in nature? For many in his setting, the objection reflected the continuing influence of a traditional notion that the diseases native to a country were best cured by remedies to be found in that country.[93] This may be part of what led Wesley to consult the health guide by Tennent when he was in Georgia. But Wesley did not seem to assume that cures were strictly geographically specific. For example, while he chastised those who treated it as a panacea for all fevers, he readily recommended "Peruvian Bark" to his British readers for certain ailments (Appendix A, #211).[94] But he made sure to include other native treatments as well, as more accessible alternatives. It appears that his main objection to an emphasis on exotic cures was that their foreign origin again imposed major limits on their availability, affordability, and familiarity of use among the poor and uneducated.[95]

This leaves the question of why Wesley favored the use of natural organic cures over their purified chemical ingredients. The issues of availability and cost surely played a strong role again—roots might be dug in the forest for free, while chemicals must be purchased from the apothecary. But, in his Preface to the *Primitive Physick*, Wesley hints at two other philosophical assumptions that reinforced this practical concern. The first is his Anglican-bred primitivism. Just as Anglican apologists assumed that Christian life and doctrine were purest at the origin of the Christian church, and sought to emulate these times, Wesley privileges the primitive origins of physick and praises the Native Americans for most closely preserving the pristine practice.[96] Closely related to this is Wesley's second apparent assumption, which concerns theodicy. Wesley refers to the "Author of nature" teaching humanity the medicinal value of plants after our sin had introduced sickness and death into creation.[97] This calls to mind Sir. 38:4: "The Lord hath created medicines out of the earth." It also echoes Wesley's frequent insistence that God would not have allowed the potential damages of human sin if God had not already prepared gracious ways to heal these damages.[98] These connections suggest that Wesley may have viewed the modern privileging of chemical medicines over plants as a failure to trust in God's long-standing provisions for dealing with the effects of sin.

Explored God's Most Ubiquitous Natural Cure—Electricity!

This possibility has to be balanced by the recognition that, in the late 1750s, Wesley became an enthusiastic supporter of exploring the most recent potential alternative to traditional therapies—electrical shock.[99] He read the groundbreaking books describing electricity and its potential uses as they were published.[100] Moved in particular by the claims of Richard Lovett about the healing benefits of electricity, he procured in 1756 an "electric machine" that delivered very low-voltage shocks through a probe and began to test its effects for a range of disorders on himself and others. His confidence in the positive results led him to procure other machines and to publicize this near "panacea."[101] Along with inserting "electrify" among his suggestions for several disorders in *Primitive Physick*, starting with the eighth edition in 1759, he added to his appended summary of the benefits of cold-bathing a similar summary for electrifying. A year later he published *The Desideratum: Or, Electricity made plain and useful* to defend the healing benefits of electrification against skeptics and scoffers in the medical profession.[102]

How do we account for Wesley's enthusiasm about electrical shock therapy? By his own admission, the evidence of its effectiveness was often ambiguous, so that alone is not sufficient. I suggest that two other factors intensified his interest. First, it could be considered part of God's creational provision like other "natural" cures. Indeed, in the opening of the *Desideratum*, Wesley speaks of electricity as the "soul of the universe," the created power permeating all other things.[103] Second, electrical shock therapy (as Wesley was practicing it) shared two important characteristics with cold-water bathing, his other favored cure—both were potentially ubiquitous and free.

Extended Care to the Whole Community

In the midst of extolling the promise of electrical treatment for health disorders, Wesley noted Richard Lovett's suggestion that this method can be perfected only if it is "administered and applied by the gentlemen of the faculty." His response was sharp:

> Nay, then . . . all my hopes are at an end. For when will it be administered and applied by them? . . . Not till the gentlemen of the faculty have more regard to the interest of their neighbours than their own; at least, not till there are no apothecaries in the land, or till physicians are independent of them.[104]

This passage is reminiscent of Wesley's negative depiction of the recent professionalizing of health care in the preface to *Primitive Physick*:

> Physicians now began to be had in admiration, as persons who were something more than human. And profit attended their employ, as well as honour; so that they had now two weighty reasons for keeping the bulk of [humanity] at a distance, that they might not pry into the mysteries of the profession. . . . Those who understood only how to restore the sick to health, they branded with the name of empirics. They introduced into practice abundance of compound medicines, consisting of so many ingredients, that it was scarce possible for common people to know which it was that wrought the cure; abundance of exotics, neither the nature nor names of which their own countrymen understood; of chemicals, such as they neither had skill, nor fortune, nor time, to prepare; yea, and of dangerous ones, such as they could not use, without hazarding life, but by the advice of a physician.[105]

There is surely room to debate the accuracy or appropriateness of Wesley's suggestions about the actual motivations of apothecaries and physicians in his day.[106] But there is little doubt that the moves to professionalize medical care in Britain in the eighteenth century served for some time to increase the disparity of access between the rich and the poor, and between those in the major cities and those in the scattered villages.[107] I suggest that the passion reflected in the Wesleyan quotations was aimed less at physicians and apothecaries per se than at this social disparity.

Wesley believed that, just as God's mercy is over *all* God's creatures, our works of mercy—to both body and soul—should be offered to all.

Early in the Methodist revival, as his ministry brought him into daily contact with the lower classes, this conviction led Wesley to set up the first free public dispensary in London. As he described this decision later:

> I was still in pain for many of the poor that were sick: there was so great expense, and so little profit.... I saw the poor people pining away, and several families ruined, and that without remedy. At length I thought of a kind of desperate expedient. "I will prepare, and give them physic myself." ... I took into my assistance an apothecary, and an experienced surgeon; resolving at the same time not to go out of my depth, but to leave all difficult and complicated cases to such physicians as the patients should choose. I gave notice of this to the society; telling them that all who were ill of *chronical* distempers (for I did not care to venture upon *acute*) might, if they pleased, come to me at such a time; and I would give them the best advice I could, and the best medicines I had.[108]

Many of the poor did come to this clinic, both those who were part of the Methodist society and those who were not. Wesley was pleased with the results that he observed, though he noted that the most common obstacle to cures was that while they might take their medicine regularly, people were less likely to follow as well the regimen he advised.[109] Without this holistic care, they were less likely to regain full health.

Within a few years, Wesley found the expenses of running this clinic too great for his limited resources and closed it. This decision is best seen not as a retreat from his concern to provide "physick for the poor" but as a refocusing of this effort. By then he had published the *Primitive Physick* and was distributing it at little or no cost across the English countryside. In this way, he was drawing upon his gifts, and the resources of his movement, to offer seasoned advice on medicine and regimen not only to the poor in London but also to the range of persons in the many cities and villages in the land. In short, he was extending his concern for holistic health and healing to the whole community.

Some Insights about "Honoring a Heritage"

There are many more details that could be offered about Wesley's concern for health and healing; however, the presentation here should be sufficient to reflect on insights that this test case sheds upon the question of how present descendants of Wesley's ministry can most appropriately honor the heritage that he bequeathed to us.

The first point that I hope the preceding discussion made clear is the importance, when evaluating any aspect of Wesley's thought and practice, of approaching it with an awareness of Wesley's cultural and historical context. Without this awareness, something like his emphasis on cold-bathing, for example, can appear purely idiosyncratic. But when one is aware that the "cool regimen" was a broadly shared model among health manuals of the day, this emphasis is less likely to be taken as a sign of Wesley's "credulity for folk tradition."[110] Likewise, Wesley's pointed comments about physicians are less likely to be taken as implying his disdain for the profession when the socioeconomic impact of the new efforts in professionalizing medical care are appreciated.

It is also important that this contextual evaluation be comparative in its own setting. A good example is Wesley's suggestion of bleeding for certain disorders, such as a fever. Readers who are aware of the role of bleeding in traditional Galenic medicine will likely take Wesley as characteristic of his age in this advice. But a careful comparative study will show that Wesley recommended bleeding (and related practices of enemas and blisters) far less often than did most standard medical texts of his time.[111] This is one of the places where his *Primitive Physick* was actually more on the leading edge of changes in medical care.

The call for contextual evaluation is not an attempt to exempt Wesley's teachings or practice from all criticism, just from anachronistic criticism. There will still be many areas where we can raise questions about the adequacy of his stance or the precedent he sets. As one example, while I can appreciate the economic reasons in his setting for Wesley defending "natural" remedies over "chemical" remedies, his implied claim that the human attempt to extract and purify the chemical medicines in various plants betrays a lack of gratitude for and trust in God's provision for our need is not convincing. Among other things, this suggestion stands at odds with Wesley's general emphasis elsewhere on our human duty to *co-operate* in God's providential care for creation.

To illustrate some other appropriate questions that we might raise to Wesley's precedent, consider the prescription he offers for venereal disease (lues venerea):

> 467. Take an ounce of quicksilver every morning, and a spoonful of aqua sulphurata in a glass of water, at five in the afternoon. I have known a person cured by this, when supposed to be at the point of death, who had been infected by a foul nurse, before she was a year old.
> »»I insert this for the sake of such innocent sufferers.[112]

While we would be tempted today to begin with questions about the wisdom of prescribing a poison (mercury) as a medicine, this was commonly prescribed in Wesley's day, and he was actually aware of its dangers, rarely prescribing it.[113] The more appropriate questions begin when we note that Wesley did not even include a treatment for venereal disease in *Primitive Physick* initially and that, when he added this one in the fifth edition (1755), it was with the qualifier that he was inserting it for the sake of "innocent sufferers." This suggests first that Wesley may not be the best guide for incorporating issues of human sexuality into a truly holistic model of health and healing. More importantly, in this case Wesley seems to have forgotten a truth that he drove home to a correspondent who had protested that he did not "deserve" good health: "Does [God] give us no more blessings than we deserve[?] . . . Not so; but mercy rejoices over judgement! Therefore expect from Him, not what you deserve, but what you want—health of soul and health of body."[114] Surely those who minister in the name of the God whose "mercy is over all his works" cannot restrict their care only to innocent sufferers!

We do not truly "honor our heritage" if we shrink from posing such challenges to the adequacy of Wesley's precedent. But we equally fail in this task if we allow awareness of the limits of Wesley's thought and practice to distract us from seeking to embody faithfully today his valuable insights into the holistic scope of salvation and holistic means to health and healing.[115] The last point that I would make is that simple repetition is not a sufficient model for this embodiment. Just as Wesley had a context, so do we, and our context differs from his on many counts. This means that our goal must be a *dynamic* continuity. For example, we can affirm his insight about the importance of regimen, making this a focus of our lives and our ministries, while recognizing the inadequacy of the specific model of the "cold regimen." Likewise, as we seek to honor the precedent of his concern to provide "physick for the poor," we will surely need to consider alternatives beyond simply publishing an up-to-date self-care health manual. While our responses might differ from those of Wesley, we can only hope that our goal will be the same—to realize as fully as possible in the present the healing of body and soul that God longs to provide to all!

Appendix A:
Selected Remedies from *Primitive Physick* (1791)

For an Ague [i.e., intermittent fever and chills]

3. Go into the Cold-Bath just before the cold fit.
   Nothing tends more to prolong an Ague, than indulging a lazy indolent disposition. The patient ought therefore between the fits to take as much exercise as he can bear; and to use a light diet, and for common drink, Lemonade is the most proper.

When all other means fail, give blue Vitriol, from one grain to two grains, in the absence of the fit; and repeat it three or four times in twenty-four hours.

4. Or, take a handful of Groundsell, shred it small, put it into a paper-bag, four inches square, pricking that side which is to be next the skin full of holes. Cover this with a thin linen, and wear it on the pit of the stomach, renewing it two hours before the fit. Tried.

5. Or, apply to the stomach a large onion slit.

6. Or, melt two-penny worth of Frankincense, spread it on linen, grate nutmeg upon it, cover it with linen, and hang this bag on the pit of the stomach. I have never yet known it to fail. . . .

9. Or, make six middling pills of cobwebs. Take one a little before the cold fit, two a little before the next fit (suppose the next day), the other three, if needs be, a little before the third fit. This seldom fails. Or, put a tea-spoonful of salt of tartar into a large glass of spring water, and drink it by little and little. Repeat the same dose the next two days, before the time of the fit.

The Apoplexy [i.e., a seizure, or stroke-like paralysis]

35. To prevent, use the cold-bath, and drink only cold water.

36. In the fit, put a handful of salt into a pint of cold water, and if possible, pour it down the throat of the patient. He will quickly come to himself. So will one who seems dead by a fall. But send for a good physician immediately.

The Asthma

41. Take a pint of cold water every morning washing the head therein immediately after, and using the cold bath once a fortnight.

42. Or, cut an ounce of stick Liquorice into slices. Steep this in a quart of water, for and twenty hours, and use it, when you are worse than usual, as common drink. I have known this give much ease.

43. Or, half a pint of Tar-Water, twice a day.

44. Or, life a fortnight on boiled Carrots only. It seldom fails.

45. Or, take an ounce of Quicksilver every morning, and a spoonful of Aqua Sulphurata, or fifteen drops of Elixer of Vitriol, in a large glass of spring-water at five in the evening. This has cured an inveterate asthma.

A Cough

211. Every cough is a dry cough at first. As long as it continues so, it may be cured by chewing immediately after you cough, the quantity of pepper-corn of Peruvian bark. Swallow your spittle as long as it is bitter, and then spit out the wood. If you cough again, do this again. It very seldom fails to cure any dry cough. I earnestly desire ever one who has any regard for his health to try this within twenty-four hours, after he first perceives a cough.

212. Or, drink a pint of cold water lying down in bed. Tried.

213. Or, make a hole through a lemon and fill it with honey. Roast it, and catch the juice. Take a tea-spoonful of this frequently. Tried

Deafness

237. Be electrified through the ear. Tried.

238. Or, use the cold bath.

239. Or, put a little salt into the ear.

240. Or, drop into it a tea-spoonful of salt water.

241. Or, three or four drops of onion-juice at lying down, and stop it with a little wool.

Extreme Fat

330. Use a total vegetable diet. I know one who was entirely cured of this, by living a year thus: she breakfasted and supped on milk and water (with bread) and dined on turnips, carrots, or other roots, drinking water.

A Fever

(In the beginning of any fever, if the stomach is uneasy, vomit; if the bowels, purge: if the pulse be hard, full or strong, bleed)

332. Drink a pint or two of cold water lying down in bed: I never knew it do hurt.

The Head-Ache

389. Rub the head for a quarter of an hour. Tried.
390. Or be electrified. Tried.
391. Or, apply to each temple the thin yellow rind of a lemon, newly pared off.

The Iliac [Ileac] Passion [i.e., obstructed bowel]

433. Apply warm flannels soaked in spirits of wine.
434. Or, hold a live puppy constantly on the belly. (Dr. Sydenham.)

For one seemingly killed with Lightning, a Damp, or suffocated

464. Plunge him immediately into cold water.
465. Or, blow strongly with bellows down his throat. This may recover a person seemingly drowned. It is still better, if a strong man blows into his mouth.

Lunacy

467. Give decoction of agrimony four times a day.
468. Or, rub the head several times a day with vinegar, in which ground-ivy leaves have been infused.
469. Or, take daily an ounce of distilled vinegar.
470. Or, boil juice of ground-ivy with sweet oil and white wine into an ointment. Shave the head, anoint it therewith, and change it in warm every other day for three weeks. Bruise also the leaves and bind them on the head, and give three spoonfuls of the juice warm every morning. This generally cures melancholy. The juice alone, taken twice a day, will cure.
471. Or, electrify. Tried.

[Lunacy:] Raging Madness

472. Apply to the head, cloths dipped in cold water.
473. Or, set the patient with his head under a great water-fall, as long as his strength will bear; or pour water on his head out of a tea-kettle.
474. Or, let him eat nothing but apples for a month.
475. Or, nothing but bread and milk. Tried.

The Measles

Immediately consult an honest Physician.
481. Drink only thin water-gruel, or milk and water, the more the better; or toast and water.

482. If the cough be very troublesome, take frequently a spoonful of barley-water sweetened with oil of sweet almonds newly drawn, mixed with syrup of maiden-hair.

Nervous Disorders

501. When the nerves perform their office too languidly, a good air is the first requisite. The patient also should rise early, and as soon as the dew is off the ground, walk. Let his breakfast be Mother of Thyme tea, gathered in June, using half as much as we do of common tea. When the nerves are too sensible, let the person breathe a proper air. Let him eat veal, chickens, or mutton. Vegetables should be eat sparingly; the most innocent is the French bean; and the best root, the turnip. Wine should be avoided carefully, so should all sauces. Sometimes he may breakfast upon a quarter of an ounce of the poser of Valerian root infused in hot water, to which he may add cream and sugar. Tea is not proper. When the person finds an uncommon oppression, let him take a large spoonful of the tincture of Valerian root.

502. But I am firmly persuaded, there is no remedy in nature, for nervous disorders of every kind, comparable to the proper and constant use of the electric machine.

To cure the Tooth-Ache

714. Be electrified through the teeth. Tried.
715. Or, apply to the aching tooth an artificial magnet.
716. Or, rub the cheek a quarter of an hour.
717. Or, lay roasted parings of turnips as hot as may be behind the ear.

Appendix B
Preface of *Primitive Physick*, §16, *Works* (Jackson) 14:314–15

For the sake of those who desire, through the blessing of God, to retain the health which they have recovered, I have added a few plain, easy rules, chiefly transcribed from Dr. Cheyne: —

I. 1. The air we breathe is of great consequence to our health. Those who have been long abroad in easterly or northerly winds should drink some thin and warm liquor going to bed, or a draught of toast and water.

2. Tender people should have those who lie with them, or are much about them, sound, sweet, and healthy.

3. Every one that would preserve health should be as clean and sweet as possible in their houses, clothes, and furniture.

II. 1. The great rule of eating and drinking is, to suit the quality and quantity of the food to the strength of our digestion; to take always such a sort and such a measure of food as sits light and easy to the stomach.

2. All pickled, or smoked, or salted food, and all high-seasoned, is unwholesome.

3. Nothing conduces more to health than abstinence and plain food, with due labour.

4. For studious persons, about eight ounces of animal food, and twelve of vegetable, in twenty-four hours, is sufficient.

5. Water is the wholesomest of all drinks; quickens the appetite, and strengthens the digestion most.

6. Strong, and more especially spirituous, liquors are a certain, though slow, poison.

7. Experience shows there is very seldom any danger in leaving them off all at once.

8. Strong liquors do not prevent the mischiefs of a surfeit, nor carry it off, so safely as water.

9. Malt liquors (except clear small beer, or small ale of due age) are exceeding hurtful to tender persons.

10 Coffee and tea are extremely hurtful to persons who have weak nerves.

III. 1. Tender persons should eat very light suppers, and that two or three hours before going to bed.

2. They ought constantly to go to bed about nine, and rise at four or five.

IV. 1. A due degree of exercise is indispensably necessary to health and long life.

2. Walking is the best exercise for those who are able to bear it; riding for those who are not. The open air, when the weather is fair, contributes much to the benefit of exercise.

3. We may strengthen any weak part of the body by constant exercise. Thus, the lungs may be strengthened by loud speaking, or walking up an easy ascent; the digestion and the nerves, by riding; the arms and hams, by strongly rubbing them daily.

4. The studious ought to have stated times for exercise, at least two or three hours a day: The one half of this before dinner; the other, before going to bed.

5. They should frequently shave, and frequently wash their feet.

6. Those who read or write much should learn to do it standing; otherwise it will impair their health.

7. The fewer clothes any one uses, by day or night, the hardier he will be.

8. Exercise, First, should be always on an empty stomach: Secondly, should never be continued to weariness: Thirdly, after it, we should take care to cool by degrees; otherwise we shall catch cold.

9. The flesh-brush is a most useful exercise, especially to strengthen any part that is weak.

10. Cold bathing is of great advantage to health. It prevents abundance of diseases. It promotes perspiration, helps the circulation of the blood, and prevents the danger of catching cold. Tender people should pour water upon the head before they go in, and walk swiftly. To jump in with the head foremost is too great a shock to nature.

V. 1. Costiveness cannot long consist with health. Therefore care should be taken to remove it at the beginning; and when it is removed, to prevent its return, by soft, cool, open diet.

2. Obstructed perspiration (vulgarly called catching cold) is one great source of diseases. Whenever there appears the least sign of this, let it be removed by gentle sweats.

VI. 1. The passions have a greater influence on health than most people are aware of.

2. All violent and sudden passions dispose to, or actually throw people into, acute diseases.

3. The slow and lasting passions, such as grief and hopeless love, bring on chronical diseases.

4. Till the passion which caused the disease is calmed, medicine is applied in vain.

5. The love of God, as it is the sovereign remedy of all miseries, so in particular it effectually prevents all the bodily disorders the passions introduce, by keeping the passions themselves within due bounds. And by the unspeakable joy, and perfect calm, serenity, and tranquillity it gives the mind, it becomes the most powerful of all the means of health and long life.

CHAPTER EIGHT

HOLY HEART, HOLY LIFE, HOLY WORK: WORK, VOCATION, AND CALLING IN THE WESLEYAN TRADITION

Rebekah L. Miles
for the Bishops of The United Methodist Church[1]

"We Wesleyans look back to look forward," observes Russell Richey.[2] In this essay, I look back to Wesley's ideas about work, vocation, and calling as resources for reflecting on those themes in the present and future. Wesley's writings provide one resource from Christian tradition to help Christians think more clearly about work and work more faithfully.[3]

Of course, to look back, I need to have confidence in the accuracy of my sources. I had no misgivings about their accuracy until I encountered Richard Heitzenrater's chapter in this book.[4] I had naively assumed that because I was relying primarily on Wesley's writings about his own ideas and activities, I was on safe ground. Wesley said it. I believed it. That settled it. Heitzenrater's exposé on myths of Methodism—including myths *about* John Wesley that were promoted *by* John Wesley—has undermined my confidence to say much about what Wesley actually believed and did. After all, I am relying only on Wesley's own words. Therefore, in light of Heitzenrater's Methodist demythology, I want to make one thing perfectly clear: I am simply reporting here on what Wesley *claimed* to have believed and done, and I am making *no* judgments at all about what Wesley *actually* believed and did.

WESLEYAN WORK HABITS

If one is searching for historical models for a healthy work life today, John Wesley is not an obvious choice. Wesley has a well-deserved reputation for living and working in overdrive. He once wrote, "Leisure and I have taken leave of one another; I propose to be busy as long as I live."[5] A young John Wesley made this startling pledge to his brother Samuel and then spent the rest of his life making it true. He gave himself and his time freely in service to God and neighbor and instructed Methodists to do the same. He exhorted them to " 'redeem the time,' crowding as much work into every day as it can contain,"[6] and he actively discouraged idleness. "A Christian abhors sloth as much as drunkenness, and flees from idleness as he does from adultery."[7] And Wesley did flee from idleness, rising early and making good use of every moment of the day.

Wesleyans have long reveled in mathematical reckonings of Wesley's diligence. He allegedly preached forty thousand sermons and traveled two hundred thousand (some say almost three hundred thousand) miles; some of those miles, Methodists love to note, were spent on horseback while reading a book.[8] In light of Heitzenrater's deconstruction of Methodist myths, I suspect that these numbers may be as many parts fiction as fact. Even so, the fact that Methodists love to calculate and recite these numbers testifies to the high value Methodists have placed on Wesley's reputation for hard work.

Wesley's habits did not change with age. Waiting impatiently for his carriage, an elderly Wesley allegedly cried out, "I have lost ten minutes, and they are lost forever." Less than six weeks before his death, an eighty-seven-year-old Wesley wrote to a friend, "I am half blind and half lame; but by the help of God I creep on still."[9] He did "creep on," and over the following weeks, according to some admirers, a half-blind and lame Wesley toiled "from early in the morning till late at night," and only stopped working (and writing) a week before he died.[10]

The year before his death, Wesley had counseled, "Let us work now; we shall rest by and by."[11] Centuries after Wesley had found that rest, Methodist clergy were still receiving his instructions on time and work. When today's United Methodist clergy (along with a host of other Methodist clergy across the history and geography of Wesleyan denominations) are voted into full clergy membership in their annual conferences, their bishops ask the historic questions and close with Wesley's stark directives about work and the use of time. "Be diligent.... Never be triflingly employed. Never trifle away time; neither spend any more time at any one place than is strictly necessary."[12] In one sense, Wesley stopped working the week before his death. In another sense, however, his work never stopped, because he had pre-arranged to have his work continue by giving work orders to those who came after him. Wesley once said, "I reverence the young because they may be useful after I am dead." For good and for ill, many Methodists still follow Wesley's work orders and continue, thereby, to be useful to his mission these many years after his death. It is precisely because so many Christians (especially Methodists) are still of use to that mission that it is fair to ask, "Is Wesley still of use to Christians?"

If one were to rely only on the image of Wesley sketched above, then he would be of limited use to many contemporary people (especially middle and upper-income people), for many people are so absorbed by their work that it is the real center of their time, energy, and devotion. For these people, Wesley's model could make things worse! Of course, some might argue that the picture of Wesley's work habits sketched here is more myth than fact; however, I wager that his reputation is well deserved. Even so, the reputation is not the whole story. If one moves beyond a focus on Wesley's micro-management of time and includes the larger pattern of his life, particularly his reflections on work, vocation, and calling, a more nuanced model emerges. This model is partly useful and partly useless to contemporary Christians.

WESLEY ON VOCATION AND CALLING

What did Wesley say about work and about the related terms—vocation and calling? I begin with the words "vocation" and "calling" because Wesley's use of them is relevant to his view of work. People today often use the words as synonyms for employment. Indeed, standard dictionaries define vocation and calling as, among other things, "occupation," "employment," "trade, "profession."[13] Within the Christian tradition, people have used the terms "vocation" and "calling" to talk about employment as well as the larger calling to faithful Christian life. Although people often think that Luther equated vocation or calling primarily with employment, his larger point was that all Christians can live out their vocations as they fulfill the tasks that accompany their various roles and stations in life. This includes, according to Luther and others, their employment as well as their roles as spouses, parents, citizens, and so forth.[14]

As we shall see, Wesley also used the word "calling" to refer to various aspects of a person's life, such as employment, marriage, and holiness. His use of the word "vocation," however, was much more limited and did not explicitly refer to a Christian's employment or role as a spouse. In the Jackson edition of *The Works of John Wesley*, Wesley used the word "vocation" thirteen times, quoting in every case the following translation of Eph. 4:1-3 (KJV): "I, therefore, the prisoner of the Lord, beseech you that ye walk worthy of the vocation wherewith ye are called, with all lowliness and meekness, with longsuffering, forbearing one another in love; endeavouring to keep the unity of the Spirit in the bond of peace." When Wesley advised Christians to "walk worthy of the vocation wherewith ye are called," he stressed the characteristics mentioned in this text—lowliness, meekness, longsuffering, and peacefulness—as well as other characteristics including cheerfulness, good humor, doing good works, and living in the love of God and neighbor.

For Wesley, "Walking in the vocation wherewith ye are called" amounted to a holiness that should extend to all of life. He wrote, "What is it to 'walk worthy of the vocation wherewith we are called'? ... It includes all our inward and outward motions, all our thoughts, and words, and actions. It takes in not only everything we do, but everything we either speak or think."[15] By this broad definition, "walking worthy" of this vocation could include employment and marriage, along with anything else a Christian did, thought, or said. Wesley, however, was not using vocation to talk specifically about employment or familial responsibilities, but, instead, about the larger life of holiness that should shape every smaller part of a Christian's life.

Although Wesley wrote about vocation using this broad definition of holiness, he used the words "call" and "calling" to refer to many different parts of Christian life, including employment. Even so, one of the most common ways that Wesley used the word "calling" was to refer to Christian life in general. As with vocation, "calling" points to the full life of holiness, "when in every motion of our heart, in every word of our tongue, in every work of our hands, we 'pursue nothing but in relation to him' ... when, whether we 'eat, or drink, or whatever we do, we do all to the glory of God.' "[16]

Wesley also wrote of the "call of God" on a congregation. Several times, after noting in his journal that attendance was up in a church, he added that a "call from God" was on them. He was referring to God's call to repentance and holiness of the entire congregation. In a journal entry from 1775, Wesley wrote, "I never saw the House thoroughly filled till now. And I am sure the people had now a call from God."[17] He made similar claims about whole towns: "There now seems to be a general call to this town; surely some will hear the voice that raises the dead."[18]

Wesley also appealed to God's extraordinary call to a specific task—often a controversial task. For example, he wrote of the call to preach—especially the call of lay preachers. It is not surprising that he stressed the calling of lay preachers, including laywomen preachers, since he was forced to defend his controversial use of them. He justified his decision by pointing to their "extraordinary call" as well as to the fruits of their ministry. In a letter to one of the first Methodist women preachers, Mary Bosanquet, Wesley wrote,

> I think the strength of the cause rests there—on your having an *extraordinary* call. So I am persuaded has every one of our lay preachers; otherwise, I could not countenance his preaching at all. It is plain to me, that the whole

work of God termed Methodism is an extraordinary dispensation of His providence. Therefore, I do not wonder if several things occur therein which do not fall under ordinary rules of discipline.[19]

Not only the preaching of laymen and laywomen, but also the whole Methodist movement, is attributed to an extraordinary call or dispensation. As proof of the call of God in the Methodist movement, Wesley often points to empirical evidence. He wrote, for example, "If [God's] work hath in fact prospered in our hands, then he hath *called* or *sent* us to do this. I entreat reasonable men to weigh this thoroughly, whether the *fact* does not plainly prove the *call*?"[20]

Wesley also justified his own controversial preaching by this appeal to an extraordinary call. In a testy letter to his brother Charles, John Wesley defended his habit of preaching without permission in the parishes of other priests: "[T]o do this I have both an ordinary call and an extraordinary. My ordinary call is, my ordination by the Bishop: 'Take thou authority to preach the word of God.' My extraordinary call is witnessed by the works God doth by my ministry."[21]

Wesley also wrote about the calling or providence of God in ordinary daily matters. He notes repeatedly in his journals and letters that he was called by God to go to one place or another, or to speak to one person or another.[22] Even natural conditions such as sickness were sometimes interpreted as a call from God. Wesley advised a Mr. Wolfe to tell a backsliding man who had fallen ill that he should "receive this stroke as a call from God."[23]

Finally, Wesley often used the words "call" and "calling" to refer to ordinary employment. In his sermon "The More Excellent Way," for example, Wesley refers to temporal employment as "worldly business" in one sentence, and "the business of their calling" in another.[24] In another reflection on temporal employment, Wesley exhorted his hearers: "[U]se all possible diligence in your calling. Lose no time. . . . If you understand your particular calling as you ought, you will have no time that hangs upon your hands. Every business will afford some employment sufficient for every day and every hour."[25]

In summary, while Wesley's use of the word "vocation" was limited to the holiness of the Christian life, he used the words "call" and "calling" to refer not only to Christian holiness, but also to other extraordinary and ordinary calls of God to engage in a particular work (e.g., lay preaching) or to take some action (e.g., traveling to a particular location). He also commonly used the word "calling" to refer to ordinary employment. Wesley's different uses of call and calling, like his use of vocation, have an underlying unity; all eventually return to the question of holiness, of right Christian life and heart.

WESLEY ON WORK

What did Wesley say about ordinary work, whether using the word "calling" or other words, such as "business," "profession," or "temporal employment"? His views were more complex than is popularly assumed.

Cautions about Work

First, Wesley, for all his commitment to hard work, was also ambivalent about it. One does not find in Wesley the grand praises of work and its glory that one finds in Luther and in other Protestant writers.[26] Indeed, Wesley offered many warnings about the dangers of temporal work. He noted that people can work too much, risking their physical and spiritual health:

> No gain whatsoever should induce us to enter into, or to continue in, any employ which is of such a kind, or is attended with so hard or so long labour, as to impair our constitution. Neither should we begin or continue in any business which necessarily deprives us of proper seasons for food and sleep in such a proportion as our nature requires.[27]

Wesley also recognized the need for time away from work: "[W]e cannot be always intent upon business: both our bodies and minds require some relaxation. We need intervals of diversion from business."[28] Because some forms of work could be bad for the body or soul of a worker, as well as for the body or soul of others (who purchased a bad product or who suffered under poor working condition), Christians should choose their employment with care.

Wesley was particularly worried that work would pull Christians away from their primary task—holiness or growth in the love of God and neighbor. He often linked the temptations of ordinary employment with the more typical temptations of the flesh—pleasure, sloth, and diversions, for example. In one sermon, Wesley exhorted his people to save "all the time you can for the best purposes; buying up every fleeting moment out of the hands of sin and Satan, out of the hands of sloth, ease, pleasure, worldly business."[29] "Never more disappoint the design of his love," Wesley wrote, "either by worldly business or idle diversions."[30] In these two examples, and in many others, "worldly business," along with sloth, pleasure, idle diversions, or any temporal activity, are seen as temptations that can draw Christians away from their primary task, distracting them from their focus on God. A "dissipated man," Wesley wrote, "is a man that is separated from God, that is disunited from his centre, whether this be occasioned by hurry of business, by seeking honour or preferment, or by fondness for diversions . . . or for any trifle under the sun."[31]

To counter the dangers of dissipation, Wesley prayed that he might pursue his business with a disengaged heart.

> Deliver me, O God, from too intense an application to even necessary business. I know how this dissipates my thoughts from the one end of all my business, and impairs that lively perception I would ever retain of thee standing at my right hand.... O teach me to go through all my employments with so truly disengaged a heart, that I may still see thee in all things.[32]

Note here that even necessary, religious business—including the business of a clergyperson—can be dissipating. Wesley was not biased against secular work. Any employment or any activity at all, however virtuous or holy, can become dissipating.

Work can also be dangerous because of the wealth it often produces. As Methodists grew wealthy, Wesley grew worried about their souls. One of Wesley's reflections on wealth begins with a line that is well known to many contemporary Methodists: "I am not afraid that the people called Methodists should ever cease to exist either in Europe or America. But I am afraid lest they should only exist as a dead sect, having the form of religion without the power."[33] Methodists today rarely note that the whole point of this essay, written less than a year before Wesley's death, was that the Methodist soul was dying because wealth and frugality were growing among the Methodists at a much faster rate than generosity:

> For the Methodists in every place grow diligent and frugal; consequently they increase in goods. Hence they proportionably increase in pride, in anger, in the desire of the flesh, the desire of the eyes, and the pride of life. So, although the form of religion remains, the spirit is swiftly vanishing away.[34]

Wesley insisted that the temptations and snares of hoarded wealth are so overpowering that "very few escape out of it." The few who are able to escape "are sorely scorched by it, though not utterly consumed. If they escape at all it is with the skin of their teeth, and with deep wounds."[35] Indeed, "the deceitfulness of riches," Wesley wrote, strikes "at the whole work of God" more than any other earthly temptation.[36] It imperils not only individual Methodists, but also the effectiveness of the whole movement. In at least one sermon, Wesley indicted irresponsible wealth as the root cause of Methodism's "inefficacy."[37]

Happily, there is a solution to the problem of the growing wealth of hard-working Methodists. If Methodists *"gain all they can"* and *"save all they can,"* they must also *"give all they can"* so that their money will not "sink [them] to the nethermost hell," but, instead, allow them to "grow in grace."[38] Wesley considered persons rich if they had anything left after taking care of necessities and conveniences for their households and businesses and paying debts. This definition would include many Methodists of his time and our time. A rich person is obliged to give the excess money away because it belongs to God and to the poor. If one spends money for unnecessary clothing, extravagant foods, or any other luxuries, one is taking from the poor. Wesley chided the wealthy, "What you put upon yourself, you are, in effect, tearing from the back of the naked; as the costly and delicate food which you eat you are snatching from the mouth of the hungry."[39] While generosity could be a means of grace or special blessing to increase holiness, misusing money and failing to help the poor undermines one's holiness.

For Wesley, this was not simply a matter of individual behavior. The larger society, especially the social habits and business practices of its wealthiest members and the policies of the government, is particularly to blame. For example, as wealthy people bought large tracts of land and formed large farming operations, they took away the livelihoods of small farmers who were previously working small portions of that land.[40] The primary causes of poverty and unemployment, claimed Wesley, were taxes, distilling, and the luxuries of the wealthy. Wesley assailed those who blamed poverty and unemployment on the idleness of the poor: "So wickedly, devilishly false is that common objection, 'They are poor, only because they are idle.' If you saw these things with your own eyes, could you lay out money in ornaments or superfluities?"[41] The luxuries of the rich and the excesses of the government, not the idleness of the poor, are primary culprits in the problems of unemployment and poverty. The only remedy "for this sore evil" of poverty and unemployment is to find work for the poor and unemployed. "They will then earn and eat their own bread."[42]

Although Wesley criticized the practices of some wealthy people and insisted that wealth could bring deadly temptations to them, he did not claim that money was bad. Indeed, money is "an excellent gift of God," precisely because it can be used to support one's household and to help the poor. Wesley wrote of money, "In the hands of [God's] children it is food for the hungry, drink for the thirsty, raiment for the naked."[43] The wealth that sometimes grows from hard work can be either an avenue for doing the work of God, or a fast road to hell.

Another benefit of wealth is that rich Christians, freed from employment and the need to provide necessities for their households, are able to help others; indeed, they have greater responsibility to do so. Wesley, writing about the important ministry of visiting the sick, noted:

> But those who "are rich in this world," who have more than the conveniences of life, are peculiarly called of God to this blessed work, and pointed out to it by his gracious Providence. As you are not under a necessity of working for your bread, you have your time at your own disposal! You may therefore allot some part of it every day for this labour of love.[44]

Given Wesley's many cautions about work, it is not surprising that he saw some advantages in having enough money to be able to avoid temporal employment and, consequently, to be able to give oneself and one's time freely to one's neighbor.

Wesley's cautions about work and wealth center on the potential temptations they bring. Wealth and work are not problems in themselves; indeed, they can be gifts of God. The problem is with the common misuse of wealth and work, which can draw people away from holiness of heart and life (including a more just relationship between their work and the poor).

Why Work?

Although Wesley saw some advantages in being free from temporal employment and spoke repeatedly about the dangers and temptations that could come with employment, he also recognized that employment was necessary for many people for pragmatic reasons: to avoid debt and to provide for their households. In the mid-1740s, Wesley wrote:

> It is the will of God, that every man should labour to "eat his own bread"; yea, and that every man should provide for his own, for them of his own household. It is likewise his will that we should "owe no man anything." ... [T]his care, to provide for ourselves and our household ... our blessed Lord does not condemn. Yea, it is good and acceptable in the sight of God our Saviour.[45]

Wesley wrote repeatedly of the importance of work for these pragmatic purposes.[46]

A person was not only allowed, but also obligated, to provide for the household. Anyone who failed to do so "hath practically 'denied the faith, and is worse than an infidel,' or heathen."[47] This duty did not justify, however, a great accumulation of wealth or a high standard of living. Methodists were to procure for their households only "the plain necessaries of life—not delicacies, not superfluities."[48] In several places, Wesley broadened these allowable provisions to include not only the "plain necessities" but also the "conveniences."[49] In a late sermon (1780), Wesley summarized his message:

> It is allowed, (1), that we are to provide necessaries and conveniences for those of our own household; (2), that men in business are to lay up as much as is necessary for the carrying on of that business; (3), that we are to leave our children what will supply them with necessaries and conveniences after we have left the world; and (4), that we are to provide things honest in the sight of all men, so as to "owe no man any thing."[50]

Note that Wesley has left room for a person to accumulate a significant amount of money, and yet still fall within these guidelines. This broad allowance permits sufficient wealth to provide for the long-term care of one's business and one's family, including necessaries, conveniences, and future security. At the same time, Methodists were to balance their needs for these things with the greater needs of their neighbors. Wesley recommended that Methodists follow "that excellent rule, 'Let our conveniences give way to our neighbour's necessities; and our necessities give way to our neighbour's extremities.' "[51] In this way, Wesley's concerns regarding work and money were quite similar to those regarding sleeping, eating, and health care, as described in Randy Maddox's chapter. Individual behavior should be tempered and health care provided in such a way that the poor could live more secure and healthy lives.

Wesley valued work, not only as a way to provide for one's household and the poor, but also as a remedy for idleness. With many others of his time, Wesley railed against idleness. In a sermon about sleep (which recommended that Christians sleep less in order to save time for more productive purposes), Wesley quoted William Law, saying that "softness and idleness" are "the bane of religion" and render a person "incapable of the fundamental duties of Christianity."[52] Wesley wrote, "Do you labour to get your own living, abhorring idleness as you abhor hell-fire? The devil tempts other men; but an idle man tempts the devil. An idle man's brain is the devil's shop, where he is continually working mischief."[53] Although temporal employment might distract a Christian from God, it is certainly better than doing nothing, and infinitely better than failing to provide for one's household or to avoid debt.

How to Choose the Right Job

As we have seen, Wesley valued work primarily for its pragmatic use and was ambivalent about work as a potential distraction from holiness. At the same time, Wesley also recognized that one's employment, carefully chosen, could be a means of holiness and care for neighbor. When he offered advice on choosing a profession for oneself or one's child, Wesley recommended that a person determine what employment would lead to greater holiness and the most good. Even here, Wesley was remarkably pragmatic, as he was in responding to a question about holiness: "Suppose, for instance, it were proposed to a reasonable man to marry, or to enter into a new business. In order to know whether this is the will of God . . . he has only to inquire, 'In which of these states can I be most holy, and do the most good?' "[54]

Likewise, Wesley believed that parents choosing a profession for their children should have as their "one consideration what calling is likely to secure . . . the highest place in heaven."[55] Wesley was critical toward those who chose "a profession or a companion for life" by looking to "the things on earth, rather than the things above." Wesley wrote to people who were overly concerned with things of this earth: "Repent, repent of your vile earthly-mindedness! Renounce the title of Christians, or prefer, both in your own case and the case of your children, grace to money, and heaven to earth."[56] The most vile offenders, according to Wesley, were men who chose to become priests with their eyes not on salvation but, instead, on "ease, honour, money, or preferment." These men, Wesley wrote, "are the pests of the Christian world, the grand nuisance of mankind, a stink in the nostrils of God."[57]

In these examples, Wesley was providing advice about how to choose (and how not to choose) employment. One determines the correct choice, the choice that is God's will, by using reason and experience to calculate which option will offer greater opportunities for "being holy and doing good." This pragmatic view of choosing employment stands in strong contrast to the assumption of some Puritans, as well as more recent Christians, that God calls each person to a particular profession or work. Wesley's view also stands in contrast to the views of Luther and other early Protestants, who believed that one's proper calling was to fulfill the responsibilities that went with one's station in society—a station that was not normally chosen, but given. (This, by the way, is why Luther's view of work is often criticized as a capitulation to the status quo.)[58] In contrast, Wesley wanted the poor to rise above "their station," in the sense of finding better work, so they could provide for themselves and their households.

How to Work Properly

As we have seen, Wesley claimed that some forms of employment could help Christians become more holy and do more good. To this end, one must not only choose one's work carefully, but also do it properly. According to Wesley, what is the proper way to work?

A Christian is to work diligently. In a series of questions about loving and serving God, Wesley asked, "Are you not slothful in business? Whatever your hand finds to do, do you do it with your might?"[59] Work is valued precisely because it is a remedy to idleness; therefore, it must not be done slothfully. When critics charged that Wesley discouraged Methodists from their temporal employment, he adamantly denied the charge, insisting instead that many Methodists, by their "diligence in business," became better, more productive workers. He wrote,

> How came you to dream again that we "condemned all regard for *temporal* concerns" . . . ? Vain dream! We on the contrary severely condemn all who neglect their *temporal* concerns . . . the Methodists, so called, do not "neglect their affairs, and impoverish their families," but by diligence in business

"provide things honest in the sight of all men." Insomuch that multitudes of them, who in time past had scarce food to eat or raiment to put on, have now "all things needful for life and godliness," and that for their families as well as themselves.[60]

Christians are to work diligently, yet with a "disengaged heart." Wesley warned, as we saw above, that the main danger of employment is that it draws one's focus away from God:

> Business itself, when it comes in such a flood upon you, must needs be one of the greatest temptations, since it naturally tends to hinder your waiting upon God (as you would desire always to do) without distraction. And when our mind is hurried it is hardly possible to retain either the spirit of prayer or of thankfulness.[61]

John Wesley often used the Gospel story of Mary and Martha to underline the importance of not being diverted from holiness by work or any other worldly activity, focusing instead on "the one thing needful." He wrote,

> And even as much serving dissipated the thoughts of Martha, and distracted her from attending to her Lord's words, so a thousand things which daily occur are apt to dissipate our thoughts, and distract us from attending to his voice who is continually speaking to our hearts. . . . We are encompassed on all sides with persons and things that tend to draw us from our centre. . . [and] distract our minds from attending to him who is both the author and end of our being.[62]

The insistence on working with a disengaged heart is also evident in several of Charles Wesley's hymns. One example is "Servant of All to Toil for Man," a hymn about human labor, in which Charles Wesley wrote,

> Careless through outward cares I go,
> From all distraction free;
> My hands are but engaged below—
> My heart is still with thee.[63]

For both Charles and John Wesley, the key human task is not just to labor, but to focus on God and to love God and neighbor in every circumstance, including one's labor. When Christians are able to work with a disengaged heart, they not only become better Christians, but also better workers. In the end, holiness is good for business. In "The Minutes from Some Late Conversations," a question is posed: "But would not one who was thus sanctified be incapable of worldly business?" On the contrary, "He would be far more capable of it than ever, as going through all without distraction."[64]

What else did John Wesley say about the proper way to work? Good work is healthy and just. As we saw above, Wesley warned against work that was "so hard or so long . . . as to impair [one's] constitution" or work that would expose the worker to toxic substances. If a person has a "weak constitution," otherwise healthy work may be unhealthy. Work, for example, that would "require many hours to be spent in writing" might be unhealthy for some people.[65] Further, good work is done justly and should not involve "sinful trades," breaking the law, or hurting the soul or body of oneself or one's neighbor. Unjust work could include selling harmful products, artificially lowering prices to hurt a competitor, providing poor working conditions, or doing anything that would hurt the soul or body of oneself or one's neighbor.[66]

Good work, according to Wesley, is not done on Sunday. Wesley was adamant that Christians should observe the Sabbath (by which he meant Sunday) by going to worship services (plural) and by giving most of the remaining hours of the day to prayer, the study of Scripture, and conversations with others about "the things of God."[67] Because the Sabbath belongs to God, Christians who work on the Sabbath "rob God."[68] Wesley scolded "Sabbath-breakers," often lumping them in a list of sinners that most often included "common swearers," "drunkards," and "whoremongers."[69] He used the word "whoremonger"—common in English Bibles, conversations of that day, and Wesley's writings (where it appeared at least two dozen times)—to refer to a fornicator and sometimes to a lecherous, idolatrous, or extremely wicked person. Sabbath-breakers were also linked, though less frequently, with other scoundrels, including adulterers, cheats, railers, thieves, extortioners, and "wolves and bears in the shape of men."[70] Evidently, Sabbath-breaking was no small sin for Wesley.

Christians are to honor the Sabbath, not simply because it is a divine command, but also because it is a day of special blessing. Wesley wrote,

> The Lord not only hallowed the Sabbath-day, but he hath also blessed it. . . . You throw away your own blessing, if you neglect to "keep this day holy." It is a day of special grace. The King of heaven now sits upon his mercy-seat, in a more gracious manner than on other days, to bestow blessings on those who observe it. If you love your own soul, can you then forbear laying hold on so happy an opportunity? Awake, arise, let God give thee his blessing! Receive a token of his love![71]

When Christians observe the Sabbath, they receive a special blessing from God.

Good work also requires the right spirit and intention. Wesley wrote, "But as our alms and devotions are not an acceptable service but when they proceed from a pure intention, so our common employment cannot be reckoned a service to him but when it is performed with the same piety of heart."[72] Good work is done toward the proper end, and one of those ends is money. Wesley wrote, "It is our bounden duty . . . to gain all we can gain."[73] As we saw above, the desire for gain cannot justify work that is unhealthy or sinful, but money, if properly earned, is good in itself and "an excellent gift of God" that can provide for one's household and the poor.

Even so, money or other human rewards can never be the ultimate goal of one's work:

> If a man pursues his business, that he may raise himself to a state of figure and riches in the world, he is no longer serving God in his employment, and has no more title to a reward from God, than he who gives alms that he may be seen, or prays that he may be heard, of men. For vain and earthly designs are no more allowable in our employments, than in our alms and devotions."[74]

In one's labor, as in every other human activity, one should aim "only at the glory of God in all."[75] A Methodist, wrote Wesley, does everything

> to the glory of God. In all his employments of every kind he not only *aims* at this . . . , but actually *attains* it. His business and refreshments, as well as his prayers, all serve this great end. . . . Whether he put on his apparel, or labour, or eat and drink, or divert himself from too wasting labour, it all tends to advance the glory of God by peace and goodwill among men. His one invariable rule is this, "Whatsoever ye do, in word or deed, do it all in the name of the Lord Jesus, giving thanks to God and the Father by him."[76]

In summary, Wesley's view of work included the following components. Work or temporal employment is necessary and good for pragmatic reasons—to avoid debt and to support one's household. The money gained from work can be a means of grace and survival not only for one's family, but also, through one's generosity, for the poor. Work can be dangerous if it draws Christians away from their primary focus on God, if it produces wealth that is then hoarded and not shared with the poor, or if it in some other way hurts the soul or body of oneself or one's neighbor. The work and wealth (or lack of work and wealth) of one individual is linked to the work and wealth of other individuals and of society as a whole. The work patterns and extravagance of wealthy classes (along with the policies of nations) can threaten the survival of the poor. Christians, Wesley insisted, should choose their work and do their work in a way that is good for their bodies and souls, as well as the bodies and souls of their neighbors. They should work in a manner that would not distract them from their primary focus on God, and they should work hard throughout the week, but never on Sundays. On any day, all of one's activities, including employment, should be done in relation to the higher vocation or calling of Christian holiness and for the glory of God.

Wesley's claims about work shared much in common with those of other Anglicans and English Puritans of the seventeenth and eighteenth centuries.[77] They too condemned idleness and recommended diligence, the good use of time, and shorter hours for sleeping. They too railed against the extravagance and excess spending of the wealthy (including those who became wealthy by their own hard work) and encouraged saving and charity. They too warned that too much work could draw one away from God. In other ways, as I will note below, Wesley's views were also in contrast to the views of many of his contemporaries.

WESLEY'S MODEL: A PIECEMEAL, PERSUASIVE, PASTORAL "THEOLOGY OF WORK"

It is easy enough to summarize Wesley's scattered claims about work. It is difficult (if not impossible) to present Wesley's comprehensive theology of work, because he did not have one. His writings on work are found in sermons, letters, and persuasive essays, in which Wesley attempted not so much to help people think more clearly about their doctrine of work, but to encourage them to work and live more faithfully. In many of his writings on work and other practical topics, he is less interested in setting out a comprehensive treatise about his position, and more interested in persuading his hearers to change their lives.[78] Although these pastoral responses do not set forth a comprehensive theology of work, they do reveal much of Wesley's pastoral theology of work, some of which is relevant for Christians today.

Holy Work, Holy Heart, Holy Life

Holiness of heart and life is the core of Wesley's model of work, vocation, and calling. This is no surprise, since Wesley holds "holiness of heart and life" at the center of Methodism.[79] This center unifies all of the smaller details—like work and calling:

> The essence of [Methodism] is holiness of heart and life; the circumstantials all point to this. And as long as they are joined together in the people called Methodists, no weapon formed against them shall prosper. But if even the circumstantial parts are despised, the essential will soon be lost. And if ever the essential parts should evaporate, what remains will be dung and dross.[80]

What is holiness of heart and life for Wesley? It is "inward and outward conformity in all things to the revealed will of God; . . . universal love filling the heart and governing the life."[81] The soul of a person who is holy of heart and life is "renewed after the image of God, in righteousness and in all true holiness." This holiness springs from the love of God. A

Methodist (or any faithful Christian) "is one who has 'the love of God shed abroad in his heart by the Holy Ghost given unto him'; one who 'loves the Lord his God with all his heart, and with all his soul, and with all his mind, and with all his strength.' God is the joy of his heart, and the desire of his soul."[82] This love of God should pervade the lives of Christians, so that in all of their thoughts, desires, dispositions, and actions they seek to love others and to do the will of God.

Holistic Holy Work

Holiness of heart and life is holistic in Wesley's writings.[83] It includes inward thoughts and emotions, and outward behavior; it includes one's action as an individual and one's relationship to larger patterns and organization of society and government; and it includes a concern for one's body, mind, and soul, as well as the body, mind, and soul of one's neighbor. It is no surprise then, that Wesley's theology of work is also holistic. Above all, good work contributes to the worker's holiness, and to the holiness of others, in all aspects of their lives. A particular job is not good for holiness if it draws the worker or others away from God; if it hurts the worker or others in body, soul, or mind; or if it participates in larger patterns within society that are bad for the body, soul, or mind of oneself or others. For Wesley, the primary Christian vocation and calling is not work, but holiness (understood holistically); good work should contribute to, and not hinder, the higher calling of holiness of heart and life.

Wesley's holistic model of work also emphasized the interrelationship between the employment of Christians on the one hand, and their saving, spending, and giving habits on the other. If one worked and gained a lot, but did not save and give a lot, one imperiled one's soul. He also emphasized the interrelationship between the working, saving, spending, and giving habits of some Christians (the wealthier ones—individually and as a social group), and the working, saving, spending, and survival of other people (the poorer ones—both individually and as a social group). Wealthier Christians who did not give away their excess wealth were taking what belonged to the poor. In addition, the extravagance of wealthier people as a social whole, as well as some practices of the government, had ripple effects that could hurt the poor by raising the prices of basic goods, such as food and housing, or increasing unemployment rates.

Although Wesley was similar to other Anglican and English Puritan thinkers on his condemnation of idleness, he was radical, in comparison, on other work-related issues, precisely because of his holistic notion of holy work described here. Wesley was unusual in his insistence that the work and consumption habits of wealthy people and nations were to blame, in large part, for poverty and unemployment. The assets and purchases of wealthy people were not private, individual matters, but had social consequences. While many of his contemporaries blamed unemployment and poverty on the idleness of the poor, Wesley blamed it, in part, on the extravagance and greed of the rich: "So wickedly, devilishly false is that common objection, 'They are poor, only because they are idle.' If you saw these things with your own eyes, could you lay out money in ornaments or superfluities?"[84] Often, when Wesley wrote about idleness and poverty in the same sentence, it was not the poor, but the rich, that he was castigating. The idleness and luxury of the rich were significant causes of poverty and unemployment.

Wesley was not denying that there were idle, sinful people among the poor. While others of his time used the distinction between the deserving and undeserving poor as a justification for helping the former and not the latter, Wesley insisted that Christians have a responsibility to seek out the sinful and idle poor, and preach to them the grace of God in Christ.[85] Indeed, he justified field preaching precisely because of its effectiveness at reaching the idle poor.[86]

While other Christian leaders called for the wealthy to give generously to the poor, Wesley insisted that they should not give just a portion of their excess, but everything left to them after providing the necessities and conveniences for their households and businesses. He also insisted that they should not give simply out of generosity, but out of a desire for justice. Excess money actually belonged to the poor, and for the wealthy to keep it for their own purposes would be stealing. Hoarding money and spending it extravagantly were bad for both the bodies of the poor and the souls of the rich.

In contrast to some Protestants, Wesley wrote about the continually increasing wealth of Christians, not so much as a sign of God's favor, but as a potential impediment or danger to Christian life. Successful work that leads to the accumulation of wealth and property over what is necessary for one's household is not a sign of God's blessing, but a sign of human unfaithfulness. It is not a predictor of one's ultimate reward in heaven, but in hell. It is no wonder that Wesley had a more radical call for giving than many of his contemporaries.

Wesley was also radical in the strength of his insistence on socially responsible work and his condemnation of bad work. Bad work would include the work of those who exploit their employees, lower prices on a product to ruin competition, provide poor working conditions, or expose workers or others to chemicals in the work environment. His emphasis on the physical dangers of some types of work or of overwork is striking. He was very aware of the effects of work on body and health. Again echoing Randy Maddox's chapter on health and healing, Wesley's view of work includes a concern for all aspects of human life—from bodily health to moral purity, and from internal peace of the soul to the external organization of society.

Pragmatic Holy Work

Wesley's holistic model of holy work was also pragmatic. One rarely finds in Wesley the high praises of ordinary work that are commonly found in Luther, Calvin, and some Puritan leaders of Wesley's time. Indeed, Wesley often focused on the temptations that work sets before Christians. Even so, he recognized that it was necessary for most people to work in order to support their households and avoid debt. If one has sufficient means not to be employed, then one has the advantage of being free to go about doing good. If one must be employed, then one should choose the employment that would best allow one to support one's household, to avoid debt, and to go about being and doing good. Wesley was pragmatic about work, both as a necessity and as a potential means to a higher end—holiness of heart and life.

There are several striking points here that distinguish Wesley's views from some common Protestant emphases. Wesley, unlike Luther, focused not on making all ordinary, secular work holy, but, instead, on calling all to holy work—to the desire for holiness in their own lives and in the lives of others. One's employment, even the ordinary business of ministry, can either help or hinder one's own holiness and the holiness of others. In the end, Wesley, like many other Christian leaders, was always clear that one's ultimate vocation or calling is the Christian call to love God and neighbor—to holiness of heart and life. One's temporal employment, or any other human activity, is appropriate only as it serves that higher calling.

Second, when Wesley offered practical advice about choosing employment (or a marriage partner) and when he insisted that Methodists should help the poor find better jobs, he went against the claims of Luther and other early Protestants. They believed that one normally fulfilled one's vocation not by *choosing* anything, but by accepting the fixed station in which one was placed and carrying out the responsibilities of that station. One's marriage or one's employment was normally determined by social position, rather than by choice. Writing in a different time and place, Wesley not only assumed that people should choose employment; he actively helped poorer people to leave their "fixed stations" and find better jobs.

Third, according to Wesley, when one chooses one's employment, one normally tries to discern God's will pragmatically, using one's experience and reason to decide what employment would allow one the greatest opportunities for being and doing good.[87] In contrast, many Christians in the seventeenth and eighteenth centuries, and up into the twenty-first century, have described Christian discernment about employment differently. The individual Christian must discern in prayer the particular occupation to which God has called him or her. Moreover, for many Christians, the key component of one's calling is thought to be one's employment. This combination sets before a person an extraordinary burden to discern the correct occupation. It also stands in sharp contrast to Wesley's model, in which one sees and chooses one's work pragmatically, based on its ability to allow one to fulfill one's responsibilities to one's household and further one's higher calling of Christian discipleship or holiness.

IS WESLEY'S VIEW OF WORK OF USE TO CHRISTIANS TODAY?

Is Wesley of use to Christians today as they work and reflect on work? What are some of the distinctive features of work patterns in the United States today?[88] For many working-class, middle-class, and upper-middle-class workers today, Wesleyans and non-Wesleyans alike, the unstated but widely practiced rules for work and wealth are these: gain all you can; spend all you can; borrow all you can; for as long as ever you can. Even the unemployed and working poor often feel pressured by these rules, although they have limited access to the game.

Many workers in the United States gain all they can by working longer hours, under conditions of increasing stress, and at the expense of their health. They gain all they can at the expense of a good night's sleep, time with family and friends, and time in their communities—including their churches. Others gain all they can at the expense of private time, including time for prayer, Scripture reading, and self-reflection. Idleness is not the prevailing sin of most workers in the United States.

Higher-paid professional people (such as doctors, attorneys, and business executives) and some lower-paid professionals (such as pastors) tend to put in the longest hours among workers in the United States. At the other end of the income scale, the lowest-paid workers are also working long hours, often at several jobs, gaining all they can but still unable to provide necessities, much less conveniences, for their families. The chronically unemployed, many living in inner-city neighborhoods with declining employment opportunities due to the flight of businesses to suburbs, smaller cities, or other countries, often find themselves caught in a spiral of poverty, poor health, poor education, violence, and crime. William Julius Wilson argues that the crisis among African-Americans living in urban poverty is caused primarily by lack of employment opportunities.[89]

Many United States workers gain all they can, working for companies that gain all *they* can at the expense of others in the United States and around the world. It is common practice in many companies today to take part in business practices that, by Wesleyan standards, are unethical and harm workers and the larger community. These practices include paying sub-survival wages to low-wage workers, firing long-time workers for the sake of short-term stockholder profits, producing products or by-products that hurt people in body and soul, selling below market prices to drive out competitors, and providing products or services that tempt others to "intemperance."

Workers in the United States spend all they can as well, frequently on unnecessary consumer goods that they do not have time to use. Often, these goods have been produced at the expense of low-wage workers at home or abroad.[90] Consumer goods are a primary marker of status across all income groups in the United States, and people, especially children, are experts at reading status and social class from a person's clothes, car, haircut, and house, as well as other indicators. According to some scholars, many workers in the United States (especially, but not only, in the middle- and upper-income ranges) spend competitively and therapeutically. They buy things in order to buy status in relation to those around them, and they "spend all they can" as an odd therapeutic response to the stress of long work hours.

Many workers in the United States also spend in response to a torrent of advertisements, designed by masters in the ancient art of temptation. This art has been perfected in the modern science of marketing, which seeks to form (some would say "deform") the desires of consumers—including the desires of children. Christians and marketers of consumer goods share a common goal—to form human desire. There are two big differences. First, marketers and Christians seek to form desire toward different ends (i.e., the purchase of a product or the love of God). Second, marketers are better at forming human desire than the average church. They design advertisements scientifically to encourage a certain group to want to buy something they do not really need with money they do not actually have. They may target, for example, eleven-year-old girls; middle-class, suburban teenage boys; or middle-aged white professionals who live in older wealthy neighborhoods, drive Hondas, and read the *New York Times*.

Many in our culture also borrow all the money they can. Indeed, credit card debt continues to rise in the United States. The average household credit card debt is more than $9,000.[91] This cycle of competitive spending and easy credit draws people across income levels and ties them to their need for longer hours of work at higher wages. This cycle perpetuates itself. More spending leads to more debt, which leads to greater pressure to gain all you can by working as hard as you can for as long as ever you can. The working poor and the unemployed poor are subject to the same desires for more money and things but have less access to the means to procure the things they need, much less the additional luxuries they desire.

Further, the profit mentality of the wealthier members of our society, and their desire for a good return on investments, are often used to justify lower-wage jobs without benefits and to excuse other practices that are devastating for low-wage workers. With increased consumer goods, prosperous workers in the United States workers report lower levels of satisfaction instead of higher ones. At the same time, low-wage workers are finding it more difficult simply to survive. As US workers have come to gain, spend, and borrow more than ever, they also give away less than ever. Methodists are not substantially (or any) different from the rest of the population in this regard. Clearly, Wesley's rules for Methodists have been turned on their head.

For many workers today, the old Wesleyan rules to save all you can and give all you can are not really ignored; they were simply never known or considered at all. We live in a culture where many people, including many good people, tend to identify others and themselves by their occupation and their consumer goods, not by their generosity, much less their religious and moral commitments or their "holiness of life and heart." Many workers in our culture, especially middle- and upper-income workers, find their identity and status through jobs and buying power. In many communities throughout the United States, those without jobs or with poorer-paying jobs, along with those who are unable to buy higher-status items, are often looked down upon. Many well-intentioned people in our culture, unwittingly, even unconsciously, view life through a market lens, making choices about what employment to seek, what city to live in, and when to marry and have children, based in part on the values of the market.[92] The problem rests not with a few greedy individuals, but with the comprehensive, often invisible, market lens through which many in the United States view the world.

It is not difficult to understand why middle- and upper-income people often fail to see the problems of the poor, much less to see their own complicity in a system that causes and perpetuates poverty. Most middle- and upper-income people in the United States live and work within spheres that do not overlap significantly with spheres of the poor. Also, the global economy is so complex that conscientious people find it difficult to fathom the impact of US economy and consumer practices on ordinary workers around the world. Because so many people in the United States have failed to see the influence of our economic system on the poor, they are still proud of our system and the values behind it, even seeking to export it to other countries. In the United States, we structure our political and economic institutions to take advantage of worldwide markets and workers for our gain and, we like to think, for their own good. A French journalist, returning to Paris from a trip to New York, "remarked that leafing through a copy of *Forbes* or *Fortune* is like reading the operating manual of a strangely sanctimonious pirate ship."[93]

In a previous article, I described the predicament of middle- and upper-income workers in the United States in this way:

> In their work life and habits, they are "Puritans without a Purpose," working extremely hard, but often without the underlying sense of divine calling

and little leisure or Sabbath. You could also call them "Puritans without a Sabbath."

In their spending and consuming habits, they are "Epicureans on a Fast." They value physical pleasure as much as any generations in recent history and purchase wildly to obtain the objects of their desires, but they have little time or energy left to indulge and to enjoy.

In their family and relational habits, they are "Emotional Ascetics who love to feel good." They value expression of emotion and feeling, perhaps as much or more than any generation before them, yet they have little time or energy for long emotionally fulfilling conversations. . . .and not much to talk about emotionally because they have so little time left in their lives to reflect on life and emotions.[94]

In light of Wesley's work, I will add one more predicament:

Many middle- and upper-income people in the United States are "Pirates with a Pulpit." They (we) not only seek their own good and goods, but also insist on calling the piracy "virtue" and "benevolence." This is less a matter of calculated deceit than of delusion. Pirates with a pulpit are often convinced that they are virtuous prophets and preachers, and, surely, in many aspects of their lives they *are* virtuous.

These predicaments are costly. People in the United States know that something is wrong. A culture would not produce so many self-help books if people did not think they needed help. The increase of stress and stress-related illnesses, of depression and the use of antidepressants, are visible signs of a deeper illness. A visit—especially a prolonged one—to chronically poor neighborhoods reveals other signs of sickness.

John Wesley and many of his contemporaries railed against the idleness of the rich who spent their time in leisure pursuits. If one uses Wesley's broad definition of the rich as those having anything left over after providing the basics for their household, then many in the United States are rich. What then can we say about the underlying problems of the rich (i.e., ordinary middle- and upper-income people) in this country?

In our day, the problem is not the idle rich, but the idolatrous rich. Most middle- and upper-income Americans have lost themselves not in idle diversions, but in extremely hard work on the job and at home and in fast spending everywhere else. Many of us have lost our center, not in the pursuit of immediate physical pleasure or ease, but in the achievements and values of the marketplace—hard work, professional success, markers of that success—and our material possessions. Even many of us who should know better find ourselves huddled around the gods of the marketplace.

And we *do* know better. One cannot read Wesley, or read Scripture for that matter, and not recognize the problem—our complicity in the poverty of others and in the diminishment of our own holiness and others' through our capitulation to market values. Christians within our culture are surely as guilty of sanctimonious piracy as any other group. Perhaps because of our complicity, or perhaps in spite of it (and by the grace of God), we have a vocabulary and framework for reflecting on human sickness—including sanctimonious piracy.

Long-running Christian discussions of sin provide a way to look at the underlying problems and possible solutions. Sin, at its root, has been understood as a turning away from God. Humans often turn away from God—their true center—and toward themselves in pride and selfishness. I have argued elsewhere that the underlying problem for many in the United States is not the sin of pride or self-centeredness, but the loss of a center.[95] Instead of turning away from God and toward self, the person loses himself or herself in finite activities or things in the world.[96] In some cases, a person turns to one focused place or center (e.g., the pursuit of money or devotion to a person). In other cases, the self turns toward multiple finite activities and things—employment, money, material possessions, body, body image, sex, relationships, and so on. Turning away from God and toward finite things (whether one or many) is idolatry.

The idolatry of our time is complicated because middle- and upper-income people often invest themselves frantically in finite things (some good and some bad) but have little opportunity, space, or time to pull back and reflect on the loss of their true center. Moreover, because these same people often have little time for religious community and, particularly, for ongoing spiritual disciplines, they lack a perspective beyond themselves and the finite activities in which they engage. This prevents them from recognizing the extent of their problem or finding in God their ultimate center. Finding one's center in God provides unity, meaning, and judgment to one's finite commitments and activities.

A key role of churches, and many other religious communities and their leaders, is to help those within their communities, and even in the wider culture, to reorient themselves away from the vain attempt to find a center in the pressured daily rush from one finite activity and person to another. Instead, churches can encourage people, even in the rush of these activities (*particularly* in the rush), to recognize their place and the place of their activity in relation to God. The church needs to be careful, of course, that it does not simply become one more finite center of frantic activity.

It is easy to imagine what Wesley might have said in response to the practice of many Christians today who gain all they can, spend all they can, and borrow all they can—for as long as ever they can—at the expense of their own souls and bodies, and those of their neighbors. He might have said to us the same things that he said to eighteenth-century Methodists: "Repent, repent of your vile earthly-mindedness: Renounce the title of

Christians, or prefer, both in your own case and the case of your children, grace to money, and heaven to earth!"⁹⁷ Or he may have said this:

> O ye Methodists, hear the word of the Lord! I have a message from God to all men; but to *you* above all. . . . I fear there is need to apply to some of *you* those terrible words of the Apostle: "Go to, now, ye rich men! Weep and howl for the miseries which shall come upon you. Your gold and silver is cankered, and the rust of them shall witness against you, and shall eat your flesh, as it were fire." Certainly it will, unless ye both save all you can, and give all you can. . . . By the grace of God, begin today!⁹⁸

I doubt that Wesley's fiery eighteenth-century style would be persuasive to most Christians today. Even so, many of Wesley's claims and emphases are remarkably fitting for our time.

In the previous pages, I have reflected on our current context and on Wesley's views; links between the two are apparent. In these final pages, I want to emphasize several ways in which a Wesleyan view of work, vocation, and calling can be relevant today. As I noted above, Wesley's writings about work are found primarily in letters, sermons, and persuasive essays, in which he was not attempting to lay out a complete theology of work, but to convince Christians to work in healthier and holier ways. He was most often speaking as a pastor and taking into account the particular needs, temptations, and problems of his eighteenth-century English context, including the social context of the people he was addressing and of the larger culture. If one begins with the picture of contemporary US society that I described here, what is an appropriate pastoral, Wesleyan response? What parts of Wesley's writings on work, vocation, and calling are useful today, and what parts are useless or even dangerous?

A Wesleyan Reversal of Wesley
(How Not to Appropriate Wesley for Our Time)

On several points, Wesley's views of work are out of place in our context. As Randy Maddox noted in the previous chapter, "We do not truly 'honor our heritage' by shrinking from" criticism of Wesley's views. We seek a "dynamic continuity" that does not simply repeat Wesley but, instead, brings key Wesleyan insights forward in ways that are appropriate for our time.⁹⁹ In relation to work, some of Wesley's teachings are not fitting today without serious revision.

First, Wesley's condemnation of idleness and praises of diligence are not fitting for much of the US population today. It is ludicrous, and even dangerous, to preach diligence to those who give almost every available moment to labor in the workplace and home, and who have only a few minutes each day to themselves and even less time for prayer. Many US workers (especially those of middle and upper incomes) work long hours and find identity in their work and the money it yields. To counsel people like this to throw themselves into their business with all diligence, putting their "whole strength to the work," sparing "no pains," and letting "nothing in [their] business be left undone"[100] is to cheer them in their idolatry. Wesley warned that a Christian should hate "sloth as much as drunkenness" and flee "from idleness as . . . from adultery."[101] For some people in the United States, overwork, not sloth, is the adulterous lover or the drug of choice from which they should flee at the peril of their own souls. Unscheduled, idle time would be a good antidote, rather than a poison, for many workers today.

Second, Wesley's advice to "redeem the time" by getting less sleep (waking up a little earlier each day until one finds the minimum amount of sleep needed) is preposterous in a sleep-deprived culture. Many people in the United States (including children) are getting less sleep than they need each night.[102] The appropriate Wesleyan advice for many people today would thus be to redeem the time by sleeping more, waking up a little later or going to bed a little earlier until one finds how much sleep one needs to feel rested and peaceful.

Third, Wesley's writings on work, calling, and vocation and his insistence on diligence rarely took into account the realities of family and household life. Wesley's own habits of hard work within the Methodist movement were made easier because he did not have children or, for most of his life, a spouse with whom he spent much time. He also had servants. Most employed people today, particularly those caring for children or other family, have tremendous household responsibilities and no servants. And, of course, some people in our culture *are* domestic "servants" (to use the old word), taking care of their own households and also those of wealthier families. A Wesleyan account of holy work must consider the realities of household life and work, and the multiple responsibilities that many people bear on the job and at home.

A Wesleyan Appropriation of Wesley on Work

While some of Wesley's advice on work and time are unhelpful, many of his key points are fitting. I summarize them here as Wesleyan guidelines for work, vocation, and calling.

1. Keep Work in Its Place.

As previously noted, Wesley is pragmatic about work. It has its place. It helps people support their households, avoid debt, and care for others. Christians should choose work by pragmatically calculating what jobs offer the greatest opportunity for being and doing good. Work and money should never be ends in themselves. Indeed, when they are treated as ends, they become dangerous. Many people live as if working, earning, and spending were the center of their lives. These people need no reminders of the great value of work; they need reminders of both the limited purposes of work and the relation of work to the higher ends of holiness.

2. Remember That Work Is Holistic.

As we saw above, Wesley did not separate people's employment from other parts of their lives. He insisted that good work would be good for the bodies and souls of workers and their neighbors; thus, people should seek work that contributes to being and doing good. Work that includes practices or products that hurt others is wrong and should be avoided. Wesley also linked people's work with how they gained, saved, and gave (or did not save and give). Good work that led to wealth that people hoarded or spent frivolously was not, in the end, good for the worker. Wesley also insisted on the link between the gaining, saving, and giving of wealthier people and the survival of poorer people. The irresponsible practices of the wealthy (spending on luxuries while failing to save or give) were a significant cause of unemployment and poverty. At the same time, the holy practices of the wealthy could be a significant remedy to poverty.

As globalization (of communications, of corporations, etc.) has fostered economic connections between various countries, it has also made it more difficult to see the effects of our individual gaining and buying because we have no regular contact with those whose lives have been affected. Wesley's insistence on the holistic nature of human work is particularly important in United States culture, which tends to compartmentalize business matters from other parts of life and to ignore the effects of our practices on other communities around the world. How can people begin to see the relationship between the ways they live, work, and spend, and the ways that others around the world are able (or unable) to live, work, and spend?

3. Avoid Dissipation.

Wesley observed that ordinary employment, like any other activity, could draw a Christian's focus away from God, leaving the Christian dissipated. A dissipated person is one who is "separated from God; that is disunited from his centre."[103] In our culture, the temptations of dissipation are even greater because of the high level of stimuli and activity, the demands for doing many things at once (i.e., multi-tasking), and the steady creep of work into Sundays, evenings, and holidays. Spending is also a source of dissipation. The science of marketing intentionally trains our desires toward consumer goods. This is a science of dissipation from our true ends and desires. If dissipation is the sickness, what is the remedy?

4. Remember the One Thing Needful.

In his sermon "The One Thing Needful," Wesley imagines a stranger, "an intelligent being," observing for the first time the inhabitants of this world.[104] Watching the way they spend their time, the stranger would "surely conclude," first, that "these creatures were designed to be busied about many things," and, second, that the varied goals that people pursued had as their common end self-gratification. "How surprised then would he be" to discover that "the one thing needful" was not any of the things they were busy pursuing, but was, instead, the restoration of the image of God.[105] Wesley described the "one thing needful" in different ways—restoration of the image of God, renewal in love, sanctification, and holiness of heart and life. All of these descriptions point to a renewal of one's nature in the image of God, so that one is holy in heart and life—in one's outward behavior and one's inner thoughts and dispositions. For Wesley, this holiness is the ultimate Christian vocation or calling. Employment and other activities are properly understood and evaluated in relation to the higher Christian vocation of holiness.

Surely, a stranger observing many parts of the United States today might easily conclude, "These creatures were designed to be busied about many things." In our time, as much as in Wesley's time, Christians need to be reminded that in all parts of life, including temporal employment, their true vocation or calling is "the one thing needful." How can people who are "busied about many things" remember the "one thing needful"?

5. Remember the Sabbath.

Wesley was convinced that a Christian could be busy at work or in some other activity and still, with the right intention, remember the "one thing needful." However, he did not give Christians a license for incessant work. He was, as we saw above, brutal in his condemnation of Sabbath-breakers who worked or indulged in diversions on Sundays. Wesley emphasized the special blessing that a Christian would receive by observing the Sabbath. This Sabbath blessing is especially needed in a culture that often makes work and earning the centers of human identity. Perhaps only when we stop working, as an act of faithfulness, are we able to see the emptiness of living as if work were the one thing needful. Daily prayer and other regular spiritual disciplines (Scripture reading, works of mercy, fasting, etc.) can also serve a similar purpose.

In an essay on the Sabbath, Martha Mendelsohn wrote,

> In this long post-Eden stretch, the punishment has become the prize. Lack of a work ethic isn't the problem: the temptation is to spend all our time working. Stalked by technology, snared by our own creations, we have become our own worst taskmasters. We work late and work out weekends, honing

our bodies, dulling our souls. Overtime is the norm. "I'm still at the office!" boasts a friend one Friday night at 10, in the tone she might have used in the past to announce she was in Paris or Hawaii. We worship a new idol: the God of Work. Should we relive the Exodus each Passover only to re-enslave ourselves the rest of the year?[106]

I suspect that, for many middle- and upper-income United States workers, the only way to see their enslavement, much less to begin freeing themselves, is to stop working. If this temporary break from work is meant to foster holiness of life and heart, it cannot be a time devoted only to fun. Instead, to grow in holiness, people must also take time to place themselves before God in the context of a worshiping community and a life of prayer. Worship and prayer remind them to see the smaller goals of their daily work in relation to the ultimate end of their lives in God, who draws them to the one thing needful—the renewal of their true natures to holiness of heart and life.

CHAPTER NINE
RECOVERING *LOS DESAPARECIDOS*[1]

Elaine A. Robinson

WHO ARE *LOS DESAPARECIDOS*?

Across Latin America, the incomprehensible reality of *los desaparecidos*, "the disappeared," permeates the fabric of society. The victims of state violence, *los desaparecidos* are a voiceless, powerless presence in the social consciousness; indeed, they are made present by their continued absence. In the specific case of Argentina, the history of *los desaparecidos* is unique. Under the military dictatorship that ousted the failed government of Isabel Martínez de Perón and held power from 1976 to 1983, not only were adults who opposed the state arrested and never seen or heard from again, but their children were also victims. The children were either born in captivity or taken from their parents as infants and given to families of the ruling military junta to raise as their own, the true identities of these children seemingly erased.[2]

The reality of *los desaparecidos* frames this paper and serves as a metaphor to help us probe the dynamics between Methodism in the United States (in particular, The United Methodist Church) and Methodism "overseas,"[3] between the center and the periphery, in an attempt to open a space where the voices and realities of the *Iglesia Evangélica Metodista Argentina* (IEMA) may become present in our consciousness and, in a larger perspective, begin the work of recovering *los desaparecidos* within the Methodist family itself.[4] My argument will proceed in three movements, exploring (1) the historical dynamics within and between Methodism in Argentina and the United States, (2) whether neocolonialism continues to inhabit The United Methodist Church (UMC) today, and (3) future trajectories for reconstituting the dynamics between what are now constructed—intentionally or not—as Methodism's center and periphery.

HISTORICAL DYNAMICS OF THE RELATIONSHIP BETWEEN US AND ARGENTINE METHODISM

To understand the historical dynamics between Methodism in the United States and in Argentina, the relationship must be placed into a broader historical context, while still focused on the religious history of the past one hundred or so years. Specifically, this context includes the colonial and postcolonial milieu of Argentina, the United Statesian[5] sense of "mission" in the nineteenth century, and the movement in Argentine Methodism for "autonomy," which began at the turn of the twentieth century and reached fruition in the turbulent era of the late 1960s. Throughout this historical overview, we must bear in mind the complexity of these dynamics and the dangers of oversimplifying the historical interrelationships therein.

The Río de la Plata was first colonized in the early sixteenth century by Spain, which introduced Catholicism throughout the region. Although free from colonial rule at a relatively early date, having declared independence in 1810, Argentina struggled to form a representative democracy. This struggle was due to tensions that, even today, exist between the privileged, wealthy center of Buenos Aires (intent on modernizing and guided by a form of liberal, though not strictly European, political ideology), and the provinces (home to gauchos and a rural cultural character, reflecting lower-class interests and a populist political ideology).[6] With the agreement in 1861 to locate the seat of government in Buenos Aires, these tensions were ameliorated sufficiently for the constitution and the federal system to be instituted, though the country has been subject to ongoing tensions between Buenos Aires and the provincial leaders. Significantly, throughout the nineteenth century, the vestiges of colonial rule haunted, or perhaps inspired, the fledgling government. The dream of becoming a modern European democracy often drove the leadership in Buenos Aires to pursue policies and relationships with the West that, in turn, led to a series of internal contestations over the nation's policies, both domestic and foreign.

To this end, Nicolas Shumway has argued that this tension between the center and periphery of Argentina was expressed as competing "guiding fictions" (i.e., the social imagination that helps to define and describe the goals and aspirations of the people). In the case of Argentina, these contradictory guiding fictions resulted in a divisive and destructive "mythology of exclusion," rather than a unifying national ideal.[7] He describes these two positions in the following way:

> [The first is] a liberal, elitist position centered in Buenos Aires and the educated upper classes that advocated success through imitation of Europe and

the United States while denigrating the Spanish heritage, popular traditions, and the mixed-blood masses. Articulate and prolific liberals, from Moreno to the Rivadavians to Sarmiento to Mitre, promoted their exclusivist ideologies while stereotyping their detractors as barbaric, unprogressive, and racially inferior.... The other current of thought... is an ideologically messy, ill-defined, often contradictory tendency (or tendencies) which could be populist (caudillos like Artigas and Güemes), reactionary (conservative ecclesiastics and Rosas), nativist (Bartolomé Hidalgo's gauchesque), or genuinely federalist and progressive (Urquiza and late Alberdi).[8]

According to Shumway, the opposition to liberalism, while never consistent in its ideological understanding, has articulated over time the most pervasive sense of Argentine "nationalism."

As these opposing and contradictory guiding fictions competed for the heart and soul of the nation, the influx of Protestant missionaries from Europe and the United States was sometimes welcomed by those in power, the liberals of Buenos Aires, despite the nation's official participation in the Roman Catholic Church. Indeed, the *culture* that these missionaries carried and conveyed was often as important as the religion to the ruling elite, since they envisioned Argentina as becoming a modern Western democracy with a thriving capitalist economy. Ironically, while Argentina was struggling to form its collective consciousness, the United States continued to deepen and pursue its own guiding fiction, a social imagination that drove US policies at home and abroad. Once known as "manifest destiny," and sometimes referred to as "the American way of life," this guiding fiction has cast its long shadow on Argentina and Latin America in a myriad of ways.

In her study of individual autonomy in the United States, Myra Jehlen argues that the ideals of liberalism that grew out of the European Reformation and the Enlightenment, such as individualism, the right to private property, and representative government, found a home and a material body in the New World, a development she refers to as "American Incarnation."[9] The concept of American incarnation suggests that

> Americans saw themselves as building their civilization out of nature itself, as neither the analogue nor the translation of Natural Law but its direct expression. Fusing the political with the natural, human volition with its object, and hope with destiny, they imagined an all-encompassing universe that in effect healed the lapsarian parting of man and his natural kingdom.[10]

Jehlen goes on to argue that the "liberal ideal fused with the material landscape" in the nation's self-understanding and turned "America" into a symbol or myth of building civilization out of wilderness through self-reliance and self-sufficiency.[11] In other words, "[t]he American Dream, whose rhetoric most often invokes family and home, is a dream of the Pilgrim's homecoming—a vision, finally, not of voyages and breached frontiers, but of safe arrivals."[12] This metaphor of the end of the Pilgrim's progress helps to flesh out Jehlen's claim that, in "the American incarnation, the Protestant soul acquired a newly powerful body."[13] It is, in a manner of speaking, this newly powerful body, this ideal of having arrived, that traveled to Latin America and Argentina with a guiding fiction that appealed directly to the liberal elites in Buenos Aires, who were struggling for control of the Republic and the validation of their social imagination and power.

The arrival of Methodism in the nineteenth century to the Río de la Plata is located amid these underlying ideological dynamics. The missionaries of The Methodist Episcopal Church (MEC) in the United States—though likely unaware of this symbolic sense of American incarnation—nonetheless brought their "American way of life" to Argentina, along with their Bibles and Methodist hymnals. The 1832 General Conference of the MEC recommended that the bishops and the Missionary Society establish a mission in South America.[14] As a result, Fountain E. Pitts made an exploratory trip to Rio de Janeiro, Montevideo, and Buenos Aires in 1835 and recommended the establishment of missions in Rio de Janeiro and Buenos Aires to the General Conference of 1836. The first missionary sent to Buenos Aires was John Dempster, who arrived in December 1836.

Due to a financial crisis, the Missionary Society curtailed its mission in Buenos Aires, and Dempster returned to the United States. The newly formed congregation in Buenos Aires continued the work that Dempster had begun. It organized a society for the promotion of Christian worship and asked the Missionary Society to permit it to use the half-completed building. The Missionary Society agreed, and the first Methodist church in South America was formally opened in 1843. This congregation took charge of the Methodist mission for some thirteen years, until, in December 1856, the Missionary Society sent William Goodfellow to direct the missionary activity in South America. Because language is such a powerful means of conveying culture, it is important to note that, up to this point, the missionary work—including worship services—had always been conducted in English.

Following some failed attempts to begin using Castellano, the national language of Argentina, Goodfellow sent a young member of the Argentine mission to study theology at Ohio Wesleyan University. Juan Francisco Thomson, a Scot raised in Argentina, returned as an ordained minister of the MEC, and on May 25, 1867, he formally began to preach in Castellano. The following year—because the Methodist mission was a regional, rather than a national body—Thomson began to preach in Castellano in Montevideo, Uruguay. From then on, although the work in

English continued, the Missionary Society focused on spreading the gospel in Castellano.

In 1893, the Methodist work in South America had grown sufficiently to become an annual conference with a bishop from the United States. Argentina, Uruguay, and Paraguay integrated into the Annual Conference of South America, along with the missions in Peru and Chile. In 1901, the Conferences of Chile and Peru organized separately. In 1910, the Annual Conference of South America changed its name to the Annual Conference of South America, East—a title that remained until 1946, when it became the Annual Conference of the Río de la Plata. In 1954, as a result of the organization of the Provisional Annual Conference in Uruguay, the Methodists in Argentina took the name of the Argentine Annual Conference. Finally, the work in the southern part of Argentina developed, and, beginning in 1963, it was organized as the Provisional Annual Conference of Patagonia. Today, the Argentine Annual Conference and the Provisional Annual Conference of Patagonia form the Evangelical Methodist Argentine Church (IEMA).

In his essay "'Por una Iglesia con Alma Nacional': Nacimiento y Ocaso de un Sueño" ("'For a Church with a National Soul': The Birth and Twilight of a Dream"), Daniel A. Bruno traces the movement to create a national church, independent of the MEC. This movement occurred in the years 1917–19, some eighty years after the first Methodist missionary arrived, and some twenty-five years after becoming an annual conference.[15] Significantly, Bruno's essay suggests that the dynamics present in the nation's politics were often replicated in the church's independence movement. He also demonstrates the control—sometimes subtle and sometimes overt—that was exercised over Argentine Methodism by the church in the United States.

The nationalization movement began in response to the 1910 Congress of Edinburgh, which deemed that Latin America was already a Christian continent and, thus, was not a proper concern for mission. As a result, representatives from the Protestant missions in the region were not invited to Edinburgh. The Annual Conference of South America stood in direct opposition to the Edinburgh statement, believing that a strong stance against Catholicism was necessary. It was disappointed further by the limited response of the General Conference of the MEC in 1912, when it considered the position of the Congress of Edinburgh. A group of clergy and lay members in Argentina began to think that nationalizing The Methodist Church was the only real option for growing the missionary work in the nation.[16] They surmised that the US church could not fully understand the needs and conditions of Argentina.

Under the direction of Bishop W. F. Oldham, this nationalizing movement petitioned the Annual Conference and voiced for the first time their desire for eventual "absolute independence." As an interim measure toward that goal, the movement requested the establishment of a national society for evangelization, arguing that the people of a country are better equipped to evangelize their own nation than outside missionaries.[17] At the same time, they emphasized that they sought neither an organic nor a sectarian separation from the "mother" church.[18] Although Bishop Oldham allowed the formation of a mission society within the Annual Conference of South America, it included both those who supported and those who opposed the idea of nationalization and, thus, made consensus impossible. Even so, through the debates and actions of this initial nationalization movement, the language and fundamental ideas for achieving autonomy were formulated.

It took another fifty years to realize the dream of an Argentine Methodist Church with a national soul. The establishment of an autonomous church arose out of the work of the Commission on the Structure of Methodism Overseas (COSMOS), which began in 1964 and officially concluded in 1972 (though the greater part of the Commission's work had been completed by 1968). COSMOS was established by the 1960 General Conference to consider the relationship between the US church (then called The Methodist Church) and the central conferences and affiliated autonomous churches. Undoubtedly, the creation of COSMOS was influenced by a number of global factors, including the revolutionary situation across Latin America, the formation of The United Methodist Church, the dissolution of the Central Jurisdiction of The Methodist Church, and the politically charged atmosphere of the United States in the 1960s. Increasingly, the Latin American Central Conference pushed for changes in the structure of The Methodist Church that would enable the Methodists of Latin America to develop churches and missions corresponding to their particular situations. For example, in 1968, the bishop and executive secretary of the Annual Conference of Argentina wrote to Bishop Richard Raines, COSMOS chairman:

> The fact that basic decisions are made by the General Conference, an organism which legislates at a great distance and in a completely different environment from the place where the testimony is made, makes it very difficult to understand the legislation and often more difficult to apply it. It seems impossible that an identical world legislation be applicable to the varying situations that the Church must confront in countries differentiated by history, tradition, race, language, environment, culture, and many other factors.[19]

The letter closes with a request for the 1968 General Conference to pass an "enabling act" that would permit The Methodist Church in Argentina to form an affiliated autonomous church.

In 1972, Carlos T. Gattinoni identified the strengths associated with autonomy. Three characteristics were highlighted: (1) "autonomous churches . . . relate more significantly to their own countries. . . . They cease to feel in any way as foreigners among their own people," (2) "[they have] flexibility in matters of structure," and (3) "autonomy favors the indigenization of the church."[20] Gattinoni also cited the sermon delivered by José Miguez Bonino at the inaugural service of the IEMA, which summarized the general sense and atmosphere of the church in Argentina when it was realizing its autonomous status: "Simply, we have tried to create a space where we can meet in search of our mission. . . . Autonomy for us is only a space, a meeting-place, a small area of liberty to let us become prisoners in the chains that belong to our condition of a servant church, here and now, servant of Jesus Christ and therefore of all."[21] The pervasive sense was that autonomy, above all else, would enable the church to better serve God and the inbreaking reign of God on earth. Although driven by contextual awareness, ultimately, they expressed a strong theological justification for the creation of a place of their own.[22]

Today, the IEMA continues as a small denominational presence in Argentina but remains only loosely "connected" to other Methodist churches in Latin America and beyond. The regional body in Latin America, the Council of Latin American Evangelical Methodist Churches (CIEMAL), was established in 1969, but it has never functioned as a legislative or administrative body of The Methodist Church in Latin America. It provides limited mutual support, planning, and programming.[23] Beyond Latin America, as an affiliated autonomous church of the UMC, the IEMA continues to receive special offerings through the General Board of Global Ministries, though less than is given to the central conferences, particularly in light of the budget cuts experienced in recent years. The IEMA is granted presence at and participation in the General Conference, but without voting privileges. Despite its wish to remain in "fellowship" with The United Methodist Church and its emphasis that it did not seek separation or isolation, the UMC, in many ways, has moved away from Argentina and toward churches that are structurally "closer to home," though not geographically closer. This seeming lack of attention to and interest in the autonomous Methodist churches in Latin America is the subject to which we now turn.

NEOCOLONIALISM AND EXILE WITHIN THE UNITED METHODIST CHURCH?

United Methodists who have participated in international gatherings of Methodists recognize, at times, an underlying framework or ideology—conscious or not—that belies the stated theology and intentions of the UMC. Until we are able to unmask these dynamics and raise the awareness of United Statesians, it seems unlikely that Latin American Methodist churches, such as the one in Argentina, will be heard and seen as full and complete members of the Methodist family. Speaking metaphorically, we might say that *los desaparecidos* must become a constant presence in our consciousness. It is this task to which we now turn: first, through highlighting the subtle ways in which the UMC continues to marginalize and render invisible the affiliated autonomous churches in Latin America; and, second, by means of postcolonial theory and diaspora theology, which enable us to better understand the dynamics that function to maintain the United States as the "center" of Methodism.

Bruce Robbins's book *A World Parish? Hopes and Challenges of The United Methodist Church in a Global Setting* provides one example of the ways in which the UMC perpetuates *los desaparecidos*. Written for a general church audience, *A World Parish?* deals directly with the question of the marginalization of autonomous (autocephalous and autochthonous) churches, while proposing a new structure for the UMC. Although Robbins, as the former general secretary of the General Commission on Christian Unity and Interreligious Concerns, recognizes, on one level, the problems related to paternalism and economic inequalities, on another level, the language of his book reinforces the patterns of center/periphery and dominance/dependency that he would seek to alter.[24] These patterns within the UMC function to render the church in Argentina—as well as Latin America as a whole—invisible or, at least, peripheral. In other words, the Methodist family in Argentina *disappears* from our consciousness in the United States and, linguistically, is rendered as *los desaparecidos*.[25]

First, the nature of the language used by Robbins serves to mark the affiliated autonomous churches as "other." Most significant is his repeated use of the adjective "American" to refer to the church in the United States. Although the examples are numerous, two will suffice to make this point. In his section entitled "Am I an American Methodist?" Robbins writes:

> Could every United Methodist answer this question positively? A quick response might be, "Of course not!" How could the thousands of United Methodists in North Katanga province of Zaire say, "I am an American Methodist"? Well, maybe their bishop does go to the United States twice a year for extended stays to attend the Council of Bishops meeting.... But they have never been to the U.S. How can they be American Methodists?[26]

At no point does Robbins acknowledge that "America" includes Canadians and Mexicans in the North, not to mention countless Central and South Americans who share the continental designation. Perhaps, because he is dealing with central conferences at this point and, thus, focuses on Africa and Asia, he is making a geographical distinction only. However, at the close of the book, Robbins refers to Methodist churches "that emerged from the American Methodist tradition" and claims that if his structural recommendations were implemented by The United Methodist Church, "then Latin American Methodists would be very interested in joining."[27] At this point, the language of the center (United Methodism in the United States) and the periphery (Latin America) becomes evident.

In calling attention to this linguistic oversight, we can turn again to Jehlen's study and her exploration of the myth of "America." In her discussion of Columbus and the "discovery" of "America," she notes that a number of contemporary scholars understand this interpretation as a later development related to the *settling* of the land, rather than to Columbus's first encounter with it. Even so, independence from Britain, the world's great power, vested the United States with a sense of destiny and power that was signified by the term "America." Jehlen explains that "the identification has never wavered: the reference to America is always clear and never signifies Canada or Mexico, let alone any country in South America."[28] In this regard, the work of Edward Said is illuminating. In his landmark study, *Orientalism*, Said wrote that "words such as 'Orient' and 'Occident' correspond to no stable reality that exists in natural fact. Moreover, all such geographical designations are an odd combination of the empirical and imaginative."[29] One can include "America" under this logic. It is a long-standing linguistic usage that continues to imply that the United States is dominant, central, and destined by God.

Robbins's language certainly is not anomalous in the United Statesian Methodist tradition or the UMC, whose linguistic practices often denote centric thinking. A case in point is the establishment of COSMOS in the 1960s, which was guilty of placing US Methodism at the center. Indeed, a few thoughtful church leaders pointed to the Commission's title, which used the word "overseas" to designate all churches beyond the geographical boundaries of the United States. In 1965, Bishop Ralph Dodge wrote that "the very name of this Commission demonstrates a prevailing concept of American Methodism and may well be a *major* cause for requesting autonomy. Every nation, every conference, every individual wishes to be at the center of things rather than on the periphery."[30] Similarly, Harry C. Spencer, general secretary of the Television, Radio, and Film Commission of The Methodist Church, also noted that "the phrase 'overseas' in the name of this Commission is an added proof of the fact that the General Conference and The Methodist Church feels itself to be based in the U.S. and is considering how the church abroad can be related to the church at home."[31]

Robbins's book offers an example—which he seeks to counter—of the ideology that places the UMC at the center. Reflecting on the November 1990 meeting of the Council of Bishops, Robbins notes that the Global

Nature of the Church Task Force reported on a plan for United Methodism to become five separate regions, located in the United States, Europe, Africa, Asia, and Latin America. He writes, "In terms of Latin America, they were envisioning that the independent Methodist churches of Latin America would 're-join' The United Methodist Church."[32] Robbins goes on to say that, despite his enthusiasm for the global vision, he was "alarmed because the UM bishops were making plans for people from other churches and had not even talked with them! None of the Latin American churches that would make up a region were part of the discussion."[33] To his credit, Robbins raised this issue with the bishops and, on their behalf, contacted the autonomous churches about the ongoing conversation on the church's global vision. Although beyond the scope of this paper, a more thorough study of the contemporary UMC would likely uncover widespread use of language and practices that continue to place the United States at the center and Latin America (as well as Africa, Asia, and Europe) at the periphery.

Theoretically, two related theories and bodies of literature would help us to understand the dynamics at work and, perhaps, also raise awareness in the UMC of the need for internal changes in ideology and theology, rather than external changes, such as new structures and programs, as the first step toward a functional connection grounded in the reality of God. These theoretical resources can be expressed as postcolonial theory and diaspora theology (or a theology of exile). While not explicitly connected with either of these theories, the work of José Miguez Bonino bears clear affinities to them and helps to deepen and develop the insights to be gleaned, particularly in relation to the dynamics between Argentine and US Methodism.

Postcolonial Theory

The relationship between The Methodist Church and its mission in Argentina can be classified as a neocolonial relationship. This assessment is based upon the original mission to the Río de la Plata, the exclusive use of the English language for over thirty years, the training of indigenous pastors in the United States, and the requirement that Central Conferences apply and be approved for autonomy by the General Conference (after first being granted an "enabling act" by the same body). In *Doing Theology in a Revolutionary Situation*, Miguez Bonino examined the "two fundamental historical projects" that occurred in Latin America: "Spanish colonialism (Roman Catholicism) and North American neocolonialism (Protestantism)." Bonino argued that "a Christian can only understand himself in Latin America when he discovers, analyzes, and takes a stand concerning these historical relationships of his faith."[34] For Miguez Bonino, "to unmask and expose the ideological misuse of Christianity as a tool of oppression" is the first step toward "a rediscovery of the true meaning of discipleship."[35] It means "awakening the Christian conscience."[36]

Postcolonial theory understands itself as "a theoretical resistance to the mystifying amnesia of the colonial [or neocolonial] aftermath. It is a disciplinary project devoted to the academic task of revisiting, remembering and, crucially, interrogating the colonial past."[37] In terms of the present study, we can suggest that postcolonial theory enables the UMC to remember and revisit its neocolonial past, in order to root out aspects that continue to impede the relationships of equality and mutuality that are demanded by the gospel. Even further, we can suggest that the almost non-existent relationship between the UMC and the affiliated autonomous church in Argentina represents a form of "amnesia," which is still filled with the persistent, "residual traces and memories" of a colonizer/colonized relationship.[38] An example of this "amnesia" is found in the archival materials of COSMOS: piercing analyses of the relationship between the United States and Latin America were written and considered by the commission, including proposals to reduce the power of the US church within United Methodism. Today, US Methodism in general has little awareness of the Latin American situation or of the need (or desire) to limit the power of the US church within the larger UMC.

At stake in the process of remembering the past is what Edward Said has referred to as "decentered consciousness," that is, a form of engagement where

> instead of seeking common unity by appeals to a center of sovereign authority, methodological consistency, canonicity, and science, . . . [we] offer the possibility of common grounds of assembly between [activities]. They are, therefore, planes of activity and praxis, rather than one topography commanded by a geographical and historical vision locatable in a known center of . . . power.[39]

Moving toward "decentered consciousness" is no easy task for the UMC, particularly in an era when the United States has conceived of itself as an "empire." Why was "America" not shocked when a senior advisor to President Bush was quoted as saying, "We're an empire now, and when we act, we create our own reality"?[40] Why did the various levels that compose the UMC in the United States, the president's official church, fail to speak out loudly and consistently against the centering of power and "reality" in the United States? While a number of reasons can be postulated, the question must here remain rhetorical. Nonetheless, as Edward Said has contended, "we should . . . take scrupulous note of how—to mention the most obvious—in Central and Latin America, as well as in the Middle

East, Africa, and Asia, the United States has replaced the great earlier empires as *the* dominant outside force."[41]

Although Said first used the term "empire" in 1975 to refer to the United States and its political and military intervention in the governments of Latin America, Miguez Bonino used the term in 1995 to illuminate "the developed world, rich, technological, democratic, and educated—which turns in upon itself and raises barriers in the face of the . . . Third World." According to Miguez Bonino, the developed world uses the countries of the "Third World" as buffer states to insulate itself and surrogate states and to feed its own interests, while ignoring *terrae incognitae*—those states that have been abandoned as of no use to the center.[42] In other words, economic and political interests are of primary concern to the United States—both despite and because of its religious language—and the UMC is a part of, and often identifies itself with, the United States. However, we could suggest that a number of Resolutions of the UMC do call those policies into question. Even so, does the practice of The United Methodist Church embody and live out its official proclamations and theological pronouncements, or does it continue to participate more directly in the vision of "America" as the preferred way of life and culture, and as God's destined nation? The affluenza that affects the United States exerts a strong pull on Christians, who are not exempt from the mythic quality of the "American way of life."

Like the United States, the UMC must confront complex issues related to economic inequalities between the "center" and the "periphery" of the church. Many central conferences and affiliated autonomous churches depend upon financial support from the US jurisdictions. In this situation, traditional liberal economic policies, emphasizing the "American dream," in which hard work can lead to economic prosperity, belie the policies that have contributed to impoverishing the two-thirds world. For example, The Methodist Church's mission in Argentina was built on the financial support of the United States. The US church even dictated how the funds were used in Argentina until the 1960s.

The IEMA sought to become financially self-sustaining as part of its quest for autonomy. Unfortunately, the complexities of economic and political policies of both the US and Argentine governments have made such self-sufficiency a difficult prospect. In fact, Argentina was once considered to be on the verge of entering the ranks of fully developed nations but experienced a dramatic reversal in 1999. Until the UMC is able to recognize the powerful draw of the "American" ideology that holds sway over its Christian commitments, financial imbalances will continue to generate dependency. This financial situation masks what is really at stake: human dignity and the flourishing of life. As Miguez Bonino has argued, "development is not seen as merely economic or structural change; rather, there is a strong emphasis on the human dimension," which is consistent with the gospel message.[43] The Christian commitment to upholding life (as Miguez Bonino has suggested, "for life and against death"[44]), a commitment to the orphan, widow, stranger, and marginalized person, suggests that human life and its ability to flourish are at the forefront of Christian discipleship. John Wesley's various and well-known social commitments certainly support this point from a Wesleyan theological perspective.

In sum, postcolonial theory suggests that the UMC must become conscious of its subtle neocolonial tendencies in relationship to churches located in nations other than the United States.[45] Moreover, the UMC is called to overcome its amnesia—the forgetfulness of who we have been and what we have done—both as a church and as participants in a larger society that claims to be "America." Building on the assertion of Miguez Bonino in 1975, that *"Latin America has discovered the basic fact of its dependence,"*[46] we are led to conclude that the United States has yet to discover the basic fact of its dominance and the debilitating and unjust consequences of its lack of consciousness and praxis.

Diaspora Theology

Closely related to postcolonial theory is the theology of exile, or diaspora theology, which argues that the marginalized must remember and reconstruct their history of marginalization and dependency in order to create a new reality. "Reality" is, thus, a function of perspective, historically and culturally located, and in constant flux. In other words, diaspora theology accepts "a multitude of constructs reflecting and engaging a variety of realities and experiences across history and culture."[47] No single culture, people, or nation has a "God's eye view" of reality. Linguistically and ideologically, a group may attempt to act as the omniscient narrator of reality, but history and the reality of God continue to disrupt this discourse.

Fernando Segovia argues that "the logic and discourse of colonialism demand, at their most fundamental level, a binomial opposition between the 'we' and the 'they': empire and possessions; colonizers and colonized; center and margins."[48] There is an inherent valuation of the superiority of the center over the margins and a demand for the margins to submit to the control of the center. Moreover, Segovia claims that "modern Christian theology has been, by and large, a theology of colonization,"[49] a description that could be applied to much of the Wesleyan theology produced over the past three hundred years. By contrast, the diaspora theology he envisions, a form of liberation theology, is located in and speaks from the margins. It is "a theology that seeks to re-view, re-claim, and re-phrase its own matrix and voice in the midst of a dominant culture and theology." Segovia's words echo those of Miguez Bonino from twenty years earlier, when he asserted, "in time we [Latin Americans] shall have to recover and incorporate both our colonial and our neocolonial past in our historical consciousness."⁵⁰ Although Segovia's theology of exile is specific to the situation of Latino/a Americans in the United States, the conceptual framework of diaspora theology enables us to re-view and re-consider the dynamics of the relationship between the UMC and the IEMA.⁵¹

Diaspora theology utilizes the motif of the journey, a movement from a place of origin to another world. The journey is defined by Segovia as "that which is known and to which one belongs is left behind for an encounter with that which is unknown and within which one dwells as 'other.' "⁵² The new and unknown situation can result in an exile that may be temporary, ongoing, or permanent. As the experience of "otherness" continues over time, it joins with the sense of "belonging," such that "the exile ends up living in two worlds and no world at the same time, with a twofold voice from no-where."⁵³ It is this sense of being in the world but not of the world, and of confronting the contradictions, challenges, and plurality between these worlds, that best characterize the "otherness" of diaspora theology. Significantly, because Segovia understands this theology to arise out of multiple experiences in diverse places under varied circumstances, he does not make the mistake of turning the "other" into an ontological category. Instead, it is out of the particularity of their context that those who live in exile must find voice and posit a reality that resists and disturbs the center.

Building upon Segovia's theological framework, the situation of the IEMA in relation to the UMC displays a twofold sense of "exile." The first "exile" of Argentine Methodists occurred in the nineteenth century, when missionaries established the Methodist presence in the Río de la Plata. The neocolonial dimensions of that relationship meant that the Methodists became the "other": "other" to the predominant Catholic tradition in Argentina, "other" to the church in the United States, and "other" to themselves, in the sense that the church leaders were from the United States, and the language of Methodism was English, not Castellano. In fact, even as the leadership began to pass into the hands of Latin Americans, it was often the case that those leaders had been trained within the US system and were "locked into dependency upon it."⁵⁴ As we discussed previously, the first uprising occurred in 1917–19 and set the stage for deepening and re-thinking the sense of being "foreigners" in their own land. This history of the first exilic period raises the question of whether today's central conferences are experiencing a first exile. Are the leaders in Africa and the Philippines imbued with a North American United Methodist consciousness and praxis? Is a sense of exile within their own countries and among their own people now present? Is the disparity between the salaries of African bishops, supported by the structures of the UMC, and the African clergy and laity one indicator of exile?

The second "exile" of Argentine Methodists, the exile from the Methodist family, occurred after they achieved autonomy, but it has unfolded in such a gradual manner as to be almost unnoticed. Although not desired by the Argentines, nor considered to be the outcome of the autonomy process, the IEMA lives, in many ways, in exile, as part of the Methodist diaspora, more than thirty-five years after achieving its autonomy. Certainly, the Argentines are not alone; other affiliated autonomous churches in Latin America and beyond are experiencing a similar sense of exile.[55] As Segovia indicates, each situation represents a unique configuration of history, culture, and perspective that should not be considered a univocal discourse. As such, we are compelled to stop short of suggesting that "a" Methodist diaspora exists.

Although we can only speculate on the causes of the second exile, several plausible, though provisional, explanations can be ventured. First, and perhaps most obvious, is the case of the limited financial resources of the United States and The United Methodist Church. A "hierarchy of needs" (though not in the sense of Maslow's theory) is established by the closeness of a church to the center. Structurally, the central conferences occupy a position nearer to the center than do the affiliated autonomous churches, and, as a result, resources are parceled out according to this sense of kinship. This hierarchy, in part, is reflected in Robbins's understanding of the need to restructure The United Methodist Church, and in his proposal to divide the UMC into five regions to create better relationships among the various structural parts and a church that is less centered on the United States. Yet, a very similar proposal to the one advocated by Robbins was rejected by COSMOS in the 1960s. As previously noted, the US bishops continued to work toward a global church during the late 1980s and early 1990s; however, their vision of the global church was envisioned and reconstructed from the center.[56] A proposal for restructuring presented to the 2008 General Conference, which failed to be ratified by the Annual Conferences, suffered from a similar centrist logic.[57]

Another possible explanation of the second exile is the desire of the Methodists in the United States to retain control or the dominant position in the church. This point relates, of course, to the question of neocolonial vestiges within the contemporary UMC. To prove such an assertion is difficult at best, especially because one cannot assume a single overarching narrative. Even so, the long-standing patterns of power imbalances—of developed/dependent worlds—driven by cultural factors beyond the church, especially foreign, defense, and economic policies, combined with the complex situation internal to Argentina, provide for a plausible explanation. In 2001, Franklin Guerrero of the General Board of Global Ministries emphasized that

Latin America has been an afterthought. Most of our funds and missionaries go to areas that need to be civilized and "Christianized" ... China, India and Africa. We're strengthening and developing the United Methodist Church in Russia. We have great opportunities to help the children of Africa and build a college in Africa. It's time to correct history and deal with the areas that have been forgotten.[58]

Concurring with Guerrero, Wilson Boots added, "Except for the conflict with Cuba, natural disasters and the drug war in Columbia, they've been forgotten after the Cold War of the 70's and 80's."[59] Lacking a decided need to pay attention to Latin America—such as the domino theory provided—and lacking a sense that Latin America needs to be civilized to benefit from the "American way of life," the region gradually "disappeared."

A remarkable study, issued as the "Report of the Latin American Task Force" by the Board of Missions of the UMC circa 1971–72, identified the goals of the Task Force, two of which are of particular note: (1) "Sensitize the United Methodist Church to the issues confronting the Latin American churches," and (2) "Raise questions that will lead to a redirection of the power of the United Methodist Church in relationship to the Latin American churches."[60] In a later section, the report called for a change in the economic relationships between the churches in the United States and Latin America, as well as support for the revolutionary struggle to overcome the systems of exploitation and dependency in Latin America. Significantly, it recommended that

> North American churches create and maintain the kind of communication and consultation with Latin American churchmen [sic] that would permit the views of those churchmen to be heard more widely among all North American Christians (not just those related to the programs of mission agencies) and enable us to face together the common religious and social problems of the hemisphere.[61]

The report seemed to wrestle with what Miguez Bonino identified as "a crisis of conscience, when Christians discover that their churches have become the ideological allies of foreign and national forces that keep countries in dependence."[62]

Today, we are compelled to ask whether the crisis of conscience that was arising in the 1960s, which was forced upon the church by the revolutionary situation in Latin America as well as in the United States and within the church itself, sputtered and died out before it had a chance to interrupt the guiding fiction and dominant ideology of the United States that is deeply embedded within the UMC. Can we, today, make the claim that the United Methodist churches in the United States understand the imbalances created by neocolonial relationships and their ongoing effects in Latin America? Can we say that our church leaders at the highest levels, or those who fill the pews every Sunday, are sensitive to the multiple ways in which the center continues to silence, minimize, and erase the periphery? From within their situation of exile, the Argentine Methodists have continued to resist, giving voice to social, economic, and political concerns rooted in a deep sense of Christian mission. However, Argentina and the IEMA cannot unmask and remake the power imbalances alone; they cannot force the United States and the UMC to hear and see. In the end, the United States and the UMC are called to accountability and to uphold justice and human dignity by working to decenter themselves—to develop a decentered consciousness. As Edward Said has suggested in building upon Adorno's theory, in contemporary societies we must "stand away from 'home' in order to look at it with the exile's detachment. For there is considerable merit in the practice of noting the discrepancies between various concepts and ideas and what they actually produce. We take home and language for granted; they become nature and their underlying assumptions recede into dogma and orthodoxy."[63]

TRAJECTORIES FOR RE-VISIONING THE DYNAMICS OF METHODISM

A pervasive ideology of the center—a lack of consciousness—continues to undermine the stated theology of Methodism in the United States. Until the UMC and, in particular, the church in the United States recognize and repent of the ongoing patterns of center/periphery and dominance/dependency, genuine theological conversation will be unable to break the stranglehold. Clearly, the ongoing work of repenting for racism against the African Americans and Native Americans in the US church is merely the tip of the iceberg.

It may seem inappropriate to speak of the UMC as needing to recover *los desaparecidos* because, in reality, the Argentine Methodists have not disappeared, but, to the contrary, are quite alive. Yet, the logic of center and periphery continues to silence and exile the Methodist Church in Argentina. The language of disappearance is not entirely unlike the history of *los desaparecidos* in Argentina, where violence perpetrated by the dominant class—at times supported by US policies or ideology—resulted in the loss of voice, life, and presence of countless persons. Perhaps the use of "violence" is a bit too strong, but strong language and a shocking metaphor might be required to "prick the ears" of United Statesians. Indeed, because the Methodists of Argentina exist fully, it is the UMC that must act to recover what has been lost to us: children of God who are our family, our brothers and sisters, our flesh and blood, our body—the Body of Christ—many of whom continue to suffer in conditions of poverty, violence, and oppression, conditions that are antithetical to the gospel of Jesus Christ. At this point, it is possible to trace only a few trajectories toward recovering *los desaparecidos* and renewing the UMC and Wesleyan theology today.

Ending Denominational Exile

I have argued that exile exists within the denomination, and it is clear that structures need to change in order to move toward greater equity and participation, despite economic imbalances that cannot easily be restructured. However, prior to structural or programmatic changes, the UMC faces a situation in which the center must become deeply aware of and sensitive to the ways in which the language and practices of the church reinforce neocolonial patterns. We can speak theologically of how such patterns are broken open and recreated by the inbreaking reign of God, but until we unmask the dynamics and become disturbed by them, we cannot live out this theology. As long as the United States prefers to take the seat at the head of the table, we will not be able to renew the church or contemporary Wesleyan theology.

Learning from the Other

Second, the logic of neocolonialism has been that of the US church and its missionaries teaching and modernizing the "overseas" churches. Yet, one need only take note of the fact that Christianity is flourishing in the Southern hemisphere and evaporating in the United States to understand that there is something that Christian sisters and brothers in Latin America, as well as Asia, Africa, and Eastern Europe, can teach the UMC.[64] Perhaps they can enlighten the UMC on the process of reconstructing a social imagination, a guiding fiction, through becoming conscious of other historical realities and narratives. Perhaps they can enable the UMC to consider how the church may better serve to voice concerns vis-à-vis the US government and its policies and practices, enabling the UMC to grasp the logic of life against death that struggles against "empire" and the "American way of life" as the only way to experience life in its fullness. Perhaps they can point the UMC toward structures that would function to empower rather than dominate the global Methodist family. Perhaps every United Methodist seminary student should be required to take a course in the history and theology of Methodism beyond the boundaries of the United States, or, better, be required to spend a semester in a Methodist-related seminary in what is referred to as the "two-thirds world" (including learning that country's language as a prerequisite to the global semester). Of course, suggestions such as these are more easily conceived than instituted, but radical changes are warranted and should be considered.

Liberating the Center

Finally, it becomes clear that a new phase of liberation theology must be pursued by Wesleyan and Methodist theologians: a liberation theology that aims now at liberating the center—Methodism in the United States. Some work in this direction has unfolded in recent years. The Oxford Institute, when it invites Néstor Miguez and J. C. Park to present plenary lectures, chips away at the center. The compilation of essays edited by Joerg Rieger and John Vincent, *Methodist and Radical*, moves in this direction and represents an important contribution.[65] Even so, these actions are only a beginning, and widespread praxis seems far away. Perhaps the General Conference of the UMC—or the dean of a United Methodist seminary—should convene a working group of Methodist theologians from around the world to meet regularly over a quadrennium to develop a communal theology that can help to liberate the center, to end the church's neocolonialism, to allow the exiles to find their way home (to a home of their choosing), and to recover *los desaparecidos*, as the work to which the Triune God calls us today.

CHAPTER TEN

PROPHETIC GRACE: A WESLEYAN HERITAGE OF REPAIRING THE WORLD

Mary Elizabeth Mullino Moore
for Russell E. Richey[1]

As we prepare this book, fear dominates the world on many fronts, whether fear of military aggression, fear of political instability and economic inequity, fear of suicide bombers, fear of street crime, or fear of diminishing peace agreements on several continents. At the same time, poverty is increasing worldwide, and environmental agreements are languishing. Now is the time to take a fresh look at prophetic traditions, both biblically and historically. Now is the time to analyze human resistance to prophecy and the power of that resistance to subvert hope. Now is the time to uncover the Wesleyan tradition of *prophetic grace*.

This chapter is one step toward retrieving and reinterpreting the living Wesleyan tradition of prophecy. Facing the complexity of Wesleyan movements and the myriad of interpretations, I recognize this chapter as a daring work, and hopefully a faithful one. In the face of world trauma, we need to engage in probing study of religious traditions, creating new patterns of dialogue and new perspectives on established traditions. The purpose of this chapter is to probe the Wesleyan tradition of *prophetic grace*, bringing John Wesley's understandings of grace into dialogue with prophetic literature and Christian life. The underlying goal is to deepen conventional understandings of prophecy and prophetic practice, particularly to propose prophetic grace as a faithful interpretation and guiding construct in the Wesleyan tradition.

Randy Maddox has argued that John Wesley's theology is centered in "responsible grace," and his view has been well accepted.[2] Building on Maddox's position, I will further claim that a theology of *prophetic grace* emanates from John and Charles Wesley and many other theologies within Wesleyan movements in the intervening centuries. It is also grounded in the Hebrew Bible and New Testament.[3] This is a large claim and cannot be fully defended in one essay. On the other hand, the theological inheritance is powerful and pervasive. To that end, this essay has three purposes. The first is to analyze prophetic traditions in the Hebrew Bible in comparison with John Wesley's understanding of Christian faith. The significance of this comparison is that the biblical prophetic tradition has a sharp edge that is present but easily missed in Wesley's words, while Wesleyan tradition has a communal emphasis that is easily missed in contemporary interpretations of the biblical tradition.[4] From this comparison, we turn to two other purposes: to explore ways that people resist prophecy and to engage with the Wesleyan tradition of prophetic grace as a source for shaping theological emphases and transformed action for the future.

PROPHETIC TRADITIONS

In reflecting on prophetic grace, we first face the question of what prophecy is.[5] The popular connotations, and much of the prophetic tradition, seem to be in tension (if not opposition) with grace. The concepts of grace in the Hebrew Bible and New Testament have a similar foundation in God's action and a similar promise of new relationships: "Just as Hosea predicted the establishment of a new relationship based on God's gracious promises to the patriarchs, Paul argued that the righteousness received by grace is based on God's promises to Abraham (Rom. 4:1-3) and David (Rom. 4:6-7)."[6] The prevalent connotations of prophecy, however, suggest more about disassembling the present world than repairing it (*tikkun olam*). The prevailing image is a person (e.g., the prophet Amos) who stands against the community in pronouncing God's judgment on the community or its leaders. However, as Abraham Heschel observed,

> The words of the prophet are stern, sour, stinging. But behind his austerity is love and compassion for mankind. Ezekiel sets forth what all the other prophets imply: "Have I any pleasure in the death of the wicked, says the Lord God, and not rather that he should turn from his way and live?" (Ezek 18:23). Indeed, every prediction of disaster is in itself an exhortation to repentance. The prophet is sent not only to upbraid, but also to "strengthen the weak hands and make firm the feeble knees" (Isa 35:3). Almost every prophet brings consolation, promise, and the hope of reconciliation along with censure and castigation. He begins with a *message of doom*, he concludes with a *message of hope*.[7]

At the heart of Heschel's understanding of prophecy is profound empathy and love. The prophet is "a witness to the divine pathos, one who bears testimony to God's concern for human beings."⁸ Such a view holds prophecy and grace quite closely together.

The biblical world is sufficiently distant from the present world that the typical twenty-first-century reader (especially in the West) assumes that the God of the Bible usually worked through an individual prophet, who in turn spoke for God to the people. Though this image is important to the tradition, the communal worldviews of the ancient world suggest that, when God spoke to Moses, Amos, Micah, or Sarah, God's messages were conveyed symbolically to the whole people, even before the prophet spoke.⁹ In recent history, the search for authoritative prophetic guidance has reinforced the more individual-based assumptions, leading many interpreters to focus on the words and actions of prophetic leaders. Even in eighteenth-century England, John Wesley lived in such a tradition of individual leadership; thus, he was willing to stand against the community, and he encouraged others to do the same when faithfulness required it.¹⁰ At the same time, he did not encourage people to trust prophetic experiences; he particularly scrutinized the occasional practice of foretelling the future. His larger concerns were to interpret the prophets of old (revealed in Scripture) and to acknowledge the ongoing work of God's Spirit in human lives.

Already in this introduction, we see some of the complexities of prophetic grace, beginning with complexities in defining "prophet" and "prophecy," and including additional complexities in cross-cultural comparisons—across centuries of time and geographical regions. To these we now turn.

Biblical Traditions of Prophecy

Even the prophetic literature in the Hebrew Bible is contested, and more than one standard is used to judge writings as prophetic.¹¹ Further, more than one Hebrew word is used in the Hebrew Bible to refer to "prophets," and these various words suggest a broad range of meanings. Four titles are given for prophet in the Hebrew Bible: *hōzeh* ("seer"), *ro'eh* ("diviner"), *'îš [hā]'ĕlōhî'm* ("man of God"), and *nābî'* ("prophet").¹² The first two have almost the same meaning¹³ and have to do with *special seeing*—seeing visions or seeing into the sacred realm. The term *ro'eh* "refers to the spokesperson who experienced the sight of God's message (by dreams or visions), as a seer (1 Sam. 9:9, 11, 18, 19)."¹⁴ Within Wesleyan tradition, the possibility of special seeing is also emphasized, especially in the prevalence of John Wesley's descriptions of faith as seeing. In "An Earnest Appeal to Men of Reason and Religion," Wesley describes faith as "the demonstrative evidence of things unseen [cf. Heb. 11:1], the supernatural evidence of things invisible, not perceivable by eyes of flesh, or by any of our natural senses or faculties."¹⁵ He even expands this to include the other senses, referring to faith as "the *eye* of the new-born soul," "the *ear* of the soul whereby a sinner 'hears the voice of the Son of God and lives,' " "the *palate* of the soul" whereby a believer "'tastes the good word, and the powers of the world to come,' " and "the *feeling* of the soul whereby a believer perceives . . . the existence and the presence of him in whom 'he lives, moves and has his being.' "[16]

The third Hebrew title for prophet is *'îš [hā]'ĕlōhî'm*,[17] or man of God. Lindblom has characterized *'îš [hā]'ĕlōhî'm* as a man "who has a close relation to God and participates in divine characteristics and powers and therefore is peculiarly well suited to be a messenger of God."[18] Frédéric Gangloff has defined such a title as "une formule de vénération ou de respect désignant le serviteur idéal de Dieu."[19] This too co-inheres with John Wesley's understanding of the nature of faith, personified in *spiritual living*. Wesley extends his previous definition of faith with these words:

> Faith is that divine evidence whereby the *spiritual man* discerneth God and the things of God. It is with regard to the *spiritual world* what sense is with regard to the natural. It is the *spiritual sensation* of every soul that is born of God.[20] (Emphases mine)

We see here a continuing emphasis on seeing as discernment and spiritual sensation, but the association is made with the life of the faithful person, or, in Wesley's words, "the spiritual man." Unlike distinctions made in the Hebrew Bible regarding prophets as special people, this spiritual person for Wesley includes "every soul that is born of God."

The fourth Hebrew title for prophet is the most common, *nābî'*, and is the term most literally translated as prophet. Some ambiguity surrounds the linguistic origins of *nābî'*; however, within the Hebrew texts, the most easily discernible meaning is in an active sense of "speaker, herald, preacher," or (more probably) in a passive sense of "one who has been called."[21] Here we see another Wesleyan emphasis, namely the stress on *God's calling and the urgency of human response*. As in the earlier comparison between Hebrew and Wesleyan understandings of a "man of God," John Wesley tends to spread the concept more broadly. He associates God's calling with all Christian people and not just with a few specially called leaders. Wesley understands calling as inextricably bound with faith and works. For him, God's calling includes obeying God's commandments and loving God and neighbor. He describes this faith as "bringing forth good works"; in fact, "without it can no good words be done."[22] Here we see Wesley's persistent attention to God's calling; the expectation of human response, made possible by God; and the extension of God's call to *all* people of faith, rather than to the leaders and to the people through them.

Prophecy across Cultures

Of course, the cultural gap between Wesley's words and those of the Hebrew Bible is great. I am boldly suggesting a comparison between the early-modern Northern European world and the ancient Middle Eastern world. Further, Wesley lived after the Renaissance, Reformation, and early Enlightenment had shifted Western understandings of human nature toward more individual and autonomous conceptualities. The Hebrew Bible reflects a world in which God's word to leaders was intended for the covenant community whom those leaders represented.[23] In short, Wesley's attention to the faith and works of all Christians reflects his world and the philosophical and theological assumptions within it. On the other hand, his emphases shift the faith discourse of his day to some of the more communal emphases of the ancient world, albeit within the worldviews of early modernity. By speaking of all Christians or all souls born of God, he is reiterating the Hebrew Bible's emphasis on the people of God and the prophet's unique role in calling the people back to God. Similarly, Wesley emphasizes the distinctive roles of people called to lead the people toward God's grace—toward justification and the unfolding fullness of sanctification. In his view, these leaders could be class leaders, lay preachers, or priests, but their role was critical all the same.

My word analysis in this chapter is not intended to be a foolish game of taking words from one context and comparing them glibly with another; it is intended rather to suggest a perspective on the Wesleyan theology of grace in relation to the prophetic tradition of the Hebrew Bible. Wesley did place considerable confidence in the Hebrew and New Testament prophets (including the prophetic word of Jesus), preaching from them, seeing their words as fulfilled over time (especially in Jesus Christ) and still being fulfilled, and using their words to proclaim a truth or argue a point.[24] On the other hand, he was suspicious of prophesying, particularly suspicious of reports that someone had exercised a spiritual gift for seeing or foreseeing the future. Such reports of dramatic religious experiences or special gifts were often linked with critiques regarding enthusiasm in the Methodist movement, so the contexts of Wesley's responses were not straightforward or uncomplicated. Even so, Wesley did not unequivocally deny or affirm that such prophecies could be true.[25] He did deny any claims to such prophetic power in himself.[26] While recognizing differences between the apostolic age and the present, Wesley developed a complex way of discerning the ancient and ongoing works of the Spirit. He recognized the extraordinary work of the Spirit in the apostolic age and the ordinary work of the Spirit into the present age; however, he further recognized that extraordinary work of the Spirit was still necessary in the present age because the Church had not yet reached maturity.[27]

On some occasions, Wesley declared certain prophecies as untrue or incompatible with the Bible.[28] On other occasions, he actively discouraged dreams, visions, and prophecies.[29] On still other occasions, he attributed an unusual occurrence to supernatural, or preternatural, movements, but without claiming that the gift of prophesying was involved.[30] He did consistently argue, however, that the Holy Spirit continues to work in the world, as promised in Scripture, which means that gifts of the Spirit persist.[31] He and people in the Methodist movement were frequently accused of enthusiasm, and he countered his critics by reference to 1 Corinthians 13:2 ("Though I have the gift of prophecy, . . . and have not love, I am nothing"), turning people to Paul's words to Christians in Corinth. Wesley kept this focus on love throughout his preaching, not just when responding to criticism. He encouraged people to live by love, and he personally delighted in loving relationships wherever he found them.[32] It is not surprising, then, that he frequently referred to the 1 Corinthians 13 text as a persistent reminder to reorient priorities around love.

Wesley's attention to divine sight, holy living, and responding to God's call on one's life suggest a prophetic flavor to his understanding of faith. At times, he is even explicit about this, as in his description of the close connection between faith and holiness, meaning faith in God's love to bestow the privilege of being children of God *and* the capacity to love and obey.[33] Further, Wesley makes a connection between faith and prophecy in the case of Job.[34] All of this is made possible only through God. No person is able to work faith in him or herself; it is pure gift. Such faith is "a new creation, and none can create a soul anew but [the One] who at first created the heavens and the earth."[35] Indeed, God's work of creating a new earth, proclaimed by prophets of old and still emerging in the present moment, is a work that will continue until "the end of the world."[36]

In this analysis, we turn, finally, to more common connotations of prophets and prophecy, namely to testify for God and God's will in the face of social and religious decay. Whatever the prophet's social location, the Hebrew prophets functioned as *intermediaries*—intermediaries between the sacred and profane, and intermediaries between those who were oppressed and powerless and those who wielded power.[37] The various titles for prophets reveal the diverse functions they performed, but these functions were for a larger purpose of calling people back to God, understood differently by different prophets and in different situations.

Further, the prophets' messages were frequently tinged with international concerns and directives; they were not simply focused on Israel. David Petersen summarizes this point:

> The prophets lived in the world of politics, both international and domestic. . . . Israel's prophets serve as heralds for a cosmic God. As such, they offer an

international perspective for what happens to Israel even as they affirm the importance of God's covenant with Israel.[38]

We see here an accent that was true also to John Wesley and the early Methodist movement—an accent that is simultaneously *local and global, particular and universal*. In John Wesley, we see a similar blending of concerns. He simultaneously focused on the qualities of a "people called Methodist," the heart of true Christianity and the larger Christian fellowship, and God's concern and eschatological promise for all creation.[39]

Prophets not only spoke to the people, but also spoke very specifically about the *ethical norms* that people should follow. For all peoples, the norms included restraint in acts of violence; for Israel, the recurring norms were justice and righteousness, and these norms were important for all of Israel (not just the leaders) to follow.[40] Again, we find a kinship with Wesleyan traditions, especially in regard to the urgency for people to live by ethical norms as found in biblical and church teachings and in their daily experiences of God and the world. The accent on holy living was part of John and Charles Wesley's childhood in the Epworth rectory, their young adult experiences with the Holy Club in early Oxford days, and their lifelong theological and liturgical emphases. To say this is to recognize that the ministries of John and Charles Wesley centered on calling people to holy living—honoring God, living according to ethical guidelines, and holding one another accountable for the sake of God and the betterment of God's world.

Further, the prophets traditionally spoke complex *words of hope*, focusing on both judgment and restoration.[41] Consider Jeremiah, for example, who judged Israel mightily but assured the people that God would save Israel (Jer. 46:27-28). Consider Isaiah, who judged both Israel and all other nations, but promised peace and restoration (Isa. 32–35). No matter how devastating the social forces were or how sinful the people of Israel and other nations became, God would continue to bring about the restoration of Israel and the world. Here we see a theme strongly conveyed by John and Charles Wesley. In John, hope is possible through God's grace working in human lives from the very beginning of life. Through prevenient grace, God works in people to awaken conscience and open them to the further work of grace. God then continues offering grace to justify and sanctify human life. Justification is "what God *does for* us" through Jesus Christ, and sanctification is what God "*works in* us" by the Spirit (emphases his).[42] This work of grace is never complete; the sanctifying work of God can even lead to perfection—a state of complete sanctification, or perfect love. We will return to these emphases, but we note here that Wesley expected the impossible from God, both for human life and for the creation. Future hope encompassed new birth for human lives and the renewal of all creation.[43]

In this journey through prophetic traditions, the prophetic nature of God's grace is abundantly clear in John Wesley's theology. I am not arguing that John Wesley was (or was not) a prophet, or that the social-critical emphases of prophetic tradition have dominated Wesleyan movements. I am simply arguing that Wesley understood the movements of God's grace as having a prophetic character insofar as they empowered special seeing, holy living, and a full-bodied response to God's call. In Wesley's view, God's grace empowers people in at least four prophetic ways: (1) to serve as intermediaries between the sacred and profane and between oppressed peoples and their oppressors; (2) to work for the well-being of God's creation, both locally and globally; (3) to live by ethical norms; and (4) to walk confidently with hope. I will later consider ways that these themes have been analyzed and emphasized in twentieth-century Wesleyan movements, but the focus here is simply on Wesley's prophetic understanding of grace. To identify Wesley's understanding of God's grace as prophetic is to identify the active character of God's grace and to accentuate the challenge of this grace for human lives.

HUMAN RESISTANCE—SUBVERTING GRACE

Thus far, my discussion functions by a thematic and comparative logic, but logic is not always the dominant force in human life. Indeed, people have enormous capacity to resist and subvert grace. Even the ways in which Christians formulate theology can be, and often are, acts of resistance and subversion. Whenever theologies of justification and sanctification are formulated in purely individual and human terms, people are resisting and subverting the social and ecological dimensions of God's grace. Whenever the theological emphasis on sin overshadows the power of grace, people are resisting and subverting the power and promises of God's grace to shape their present and future lives. Whenever theology values one people to the exclusion of others, people are resisting the reach of God's grace to all peoples and all creation. Whenever one set of ethical norms is identified as ultimate to the exclusion of others, people are resisting the power of God's grace to move differently in different situations and to stir critique of any set of ethical norms, humanly understood. Whenever theologies of grace emphasize the total passivity and hopelessness of human response, people are resisting the power of God's grace to imbue them with courage and strength to respond to God's prophetic call.

Because people can find many ways to resist and subvert God's grace, they (we) also resist God's claim on their (our) lives. For Wesley, this tendency toward resisting God and the work of God's grace is attributed to original sin.[44] Whether or not his view of original sin is deemed adequate, he does underscore the human propensity to resist God. Through self-deception, even theological self-deception, people are often quite skillful in denying the wondrous works that God has done in the world and the wondrous work that God does in their own lives. This deception is manifested in several forms of resistance, five of which are briefly described here: self-absorption, determinism, tribalism, competition, and despair. Each pattern of resistance is well documented in social science literature and in theological traditions. A small sample of that literature is offered here to illumine and support the description of human resistance.

Self-Absorption

Self-absorption is caring only for oneself and one's inner circle, whether one's family or friendship circle. It is grounded in a belief that only the self matters, though the self is sometimes expanded to include persons with whom one identifies as an extension of oneself (as one's children or partner). In psychological and sociological literature, this is often discussed in relation to narcissism. Self-absorbed thinking is based on assumptions that human beings are autonomous, individual selves; thus, communities and the natural world exist simply to support the individual and his or her loved ones.[45] Self-absorbed people further assume that they are entitled to anything they want or need for personal benefit; their sense of entitlement shapes their relationships with other people, their social communities, and the natural world.

Self-absorption takes many forms and is seemingly rampant in United States society. In one study of two hundred thousand college students, researchers asked which of twenty goals influenced respondents to decide to go to college. Sixty percent of the students chose the option "being well off financially."[46] Such a response points to self-absorption in a materialist form. On the other hand, psychological studies of altruism reveal the limits of self-absorption. The human ability to function in social relationships and to experience satisfaction in life are substantially enhanced through the social processes of bonding, empathizing, learning caring norms, participating in caring behaviors, diversifying, networking, developing problem-solving strategies, and forming global connections.[47] These processes contribute to a propensity for altruistic behavior and also a sense of personal well-being; concerning oneself with others thus enhances both communal and personal values. Self-absorption denies people the plentitude of altruism.

Determinism

Determinism is feeling imprisoned by the past. It is grounded in the belief that the past determines the future and is often influenced by the scientific method and theories of causation.[48] Deterministic thinking does not allow for the possibility that God might do something new or that God might transform the world (indeed our own lives) in radical ways. Certainly, the dream of a future of justice and righteousness is foolish when you reflect on human history. Surveying the history of war, oppression, and abuse is sufficient reminder that optimism is impossible in the face of human tragedy—even more so when human abuse of the cosmos is taken into account. The dream of a just and righteous future is possible only if you trust a power greater than your own. That power might be humankind, taken as a whole; it might be an unknowable force in the universe. For most Christian theology, that power is God. Unfortunately, in most major theological systems, the structures of hope are vague or ineffable, offering little guidance other than a mandate to trust.

Determinism can represent a lack of trust in transcendence, either in divine power or in the capacity of the human family to transcend itself and the present disasters that beset it. In one study, Chitra Golestani asked classes at the University of California at Los Angeles, "Do you believe a better world is possible? Do you believe that peace is possible?"[49] Only 5 percent of the students responded positively to these questions. This echoes the studies of rising fundamentalism, with its grim future predictions, conducted by Robert Jay Lifton in the latter part of the twentieth century.[50] All of this research suggests a strong sense of determinism in US culture.

Some of the most compelling testimony to the dangers of determinism comes from Viktor Frankl, who witnessed in Auschwitz that the people who were able to search for (or reach toward) meaning beyond the death camp were the ones most able to survive.[51] For most of these people, the strength to hope beyond their devastating situation emerged from a rich inner life, which had been nourished by religious faith, intellectual reflection, human relationships, and so forth. The people who could focus on a future vision (completing a life work, walking with a loved one, or reuniting with family) were able to find some degree of strength as they sought to endure the daily suffering of prison life. Though they could not control their fates in the death camp, their spirits were not determined by determinism.

Tribalism

Tribalism is showing allegiance to one's own people above or exclusive of all others. Sociologically, tribalism places the focus on ethno-religious identity. Tribalism is also an ideological stance in which groups are seen as competitive, hierarchical, and isolated in relationship to one another. It is grounded in the belief that competing for the goods of life is necessary or inevitable in human life. At best, people tolerate one another and think of different tribes as sufficiently independent such that some issues belong to some people, and other issues to others. The problem with tribalism and competing tribes is that people assume they can limit their concern to their own kind of people; thus, each part of the human family has to carry its own issues, often in competition with other peoples and their issues. Such a view is rampant in several modern forms of fundamentalism and sectarianism.[52] Found in diverse religious traditions, such movements are often accompanied by "essentialization and totalization of tradition—often in a utopian mode."[53] Thus, they represent reactions to social challenges of modernity and postmodernity.

Tribalism is distinct from loyalty to or love of one's distinctive people. Tribalism gives rise to racist, classist, sexist, homophobic, ageist, and anthropomorphic thinking. People classify the human race and God's creation into discrete categories, inevitably valuing some categories as superior to others. With such thinking, Nazis justified exterminating six million Jews, along with people who were disabled, homosexual, aged, infirm, or ideologically critical of their views and actions. With such thinking, the white-dominated Southern United States justified Jim Crow laws and the consequent strictures on African Americans throughout much of the post–Civil War and twentieth-century eras. With such thinking, in more subtle forms, people identify environmental issues with the Western white middle class, or racial concerns with ethnic minority peoples. Tribalism finally leads to exclusionary relationships among people and inadequate understanding of all the issues that diverse peoples bring to the common table of humanity.

Violence studies illumine the dynamics of tribalism. Much critical work builds on Rene Girard, for whom the practice of scapegoating is seen as the root of violence.[54] Girard, a literary scholar, sees within biblical traditions the potential both to validate and to critique violence—to justify sacrificial victimization or to contribute to the transformation of victims and victimizers. Extending Girard's work, others have shown how societies have perpetuated racism and oppressive politics by scapegoating, often in subtle, unconscious ways.[55] Even daily patterns of interaction are tinged by this dynamic—one group's marking another as the source of problems for their institution, community, or society. In fact, the very attempt to eradicate violence is often marked with scapegoating offenders, subtly enhancing the cycle of violence while claiming to denounce it. Tribalism thus permeates social structures, community life, and daily interactions within families and neighborhoods.

Interestingly, studies of learning suggest that children learn best within an ethos where diverse ages, genders, races, and cultures are actively engaged, and diverse experiences are valued.[56] Such studies suggest that moving beyond tribalism is healthy for children and other human beings.

Competition

The discussion of tribalism leads naturally to another form of resistance—competition. *Competition is contesting with others to attain an end or to defend what one owns or values.* This tension is described in sociology in terms of in-groups and out-groups. It is grounded in a belief that the "goods" of creation (whether material, mental, or spiritual) are limited; therefore, only some people can have access to these goods. This understanding extends to the ethical realm as well. Values are understood as competing with one another; thus, some priorities must be sacrificed for other priorities. The further assumption is that competition is a necessary way of framing issues and some concerns have to be sacrificed if other concerns are to be addressed. With such assumptions, people frequently frame religious and ethical relationships as competitive.[57] In more extreme forms, such competition is expressed by one religious community declaring apocalyptic judgments on others, even enacting violence to force the coming of an end time. All of this is done with an appeal to spiritual insights and traditions, supporting a very deadly form of competition.[58]

Competition is often considered necessary to inspire human accomplishment. Sports, for example, are seen as healthy forms of competition, as are grades and contests in school. Such contests even exist in churches—contests for memorizing Scripture, for the best cake, for the best attendance. The purpose here is not to indict such activities entirely, but to pose questions about when and where such competition contributes to social health and when and where it undermines a community's identified goals. Parallel to the discussion of tribalism, studies of learning suggest that children's intellectual and social development are enhanced in noncompetitive educational settings, especially where they study the needs, suffering, and hopes of children in different parts of the world and engage in global partnership projects.[59] This suggests that motivation is often enhanced by cooperation and collaboration more than by competition.

Despair

Finally, we see the problem of *despair, or believing that bad situations are irreversible and people cannot make a difference, no matter how hard they try.* Ironically, human science research of the past three decades reveals that despair can be countered by active engagement in empathy and transformation.[60] Opening to others and working for change are seemingly antidotes to hopelessness. Further, Jewish and Christian traditions repeatedly emphasize the significance of human effort, not as a substitute for God's work, but as an extension. People are called to act with love, justice, and righteousness, all the while guided by God's wisdom and empowered by God's Spirit.

In *The Redemption of God*, Carter Heyward argues that God *needs* human beings to do the work of redemption in this torn-apart world.[61] She argues that God is limited in power and God needs people to exercise what powers they have for the good of creation. Despair is not only a lack of trust in God's goodness and will for creation, but also a lack of trust in human abilities to participate in God's work.

Victor Frankl illumined the problems of despair in stark terms when he reflected on the experience of people in death camps during the Holocaust (*Shoah*). As described above, the search for meaning—the decision to find an anchoring vision—was vital for daily living in those camps. Frankl identified three primary avenues by which people search for meaning—creating work ("doing a deed"), engaging in relationships (love), or rising above oneself.[62] As he developed these ideas long after the Holocaust, Frankl argued that "when the self-transcendence of existence is denied, existence itself is distorted."[63] Without denying the reality and horror of suffering, Frankl offered a vision of life that is not dominated by despair, but by a search for meaning. Meaning arises from a person's (or community's) decision to live life in such a way as to transcend the confines imposed from the outside.

These various patterns of resistance represent much that destroys the well-being of the world and its potential for transformation. Situations such as these once called forth the prophetic proclamations and actions of Hebrew prophets, the leadership of John Wesley in a seventeenth-century Christian renewal movement, and the leadership of many others in the Wesleyan movements of intervening centuries. Situations such as these underscore the significance of naming and recovering traditions of prophetic grace.

Prophetic Grace in Wesleyan Traditions

Turning now to prophetic grace in Wesleyan movements, we begin with a brief look at the larger Christian movement. Jesus himself was a prophet. Jesus ate with tax collectors and sinners, called the poor and the wealthy, and included women as followers—realities often obscured by the Gospels themselves. The radical Jesus traditions were sufficiently visible, however, to be controversial; the Gospels point repeatedly to controversies surrounding Jesus' words and actions. The mixed communities of early Christianity were also controversial, stirring contention and ambivalence, both within and without. Paul, for example, could argue in one moment that, in Christ, there was "neither Jew nor Greek, . . . slave nor free, . . . male nor female" (Gal. 3:28 WEB); yet, in other moments, he could put forth a very different view (Rom. 9:31-33; 1 Cor. 11:3-12; Eph. 5:22-24; 6:5-6).[64] Within this one man, ambivalence toward women, slaves, and people of his own Jewish tradition helped limit his bold sense of prophetic grace.

Recent scholarship has added to the picture, uncovering more obscure threads of the tradition that intensify the evidence of Jesus' radicality.[65] Similarly, exegetes have increasingly uncovered the radicality of early

Christians as regards crossing boundaries of social class and gender.[66] Elisabeth Schussler-Fiorenza, for example, focuses on texts that reveal women and men struggling against the powers of patriarchal domination. Reading texts suspiciously, she searches for emancipatory elements and reconstructs a picture of Christian origins that includes those who were lowly and rejected in the larger society.[67] Further, she engages in counter-hegemonic inquiries in Christology, seeking to identify an "ekklesia of wo/men" that challenged kyriarchy in antiquity and continues to do so in modernity.[68] She also uses rhetorical analysis of Revelation to uncover prophetic vision.[69] In all of these ways, Schussler-Fiorenza seeks to uncover vision for the future.

We can see here a push in Jewish and early Christian communities toward inclusion, even toward a "discipleship of equals."[70] The prophetic strains were stirring visions—new ways of seeing, challenging people toward spiritual lives—holy living, and calling people to action—to particular tasks and roles. In spite of these radical movements, people resisted and squabbles arose. Indeed, their responses resembled the human resistances discussed above—the ones we do so well today. This is not to say that all human situations are the same, but only that patterns of resistance endure over time, taking many different forms, but obscuring the fullness of God's creation and God's intentions for the world.

Because these patterns of resistance are themselves resistant to change, God calls people to take up the role of prophet. And because the patterns pervade the entire community, God calls *all* people to prophecy. Because prophecy has to do with seeing, spiritual living, fulfilling particular roles, mediating God in particular and global situations, proclaiming ethical norms, and walking in hope, the prophets may be few, but the calling to live prophetically is shared by all. Because prophecy is an impossible calling, God gives it together with the gift of grace; it is God's grace that inspires, invokes, requires, and empowers human response. But what is prophetic grace, and what theological tenets and Christian action does it inspire?

John Wesley and the Wesleyan movements that flowed from his ministry have focused largely on the *fullness of God's grace as the power and source for radical living in the world*; thus, one can appropriately describe a Wesleyan theology as grounded in prophetic grace.[71] The tradition embraces contradictions, to be sure, but that is true of prophecy in general. As evidenced in the discussion earlier in this chapter, prophecy is often wrought by the contradictions that emerge from its embeddedness within a particular tradition and its simultaneous pattern of pointing beyond itself to future possibilities. It is also wrought by the contradictions of fallible prophets. The Wesleyan prophetic grace traditions are no exception to this pattern of contradiction and hubris. Even with these realities of fallibility and contradiction, the theological commitments associated with prophetic grace have potential to counter human resistance and to guide Christian practice in the future. To these commitments we now turn.

Trust in the Transcendent Immanent God of Justice

The God of the prophets is One who messes around in the world. At the same time, God is far greater than the world. Amos proclaims judgment on all of Israel's neighbors, saying, "The LORD roars from Zion" (Amos 1:2a). Then, Amos declares judgment in a litany:

> Thus says the Lord: For three transgressions of Damascus, and for four, I will not revoke the punishment; . . . For three transgressions of Gaza, and for four, I will not revoke the punishment; . . . For three transgressions of Tyre, and for four, I will not revoke the punishment; . . . For three transgressions of Edom, and for four, I will not revoke the punishment; . . . For three transgressions of the Ammonites, and for four, I will not revoke the punishment; . . . For three transgressions of Moab, and for four, I will not revoke the punishment; . . . For three transgressions of Judah, and for four, I will not revoke the punishment; . . . For three transgressions of Israel, and for four, I will not revoke the punishment; (Amos 1:3–2:8)

These words are delivered in the name of God, who knows what is going on in the world, who is present to every transgression, and who judges from the heights and depths of a larger reality. This is a transcendent immanent God of justice.

This same judging God also pleads for the people to live in the ways of the Lord:

> I hate, I despise your festivals, and I take no delight in your solemn assemblies . . . Take away from me the noise of your songs; I will not listen to the melody of your harps. But let justice roll down like waters, and righteousness like an ever flowing stream. (Amos 5:21-24)

The book of Amos, taken as a whole, is a prophetic picture of God's grace—judging, lamenting, promising, and calling.

One can argue that John Wesley proclaimed God's prophetic grace as well, whether in judging the lukewarm religion of his contemporaries or condemning slave trade or pleading to a government official on behalf of a poor widow. On the other hand, both John Wesley and the Wesleyan movements have fallen short of the visions they have proclaimed, and their visions have often been inadequate as well. One vivid example is presented by the South African theologian Peter Grassow, who critiques the inadequacy of Wesley's political theology, arguing that Wesley's belief in the divine sanction of his own country's government made it impossible for him to connect his sympathy for the American situation during the

Revolutionary period and his endorsement of the British political structures that obscured their freedom.[72]

Grassow calls for a reconstruction of Wesleyan theology, critiquing John Wesley on three points, which he identifies as challenges for South African Methodists today. First is the inadequacy of Wesley and early Methodist leaders in analyzing and interpreting the political and economic realities of their situation:

> Like Wesley, South African Methodists have a sincere concern for the poor. If we are to avoid Wesley's inadequacies we need to develop a rigorous social analysis. At the same time—drawing some precedent from Wesley!—the church needs to geographically relocate its leadership and administrative functions to the areas of the poor . . . , for it is only here that it can develop a perspective that will be liberating for all our people.[73]

Second, Grassow critiques the personal focus of Wesley's doctrine of salvation, recognizing that his understanding of social holiness, combined with his teleological focus in the doctrine of perfection, provide a ground for more revolutionary implications than Wesley was able to draw. Wesley's understanding of salvation leads naturally to a teleological vision and commitment to social holiness and, consequently, to a sharp critique of "every interim-ethic."[74] The commitment today needs to be a commitment to social holiness grounded in the authority and sovereignty of God. Third, Grassow challenges South African Methodists to go beyond Wesley's limitations as regards social holiness, and to seek "a holiness committed to the social order," or "to bring salvation to every aspect of our society."[75] To do this requires giving priority to social reconstruction over ideological agreement, for the reconstruction of South Africa is more urgent than theological or ideological differences.

Grassow, like Amos, is speaking a prophetic word to his people of South Africa, and by extension to us. He speaks on behalf of the transcendent immanent God who calls people to see the real possibility of justice beyond their imaginations and to take up the work that they are incapable of doing save by the grace of God. This is prophetic grace, which invites people today to study the praxis of God in its fullness, thus subverting dualistic assumptions about God's immanence and transcendence and uncovering the pervasive witness to God's justice in Jewish and Christian traditions.

Trust in the Movements of God—Transforming the Past with Hope

A second commitment stirred by prophetic grace is trust in the movements of God. Countering determinism, trusting in God allows people to hope for and work toward the transformation of evil, past and present. In spite of the dominance of determinism, hope has been central to the

Wesleyan movements. John Wesley began most sermons and theological affirmations with the possibilities of what God can do, even transforming evil into good. The Wesleyan conviction is that God is at work in every moment, moving the world toward a new creation. This conviction is itself prophetic. John Wesley trusted in God's undying devotion to the creation and every person in it; thus, he trusted that God always acts for the good of creation and for the good of each part. Wesleyan movements have grounded hope largely in the movements of God. Their emphasis on the overflowing of God's love also offers hope and guidance for people to contribute through their own life work to transforming the future of God's creation. In this view, the past is never a first or last word; God's love is.

If people genuinely want to transform the future, their trust in the powerful love of God will be a source of strength and hope. This trust will empower them to respond by reshaping their own orientations to the past and present. Nelson Mandela, part of the Wesleyan tradition himself, was a man who trusted in the movements of God to transform the past and immediate problems of his country. He, thus, made deliberate attempts to reframe the past when apartheid finally ended and his country of South Africa began the long, slow process of building a new society.

Mandela worked on social transformation through confessional acts (as in the Truth and Reconciliation Commission), through government reorganization, through encouragement to his people to build the New South Africa, and through a deliberate choice to reframe the past as a source of hope. These acts were attempts to cleanse and transform the past. On the occasion of Mandela's return to Robben Island Maximum Security Prison, where he was imprisoned for twenty years, he declared that he would now think of this as Robben Island University. That spirit has been adopted by other former prisoners. One told me, "We do not call this Robben Island Maximum Security Prison but Robben Island University because we turned what we learned here into good, not into bad as the apartheid government expected." Another former prisoner added, "Robben Island has become a symbol of the triumph of the human spirit." Like Mandela, these men have chosen to reshape their memory of Robben Island so it can be a force for good rather than evil. They have chosen to shift from the role of victim to that of victor.

These quotations reveal the power of reframing the past, both for individuals and for a nation. I had the privilege to visit Robben Island with an international group of theologians. At one point, we sat on hard benches and heard stories of the torture and punishments at Robben Island during Apartheid years. I was seated beside a German colleague whose eyes filled with tears. He leaned toward me and said, "This is what my people did to the Jews; I am overcome that these men at Robben Island could now love the people who did these terrible things." He was making connections between what he heard and the history of his own country, as I was simultaneously making connections with racism in the United States. We were all being challenged to transform the meanings of the past for the sake of future. Determinism was not to have the last word. Whether in our personal lives or in our theological formulations, the Wesleyan tradition and movements of recent history challenge us to reject determinism and to be aware of the psychological, sociological, and theological potency of trust in God.

Commitment to All of God's Creation

Prophetic grace further involves a commitment to all of God's creation. Countering tribalism, this is a commitment that has been well developed in recent works on the Wesleyan tradition. Ted Runyon argues that John Wesley was concerned for all of God's creation, and that Wesley included the whole of creation in his understanding of grace.[76] Others have built in similar directions.[77] This new work offers directions for rethinking God's love of creation, and our responsibility to and for it.

Such reinterpretations, reformulations, and shifting of accents are necessary if prophetic grace is to flower. Prophetic grace invites Christian people to frame their lives, and Christian theologians to frame their work, in relation to preserving and enhancing life in *all* of creation. Such a perspective critiques much religious and political practice in the present world. It critiques the anthropocentric focus of much theology and environmental rape for the sake of human comfort. It critiques international policies that focus solely on national interests. It critiques national or religious isolation and pushes toward global, ecumenical, and interreligious collaboration for the good of creation. With such commitment in mind, practical theologians need to engage in critical discourse with theological traditions and in re-forming theological constructs and practices for the well-being of creation. Prophetic grace requires Wesleyan peoples to join with all peoples in preserving and enhancing life for God's creation. Such a perspective critiques US international policy when it is concerned only with the interests of the United States. It critiques environmental rape for the sake of human comfort. It critiques denominational or Christian isolation, including Wesley's own diatribes against Jews, "Mahometans," "Heathens," "Pagans," "Popists," and others. A focus on God's creation pushes toward ecumenical and interreligious respect and collaboration for the good of God's cosmos.

Valuing of All God's People

A fourth commitment stirred by prophetic grace is valuing all people. Wesleyan movements have a messy history in this regard, but valuing all of God's people is an important quality to counter competition. Mercy Amba

Oduyoye describes the tenuous relationship between Christian missions and African people, and between Christian theology and practice and traditional African culture.[78] Similar issues are raised in this volume with regard to Methodism in Argentina (Elaine Robinson's chapter) and the relationship of Methodism, particularly United Methodism, with African Americans in the United States (William Bobby McClain's chapter). Another example is found in the Methodist missions of the Caribbean, where many people experienced conversion to Christianity. Their individual lives were changed, but the Methodist people continued to own slaves and support the system of slavery. In spite of the contradictions, many Caribbean Methodists sought ways to embrace all people, as when the Methodists in Antigua "succeeded in bringing together small groups of whites, free coloureds and slaves in Christian fellowship."[79] Methodists there continued to attract free colored and white people in the towns, and the news of John Wesley's stand against slavery influenced the Methodist missionary centers.[80] Further, Methodists in other parts of the Caribbean engaged in modest mission with the Indians.[81]

The history of contradictions continues. For example, The United Methodist Church, since 1980, has included increasingly judgmental and limiting language in *The Book of Discipline* regarding the value of gay and lesbian persons and their relationship to the church.[82] Persons in the Church still vary in their understandings and judgments about homosexuality, but the quickness with which the Church has been willing to allow this one set of issues to dominate debates of theological orthodoxy, boundaries of ordination, and legal-judicial proceedings reveals something of the difficulty in The United Methodist Church regarding the value of all God's people.

Writing from Argentina, José Miguez Bonino offers a countering word—evoking what I have identified as Wesley's implicit doctrine of prophetic grace. He argues that Wesley's view of prevenient grace has potential for joining with Gustavo Gutierrez in seeing the people who have been reduced to "'non-persons' " as "being the focus of God's liberating word."[83] Miguez Bonino credits the nineteenth-century British theologian William B. Pope for developing these ideas beyond the scope of Wesley's own theology. Further, Miguez Bonino insists that sanctification be understood more fully as restoration, linking Wesley's concerns for the social realities of his day with his theology. He celebrates the recent uncovering of Wesley's own concerns for "full restoration of humanity in the image of God (which involves the totality of human life—spiritual, moral, political, and more) and the restoration of the whole creation (which had been entrusted to human care and disrupted by human sin.)"[84]

To take seriously Wesley's large view of God's grace and its prophetic work is to value all God's people—all those created by God—for God is working in all peoples from the beginning to the end of their lives. When

Christian theologians draw limits and judgments on other peoples and other perspectives without giving equal attention to critiquing the limits and judgments of their own views, they are engaged in hubris of a most destructive kind. When Christian theologies are not judged on the basis of their effects on other peoples, they are likely to be trivial or dangerous. The ability to value all of God's people escapes the human capacity, of course; however, people *are* able to move toward universal valuing of all people through the prophetic grace of God. Indeed, human theologies and Christian practice toward others will never be as profound as the movements of God's prophetic grace—forming, judging, transforming, and redeeming God's beautiful and broken world.

Commitment to the Human Vocation of Working with God

As regards the human vocation, Wesley expressed a seemingly impossible view in his doctrine of perfection. In this doctrine, he expressed hope that the ideal of holy living might become real; he believed this possible by God's grace. Such a doctrine does not, and cannot, eradicate the sinfulness and horrors of this world; yet, it mediates against despair in holding forth hope in seemingly hopeless situations. It bears some resemblance to Viktor Frankl's emphasis on the human ability to make meaning and to choose one's responses, even within the limits of desperate situations. Such a view does not encourage glib confidence in positive thinking, but it does encourage people to live as fully as possible within the bounds of their particular situations. Such a view, in the Wesleyan sense, encourages people to see themselves as called and strengthened by God for holy living.

To follow such a calling requires repentance—or turning around.[85] It requires a giving of one's life to God, which is possible only through the prophetic grace of God—God's moving in human lives to love, judge, forgive, call, bless, and empower people to live in intimate relation with God and to walk in the ways of God. How does this relate to perfection? Wesley explained perfection as "loving God with all our heart, mind, soul, and strength." For him, this meant "that no wrong temper, none contrary to love, remains in the soul; and that all the thoughts, words, and actions, are governed by pure love."[86] Lively discussion has raged as to whether Wesley understood perfection as a sinless state. He himself was ambiguous on this point, allowing for the possibility that mistakes could still be made. Despite the ambiguity, Wesley clearly asserted that, through God's grace, perfection is possible. Even as an ideal, however, perfection is not static; it is a continuing process of growing in perfect love.

On this subject of perfection in love, many in the Wesleyan movements have built arguments to decry slavery and appeal for the ordination of African Americans, women, and gay and lesbian persons. The centrality of love in biblical and Wesleyan traditions has been the central argument for inclusiveness within the Christian community, for efforts toward international justice and peace, and for pietistic living in daily life. Miguez Bonino underscores this from a Latin American perspective:

> The full recreation of God's image is, in the last resort, for Wesley, nothing but the total control of human intention, purpose, and action by God's love. It is the work of the Holy Spirit . . . it is the culmination and perfection of God's redemptive action. "Perfection" is not so much a measure to be filled as a fullness that has no limits. The insistence on "social holiness" or "social Christianity," rather than a sociological conception, is but a way of underlining the centrality of love.[87]

Miguez Bonino challenges partial or simplistic views of God's work and the human vocation of working with God. He uses the Wesleyan tradition to critique the Wesleyan tradition, which is the kind of critical retrieval that is needed if the human vocation is taken seriously.

Joining with Miguez Bonino and John Wesley, people who participate in the living Wesleyan traditions today need to engage in more thorough analysis of God's work and the human vocation, and to do so with full attention to personal, social, and structural dimensions. This calls people to analyze social structures and human practices, as well as the beliefs and values embodied in them. It calls people to engage critically with theological constructs and to re-imagine the human vocation in a complex and debilitating world. It calls people to reflect upon and develop theologies of prophetic grace, which deconstruct theories of human passivity and hopelessness and acknowledge the power of God's prophetic grace to imbue people simultaneously with the assurance of God's everlasting love, the urgency of God's call on human life, and the courage and strength of God's presence to guide human response. Thus, people are called to be bearers of God's overflowing of love into every corner of their individual lives and every dimension of the larger world.

In conclusion, we can view John Wesley's theology as grounded in prophetic grace, partially expressed and embodied. Wesleyan movements carry that tradition, however humbly and inadequately. The challenge before "the people called Methodist" today is to claim and reconstruct theologies of prophecy and grace, recognizing their inseparability, and to analyze contemporary realities and religious practice with the intent of reconstructing both belief and practice for the future. The most fundamental challenge is to open ourselves to the prophetic grace of God and the commitments it will stir in us. The challenge is vast, and perhaps impossible, but prophetic grace is a divine gift, renewed every morning and persisting to the end of time.

NOTES

1. ENGAGING THE PAST—ENGAGING THE FUTURE

1. The present volume complements, but builds in different directions from, historical works such as Frank Baker, *John Wesley and the Church of England* (London: Epworth, 2000); David Hempton, *Methodism: Empire of the Spirit* (New Haven: Yale University Press, 2005); John H. Wigger and Nathan O. Hatch, eds., *Methodism and the Shaping of American Culture* (Nashville: Kingswood Books, Abingdon, 2001).

2. A few examples will suffice, pointing to praxis in relation to poverty, ethnicity, spirituality, and ethics: Joerg Rieger and John J. Vincent, eds., *Methodist and Radical: Rejuvenating a Tradition* (Nashville: Kingswood Books, Abingdon, 2003); Richard Heitzenrater, *The Poor and the People Called Methodists* (Nashville: Kingswood Books, Abingdon, 2002); Theodore Jennings, *Good News to the Poor: John Wesley's Evangelical Economics* (Nashville: Abingdon, 1990); Pamela D. Couture, *Blessed are the Poor?* (Nashville: The United Methodist Publishing House, 1991); M. Douglas Meeks, ed., *Portion of the Poor: Good News to the Poor in the Wesleyan Tradition* (Nashville: Kingswood Books, Abingdon, 1995); Grant S. Shockley, Karen Y. Collier, and William B. McClain, eds., *Heritage and Hope: The African American Presence in United Methodism* (Nashville: Abingdon Press, 1991); Paul W. Chilcote, *Early Methodist Spirituality: Selected Women's Writing* (Nashville: Kingswood Books, Abingdon, 2007); Manfred Marquardt, *John Wesley's Social Ethics: Praxis and Principles*, trans. John E. Steely and W. Stephen Gunter (Nashville: Abingdon, 1992); Theodore R. Weber, *Politics in the Order of Salvation: Transforming Wesleyan Political Ethics* (Nashville: Kingswood Books, Abingdon, 2001).

3. Erich S. Gruen, *Heritage and Hellenism: The Reinvention of Jewish Tradition* (Berkeley: University of California Press, 2002, 1998).

4. Ullrich Kockel and Mairead Nic Craith, eds., *Cultural Heritages as Reflexive Traditions* (Basingstoke, UK: Palgrave, 2007).

5. Theodore Runyon, *The New Creation: John Wesley's Theology Today* (Nashville: Abingdon, 1998); M. Douglas Meeks, ed., *Wesleyan Perspectives on the New Creation* (Nashville: Kingswood Books, Abingdon, 2004).

6. Albert C. Outler, *God Is Love: Theology in the Wesleyan Spirit* (Nashville: Discipleship Resources, 1994); W. Stephen Gunter, *The Limits of Love Divine* (Nashville: Kingswood Books, Abingdon, 1989); Bryan P. Stone and Thomas Jay Oord, eds., *Thy Nature and Thy Name is Love: Wesleyan and Process Theologies in Dialogue* (Nashville: Abingdon, Kingswood Books, 2001).

7. Heitzenrater, *The Poor and the People Called Methodists*; Rieger and Vincent, *Methodist and Radical*.

8. Christopher Boyd Brown, *Singing the Gospel: Lutheran Hymns and the Success of the Reformation* (Cambridge, MA: Harvard University Press, 2005).

9. Catharina Raudvere and Leif Stenberg, eds., *Sufism Today: Heritage and Tradition in the Global Community* (London: I. B. Tauris & Co., 2009).

10. Thaddeus W. W. Pace, Lobsang Tenzin Negi, Daniel D. Adame, Steven P. Cole, Teresa I. Sivilli, Timothy D. Brown, Michael J. Issa, and Charles L. Raison, "Effect of Compassion Meditation on Neuroendocrine, Innate Immune and Behavioral Responses to Psychosocial Stress," *Psychoneuroendocrinology* 34 (2009): 87–98.

11. Walpola Rahula, *Heritage of the Bhikkhu: The Buddhist Tradition of Service*, trans. K. P. G. Wijayasuendra and K. P. Wijayasurendra (New York: Grove/Atlantic, Inc., 2003); Esther De Waal, *The Way of Simplicity: The Cistercian Tradition* (Maryknoll, NY: Orbis, 1998); De Waal, *Every Earthly Blessing: Rediscovering the Celtic Tradition* (New York: Church Publishing, Inc., 1999); De Waal, *Celtic Way of Prayer: The Recovery of the Religious Imagination* (New York: Bantam Books, 1999).

12. Richard P. Heitzenrater, *The Elusive Mr. Wesley*, 2nd ed. (Nashville: Abingdon, 2003); W. Reginald Ward and Heitzenrater, eds., *The Works of John Wesley: Journals and Diaries, Bicentennial Edition*, vols. 18–24 (Nashville: Abingdon, 1988–2003); Maddox, *Responsible Grace: John Wesley's Practical Theology* (Nashville: Kingswood Books, 1994); Jennings, *Good News to the Poor*; José Míguez Bonino, "Wesley in Latin America: A Theological and Historical Reflection," in *Rethinking Wesley's Theology for Contemporary Methodism*, ed. Randy L. Maddox (Nashville: Kingswood Books, Abingdon, 1998), 169–82; Rieger and Vincent, *Methodist and Radical*; Couture, *Blessed are the Poor?*; Meeks, *Portion of the Poor*; Heitzenrater, *The Poor and the People Called Methodists*; Russell E. Richey, with William B. Lawrence and Dennis M. Campbell, *Marks of Methodism: Practices of Ecclesiology* (Nashville: Abingdon, 2005); Richey, *Extension Ministers: Mr. Wesley's True Heirs* (Nashville: General Board of Higher Education and Ministry, UMC, 2008); Richey and Thomas Edward Frank, *Episcopacy in the Methodist Tradition: Perspectives and Proposals* (Nashville: Abingdon, 2004); Richey, *Doctrine in Experience: A Methodist Theology of Church and Ministry* (Nashville: Kingswood Books, Abingdon, 2009); Mary Elizabeth Moore, *Covenant and Call* (Nashville: Discipleship Resources, UMC, 2000); Moore, "Commissioning the People of God: Called to Be a Community in Mission," *Quarterly Review* 23, no. 4 (Winter 2003): 399–411; McClain, *Black People in the Methodist Church: Whither Thou Goest?*, 2nd ed. (Cambridge, MA: Schenkman Publishing Company, 1984); Shockley, Collier, and McClain, *Heritage and Hope*; William Gravely and Gilbert Haven,

Methodist Abolitionist: A Study in Race, Religion, and Reform (Nashville: Abingdon, 1973); Melvin Easterday Dieter, Donald W. Dayton, and Kenneth E. Rowe, eds., *The Holiness Revival of the Nineteenth Century* (Lanham, MD: Rowman & Littlefield, 1996); Rosemary Skinner Keller, ed., *Spirituality and Responsibility* (Nashville: Abingdon, 1993); Paul W. Chilcote, *Her Own Story: Autobiographical Portraits of Early Methodist Women* (Nashville: Kingswood Books, Abingdon, 2001); Chilcote, *Early Methodist Spirituality: Selected Women's Writings*; Diane Leclerc, *Singleness of Heart: Gender, Sin, and Holiness in Historical Perspective* (Lanham, MD: Rowman & Littlefield, 2001); Rob Weber and Elaine Robinson, eds., *Considering the Great Commission: Evangelism and Mission in the Wesleyan Spirit* (Nashville: Abingdon, 2005); Henry Knight and F. Douglas Powe, *Transforming Evangelism: The Wesleyan Way of Sharing Faith* (Nashville: Discipleship Resources, UMC, 2006); John Sungschul Hong, *John Wesley the Evangelist* (Lexington, KY: Emeth Press, 2006); Marquardt, *John Wesley's Social Ethics*; Weber, *Politics in the Order of Salvation*; Gregory S. Clapper, *As If the Heart Mattered: A Wesleyan Spirituality* (Nashville: Upper Room Books, 1997); and Sondra Higgins Matthaei, *Making Disciples: Faith Formation in the Methodist Tradition* (Nashville: Abingdon, 2000).

13. A few classic examples are James H. Cone, *God of the Oppressed*, rev. ed. (Maryknoll, NY: Orbis, 1997); Cone, *Black Theology and Black Power*, rev. ed. (Maryknoll, NY: Orbis, 1997); Rosemary Radford Ruether, *Women and Redemption: A Theological History*, rev. ed. (Minneapolis: Augsburg/Fortress, 1998); Ruether, *Gaia and God: An Ecofeminist Theology of Earth Healing* (New York: HarperCollins, 1994); Ruether, *New Woman, New Earth: Sexist Ideologies and Human Liberation*, reprint (Boston: Beacon, 1995, 1975); José Míguez Bonino, *Doing Theology in a Revolutionary Situation* (Minneapolis: Fortress, 2007, 1975); Míguez Bonino, *Toward a Christian Political Ethics* (Minneapolis: Fortress, 2007, 1983); Mercy Amba Oduyoye and Musimbi R. A. Kanyoro, *The Will to Arise: Women, Tradition, and the Church in Africa* (Maryknoll, NY: Orbis, 1992); Oduyoye, *Daughters of Anowa: African Women and Patriarchy* (Maryknoll, NY: Orbis, 1995); Delores S. Williams, *Sisters in the Wilderness: The Challenge of Womanist God-Talk* (Maryknoll, NY: Orbis, 1995); and Hyun Kyung Chung, *Struggle to Be the Sun Again: Introducing Asian Women's Theology* (Maryknoll, NY: Orbis, 1990). Some of these authors themselves are writing from their own Methodist theological traditions, for example, Cone, Míguez Bonino, and Oduyoye; however, they are not explicitly addressing that tradition in most of their theological writing. Others write more explicitly from and to the Wesleyan traditions, such as Leclerc, *Singleness of Heart*; McClain, *Black People*; and Rieger and Vincent, *Methodist and Radical*.

14. Rieger and Vincent, *Methodist and Radical*.

15. Steven L. McKenzie and M. Patrick Graham, eds., *The History of Israel's Traditions: The Heritage of Martin Noth* (New York: Continuum, 1994).

16. Richard P. Heitzenrater, *Wesley and the People Called Methodists* (Nashville: Abingdon, 1993); Phyllis Mack, *Heart Religion in the British Enlightenment: Gender and Emotion in Early Methodism* (Cambridge: Cambridge University Press, 2008); W. J. Gaines and W. S. Scarborough, eds., *African Methodism in the South: or Twenty-Five Years of Freedom* (Atlanta: Emory University Digital Library Publications, Franklin Publishing House, 1890); Clive Marsh, Brian E. Beck, Angela Shier-Jones, and Helen Wareing, eds., *Unmasking Methodist*

Theology Today: A Way Forward (New York: Continuum, 2006); Míguez Bonino, "Wesley in Latin America"; S. T. Kimbrough, Jr., ed., *Methodism in Russia and the Baltic States: History and Renewal* (Nashville: Abingdon, 2008); Charles Henry Crookshank, *History of Methodism in Ireland* (BiblioLife, 2009, 1888); and Patrick P. Streiff, *Methodism in Europe: 19th and 20th Centuries* (Tallinn, Estonia: Baltic Methodist Theological Seminary, 2003).

17. Albert C. Outler, *Evangelism and Theology in the Wesleyan Spirit*, reprint (Nashville: Discipleship Resources, 2003); Paul W. Chilcote, *John Wesley and the Women Preachers of Early Methodism* (Lanham, MD: Rowman & Littlefield, 1991); Chilcote, *She Offered Them Christ: The Legacy of Women Preachers in Early Methodism* (Eugene, OR: Wipf & Stock, 2001); Jean Miller Schmidt, *Grace Sufficient: A History of Women in American Methodism, 1760–1939* (Nashville: Abingdon, 2004); John R. Tyson, *Assist Me to Proclaim: The Life and Hymns of Charles Wesley* (Grand Rapids: Eerdmans, 2008); Tyson, *Charles Wesley: A Reader* (Oxford: Oxford University Press, 2000); S. T. Kimbrough, Jr., *Charles Wesley: Poet and Theologian* (Nashville: Kingswood Books, Abingdon, 1992); Carlton R. Young, *Music of the Heart: John and Charles Wesley on Music and Musicians* (Carol Stream, IL: Hope Publishing Co., 1995); and Brian E. Beck, *Exploring Methodism's Heritage: The Story of the Oxford Institute of Methodist Theological Studies* (Nashville: General Board of Higher Education and Ministry, UMC, 2004).

18. Orlando O. Espin, "Traditioning: Culture, Daily Life and Popular Religion, and Their Impact on Christian Tradition," in *Futuring Our Past: Explorations in the Theology of Tradition*, ed. Espin and Gary Macy (Maryknoll, NY: Orbis, 2006), 2. The other chapters in *Futuring Our Past* exemplify the study of complex interactions between traditions and living communities.

19. Jeanette Rodriguez, *Our Lady of Guadalupe: Faith and Empowerment among Mexican-American Women* (Austin: University of Texas Press, 1994); Virginia Ortiz, *Tradition and Heritage: A History of the Parish of Our Lady of Guadalupe in Péna Blanca, New Mexico* (Los Ranchos de Albuquerque, NM: Rio Grande Books, 2007).

20. Gary Riebe-Estrella makes an explicit case for such an approach to theology in "Tradition as Conversation," in *Futuring Our Past*, 141–56.

21. Janet F. Fishburn, ed., *People of a Compassionate God: Creating Welcoming Congregations* (Nashville: Abingdon, 2003).

22. Maddox, *Responsible Grace*.

23. Laurent A. Daloz, *Mentor: Guiding the Journey of Adult Learners* (San Francisco: Jossey-Bass, 1999); Sondra Higgins Matthaei, *Faith Matters: Faith Mentoring in the Faith Community* (New York: Continuum, 1996).

24. Elizabeth Tonkin, *Narrating Our Past: The Social Construction of Oral History* (Cambridge: Cambridge University Press, 1992), 1.

25. Ibid., 1–2.

2. The Wesleyan Tradition and the Myths We Love

1. In this article, we are using "myth" and "legend" interchangeably to mean traditional stories of ostensibly historical ideas or events that relate

to a person or group's self-understanding or stories from the past that are popularly regarded as true, though historically unverifiable. Different versions of this paper were presented at the conference at Emory University in January 2003 and at the tercentenary conference sponsored by the University of Manchester, England, in June 2003.

2. Their marriage was marred by frequent marital turmoil and family discord, even causing at least one period of separation. The number of children born to the Annesleys is uncertain—the father thought perhaps twenty-four or twenty-five.

3. Samuel was the rector of the Epworth parish; therefore, his home was a rectory, not a parsonage (vicars have a vicarage, etc.). He recounted that Susanna had given birth to "eighteen or nineteen" children (there is no accurate record), of which only ten survived, and only five or six would have been children living at home at any given time.

4. John had no middle name, as a copy of his baptismal record in the Lincolnshire archives confirms. Earlier siblings John and Benjamin died at birth or in infancy, as did a subsequent John Benjamin—all before 1703.

5. Most accounts say six, but at the time of the fire in February 1709, he was four months short of that age.

6. There is no evidence that Susanna ever used this phrase in reference to John, much less at that early point.

7. This idea comes from a presumptive reading of her private journal and is contradicted by John's later correspondence with Samuel Badcock.

8. The time and day is conjectural, based on ambiguous evidence ("S. J."), a designation that is never otherwise used for John.

9. There is no evidence that Susanna knew languages beyond English, and her theology is not especially sophisticated. Two hundred people could not possibly have fit into the kitchen at Epworth, including those peering in the windows.

10. John and Charles's college in Oxford was and is normally called Christ Church; "Student" is a special designation for pupils named to the college foundation (similar to "Fellow"), which is true later for Charles but not for John.

11. The only development before John returned was that Charles and one of his neighbors began to study together and attend church regularly. No group is evident until both brothers are together at Oxford in the summer of 1729; no regular group meetings take place until 1730. The term "Holy Club" was not used (and then only briefly) until the fall of 1730.

12. As the group emerged in 1730, it met in rotation at the rooms of the four members in different colleges around the university.

13. Whitefield did not meet with Charles until after 1733 and not with John's group at all. By that time, the term "Holy Club" was no longer in use by anyone, having been superseded by other names that eventuated into "Methodist."

14. There is no evidence of a theology of works righteousness among the Oxford Methodists; grace (including prevenient grace, which obviates any argument for works righteousness) was central to the Wesleyan theology even at this early stage.

15. The Methodists exhibited a great variety of viewpoints on theology and mission, some of which varied markedly from Wesley's.

16. In this study, we will be concerned primarily with present understandings of eighteenth-century events and ideas, without looking at parts of the tradition that are attributable to the nineteenth century or beyond.

17. John Wesley, "A Short History of the People called Methodists," §1, in *The Methodist Societies*, ed. Rupert E. Davies, in the *Bicentennial Edition of the Works of John Wesley* (Nashville: Abingdon Press, 1976–), 9:426 (hereafter cited as *Works*).

18. "A Short History of Methodism," §3, in *Works*, 9:368. See also Wesley's self-professed approach in his sermon on "The Late Work of God in North America," I, in *Sermons III*, ed. Albert C. Outler, in *Works*, 3:596—"barely to give a simple and naked deduction of a few well known facts."

19. Account written in 1732, John's letter to Mr. Richard Morgan, in *Journal and Diaries I*, ed. W. Reginald Ward and Richard P. Heitzenrater, in *Works*, 18:124.

20. "The Character of a Methodist" (1742), in *Works*, 9:32.

21. "Above ten years ago, my brother and I. . . ." "A Plain Account of the People called Methodists" (1749), in *Works*, 9:254.

22. Sermon 112, "On Laying the Foundation Stone" (1777), I.1, in *Works*, 3:580.

23. See Charles's letter to Dr. Samuel Chandler in April 1785, when he first claims to have been the original "Methodist," starting a group at Oxford that his brother later joined. The story is without basis in the available information concerning the developments of the time and tries to support a claim that Charles had never made in the previous fifty years.

24. "Against Heresy," IV.32; see also Eph. 4:5.

25. The manuscript of that sermon, in Wesley's own hand, states that it was the first sermon he wrote, as the numeral one on the cover confirms, and the actual date of preaching is contained in a list of preaching locations and times on the back cover. See my first publication, "John Wesley's Early Sermons," in *Proceedings of the Wesley Historical Society* 37 (February 1970): 110–28. Ralph Bates picked up my observation on this point and crafted it into an article, "John Wesley's First Preaching Sunday," in *Proceedings of the Wesley Historical Society* 40 (February 1975): 7–16.

26. *Journal and Diaries I* (account leading up to May 24, 1738), in *Works*, 18:244.

27. Ibid., 18:249.

28. In "A Short History of the People Called Methodists," see *Works*, 9:429.

29. See *Journal and Diaries I* (June 10, 1735), in *Works*, 18:160.

30. For more information on this development, see my article "The Second Rise of Methodism—Georgia," in *Methodist History* 28 (Jan. 1990):117–32.

31. *Journal and Diaries II*, in *Works*, 19:325n6.

32. That particular part of the journal, covering the period May 6, 1760 to Oct. 28, 1762, was prepared for the press in January 1767. He may have simply misplaced the material. *Journal and Diaries IV*, in *Works*, 21:355.

33. *Journal and Diaries V*, in *Works*, 22:307.

34. The critic, writing in the *Gentleman's Magazine*, was comparing Wesley's preface to *Hymns and Sacred Poems* (1739) and his published sermon on "Salvation by Faith" (1738, on Eph. 2:8). See *The Elusive Mr. Wesley*, 283.

35. In one instance in particular, in a comment to Melville Horne in the 1780s, he marvels that the people of England did not stone him and his brother for preaching such. Robert Southey, *The Life of Wesley* (New York: Gilley, 1820), 1:258.

36. These later comments are all included in his list of corrections (errata) in the 1774 edition of his *Works* (vol. 26), published by William Pine in Bristol. See *Journal and Diaries I*, in *Works*, 18:214–15.

37. For more on this issue, see the debate between Theodore Jennings and Kenneth Collins in *Quarterly Review* 8 (1988–89): Jennings, "John Wesley Against Aldersgate" (No. 3, Fall): 3–22; Collins, "The Continuing Significance of Aldersgate: A Response to 'John Wesley Against Aldersgate'" (No. 4, Winter): 90–99; and Jennings, "Reply to Kenneth Collins" (No. 4, Winter): 100–105.

38. *A Plain Account of Christian Perfection* (1777), ¶¶ 12, 19, in *The Works of John Wesley*, ed. Thomas Jackson (London: Conference Office, 1872), vol. 11, hereafter cited as *Works* (Jackson). See also Sermon 40, "Christian Perfection" (1741), II.20–28, in *Works*, 2:116–20.

39. See *Works*, 1:317–34, esp. n102.

40. See *Journal and Diaries I*, in *Works*, 18:243, ¶ 2. Even though he canonized these three points in his General Rules, his critical view that religion was more than doing good, avoiding evil, and using the means of grace (or just fearing God and doing righteousness) is evident through much of his writing (sometimes claiming that such people have the form but not the power of godliness), for example, Sermon 2, "The Almost Christian," I.10, and Sermon 22, "Sermon on the Mount, II" (1748), II.4, in *Works*, 1:136, 496–97. In his later years, the attempt to follow these rules was seen in a more positive light, as a mark of the aspiring Christian—having the "faith of a servant." See Sermon 80, "On Friendship with the World," §12; Sermon 89, "The More Excellent Way," §5; Sermon 106, "On Faith," §I.10, II.4. See also Sermon 121, "Prophets and Priests," §21, and *Journal and Diaries, VII* (August 26, 1789). *Works*, 3:132, 265, 497, 500; 4:83–84; 24:152.

41. In another sermon, Wesley tries to prove the point that his views have not changed by quoting a previous sermon on the subject, but in fact he alters the text of the previous sermon—not really fair, given the point he is trying to make. In fact, he follows the quotation by saying, "Neither do I conceive how any of these expressions may be altered so as to make them more intelligible," which is exactly what he has just done. Sermon 11, "The Witness of the Spirit, II" (1767), II.2, in *Works*, 1:287; cf. Sermon 10, "The Witness of the Spirit, I" (1746), I.7, in *Works*, 1:274. The changes are didactic rather than substantive, but they demonstrate not only what Albert Outler calls "his habitual indifference to exact quotation" but also a rather cavalier attitude toward the matter of consistency over time.

42. See above, fn. 28; Crowther, *A True and Complete Portraiture of Methodism* (London: Edwards, 1811); and Robert Moore, *John Wesley and Authority: A Psychological Perspective* (Missoula, MT: Scholars Press, 1979). Moore claims that Wesley's sense of importance and destiny was the result of his trying

to fulfill the lives of the two deceased siblings for whom he was supposedly named (an interesting theory, which actually would have applied to more than one other brother and sister, who were named for previously deceased siblings).

43. John Hampson, *Memoirs of the Late Rev. John Wesley, A.M.* (Sunderland: Graham, 1791), 3 vols.

44. *The Life of the Rev. John Wesley, A.M.* (London: Paramore, 1792).

45. *The Life of the Rev. John Wesley, M.A.* (London: Couchman, 1793–96), 2 vols.

46. *The Life and Times of the Rev. John Wesley* (London: Hodder & Stoughton, 1870–71), 2 vols. A survey of the interpretive history of Wesleyan biography may be found in Part 3 of *The Elusive Mr. Wesley*, 2nd ed. (Nashville: Abingdon, 2004), 345–94.

47. Much of the material is made up by anonymous and untraceable sources and copied by dozens of others, replicating misinformation (though it may sound or look interesting) at an amazing rate.

48. The Hebrew grammar is only eleven pages long; the French is thirty-five. He mentions learning Spanish while in Georgia in order to speak with some Spanish Jewish settlers, and he read the Sunday service in Italian one time to a few Vaudois.

49. A similar exaggeration is often extended to John's mother. The idea that Susanna Wesley had studied the classics and knew many languages paints an appealing picture of her as the mother of Methodism, but it just does not bear up to historical scrutiny. The story began somewhere in the nineteenth century and has been circulating ever since. Never mind that the entire corpus of Susanna's extant writings contains not one phrase in Latin, Greek, Hebrew, French, or German, or any reference from any book in those languages. This fact is conveniently overlooked in order to propagate the Susanna myth. See Charles Wallace, Jr., ed., *Susanna Wesley: The Complete Writings* (New York: Oxford, 1997). She does occasionally end a letter with "Adieu," as on December 7, 1725 (ibid., 123). The children most likely learned their Latin and biblical languages from their father, Samuel, whose scholarship exhibits a close knowledge of several languages.

50. His method of developing lists of Particular Resolutions for each day and General Resolutions for every day, and of keeping charts indicating his adherence to them, is in keeping with the specific suggestions made in Ignatius of Loyola's introduction to the *Spiritual Exercises*, though there is no indication that Wesley ever read that work himself. His selection of categories for the Particular Resolutions, based on virtues for each day of the week, comes directly from Robert Nelson's work *The Practice of True Devotion* (London: Downing, 1715).

51. This saying was attributed to Wesley as early as 1904 by George Eayrs (and from there, cited in *Bartlett's Famous Quotations*), but there is no evidence in any early writings by or about Wesley that he had any connection whatsoever with the saying. The best one can say is that it sounds like something Wesley might have said.

52. The saying seems to have come from the work of Rupertus Meldenius in the previous century and was quoted by people such as Richard Baxter, whom Wesley read. There is no evidence that Wesley ever used this phrasing,

although the ideas expressed therein come close to expressing ideas that are similar to some of his thoughts. See Heitzenrater, "Unity, Liberty, Charity in the Wesleyan Heritage," in *Unity, Liberty, and Charity*, ed. Donald E. Messer and William J. Abraham (Nashville: Abingdon, 1996), 29–45.

53. Like many other sayings that have spread by Internet, there are many variations, but all of them have the same egoistic self-righteousness that is foreign to Wesley's thought—he would never claim that he set himself on fire. Some of the sites attribute a similar phrase to Augustine, with a more believable sense: "Lord, set me on fire...."

54. See Eric Hobsbawm and Terence Ranger, *The Invention of Tradition* (Cambridge: Cambridge University Press, 1983), 1–2.

55. See "The Quest of the First Methodist," in *Mirror and Memory* (Nashville: Kingswood Books, Abingdon, 1989), 63–77, and especially 221n22, 233n16, all of which contradicts the basic assumption underlying Frederick Gill's book, *Charles Wesley, the First Methodist* (Nashville: Abingdon, 1964).

56. As referenced in V. H. H. Green, *John Wesley* (London: Thomas Nelson, 1964), 32.

57. Letter from John Clayton to John Wesley (September 4, 1732), in *The Journal of the Rev. John Wesley, A.M.*, ed. Nehemiah Curnock, 8 vols. (London: Epworth, 1938), 8:279.

58. Dean B. McIntyre, "Did the Wesleys Really Use Drinking Song Tunes for Their Hymns?" *Worship*, April 17, 2001, http://www.gbod.org/worship. See also Larry Witham, "Bar Tunes Not Wesley's Way; Exposing the Vulgar Myth behind Methodist Hymns," *Insight on the News 18* (September 2002). For more information on the tunes associated with the Wesleyan hymns, see Nelson Adams, *The Musical Sources for John Wesley's Tune-Books: The Genealogy of 148 Tunes* (PhD diss., Union Theological Seminary, 1973).

59. There is the traditional (unsubstantiated) story that Charles wrote words for bawdy ballads that he heard sung in the streets, saying "Why should the Devil have all the good tunes?"—a myth also applied to Martin Luther. The quotation is most often attributed to Rowland Hill in the nineteenth century ("The devil should not have all the best tunes"). The story relates to the origin of his hymn "The True Use of Music," which was supposedly written to the tune of the song "Nancy Dawson." See John Tyson, *Charles Wesley* (New York: Oxford, 1989), 221.

60. To the instituted means, Wesley adds a list of "prudential means," which are often seen as original with him, although he borrowed the idea directly from John Norris's book *A Treatise Concerning Christian Prudence* (London: Manship, 1710; see esp. p. 176), which Wesley read the day before he broached the concept to his mother Susanna in a letter of June 11, 1731 (see also letter to brother Samuel, November 17, 1731), in *Works*, 25:283–84, 321–22.

61. Found in every edition during Wesley's lifetime, beginning in 1763. *Minutes of Conference*, in *Works*, 10:856–57. In his sermon on "Self Denial" (1760), Wesley lists some of the same things under works of piety but uses the term "religious conference" rather than "Christian conference."

62. It is hard to imagine how it could be confused with the meetings of an annual (or general, district, or charge) conference when Wesley presses the matter further (in that same section) by asking, "Do not you converse too long at a time? Is not an hour commonly enough? Would it not be well

always to have a determinate end in view, and to pray before and after it?"

63. Luke Tyerman, *The Life and Times of the Rev. John Wesley* (London: Hodder & Stoughton, 1870–71), 2 vols.

64. Letter to Sarah Crosby (February 14, 1761).

65. In 1789, Sarah Mallet received written permission from the conference to preach within her local circuit, under a new provision to control the presence of "outsiders" in the pulpit by requiring that they get conference permission to preach in a given circuit for a year.

66. This information was transmitted to me by the pastor of the congregation, who witnessed the debacle.

67. The discussion begins with William Hawes, *An Examination of the Rev. Mr. John Wesley's Primitive Physic* (London: Dodsley, 1776). See Randy Maddox's chapter in this book for more on Wesley's medical practices.

68. See *Fanatical Conversion* (1779), quoted in *The Elusive Mr. Wesley*, 2nd ed. (Nashville: Abingdon, 2003), 298.

69. Henry Abelove, *The Evangelist of Desire: John Wesley and the Methodists* (Stanford, CA: Stanford University Press, 1990), 58, 65, 72.

70. These are just a couple of the wild claims made in Abelove's book *The Evangelist of Desire*, 71 and passim. Abelove manages to create more preposterous myths in his 115 pages than nearly all the anti-Methodists of the eighteenth century put together.

71. For instance, the mere mention of the Methodist preacher's pledge to "go on to perfection," probably as misunderstood today as then although it is the linchpin of the Wesleyan view of Christian living, can still bring snickers to groups of Methodists (especially preachers) if mentioned in a lighthearted, joking way.

72. Reproduced as Illustration 13 in *The Elusive Mr. Wesley* (after p. 208).

73. *Account of the Circumstances Relative to the Departure of the Late Rev. Mr. Wesley* (London: n. p., 1791), dated March 8, six days after Wesley's death; reprinted in Curnock's edition of *Wesley's Journal*, 8:133 passim 44, which also includes an engraving of Claxton's painting of the deathbed scene.

74. The other tendency is for people to assume that these ideas in Wesley are all post-Aldersgate, whereas most of them are evident from references in his diaries to readings and conversations prior to 1738.

75. The terminology, as well as the idea, was borrowed by Outler from the Chicago-Lambeth Quadrilateral of the 1880s, although the four terms are somewhat different: Holy Scriptures, Apostle's Creed, Two Sacraments, and Historic Episcopate (Lambeth); and Scripture, tradition, reason, and experience. See Ted Campbell, "The 'Wesleyan Quadrilateral': The Story of a Modern Methodist Myth," in *Doctrine and Theology in The United Methodist Church*, ed. Thomas A. Langford (Nashville: Kingswood Books, Abingdon, 1991), 154–61.

76. Wesley's voice, as described by firsthand observers, was clear but not strong. His manner was calm and not dramatic. One observer pointed out that if he had not occasionally moved his hand to turn the page of his sermon manuscript, one would have thought he was a "speaking marble statue." See analysis of Wesley's oral preaching style in *Sermons IV* (Appendix B), in *Works*, 4:515–16.

77. The theory, introduced by English historian W. E. H. Lecky, *A History of England in the Eighteenth Century* (London: Longmans, 1878–90) and focused by Elie Halévy in two articles published in the Revue de Paris in 1906, was given wider circulation in a translation of the French articles by Bernard Semmel in *The Birth of Methodism* (Chicago: University of Chicago Press, 1971). The theory has provoked widespread reaction, pro and con.

78. His obituary in the *Gentleman's Magazine* makes a particular note of his energy in old age. See *The Elusive Mr. Wesley*, 335–40, 347.

79. Bouts with illness that he considered to be potentially life threatening started in the 1750s. He wrote and re-wrote his will at least three times, in 1768, 1771, and 1789. His birthday reflection in 1786 is typical: "I entered into the eighty-third year of my age. I am a wonder to myself. It is now twelve years since I have felt any such sensation as weariness" (June 28, 1786), in *Works*, 23:400–401.

80. That is the number he gives for his preaching at Gwennap Pit at 5:00 p.m. on August 22, 1773. He describes the crowd at the "amphitheatre" as filling the depression and covering the ground around it "to a considerable distance," *Works*, 22:387. Granted, even Wesley's apparent exaggerations are not as fanciful as the common portrayal of the occasion in the familiar painting done in the mid-nineteenth century by William Overend Geller, which makes the pit look like it is at least a half mile across. The topography, sky, and some characters in that painting are actually modeled after an earlier painting by John Martin portraying "Joshua Commanding the Sun to Stand Still" (1816).

81. He figures the space to be eighty yards square (six hundred forty square yards), and calculates the total on the basis of five persons per square yard, which is a very tight crowd. Granted, the site of the pit has changed since the eighteenth century, but the general topography of the location does not allow for a much larger natural amphitheater.

82. Similar questions could be raised about the numbers reported for other events. Susanna Wesley also started a myth of her own, by claiming that two hundred people met in her kitchen for family prayers while Samuel was gone from Epworth "and yet many went away for want of room." Wallace, *Writings of Susanna Wesley*, 80. And how many people could squeeze into Wesley's bedroom on the day he died in his house on City Road? The traditional picture of the occasion shows everyone who was mentioned in Elizabeth Ritchie's account as having visited him during the last week of his life. Painting by Marshall Claxton, presently at the Museum of Methodism at Wesley's Chapel in City Road, London; see fn. 73.

83. See fn. 87.

84. John's journal entry for October 20, 1743, summarizes the tumultuous events: "From the beginning to the end, I found the same presence of mind as if I had been sitting in my own study," *Works*, 19:346. Charles's journal entry for October 21 (cf. October 25) comments, "My brother came, delivered out of the mouth of the lion! He looked like a soldier of Christ. His clothes were torn to tatters." See the documents compared in *The Elusive Mr. Wesley*, 124, 266–67.

85. This is the subtitle of his book *Charles Wesley, the First Methodist* (New York: Abingdon, 1964).

86. This letter is cited several times by Frank Baker in *Charles Wesley as Revealed in His Letters* (London: Epworth, 1948), see esp. p. 20.

87. For the definitive 1780 Collection, John included at least 477 hymns that seem to have been by Charles (of the 525 total). That represents about 5 percent of Charles's poetic production. Oliver Beckerlegge and Franz Hildebrandt, eds., "The Sources of the Collection," in *A Collection of Hymns for the Use of the People Called Methodists,* in *Works,* 7:31–38. See also Frank Baker, *Charles Wesley's Verse* (London: Epworth, 1988), 92.

88. Kenneth Shields tries to dissect the reasons for the lack of interest in Charles's poetry in "Charles Wesley as Poet," in *Charles Wesley: Poet and Theologian,* ed. S. T. Kimbrough (Nashville: Kingswood Books, Abingdon, 1992), 45–71.

89. *Works,* 7:56–57.

90. *Son to Susanna* (London: Nicholson and Watson, 1937). Her misportrayal of Samuel's role during the rectory fire of 1709 is especially prejudicial, as is her pejorative view of his scholarship.

91. Many of her stories can be found in previous works on Methodist women heroes of the faith, going back at least to the mid-nineteenth-century work of Abel Stevens, *Women of Methodism* (New York: Carlton & Porter, 1866); John Kirk, *The Mother of the Wesleys* (Cincinnati: Poe & Hitchcock, 1867); and Margaret Martin, *Heroines of Early Methodism* (Nashville: Southern Methodist Publishing House, 1887).

92. Such an endeavor is also important in order to advance theological and ethical analysis, as represented in this volume by Diane Leclerc's analysis of sin and Rebekah Miles's development of a Wesleyan perspective on work and vocation.

93. Grant Wacker, private communication, 2006.

94. There is no evidence that this saying was ever used by Wesley; see fn. 52.

95. In his sermon on "Catholic Spirit" (1750), Wesley speaks about the requirements and responsibilities of a "right heart," showing that it is more than the broad tolerance that most people associate with the term. Sermon 39, *Works,* 2:81–95.

96. "Reports of Wesley as Preacher," in *Works,* 4:515–16 (Appendix B).

97. The same point can be made concerning other "powerful" preachers, whose deliveries seem to have been less spectacular than one might suspect, such as Jonathan Edwards. See Jim Ehrhard, "A Critical Analysis of the Tradition of Jonathan Edwards as a Manuscript Preacher," *Westminster Theological Journal* 60, no. 1 (Spring 1998): 71–84.

98. Cf. Heitzenrater, "Inventing Church History," *Church History* 80 (December 2011): 737–48.

99. The successive editions of the Enoch Wood bust of Wesley (orig. 1780s, from life) become an artistic symbol of this tendency, as the distortions of recasting and copying the bust result in Wesley's head and eyes becoming more and more tilted up in a more saintly pose.

100. In fact, Wesley went so far as to say, "While I live, I will bear the most public testimony I can to the reality of witchcraft. The denial of this springs originally from the Deists; and simple Christians lick up their spittle. I hereby set them at open defiance." Letter to Thomas Tattershall (November 13, 1785), in *Letters* (Telford), 7:300 (with corrections from holograph).

101. See *Explanatory Notes* (1 Cor. 14:34), where Wesley says (his

commentary on the text is in non-italic), "Let your women be silent in the churches—unless they are under an extraordinary impulse of the Spirit. For in other cases, it is not permitted them to speak—by way of teaching in public assemblies; but to be in subjection—to the man, whose proper office it is, to lead and to instruct the congregation." See also his comment on Eph. 5:25: "In all indifferent things, the will of the husband is a law to the wife." (First edition, London: Bowyer, 1755), 457, 520.

102. Ibid. (Rev. 13:1, 15), 720–25, 728, where Wesley has a long discourse explaining that the Roman papacy is the Beast and that all popes since Gregory VII are identified as Antichrist.

103. Sermon 141, "The Image of God," II.1, in *Works*, 4:297.

104. See his "Serious Thoughts occasioned by the late Earthquake in Lisbon" (London: 1755), in *Works* (Jackson), 11:1–13 (written in late November, within a month of the event). Wesley draws many parallels with recent events in England that had commonly been attributed to "natural causes" but which, he argues, demonstrate continuing visible evidence of the hand of God working "to shake terribly the earth." He also mentions Edmund Halley's calculations (in 1705) that the return of the great comet in 1758 would cross orbits with that of the earth, with unknown consequences.

105. See the "Large" *Minutes*, in *Works*, 10:857. He also recognized that many "wise and good" people had recommended the same thing. Sermon 79, "On Dissipation," §19, in *Works*, 3:123.

106. Part Two of the Discipline contains doctrinal material, including a section on Wesleyan Distinctives, which discusses his views on prevenient grace, the linkage of faith and good works, the assurance of faith, and entire sanctification (Christian perfection), to name a few. *The Book of Discipline* (Nashville: United Methodist Publishing House, 2004), ¶¶ 101–4.

107. Phil. 2:12, one of Wesley's consistent descriptions of the goal of the Christian life, or "Christian perfection."

108. "Thoughts upon Methodism" (1786), in *Works*, 9:527.

3. AFRICAN AMERICAN METHODISTS AND UNITED METHODISM

1. William B. McClain, "African American Methodists: A Remnant and a Reminder," in *Connectionalism: Ecclesiology, Mission, and Identity*, ed. Russell E. Richey, Dennis M. Campbell, and William B. Lawrence, vol. 1 (Nashville: Abingdon Press, 1997), 77.

2. William B. McClain, "Reclaiming Our Heritage," in *Heritage and Hope: The African American Presence in United Methodism*, ed. Grant S. Shockley, Karen Y. Collier, and William B. McClain (Nashville: Abingdon Press, 1991), 286.

3. Richard Allen, *The Life Experience and Gospel Labors of the Rt. Rev. Richard Allen*, ed. George Singleton (Nashville: Abingdon, 1960), 30.

4. Allen, *The Life Experience*, 15–16 (emphasis added).

5. Ibid., 29–30.

6. Ibid., 29 (emphasis added).

7. It should be noted that there were five other, smaller African American groups who were associated with Methodism. The Union American Episcopal

Church (originally called "the Union Church of Africans"), which is actually the oldest of all Black Methodist denominations, was founded by Peter Spencer in Wilmington, Delaware, in 1813. Other groups separated themselves from the AME and the AME Zion Churches. They include The Reformed Methodist Union Episcopal Church (1885), The Reformed Zion Union Apostolic Church (1881), and The Independent African Methodist Episcopal Church (1907). Finally, The African Union First Colored Methodist Protestant Church (commonly known as AUMP) was a merger of the Union Church of Africans, a split-off from the original Union Church of Africans, and The First Colored Methodist Protestant Church. See C. Eric Lincoln and Lawrence H. Mamiya, *The Black Church in the African American Experience* (Durham: Duke University Press, 1990), 47–49. See also the writings of Professor Lewis V. Baldwin, especially his doctoral dissertation published as Baldwin, *"Invisible" Strands in African Methodism: A History of the African Union Methodist Protestant and Union American Methodist Episcopal Churches, 1805–1980* (Metuchan, NJ: Scarecrow Press, 1983).

8. William B. McClain, *Black People in the Methodist Church: Whither Thou Goest?*, 2nd ed. (Cambridge, MA: Schenkman Publishing Company, 1984), 7–9.

9. Frederick A. Norwood, *The Story of American Methodism: A History of the United Methodists and Their Relations* (Nashville: Abingdon, 1974), 166; and Harry VanBuren Richardson, *Dark Salvation: The Story of Methodism as It Developed Among Blacks in America* (Garden City, NY: Anchor Press, 1976), 35. In the official history of AMEZ, the author points out that, of the 360 members of the John Street Church in 1789, seventy were African Americans. See William J. Walls, *The African Methodist Episcopal Zion Church: Reality of the Black Church* (Charlotte, NC: A.M.E. Zion Publishing House, 1974).

10. Joshua E. Licorish, *Harry Hosier, African Pioneer: Including Brief History of African Zoar Methodist Church, founded 1794, Philadelphia, Pennsylvania* (Philadelphia: Afro-Methodist Associates, 1967). The Rev. Joshua E. Licorish, now deceased, was the pastor of African Zoar United Methodist Church in Philadelphia for many years, and a fine historian in his own right. He credits Hosier for founding the African Zoar Church (the first lot was purchased, and the first edifice was constructed, in 1794) around the time when Allen and others left St. George's M. E. Church to form Bethel African Methodist Episcopal Church (under the leadership of Allen) and African St. Thomas Episcopal Church (under the leadership of Absalom Jones). Licorish devoted many years to collecting material on Hosier. He published some of this but did not make much (or most) of it available to scholars and the general public. If this research is ever found and made available, these materials, along with the tedious and painstaking research of an archrival, William Jason, Jr., would be valuable sources for additional information and insights into Harry Hoosier.

11. Abel Stevens, *History of the Methodist Church* (New York: Carlton and Porter, 1866), 174. See also Warren Thomas Smith, *Harry Hoosier: Circuit Rider* (Nashville: The Upper Room, 1981), 24; McClain, *Black People in the Methodist Church*, 41–46.

12. Smith, *Harry Hosier*, 25.

13. Smith, *Harry Hosier*, 29.

14. A quotation from an address given by President Matthew Simpson Davage of Clark University, Atlanta, GA, on May 9, 1939. See "Methodism—Our Heritage and Hope," *The Daily Christian Advocate*, no. 14, May 11, 1939, 474. To the credit of the Eastern Pennsylvania Annual Conference, one of the districts of the conference has been renamed "The Harry Hoosier District," which covers part of Philadelphia, including where Harry served.

15. Allen, *The Life Experience*, 30.

16. Lewis V. Baldwin, "Early African American Methodism: Founders and Foundations," in *Heritage and Hope*, 23–38. See also Baldwin, "New Directions for the Study of Blacks in Methodism," in *Rethinking Methodist History: A Bicentennial Historical Consultation*, ed. Russell E. Richey and Kenneth E. Rowe (Nashville: Kingswood Books, Abingdon, 1985), 185–93. Of the list given, Harry Hoosier and Henry Evans remained in the predominantly white Methodist Episcopal Church, now The United Methodist Church. The others who remained Methodists gave outstanding pastoral and administrative leadership to the founding and development of the independent African Methodist Church (AME and AME Zion Churches). Absalom Jones, it will be remembered, broke away and became the first African Episcopal priest in America.

17. *The Book of Discipline of The United Methodist Church, 2008* (Nashville: The United Methodist Publishing House, 2008), 11. This historical fact is recorded in other primary and secondary sources but is significantly included in the brief historical account of *The Book of Discipline*.

18. John Thompson, *The Life of John Thompson: A Fugitive Slave* (New York: Negro Universities Press, 1968), 18–19. Originally published: (Worcester, MA: John Thompson, 1856). Quoted in: Albert J. Raboteau, *Slave Religion* (New York: Oxford University Press, 1980), 133.

19. Donald G. Mathews, "Evangelical America—The Methodist Ideology," in *Rethinking Methodist History*, 92.

20. Ibid., 92 (emphasis added).

21. Clarence C. Goen, *Broken Churches, Broken Nation: Denominational Schisms and the Coming of the American Civil War* (Macon, GA: Mercer University Press, 1987).

22. See Gayraud Wilmore, "Three Generals in the Lord's Army," in *Black Religion and Black Radicalism*, 3rd ed. (New York: Marynoll Press, 2004), 77ff.

23. The *Large Minutes*, being "Minutes of several conversations between the Rev. Mr. Wesley and others from the year 1744 to the year 1789," containing the plans of discipline as practiced in the Methodist connection during the life of Mr. Wesley, asks in Question 3: "What may we reasonably believe to be GOD'S design in raising up the people called Methodists?" and answers: "Not to form a new sect, but to reform the nation, particularly the Church, and to spread Scriptural holiness over the land."

24. Francis Asbury, "Journal for 1 February 1809," *The Journal and Letters of Francis Asbury*, ed. Elmer T. Clark, 3 vols. (London: Epworth; Nashville: Abingdon, 1958), 2:591. Cited by Baldwin, "Early African American Methodism," in *Heritage and Hope*, 27.

25. William H. Williams, "The Attraction of Methodism: The Delmarva Peninsula as a Case Study, 1769–1802."

26. The many works of Martin E. Marty are good places to start: Marty, *A Nation of Believers* (Chicago: University of Chicago Press, 1976); Marty, *The Public Church: Mainline, Evangelical, Catholic* (New York: Crossroad, 1981); and Marty and R. Scott Appleby, *The Glory and the Power: The Fundamentalist Challenge to the Modern World* (Boston: Beacon Press, 1992). See also Wade Clark Roof, *A Generation of Seekers: The Spiritual Journeys of the Baby Boom Generation* (San Francisco: Harper Collins, 1993); William Strauss and Neil Howe, *Generations: The History of America's Future, 1584 to 2069* (New York: William Morrow, 1991); and Dean R. Hoge, Benton Johnson, and Donald A. Luidens, *Vanishing Boundaries: The Religion of Mainline Protestant Baby Boomers* (Louisville: Westminster John Knox Press, 1994).

27. McClain, "A Vision of Hope," in *Heritage and Hope*, 299. This reference is not far from the vision of John Wesley for his preachers: "to reform the nation and spread scriptural holiness over the land."

28. Henry Clay Work, "Kingdom Coming (Year of Jubilo)," in Benjamin Tubb, *The Music of the American Civil War (1861-1865)*, accessed July 1, 2009, http://www.civilwarpoetry.org/union/songs/jubilo.html.

29. "The World Didn't Give It to Me," traditional gospel song, accessible at http://www.bensonsound.com/lyrics/0638.htm, accessed June 19, 2013.

30. William Capers was his successor at Fayetteville, and later bishop of the southern Methodist church. See William M. Wightman, *Life of William Capers, D.D., One of the Bishops of The Methodist Episcopal Church, South, Including an Autobiography* (Nashville: Southern Methodist Publishing House, 1858), 124.

31. Ibid., 129.

32. Shockley, "The Methodist Episcopal Church: Promise and Peril, 1784-1939," in *Heritage and Hope*, 40.

33. See the works of theologians, such as Roy Sano, Justo Gonzalez, Ignacio Castuera, and others. See especially Ignacio Castuera, William B. McClain, and Roy I. Sano, "Biblical and Theological Foundations for Racial and Ethnic Minority Persons in Mission," in *Black People in the Methodist Church*, 110–21. See also Justo L. Gonzalez, *Out of Every Tribe and Nation: Christian Theology at the Ethnic Roundtable* (Nashville: Abingdon Press, 1992). Also available are documents, proceedings, and publications of The Roundtable of Ethnic Theologians, sponsored for two quadrennia by the General Board of Higher Education and Ministry (UMC), as well as documents from the several ethnic minority caucuses.

34. Gonzalez, *Out of Every Tribe and Nation*.

35. Shockley, "The Methodist Episcopal Church," in *Heritage and Hope*, 41.

36. "I'm Gonna Sit at the Welcome Table," in *Sing for Freedom: The Story of the Civil Rights Movement through Its Songs* (Smithsonian Folkways Recording, 1992).

4. Susanna Annesley Wesley

1. In a letter to her oldest son, Samuel Wesley, Jr., dated October 11, 1709, she wrote: "And because I was educated among the Dissenters, and there was somewhat remarkable in my leaving 'em at so early an age, not being full 13, I had drawn up an account of the whole transaction, under which head I had included the main of the controversy between them and the Established

Church as far as it had come to my knowledge; and then followed the reasons that determined my judgment to the preference of the Church of England." Cf. Charles Wallace, *Susanna Wesley: The Complete Writings* (New York: Oxford University Press, 1997), 71.

2. Cf. Vivien Jones, ed., *Women in the Eighteenth Century: Constructions in Femininity* (New York: Routledge, 1990), 244–48.

3. M. Astell, *Letters Concerning the Love of God, between the Author of the Proposal to the Ladies and Mr. J. Norris* (London: Samuel Manship & Richard Wilkin, 1695). Also (London: S. Manship, 1705) and (London: Edmund Parker, 1730).

4. See especially John C. English, "John Wesley's Indebtedness to John Norris," *Church History* 60, no. 1 (March 1991): 55–69.

5. Hester Chapone, *Letters on the Improvement of the Mind, Addressed to a Young Lady*, 2 vols. (London: J. Walter, 1773). Subsequent editions from the same printer appeared in 1774, 1787, and 1793, as well as a recent reprint (London: Pickering and Chatto, 1996); Chapone, *Miscellanies in Prose and Verse* (London: E. & C. Dilly with J. Walter, 1773). A second edition appeared in 1775 by the same printer.

6. C——— (M—y), *The Ladies' Defence: or, the Bride-woman's Counsellor Answer'd: A Poem . . . Written by a Lady* (London: John Deeve, 1700, 1701). Also, (London: Bernard Lintott, 1709).

7. Catherine Macaulay Graham, *The History of England from the Accession of James I to that of the Brunswick Line*, 8 vols. (London: J. Nourse, 1763–83).

8. The original *Female Spectator* was the first woman's English periodical written by a woman, appearing as a monthly in 1744 and ending its published circulation in 1746. It was later collected into a four-volume set that went through thirteen printings, the last in 1771. A selection from the 1748 second edition is in Mary Priestly, ed., *The Female Spectator. Being Selections from Mrs. Eliza Haywood's Periodical, 1744–1746* (London: John Lane, 1929).

9. Eliza Haygood, *The History of Miss Betsy Thoughtless* (London: T. Gardner, 1751).

10. *Morning Chronicle*, January 6, 1794.

11. Vivien Jones teaches English Literature at Leeds University, and her seminar, "Eighteenth Century Fiction—A Feminist Perspective," was the source for her book.

12. Edmund Burke, *A Philosophical Enquiry into the Origin of Our Ideas of the Sublime and the Beautiful* [1757], ed. J. T. Boulton (London: Routledge & Kegan Paul, 1958), 110.

13. Jones, *Women in the Eighteenth Century*, 3.

14. See Nancy Armstrong, "The Rise of the Domestic Woman," in *The Ideology of Conduct: Essays on Literature and the History of Sexuality*, ed. N. Armstrong and Leonard Tennenhouse (London and New York: Methuen, 1987); Nancy Armstrong, *Desire and Domestic Fiction: A Political History of the Novel* (Oxford: Oxford University Press, 1987); Sylvana Tomaselli, "The Enlightenment Debate on Women," *History Workshop Journal* 19 (1985): 101–24.

15. Francois de Salignac de la Mothe-Fénélon, *Treatise on the Education of Daughters* (1687), trans. Rev. T. F. Dibbin (1805). [First English translation in 1707; this went through no fewer than twenty-seven printings.]

16. Antonia Fraser, *The Weaker Vessel, Woman's Lot in Seventeenth Century England*, 1st ed. (Mandarin, 1984), Wiedenfield and Nicolson, 45.

17. Vicesimus Knox, "On the Insensibility of Men to the Charms of a Female Mind Cultivated with Polite and Solid Literature. In a Letter," in *Essays Moral and Literary*, 2 vols. (London: E. & C. Dilly, 1778–79). These volumes went through no fewer than twenty-four reprintings, the most recent being a reprint from the first edition (New York: Garland Publishing, 1972). Cited by V. Jones, *Women of the Eighteenth Century*, 106–8.

18. Mary Wollstonecraft, "Unfortunate Situation of Females, Fashionably Educated, and Left without a Fortune," in *Thoughts on the Education of Daughters: With Reflections on Female Conduct in the More Important Duties of Life* (London: J. Johnson, 1787, 1788). Also (Dublin: W. Sleuter, 1788). Reprinted with Mary Wollstonecraft Godwin as author (Clifton, NJ: Augustus M. Kelly, 1972), from which my citation is taken, 69–77.

19. Catherine Macaulay Graham, "Part One, Letter IV," in *Letters on Education* (London: C. Dilly, 1790). Reprinted (Oxford: Woodstock, 1994). Cited by V. Jones, *Women of the Eighteenth Century*, 112–14.

20. Mary R. Mahl and Helene Koon, eds., *The Female Spectator: English Writers Before 1800* (Bloomington & London: Indiana University Press, 1977), 6–9.

21. In the *Dictionary of National Biography* and elsewhere, Bathsua is identified as Bathsua Pell Makin, the daughter of a clergyman and sister of the mathematician John Pell. This is now known to be inaccurate. For a discussion of how the misidentification occurred, see Frances N. Teague, *Bathsua Makin: Woman of Learning* (Lewisburg: Bucknell University Press, 1998), 12–17.

22. See (British Library, London) Edward Millington, Bibliotheca Annesleiana: Or a Catalogue of Choice Greke, Latin and English Books . . . Being the Library of the Reverend Samuel Annesley, L.L.D. (London: 1696–97).

23. Charles Wallace, *Susanna Wesley*, Part III, 365–484.

24. See John Newton, *Susanna Wesley and the Puritan Tradition in Methodism* (London: Epworth, 1968) and A. A. Dallimore, *Susanna: The Mother of John and Charles Wesley* (Darlington: Evangelical Press, 1992). For an analysis of attempts at biography that preceded his own, see John Newton, "Susanna Wesley (1669–1742): A Bibliographical Survey," *Proceedings of the Wesley Historical Society* 37 (1969–70): 37–40.

25. Adam Clarke, *Memoirs of the Wesley Family; Collected Principally from Original Documents* (New York: N. Bangs and T. Masor, 1824), 292.

26. Charles Wallace, *Complete Writings*, 18.

27. See Gerald R. Cragg, *The Church and the Age of Reason, 1648–1789* (New York: Atheneum, 1961), esp. 65–70, 157–73.

28. Wesley, "Letter to Mr. C. Glascott, Jesus College, Oxford," in *Works* (Jackson), 13:67.

29. Quoted by Cragg, 158.

30. John Wesley, *Letters* I, in *Works*, 25:175–76.

31. *Susanna Wesley: The Complete Writings*, 112. See also John Wesley, *Letters I* in *Works*, 25:179.

32. *Susanna Wesley: The Complete Writings*, 118. See also John Wesley, *Letters I* in *Works*, 25:183.

33. John Wesley, *Letters I* in *Works*, 25:188.

34. Charles Wallace, "Susanna Wesley's Spirituality: The Freedom of a Christian Woman," *Methodist History* 22, no. 3 (April 1984): 158–73.

35. Susanna Wesley, *The Complete Writings*, 262, journal entry number 95.

36. The following summary is taken from *Susanna Wesley: The Complete Writings*, 78–81.

5. HOSPITALITY AS A LIVING WESLEYAN TRADITION

1. Jaroslav Pelikan, *The Christian Tradition: A History of the Development of Doctrine*: vol. 1, *The Emergence of the Catholic Tradition (100–600)* (Chicago: University of Chicago Press, 1971), 9.

2. Much of the material in the section on early Christian hospitality is from my research on hospitality: Amy Oden, *And You Welcomed Me: Sourcebook on Hospitality in Early Christianity* (Nashville: Abingdon Press, 2001).

3. Many contemporary writers have offered extended discussion on the nature of hospitality, its definition, and its characteristics. For a more developed reflection, see Thomas W. Ogletree, *Hospitality to the Stranger: Dimensions of Moral Understanding* (Philadelphia: Fortress Press, 1985); Christine D. Pohl, *Making Room: Recovering Hospitality as a Christian Tradition* (Grand Rapids: Eerdmans, 1999); Henri J. M. Nouwen, *Reaching Out: The Three Movements of the Spiritual Life* (Garden City, NY: Doubleday, 1975); Parker J. Palmer, *The Company of Strangers: Christians and the Renewal of America's Public Life* (New York: Crossroad, 1981); John Koenig, *New Testament Hospitality: Partnership with Strangers as Promise and Mission* (Philadelphia: Fortress Press, 1985).

4. Interestingly, language itself provides the strong connection between host and guest. In Latin, *hospes* can refer to either host or guest. The Greek *xenos* carries the same double meaning, as do *hote* (French) and *ospite* (Italian).

5. Koenig argues that Paul uses "feast" as the image for new life in Christ, so everyday meals become signs of life in Christ as feast. See especially Koenig, *New Testament Hospitality*, 52–57.

6. For a case study on the notion of hospitality in the New Testament, see G. C. Nicholson, "Houses for Hospitality: 1 Cor 11:17–34," *Colloquium* 19, no. 1 (October 1986): 1–6. Greek and Roman cultures both had highly developed concepts of hospitality as well. See Ladislaus J. Bolchazy, *Hospitality in Early Rome: Livy's Concept of Its Humanizing Force* (Chicago: Ares Publishers, 1977), particularly 1–34.

7. For other Hebrew Bible references to the status of stranger, see Gen. 23:4; 47:4, 9; Lev. 19:34; 25:23; 1 Chr. 29:15; Ps. 39:12. All biblical citations are from the *New Revised Standard Version* (NRSV) of the Bible.

8. Jesus discusses spiritual sight and hearing most explicitly in Matt. 13:9-17.

9. I explore these marks of hospitality in my book *God's Welcome: Hospitality for a Gospel-Hungry World* (Cleveland, OH: Pilgrim Press, 2008).

10. For a thoughtful discussion of the trivialization of the notion of hospitality, see: Pohl, *Making Room*, 3–8, 36–39; Nouwen, *Reaching Out*, 46–47.

11. For discussion of hospitality as a moral category in early Christianity, see Ogletree, *Hospitality to the Stranger*; Rowan A. Greer, "Hospitality," in

Broken Lights and Mended Lives: Theology and Common Life in the Early Church (University Park: The Pennsylvania State University Press, 1986), 119–40.

12. Paul Ricoeur, *Freedom and Nature: The Voluntary and the Involuntary*, trans. Erazim V. Kohák (Evanston, IL: Northwestern University Press, 1966), 126.

13. Thomas Ogletree offers an insightful discussion of the way hospitality reveals the moral bankruptcy of the community's or individual's frame of reference and thus leads to repentance. See Ogletree, *Hospitality to the Stranger*, 1–9.

14. John Wesley, "A Plain Account of Genuine Christianity," in *John Wesley*, ed. Albert Outler (New York: Oxford University Press, 1964), 187.

15. For a discussion of the societies as fields of "social probation" for the poor, see Manfred Marquardt, *John Wesley's Social Ethics* (Nashville: Abingdon Press, 1992), 33–34.

16. Marquardt, *John Wesley's Social Ethics*, 34. He is quoting Wesley in *Journal* 3:301.

17. See MacQuiban, *Pure, Universal Love: Reflections on the Wesleys and Inter-faith Dialogue* (Oxford: Applied Theology Press, 1995).

18. Online exhibit, "Strangers Friend Society Cashbook," *British Methodism and the Poor, 1739–1999*, An Exhibition by the Methodist Archives and Research Centre (John Rylands University Library, Manchester, March 2004), accessed January 20, 2011, http://www.library.manchester.ac.uk/specialcollections/exhibitions/web/britishmethodismandthepoor/earlymethodism/thestrangersfriendsociety/.

19. "Strangers Friend Society Cashbook."

20. John Wesley, letter to Adam Clark, *The Works of John Wesley*, ed. T. Jackson, 3rd ed. (London, 1872), 13:140.

21. "Strangers Friend Society Cashbook."

22. Online exhibit, "Report of the Strangers Friend Society," *British Methodism and the Poor, 1739–1999*.

23. "Report of the Strangers Friend Society."

24. "Report of the Strangers Friend Society."

25. "Report of the Strangers Friend Society."

26. Certainly, Wesley's own life experiences contributed to that keen sense, both growing up at Epworth and subsequently experiencing alienation from others and from God.

27. Sermon 43, "Scripture Way of Salvation," III.8–10, *Works* 2:166. In other places, Wesley argues that such acts of holiness bring happiness: Sermon 49, "The Cure of Evil-Speaking," I.6, *Works* 2:257; Sermon 59, "God's Love to Fallen Man," I.9, *Works* 2:430–31.

28. Matt. 25:37-40.

29. Sermon 26, "Upon Our Lord's Sermon on the Mount (VI)," I.1, *Works* 1:573.

30. Sermon 23, "Upon Our Lord's Sermon on the Mount (III)," II.4-5, *Works* 1:518–9.

31. "A Short History of the People Called Methodists," §39, *Works* 9:447–48.

32. Sermon 51, "The Good Steward," III.5, *Works* 2:295.

33. The presence and identity of the stranger has been addressed with insightful reflections by several recent writers. See Christine D. Pohl,

"Hospitality, Dignity and the Power of Recognition," *Making Room*, 61–84. Also see Thomas W. Ogletree, *Hospitality to the Stranger*; Parker J. Palmer, *The Company of Strangers*; Henri J. M. Nouwen, *Reaching Out*; John Koenig, *New Testament Hospitality*, 1–14; Francis W. Nichols, ed., *Christianity and the Stranger: Historical Essays* (Atlanta: Scholars Press, 1995).

34. Ogletree reminds us not to romanticize the stranger, for that trivializes the genuine risk of hospitality. See Ogletree, *Hospitality to the Stranger*, 39–45.

35. The identification of the stranger with the divine is commonplace in classical literature. Visitation of gods disguised as humans, or *theoxenia*, is a frequent motif in Greek literature. See H. J. Rose, "Divine Disguisings," *Harvard Theological Review* 49, no. 1 (January 1956): 63–72; Sheila Murnaghan, *Disguise and Recognition in the Odyssey* (Princeton, NJ: Princeton University Press, 1987); A. Denaux, "The Theme of Divine Visits and Human (In)Hospitality in Luke-Acts: Its Old Testament and Graeco-Roman Antecedents," in *The Unity of Luke-Acts*, ed. Jozef Verheyden (Leuven: Leuven University Press, 1999), 263–8; Julian Pitt-Rivers, "The Stranger, The Guest and The Hostile Host: Introduction to the Study of the Laws of Hospitality," in *Contributions to Mediterranean Sociology: Mediterranean Rural Communities and Social Change*, ed. John G. Peristiany, Acts of the Mediterranean Sociological Conference, Athens, July 1963 (Paris: Mouton & Co, 1968). For treatment of this theme in an eastern religious tradition, see Teigo Yoshida, "The Stranger as God: The Place of the Outsider in Japanese Folk Religion," *Ethnology* 20 (1981): 87f.

36. Sarah Sloan Kruetziger, "Wesley's Legacy of Social Holiness: The Methodist Settlement Movement and American Social Reform," in *Connectionalism: Ecclesiology, Mission and Identity*, 143.

37. Kruetziger, "Wesley's Legacy," 140.

38. In addition to Kruetziger, see Noreen Dunn Tatum, *A Crown of Service: A Story of Women's Work in the Methodist Episcopal Church, South, from 1878–1940* (Nashville: Parthenon Press, 1960).

39. Kruetziger, "Wesley's Legacy," 140.

40. For more on the history of the deaconess movement, see Carolyn De Swarte Gifford, ed., *The American Deaconess Movement in the Early Twentieth Century* (New York: Garland, 1987). This includes reprints of Isabelle Horton, *The Burden of the City* (1904), and Women's Home Missionary Society, *The Early History of Deaconess Work and Training Schools for Women in American Methodism, 1883–1885* (1912?). See also Priscilla Pope-Levison, "A 'Thirty-Year War' and More: Exposing Complexities in the Methodist Deaconess Movement," *Methodist History* 47, no. 2 (January 2009): 101–16; Laceye C. Warner, *Methodist Episcopal and Wesleyan Methodist Deaconess Work in the Late Nineteenth and Early Twentieth Centuries: A Paradigm for Evangelism* (PhD diss., Trinity College, University of Bristol, 2000).

41. See Pseudo-Clementine, *First Epistle Concerning Virginity*, chap. 12; Commodianus, *The Instructions of Commodianus in Favor of Christian Discipline: Against the Gods of the Heathens*, 71–72; and especially the account of Christians visiting the contagious sick during an epidemic in Alexandria in Dionysius the Great, Epistle 12: *To the Alexandrians*. All excerpts are quoted in *And You Welcomed Me*, 150–3.

42. Pseudo-Clementine, *First Epistle*, in *And You Welcomed Me*, 150.

43. For further discussion and primary source examples, see *And You Welcomed Me: Sourcebook on Hospitality in Early Christianity*, Chapter Three: "Having Eyes to See: Recognizing the Stranger."

6. RECONSIDERING SIN

1. For Virginia Burrus, PhD. Virginia Burrus was my mentor and dissertation advisor at Drew University, where she is Professor of Early Church History and Women's Studies. She invested much time in my work, and also in me as a person. Most important for the chapter presented here, she taught me feminist theory, in all of its complex nuances. In return, I taught her Wesley. It was a perfect match. As in all my work, her voice is always just below the surface of my own, for which I thank her here.

2. Catherine Keller, *From a Broken Web: Separation, Sexism, and Self* (Boston: Beacon Press, 1986), 40. Italics mine.

3. Valerie Saiving Goldstein, "The Human Situation: A Feminine View," in *Womanspirit Rising*, ed. Carol P. Christ and Judith Plaskow (San Francisco: Harper and Row, 1979), 37 (reprinted from *Journal of Religion* 40 [1960]:100–112). Working closely with the Danish text, Sylvia Walsh interprets a key passage in Kierkegaard that is suggestive of the feminist understanding of sin: "In abandoning or throwing herself altogether into that which she devotes herself, woman tends to have a sense of self only in and through the object of her devotion. When the object is taken away, her self is also lost. Her despair, consequently, lies in not willing to be herself, that is, in not having any separate or independent self-identity." Sylvia I. Walsh, "On 'Feminine' and 'Masculine' Forms of Despair," in *International Kierkegaard Commentary: The Sickness unto Death*, ed. Robert L. Perkins (Macon, GA: Mercer University Press, 1987), 124.

4. Judith Plaskow, *Sex, Sin, and Grace: Women's Experience and the Theologies of Reinhold Niebuhr and Paul Tillich* (Washington, D.C.: University Press of America, 1980), 3.

5. Daly and others ask how women can be blamed for the "sin" or failure to self-actualize when social and cultural conditions, namely oppression, prevent them from doing so. In Daly's early work, when she was still interested in traditional theological categories, she offers a shift in the definition of original sin. For Daly, a woman's original sin is the "internalization of blame and guilt." She continues, "The phrase 'original sin' is then torn from its original semantic context. The new sense retains the connotation of an inherited defect. However, it is understood that the 'sin' is inherited through socialization processes. It is the inherited burden of being condemned . . . . The fault should not be seen as existing primarily in victimized individuals, but rather in demonic power structures which induce individuals to internalize false identities." Daly believes that, rather than reinforcing stereotypes by labeling sin "masculine" or "feminine," healing will come when members of both sexes move toward "androgynous being." She states, "For women, this means exorcism of the internalized patriarchal presence, which carries with it feelings of guilt, inferiority, and self-hatred." Mary Daly, *Beyond God the Father: Toward a Philosophy of Women's Liberation* (Boston: Beacon Press, 1973), 49–50.

6. See Mary McClintock Fulkerson, "Sexism as Original Sin: Developing

a Theacentric Discourse," in *Journal of the American Academy of Religion* 59, no. 4 (Winter 1991): 653–75.

7. Marjorie Hewitt Suchocki, *The Fall to Violence: Original Sin in Relational Theology* (New York: Continuum, 1994), 32.

8. The task of providing historical foundations for these and other feminists' alternative "gendered" doctrine of sin is the subject of my book *Singleness of Heart*. There I examine Augustine's contemporaries, Jerome and John Chrysostom, and their rhetoric around women's devotion; John Wesley's correspondence with Methodist women; and Phoebe Palmer's doctrines of sin and holiness. This article draws heavily upon Chapter 3: "Women and the Unwitting Wisdom of John Wesley" and draws also from the constructive Chapter 5: "Sin of the (M)other: A Wesleyan-Holiness-Feminist Hamartiology." Diane Leclerc, *Singleness of Heart: Gender, Sin, and Holiness in Historical Perspective* (Lanham, MD: Scarecrow Press, Inc., 2001).

9. In sum, the debate over essentialism focuses on the fact that affirming a female essence potentially reinstates and reinforces the very abuses feminism intends to fight, and actually makes women collaborators of patriarchy. Thus, some have determined to eradicate the evils of essentialism from feminist theory; for them, any notion of an ontological foundation that affirms a "female" nature, and anyone who might hold to such a position, has been relegated to the realm of the contemptible. Teresa De Lauretis points out there are others who believe that debate, fought on such terms, has ceased to be productive. "Many have grown impatient with this word—essentialism—time and again repeated with its reductive ring, its self-righteous tone of superiority, its contempt for 'them'—those guilty of it." See Teresa De Lauretis, "The Essence of the Triangle or, Taking the Risk of Essentialism Seriously: Feminist Theory in Italy, the U.S., and Britain," in *The Essential Difference*, ed. Naomi Schor and Elizabeth Weed (Indianapolis: Indiana University Press, 1994), 1. Naomi Schor furthers the description of the polarized nature of the debate: "What revisionism, not to say essentialism, was to Marxism-Leninism, essentialism is to feminism: the prime idiom of intellectual terrorism and the privileged instrument of political orthodoxy. . . . The word essentialism has been endowed within the context of feminism with the power to reduce to silence, to excommunicate, to consign to oblivion. Essentialism in modern-day feminism is anathema." Naomi Schor, "This Essentialism Which is Not One: Coming to Grips with Irigaray," in *The Essential Difference*, 42.

10. Gayatri Chakravorty Spivak articulates that "to an extent, we have to look at where the group—the person, the persons, or the movement—is situated when we make claims for or against essentialism. A strategy suits a situation; a strategy is not a theory." Gayatri Chakravorty Spivak with Ellen Rooney, "In a Word. Interview," in *The Essential Difference*, 154.

11. Deborah Rhode summarizes the debate on difference: "[F]eminists generally have taken two approaches, both of which remain critical in contemporary debates over difference. One strategy has been to deny the extent or essential nature of differences between men and women. A second approach has been to celebrate difference—to embrace characteristics historically associated with women and demand their equal social recognition. A third, more recent strategy attempts to dislodge difference—to challenge its centrality and its organizing premises and to recast the terms on which gender relations have

traditionally been debated." Deborah L. Rhode, "Theoretical Perspectives on Sexual Difference," in *Theoretical Perspectives on Sexual Difference*, ed. Deborah L. Rhode (New Haven: Yale University Press, 1990), 3.

12. Regenia Gagnier articulates that, in a postmodern scheme, "microresistances" replace "identities" and are "characterized by fluidity, the ability to mobilize and then disperse." Regenia Gagnier, "Feminist Postmodernism: The End of Feminism or the Ends of Theory?" in *Theoretical Perspectives*, 23.

13. See Judith Butler's advocacy of understanding gender as pure "performance" in Judith Butler, *Gender Trouble: Feminism and the Subversion of Identity* (New York: Routledge, 1990). Elsewhere she argues, "We may seek to return to matter as prior to discourse in order to ground our claims about sexual difference, only to discover that matter is fully sedimented with discourses on sex and sexuality that prefigure and constrain the uses to which that term can be put. Moreover, we may seek recourse to matter in order to ground or to verify a set of injuries or violations, only to find that matter itself is founded through a set of violations, ones that are unwittingly repeated in the contemporary invocation. Indeed, if it can be shown that in its constitutive history this 'irreducible' materiality is constructed through a problematic gendered matrix, then the discursive practice by which matter is rendered irreducible simultaneously ontologizes and fixes that gendered matrix in its place. . . . [A]gainst those who would claim that the body's irreducible materiality is a necessary precondition for feminist practice, I suggest that prized materiality may well be constituted through an exclusion and degradation of the feminine that is profoundly problematic for feminism," Judith Butler, "Bodies that Matter," in *Engaging with Irigaray*, ed. Carolyn Burke, Naomi Schor, and Margaret Whitford (New York: Columbia University Press, 1994), 143. For a historical overview of gender differentiation, see Thomas Walter Laqueur, *Making Sex: Body and Gender from the Greeks to Freud* (Cambridge, MA: Harvard University Press, 1990).

14. Gagnier reminds, "It cannot be overemphasized that . . . critiques of earlier feminist theorizing are rejecting precisely the stories of oppression that gave earlier feminism its discursive unity, the stories that provided slogans that incited action." Gagnier, "Feminist Postmodernism," 22–23. Karen Offen adds, "The fragmentation of identities [postmodernism] proposes, specifically the dissolution of the category women, threatens the historical feminist project." Offen, "Feminism and Sexual Difference in Historical Perspective," in *Theoretical Perspectives*, 15.

15. De Lauretis argues, "If 'woman' is a fiction . . . and if there are no women as such, then the very issue of women's oppression would appear to be obsolete and feminism itself would have no reason to exist (which, it may be noted, is a corollary of poststructuralism and the stated position of those who call themselves 'post-feminists')." De Lauretis, "The Essence," 10.

16. Susan Bordo states, "Assessing where we are now, it seems to me that feminism stands less in danger of the totalizing tendencies of feminists than of an increasingly paralyzing anxiety over a fall (from what grace?) into ethnocentrism or 'essentialism.' " Susan Bordo, *Unbearable Weight: Feminism, Western Culture, and the Body* (Berkeley: University of California Press, 1993), 225. It can be argued that the intensity of the anxiety over a lost identity is unfounded. Such anxiety fails to acknowledge the tenacity of a "mere" construction;

anti-essentialism is unlikely to overthrow or undermine the agenda of feminism, even if feminism itself is seen as a construction.

17. De Lauretis, "The Essence," 5.

18. Bordo, *Unbearable Weight*, 242.

19. De Lauretis, despite the arguments of "post-feminism," still claims that "there is, undeniably, an essential difference between a feminist and a non-feminist understanding of the subject and its relation to institutions; between feminist and non-feminist knowledges, discourse, and practices of cultural forms, social relations, and subjective processes; between a feminist and a non-feminist historical consciousness." (And I would add, between a feminist and a non-feminist theological consciousness.) De Lauretis continues, "That difference is essential in that it is constitutive of feminist thinking, and thus of feminism: it is what makes [this] thinking ... into the historically diverse and culturally heterogeneous social movement which, qualifiers and distinctions notwithstanding ... we continue with good reasons to call feminism." De Lauretis, "The Essence," 1–2. De Lauretis's discourse, although not explicitly addressing the study of theology, certainly legitimates the purposes of feminist theology.

20. See Paul Wesley Chilcote, *John Wesley and the Women Preachers of Early Methodism*, and Earl Kent Brown, *Women of Mr. Wesley's Methodism* (New York: E. Mellen Press, 1983). Other historic studies include George Coles, *Heroines of Methodism: or, Pen and Ink Sketches of the Mothers and Daughters of the Church* (New York: Carlton & Porter, 1857); Maldwyn Edwards, *My Dear Sister: The Story of John Wesley and the Women in His Life* (Manchester: Penwork, Leeds, 1980); Abel Stevens, *The Women of Methodism: Its Three Foundresses, Susanna Wesley, the Countess of Huntingdon, and Barbara Heck; with Sketches of Their Female Associates and Successors in the Early History of the Denomination* (New York: Carlton & Porter, 1866); and Zechariah Taft, *Biographical Sketches of the Lives and Public Ministry of Various Holy Women: Whose Eminent Usefulness and Successful Labours in the Church of Christ, Have Entitled Them to be Enrolled Among the Great Benefactors of Mankind*, 2 vols. (London: Mr. Kershaw, 1825–28).

21. Chilcote, *Women Preachers*, 4–17. Chilcote reviews similar "feminist" activities just prior to Methodism's inception.

22. Letter to Mary Bosanquet (June 3, 1771), *Letters* 5:257.

23. Chilcote, *Women Preachers*, 192–218, esp. 192–98.

24. After explaining his reasons for moving a certain preacher from her society, Wesley tells Sarah Baker to "Feed the lambs!" See Letter to Sarah Baker (July 30, 1785), *Letters* 8:275. Also see Letter to Mrs. Downes (October 1776), *Letters* 6:233. Here Wesley gives his rationale for allowing Mrs. Downes to lead even mixed classes.

25. They were also a part of their own type of circle. Edwards alludes to an almost convent-like environment in their household. See Edwards, *My Dear Sister*, 87–88.

26. Alexander Knox, "Remarks on the Life and Character of John Wesley," *The Life of Wesley: And the Rise and Progress of Methodism*, ed. Robert Southey (London: Oxford University Press, 1925), 2:339.

27. John Fletcher can be considered Wesley's closest male friend. Wesley appointed him as his successor in the leadership of Methodism, although in the end Wesley outlived him. Edwards, *My Dear Sister*, 93–97.

28. Letter to Mary Fletcher (October 2, 1785), *Letters* 7:295.
29. Letter to Sarah Ryan (January 20, 1758), *Letters* 4:4.
30. Letter to Sarah Crosby (September 12, 1766), *Letters* 5:25–27.
31. Letter to Mary (Bosanquet) Fletcher (July 12, 1782), *Letters* 7:128.
32. It should be noted that one study is available that implicates Wesley as a rank misogynist and interprets his leadership of the Methodist movement in terms of sexual seduction. See Henry Abelove, *The Evangelist of Desire: John Wesley and the Methodists* (Stanford, CA: Stanford University Press, 1990). Many Wesley scholars, including myself, are at great odds with Abelove's driving thesis. See the following critique: Richard P. Heitzenrater, "Book Review: Henry Abelove, The Evangelist of Desire; John Wesley and the Methodists," *Methodist History* 30, no. 2 (1992): 118–20.
33. John Wesley, *Explanatory Notes upon the New Testament* (London: Epworth Press, 1954), Acts 17:4.
34. *NT Notes*, 1 Cor. 13:34.
35. *NT Notes*, 1 Pet. 3:7.
36. Letter to Sarah Crosby (July 1, 1757), *Letters* 3:219.
37. John P. Briggs and John Briggs, "Unholy Desires, Inordinate Affections: A Psychodynamic Inquiry into John Wesley's Relationship with Women," *Connecticut Review* 13 (1991): 1.
38. There is some debate as to whether Wesley's proposal actually denoted marriage in light of English law prior to 1754 (when Lord Hardwicke's "Marriage Act" was initiated). Frank Baker argues that the type of proposal Wesley offered in fact made Grace Murray his legal wife. See Frank Baker, "John Wesley's First Marriage," *London Quarterly and Holborn Review* 36, no. 4 (October 1967): 305–15.This argument is refuted by Frederick Maser, who adds that, according to law, a proposal does not denote marriage if conditions are placed on the contract. In Maser's analysis, Wesley had such conditions. Frederick E. Maser, "John Wesley's Only Marriage: An Examination of Dr. Frank Baker's Article 'John Wesley's First Marriage,'" *Methodist History* 16, no. 1 (October 1977): 33–41.
39. Henry D. Rack, *Reasonable Enthusiast: John Wesley and the Rise of Methodism* (Nashville: Abingdon Press, 1993), 261.
40. Rack, *Reasonable Enthusiast*, 264.
41. Southey, *The Life of Wesley*, 2:152. Southey compares Mrs. Wesley to Xantippi, spouse of Socrates, and the wife of Job.
42. Nehemiah Curnock, ed., *The Journal of Rev. John Wesley*, 8 vols. (London: Epworth Press, 1909–16), 3:512.
43. See Rack, *Reasonable Enthusiast*, 265–66.
44. Rack, *Reasonable Enthusiast*, 262.
45. Rack refutes this in light of the time that had passed. See Rack, *Reasonable Enthusiast*, 265.
46. See: Letter to Mrs. Wesley (March 27, 1751) and Letter to Mrs. Wesley (March 30, 1751), *Letters* 3:63–66.
47. Journal for 19 March 1751, *Works*, 20:380; see also 1 Cor. 7:29.
48. Mrs. Wesley eventually "stole" her husband's letters, apparently giving them to his opponents, the Calvinists, to use as ammunition against him. This, for Wesley, was nearly the unforgivable sin.
49. What this actually meant is never stated directly.

50. Letter to Sarah Ryan (January 27, 1758), *Letters* 4:4.
51. Letter to Mrs. Wesley (December 23, 1758), *Letters* 4:49.
52. See: Letter to Mrs. Wesley (October 23, 1759), *Letters* 4:74–78.
53. See: Letter to Mrs. Wesley (October 2, 1778), *Letters* 8:273–74.
54. Maldwyn Edwards, "The Reluctant Lover: John Wesley as Suitor," *Methodist History* 12, no. 2 (January 1974): 62.
55. Samuel J. Rogal, "John Wesley at Edinburgh: 1751–1790," in *Trinity Journal* 4, no. 1 (Spring 1983): 18.
56. Kenneth J. Collins, "John Wesley's Relationship with His Wife as Revealed in His Correspondence," *Methodist History* 32, no. 1 (October 1993): 5.
57. Collins, "John Wesley's Relationship," 18.
58. See Briggs, "Unholy Desires," 5. I have chosen not to include an account of the impact of Wesley's enormously influential mother, Susanna, on his life. Such studies are numerous. For one of the more controversial, see G. Elsie Harrison, *Son to Susanna: The Private Life of John Wesley* (Nashville: Cokesbury, 1938).
59. Although not my main emphasis here, it is important to note that aspects of Wesley's "gender theory" show evidence of development and change. Paul Chilcote highlights Wesley's progressive acceptance of women preachers. He relates that, "Unlike his noted contemporar(ies), Wesley's initial prejudice against the preaching of women gradually dissipated as, step by step, in response to the exigencies of extraordinary situations, he followed the internal promptings of the Holy Spirit, always testing them with the authority of Scripture, reason, experience, and tradition. His attitude toward the whole question began to change over the course of the revival's third decade, just as his views on lay preaching were necessarily transformed a generation earlier." Chilcote, *Women Preachers*, 117. Randy Maddox adds, "In 1754 [Wesley] invoked with no qualifications the common supposition that Eve's creation subsequent to Adam demonstrated that women were originally intended to be subordinate to men. However, by 1765 he inclined more to the view that male and female were created by God to be equal in all ways with women's subjection to men being one of the results of the Fall." Maddox, *Responsible Grace*, 72. My assessment of Wesley's changing views is that he did change his views on women in ministry, but he did not change his view of women in the domestic sphere.
60. See Collins, "John Wesley's Relationship," 4–18; Rogal, "John Wesley at Edinburgh," 18–34. Rogal offers one of the more objective accounts of Wesley's marriage.
61. While my argument here utilizes the definition of misogynism given by Ann Ewing Hickey, who asserts that "a freedom which demands denial of the maternal has limited authenticity for women," it is my intention to oppose Hickey's presupposition. Anne Ewing Hickey, *Women of the Roman Aristocracy as Christian Monastics, Studies in Religion*, no. 1 (Ann Arbor, MI: UMI Research Press, 1987), 20.
62. See Schor, "This Essentialism," 50.
63. "Thoughts on a Single Life," *Works* (Jackson), 11:456–63. Note that Wesley was himself married between revisions.
64. "Thoughts on a Single Life," §14, *Works* (Jackson), 11:462.

65. "Thoughts on a Single Life," §6, *Works* (Jackson), 11:459.
66. "A Thought upon Marriage," *Works* (Jackson), 11:463–65.
67. Rack, *Reasonable Enthusiast*, 264.
68. See: Letter to Charles Wesley (September 2, 1749), *Works* 26:380–88.
69. I am not arguing here against the premise that Wesley held to the conviction that the celibate life was preferable for anyone, male or female, in ministry.
70. Letter to Jane (Hilton) Barton (July 22, 1766), *Letters* 5:24.
71. Letter to Jane (Hilton) Barton (April 9, 1769), *Letters* 5:131.
72. See: Chilcote, *Women Preachers*, 253–54.
73. Letter to Jane (Bisson) Cock (May 20, 1788), *Letters* 8:60.
74. Letter to Jane (Bisson) Cock (December 27, 1788), *Letters* 8:109.
75. Letter to Jane (Bisson) Cock (April 7, 1789), *Letters* 8:128.
76. Letter to Jane (Bisson) Cock (August 3, 1789), *Letters* 8:159.
77. Letter to Jane (Bisson) Cock (November 9, 1790), *Letters* 8:247–48.
78. See Chilcote, *Women Preachers*, 275–76.
79. Letter to Penelope Newman (October 1, 1782), *Letters* 7:143.
80. Introduction to Letter to Peggy Dale (May 20, 1769), *Letters* 5:136.
81. Letter to Peggy Dale (May 20, 1769), *Letters* 5:136.
82. Letter to Elizabeth Ritchie (November 29, 1775), *Letters* 6:194.
83. Letter to Elizabeth Ritchie (February 12, 1779), *Letters* 6:340.
84. Letter to Martha Chapman (November 3, 1784), *Letters* 7:246.
85. Letter to Ann Bolton (February 13, 1768), *Letters* 5:80.
86. Letter to Ann Bolton (August 12, 1770), *Letters* 5:197.
87. Letter to Ann Bolton (December 28, 1771), *Letters* 5:295.
88. Letter to Ann Bolton (November 28, 1772), *Letters* 5:348.
89. Letter to Ann Bolton (January 15, 1773), *Letters* 6:10.
90. Letter to Ann Bolton (January 20, 1774), *Letters* 6:69–70.
91. Letter to Ann Bolton (February 17, 1774), *Letters* 6:73.
92. Letter to Ann Bolton (September 15, 1777), *Letters* 6:279–80.
93. Letter to Ann Bolton (May 8, 1780), *Letters* 7:18.
94. Letter to Mrs. Woodhouse (January 1, 1770), *Letters* 5:174.
95. Letter to Ellen Gretton (July 23, 1782), *Letters* 7:130.
96. Chilcote, "John Wesley as Revealed by the Journal of Hester Ann Rogers," *Methodist History* 20, no. 3 (April 1982): 113. See also Hester Ann Rogers, *Autobiography of Hester Ann Rogers*, reprint (Hampton, TN: Harvey and Tait, 1981).
97. Letter to Sarah Wesley (June 30, 1788), *Letters* 8:69.
98. Letter to Jane (Hilton) Barton (December 30, 1774), *Letters* 6:135.
99. Letter to Jane (Hilton) Barton (April 23, 1783), *Letters* 7:175.
100. Letter to Martha (Wesley) Hall (November 17, 1742), *Works* 26:90–91.
101. Frank Baker observes, "Most of the women with whom Wesley corresponded were either single, widowed, or separated from their husbands." Frank Baker, "Introduction," *Works* 25:86.
102. Wesley quotes Chrysostom directly in "A Farther Appeal to Men of Reason and Religion," Part I: "His comment on the twenty-sixth verse [of John 14] is as follows: Such is that grace (of the Comforter) that if it finds sadness, it takes it away; if evil desire, it consumes it. It casts out fear, and suffers him that receives it to be a man no longer, but translates him, as it were, into heaven.

Hence 'none of them counted anything his own', but 'continued in prayer, with gladness and singleness of heart'." "A Farther Appeal to Men of Reason and Religion," Part I, V.16, *Works* 11:155.

103. Maddox argues that Wesley's theology, particularly the doctrine of Christian perfection, must be evaluated through a chronological survey. See Maddox, *Responsible Grace*, 180–87. Maddox also refers to the use by Wesley's recent interpreters of an "early," "middle," and "late" Wesley; these represent stages in his theological development. See Maddox, *Responsible Grace*, 20.

104. Letter to Rebecca Yeoman (August 4, 1770), *Letters* 5:195

105. Letter to Rebecca Yeoman (February 5, 1772), *Letters* 5:304.

106. Letter to Ann Taylor (March 8, 1787), *Letters* 7:374.

107. Sarah Mallet began "preaching" during "fits" of unconsciousness. Wesley's journal records Mallet's experience. "Some years since, it was strongly impressed upon her, that she ought to call sinners to repentance. This impression she vehemently resisted, believing herself quite unqualified both by her sin and her ignorance, till it was suggested, 'If you do it not willingly, you shall do it whether you will or no.' She fell into a fit and, while utterly senseless, thought she was in the preaching house in Lowestoft, where she prayed and preached for near an hour, to a numerous congregation. She then opened her eyes, and recovered her senses. In a year or two, she had eighteen of these fits, in every one of which she imagined herself to be preaching in one or another congregation. She then cried out, 'Lord, I will obey Thee; I will call sinners to repentance.' She has done so occasionally from that time. And her fits returned no more." Journal from December 4, 1786, *Works* 23:426–27.

108. Letter to Sarah Mallet (March 11, 1788), *Letters* 8:44.

109. Letter to Elizabeth Baker (August 26, 1788), *Letters* 8:85.

110. Umphrey Lee, *John Wesley and Modern Religion* (Nashville: Abingdon-Cokesbury, 1936), 120.

111. John Wesley, "The Doctrine of Original Sin," Preface, ¶4, *Works* (Jackson), 9:194.

112. Robert Chiles, *Theological Transitions in American Methodism: 1790–1935* (New York: Abingdon, 1965), 121–23. Reprint: (Lanham, MD: University Press of America, 1983).

113. John R. Tyson, "Sin, Self and Society: John Wesley's Hamartiology Reconsidered," *Asbury Theological Journal* 44, no. 2 (Fall 1989): 79. Although this is not Tyson's major thesis in an essay in which he "reconsiders" Wesley's hamartiology, Tyson says nothing that would align Wesley with Augustine on the doctrine of original sin and gives several references for Wesley's emphasis on idolatry: Sermon 44, "Original Sin," II.3–9, *Works* 2:177–80; Sermon 52, "On Eternity," §15–16, *Works* 2:367; Sermon 76, "On Perfection," §7, *Works* 3:78; Sermon 78, "Spiritual Idolatry," *Works* 3:103–14; Sermon 80, "On Friendship with the World," §11, *Works* 3:131–32.

114. Craig Alan Blaising, "John Wesley's Doctrine of Original Sin" (ThD diss., Dallas Theological Seminary, 1979), abstract, i.

115. Of note, due to Blaising's extensive review of historical precursors and due to this broader interest, the section that actually reviews Wesley's doctrine of original sin is quite scant: pages 186–217.

116. Blaising, "John Wesley's Doctrine," 186.

117. Sermon 57, "On the Fall of Man," I.1, *Works* 2:402–3. Interestingly, Wesley seems to be interpreting Genesis through the eyes of Milton here.
118. See Blaising, "John Wesley's Doctrine," 198. The "great man" Wesley quotes here is, in fact, Augustine.
119. Blaising, "John Wesley's Doctrine," 198.
120. In *The City of God* (book 14:13), Augustine argues that Adam "preferred the request of his wife to the command of God"; he transgressed by "cleav[ing] to the partner of his life even in a partnership of sin." Saint Augustine, *The City of God*, vol. 2, §14.3, trans. and ed. Marcus Dods (New York: Hafner Publishing Company, 1948), 26. This is a reprint of the original: (Edinburgh: T. & T. Clark, 1872). Yet Augustine fails to see the ramifications of his own interpretation and names this sin as pride.
121. Blaising, "John Wesley's Doctrine," 198. Italics mine.
122. Sermon 57, "On the Fall of Man," I.1, *Works* 2:403.
123. Sermon 57, "On the Fall of Man," I.1, *Works* 2:403.
124. Barry Edward Bryant, "John Wesley's Doctrine of Sin" (PhD diss., King's College, University of London, July 1992), 169.
125. Bryant, "John Wesley's Doctrine," 170. Bryant quotes from John Wesley, "A Thought upon Marriage," 6, *Works* (Jackson), 11:465.
126. Bryant, "John Wesley's Doctrine," 170.
127. Seung-An Im, "John Wesley's Theological Anthropology: A Dialectical Tension between the Latin Western Patristic Tradition (Augustine) and the Greek Eastern Patristic Tradition (Gregory of Nyssa)" (PhD diss., Drew University, 1994, Ann Arbor, MI: UMI Dissertation Services, 1995), 152.
128. A helpful essay on the topic of Wesley's doctrine of sin is offered by John Chongnahm Cho. However, only one sentence of this essay deals with the content of original sin; Cho follows the Augustinian interpretation. "Man's faculties of reason, will and liberty were then corrupted and man's love and obedience to God were replaced by self-love and self-will." John Chongnahm Cho, "John Wesley's View of Fallen Man," in *A Spectrum of Thought: Essays in Honor of Dennis F. Kinlaw*, ed. Michael L. Peterson (Wilmore, KY: Francis Asbury Publishing Company, Inc., 1982), 68.
129. See Leon O. Hynson, "Original Sin as Privation: An Inquiry into a Theology of Sin and Sanctification," *Wesleyan Theological Journal* 22, no. 2 (Fall 1987): 65–83.
130. See Carl O. Bangs, *Arminius: A Study in the Dutch Reformation* (Nashville: Abingdon Press, 1971).
131. Hynson, "Original Sin," 70. Also see Mildred Bangs Wynkoop, *A Theology of Love: The Dynamic of Wesleyanism* (Kansas City: Beacon Hill Press, 1972), 155–58. Although it is clear that simply adopting a relational theology will not automatically delete error from one's interpretation of Wesley, I concur with Hynson's appreciation of Wynkoop, despite her interpretation that places Wesley in Augustinian categories. She writes, "[People] find themselves locked by their own love into an orbit about a center. Sin is love locked into a false center, the self. . . . The epitome of pride and carnal arrogance is to raise one's own miserable self to the pretension of being a god." Wynkoop, *A Theology of Love*, 158. However, there seems to be some latitude in Wynkoop's own analysis. Elsewhere she states, "Sin must be interpreted

in keeping with the 'existential' terminology of Scripture. . . . In the Bible [sin] is an active spirit of 'yielding' or dedication, to any center outside of God." Wynkoop, *A Theology of Love*, 150. Italics mine.

132. For further treatments of John Wesley's doctrine of sin that focus on the issue of depravity, see Donal Dorr, "Total Corruption and the Wesleyan Tradition," *Irish Theological Quarterly* 31 (1964): 303–21; Daniel Joseph Luby, *The Perceptibility of Grace in the Theology of John Wesley: A Roman Catholic Consideration* (Rome: Apud Pontificia Universitatem S. Thomae in Urbe, 1994).

133. Maddox, *Responsible Grace*, 73–74.

134. John Wesley, "The Doctrine of Original Sin," Preface, ¶4, *Works* (Jackson), 9:194.

135. My survey was based on the Journals in *Works* (Jackson), vols. 1–4.

136. In Wesley's journals, pride appears with various combinations of the following words: fear, anger, revenge, unbelief, levity, desire, impatience, lust, worldliness, carelessness, self-will, guile, covetousness, love of the world, darkness of mind, love of money, bitterness, bigotry, self-indulgence, envy, fretfulness, peevishness, enthusiasm, uncharitableness, prejudice, offense, resentment, evil-habits, folly, vanity, and affection.

137. For the sake of continuity and comparison, the sermons examined here are the same sermons used by Im to support his claim that the content of original sin is pride. See Im, "Wesley's Theological Anthropology," 152–54.

138. Sermon 5, "Justification by Faith," III.3, *Works* 1:192.

139. See Sermon 62, "The End of Christ's Coming," I.8, *Works* 2:476; Sermon 5, "Justification by Faith," IV.8, *Works* 1:197; Sermon 128, "The Deceitfulness of the Human Heart," I.1, *Works* 4:152.

140. Sermon 128, "The Deceitfulness of the Human Heart," I.1, *Works* 4:152. Italics mine.

141. Maddox, *Responsible Grace*, 81. Maddox references the following sermons as examples: Sermon 7, "The Way to the Kingdom, II.2, *Works* 1:226; Sermon 78, "Spiritual Idolatry," I.5–15, *Works* 3:105–9; Sermon 84, "The Important Question," I.2–4, *Works* 3:183–85. Maddox, *Responsible Grace*, 296n120.

142. Maddox, *Responsible Grace*, 81–82.

143. Sermon 14, "The Repentance of Believers," I.3, *Works* 1:337.

144. Sermon 14, I.5, *Works* 1:338.

145. Ibid.

146. Sermon 44, "Original Sin," II.1–10, *Works* 2:176–81.

147. Sermon 44, II.7, *Works* 2:179.

148. Sermon 44, II.9, *Works* 2:179–80.

149. Sermon 78, "Spiritual Idolatry," I.18, *Works* 3:110–11.

150. Letter to Sarah Crosby (May 11, 1780), *Letters* 7:19.

151. From Sarah Ryan to John Wesley (May 4, 1764), *Letters* 4:240.

152. Sermon 57, "On the Fall of Man," I.4, *Works* 2:404–5.

153. Maddox, *Responsible Grace*, 73.

154. Baker, "Introduction," *Works* 25:86.

155. Saiving Goldstein, "The Human Situation," 37.

7. A Heritage Reclaimed

1. This essay is dedicated to Paul M. Bassett on the occasion of his retirement as Professor of the History of Christianity at Nazarene Theological Seminary after thirty-five years of service. It was Dr. Bassett who instilled in me a deep appreciation for the historical rooting of current faith and practice, and who modeled for me the passionate, yet careful, study of this traditioning process.

2. For more on this, see Randy L. Maddox, "Reclaiming an Inheritance: Wesley as Theologian in the History of Methodist Theology," in *Rethinking Wesley's Theology for Contemporary Methodism*, ed. R. L. Maddox (Nashville: Kingswood Books, Abingdon, 1998), 213–26.

3. The quotation is from Foster, *Studies in Theology, Vol. 1: Prolegomena: Philosophic Basis of Theology; or, Rational Principles of Religious Faith* (New York: Hunt & Eaton, 1891), vi–vii. The only reference to Wesley I have found is in *Vol. 6: Sin* (1899), 179–81.

4. David F. Ford, *The Shape of Living: Spiritual Directions for Everyday Life* (Grand Rapids: Baker Book House, 1997), 21.

5. See respectively, Ronald H. Stone, *John Wesley's Life and Ethics* (Nashville: Abingdon, 2001), 157; and John Munsey Turner, *John Wesley: The Evangelical Revival and the Rise of Methodism in England* (Peterborough: Epworth, 2002), 41–42.

6. Cf. A. W. Sloan, *English Medicine in the Seventeenth Century* (Durham: Durham Academic Press, 1996), 138–40; and Robert Heller, " 'Priest-Doctors' as a Rural Health Service in the Age of the Enlightenment," *Medical History* 20 (1976): 361–83.

7. In addition to *Boyle's Medicinal Experiments; or, A Collection of Choice Remedies, for the Most Part Simple, and Easily Prepared*, 3 vols. (London: Sam Smith, 1692–94), and *Of the Reconcileableness of Specific Medicines to the Corpuscular Philosophy; to which is annexed a discourse about the advantages of the use of simple medicines* (London: Samuel Smith, 1685); he read during this time at least John Allen, *Dr. Allen's Synopsis Medicinae*, 2 vols. (London: Pemberton & Meandows, 1730); George Cheyne, *An Essay of Health and Long Life* (London: George Strahan, 1724); George Cheyne, *A New Theory of Acute and Slow Continued Fevers* (London: George Strahan, 1702); John Drake, *Anthropologia Nova; or, A New System of Anatomy*, 2 vols. (London: William Innys, 1727–28); John Floyer, *Pharmako-Basanos; or, the Touch-stone of Medicines*, 2 vols. (London: Michael Johnson, 1687–90); and Daniel Le Clerc, *The History of Physick* (London: Brown, et al., 1699).

8. Thomas Sydenham, *Complete Method of Curing Almost All Diseases* (London: Randal Taylor, 1694), see *Works* 18:447; John Tennent, *Every Man His Own Doctor: or, The Poor Planter's Physician* (Williamsburg, VA: William Parks, 1734), see *Works* 18:443; and Daniel Turner, *The Art of Surgery* (London: C. Rivington & J. Clarke, 1722), see *Works* 18:385. Note also Wesley's comment about studying physick "properly" in preparation for his time in America, in "Plain Account of the People Called Methodists," §XII.2, *Works* 9:275.

9. "To the Editor of Lloyd's Evening Post" (January 23, 1776), in *Lloyd's Evening Post* (January 26–29, 1776): 102. While Wesley may have drawn on

his transcription of Tennent during his Georgia years, there is little direct dependence in the *Primitive Physick*, likely reflecting Tennent's own claim to be giving prescriptions suited to North America.

10. See James G. Donat, "Empirical Medicine in the 18th Century: The Rev. John Wesley's Search for Remedies That Work," *Methodist History* 44 (2006): 216–26.

11. These will all be included in the future Volume 17 of Wesley's *Works*. For an analysis of the two extracts from Tissot, see James G. Donat, "The Rev. Mr. John Wesley's Extractions from Dr. Tissot: A Methodist Imprimatur," *History of Science* 39 (2001): 285–98.

12. Cf. Dorothy Porter and Roy Porter, *Patient's Progress: Doctors and Doctoring in Eighteenth Century England* (Stanford, CA: Stanford University Press, 1989); Irvine Loudon, "Medical Practitioners 1750–1850 and the Period of Medical Reform in Britain," in *Medicine in Society*, ed. Andrew Wear (New York: Cambridge University Press, 1992), 219–47; and Roy Porter, "The Eighteenth Century," in *The Western Medical Tradition*, ed. Lawrence Conrad (New York: Cambridge University Press, 1995), 371–475.

13. Note his rejection of this explicit suggestion in Letter to John Smith (March 25, 1747), *Works* 26:236.

14. "A Farther Appeal to Men of Reason and Religion," Pt. I, §3, *Works* 11:106.

15. For more on the "healing" emphasis in Wesley's understanding of salvation, see Randy L. Maddox, *Responsible Grace*, 144–47.

16. Letter to Alexander Knox (October 26, 1778), *Letters* (Telford) 6:327. Another good example is Letter to Miss Agnes Gibbes (April 28, 1784), *Methodist History* 6, no. 3 (1968): 53.

17. See in this regard George Whitefield's Letter to John Wesley (September 25, 1740), *Works* 26:31–33.

18. Cf. David Harley, "John Hart of Northampton and the Calvinist Critique of Priest-Physicians: An Unpublished Polemic of the Early 1620s," *Medical History* 42 (1998): 362–86. An excellent example of the contrary view that offering medical advice was central to the role of a country parson is George Herbert, *A Priest to the Temple; or the Country Parson* (London: T. Garthwaite, 1652), Chapter 23 (Wesley's Oxford diary records that he read this volume in July 1730).

19. See *Bibliotheca Annesleiana; or a Catalogue of Choice Greek, Latin and English Books, both Ancient and Modern*, . . . being the library of the Reverend Samuel Annesley . . . sold by auction on Thursday the Eighteenth of March, 1696, by Edward Millington (copy in British Library). The medical volumes, by such authors as Boyle, Culpepper, Digby, and Helmont, can be found on pp. 7–8, 18.

20. For a few examples, see "Large Minutes," Q. 42, *Works* (Jackson) 8:319; To the Societies at Bristol (1764), *Letters* (Telford) 4:272; Letter to Christopher Hopper (November 20, 1769), *Letters* (Telford) 5:161; and Letter to Joseph Taylor (September 9, 1782), *Letters* (Telford) 7:139.

21. Compare the list recommended for Assistants in "Minutes" (August 3, 1745), *Minutes of the Methodist Conferences, from the First, held in London, by the Late Rev. John Wesley, A.M., in the Year 1744* (London: John Mason, 1862), 1:29; to a list recommended to all readers in the Appendix of *Reflections upon*

the Conduct of Human Life: with reference to Learning and Knowing, extracted [by Wesley] from John Norris, 3rd edition (London: William Strahan, 1755); and his recommendation in Letter to Margaret Lewen (June 1764), *Letters* (Telford) 4:249, that were later published as "A Female Course of Study," *Arminian Magazine* 3 (1780): 602–4.

22. Note in this regard that the letter that John and Charles Wesley sent on June 25, 1751 to James Wheatley, a Methodist itinerant who had been caught in sexual impropriety, instructed him to desist not only from preaching but from practicing physic (see *Works* 26:465).

23. Cf. "Plain Account of the People Called Methodists," §XI.4, *Works* 9:274.

24. Philip Wesley Ott has made this point well in "John Wesley on Mind and Body: Toward an Understanding of Health as Wholeness," *Methodist History* 27 (1989): 61–72; and "John Wesley on Health as Wholeness," *Journal of Religion and Health* 30 (1991): 43–57.

25. Letter to Samuel Bradburn (March 13, 1788), *Letters* (Telford) 8:45.

26. Cf. the prescriptions for apoplexy and measles in Appendix A. See also his Postscript to the Preface of *Primitive Physick*, §5, *Works* (Jackson) 14:317.

27. See particularly Journal (January 4, 1785), *Works* 23:340–41.

28. Journal (September 30, 1786), *Works* 23:420.

29. Note his warning against such practice in medicine, and in many other fields, in Sermon 50, "On the Use of Money," §I.5, *Works* 2:272. Cf. *Primitive Physick*, Preface, §14, *Works* (Jackson) 14:312–13.

30. For good surveys of this tension, see Doreen Evenden Nagy, "The Intellectual Climate: Religion and Popular Medicine," in *Popular Medicine in Seventeenth-Century England* (Bowling Green, OH: Bowling Green State University Popular Press, 1988), 34–42; and Roy Porter, "Medicine and Religion in 18th Century England," *Ideas and Production* 7 (1987): 4–17.

31. For some examples in his journal, see December 20, 1742 (*Works* 19:306), November 12, 1746 (*Works* 20:145), September 22–October 3, 1756 (*Works* 21:78), and October 7, 1790 (*Works* 24:191). See also the published accounts in *Arminian Magazine* 5 (1782): 251–57, 312–18; 9 (1786): 43–44; and 10 (1787): 35–37.

32. *Advice with Respect to Health*, Preface, §9, *Works* (Jackson) 14:258. Cf. *Primitive Physick*, Preface, §15, *Works* (Jackson) 14:314; and Letter to Robert Carr Brackenbury (February 13, 1784), *Letters* (Telford) 7:209.

33. This point is demonstrated in further detail in Henry D. Rack, "Doctors, Demons, and Early Methodist Healing," in *The Church and Healing*, ed. W. J. Sheils (Oxford: Basil Blackwell, 1982), 137–52.

34. For example, Michael MacDonald, "Religion, Social Change, and Psychological Healing in England, 1600–1800," in *The Church and Healing*, 101–25, esp. 106 and 125; and Roy Porter, *Mind Forg'd Manacles: A History of Madness in England from the Restoration to the Regency* (London: Athlone, 1987), 68–72.

35. Wesley notes such early reactions in his journal for January 21, 1739 (*Works* 19:32), March 1, 1740 (*Works* 19:140), August 23, 1740 (*Works* 19:166), and September 17, 1740 (*Works* 19:168–69).

36. Note this defense in his journal (September 21, 1739), *Works* 19:99. Continuing debate over this defense can be traced in "A Farther Appeal to Men

of Reason and Religion," Part I, §VII.13–17, *Works* 11:197–201; "Answer to Mr. Church's Remarks," §III.10, *Works* 9:119–20; and "Principles of a Methodist Farther Explained," §IV.7–10, *Works* 9:207–11.

37. See "A Farther Appeal to Men of Reason and Religion," Part I, §VII.14, *Works* 11:198.

38. See the journal entries for May 2, 1739 (*Works* 19:54–55), October 12, 1739 (*Works* 19:104), October 25–26, 1739 (*Works* 19:110–11), July 15, 1742 (*Works* 19:282), and January 13, 1743 (*Works* 19:311–12).

39. See George Cheyne, *The Natural Method of Curing the Diseases of the Body and Disorders of the Mind Depending on the Body* (London: Strahan, 1742), 78–95, esp. 90. Wesley notes reading this volume in his journal (March 12, 1742), *Works* 19:256. Cheyne emphasizes a sparse diet and cold baths for the cure.

40. Journal (September 24, 1742), *Works* 19:299.

41. Cf. Journal (June 5, 1753), *Works* 20:461–63; Journal (September 8–11, 1755), *Works* 21:28–29; and Journal (July 2, 1766), *Works* 22:48. Note as well Journal (April 27, 1752), *Works* 20:421, where Wesley describes a woman as either raving mad or possessed, and then makes clear that it was demonic possession, since a prayer for deliverance was effective.

42. Cf. Journal (December 21, 1762), *Works* 21:400. For a comparison of Bedlam, which did not focus on medicinal treatment of patients, with Saint Luke's Hospital, see G. S. Rousseau, "Science," in *The Eighteenth Century*, ed. Pat Rogers (New York: Holmes & Meier, 1978), 153–207, esp. 180–82; and the recent more nuanced account in Jonathan Andrews and Andrew Scull, *Undertaker of the Mind: John Monro and Mad-Doctoring in Eighteenth-Century England* (Berkeley: University of California Press, 2001).

43. Cf. Sermon 72, "On Angels," §II.13, *Works* 3:26; and Sermon 132, "On Faith," §8, *Works* 4:194. Wesley is citing Thomas Deacon (1697–1753), another priest/physician. Deacon trained under Richard Mead (1673–1754), a leading physician, who shared this view of the causes of insanity. See Henry Broxap, *A Biography of Thomas Deacon* (Manchester: University Press, 1911), 21–22, 81–88.

44. This point is well argued, against MacDonald and Porter, in Paul Laffey, "John Wesley on Insanity," *History of Psychiatry* 12 (2001): 467–79. A good example of the elder Wesley attributing madness to natural causes is Sermon 41, "Wandering Thoughts," §II.3, *Works* 2:129.

45. The most insightful study of Cheyne is Anita Guerrini, *Obesity and Depression in the Enlightenment: The Life and Times of George Cheyne* (Norman: University of Oklahoma Press, 2000).

46. Note his comment about the book in his Letter to Susanna Wesley (November 1, 1724), *Works* 25:151. For publication details of *Essay*, see note 7.

47. *Primitive Physick*, Preface, §16.VI (see Appendix B); cf. Cheyne, *Essay*, 170–72.

48. Journal (May 12, 1759), *Works* 21:191.

49. Cheyne, *Essay*, 171.

50. Cheyne, *The English Malady; or, A Treatise of Nervous Diseases of all Kinds, as spleen, vapours, lowness of spirits, hypochodriacal, and hysterical distempers* (London: George Strahan, 1733). His title reflects the fact that many on the continent were claiming that the English were particularly susceptible to these diseases. See p. x for his main thesis.

51. The entry in his Oxford diary for September 9, 1734 mentions reading "Cheyne" but does not list a title. *English Malady* is item 75 in the list of books in Randy L. Maddox, "Kingswood School Library Holdings (ca. 1775)," *Methodist History* 41, no. 1 (2002): 342–70.

52. "Thoughts on Nervous Disorders," §§1–5, *Works* (Jackson) 11:515–17. The reference at the end is to William Cadogan, *A Dissertation on the Gout, and All Chronical Diseases, Jointly Considered, as Proceeding from the Same Causes; What These Causes Are; and a Rational and Natural Method of Cure Proposed* (London: Dodsley, 1771). Wesley read Cadogan in 1771 and published an extract three years later in Volume 26 of his *Works* (Pine edition).

53. Sermon 84, "The Important Question," §III.7, *Works* 3:193.

54. Cf. his comments on "lowness of spirits" in Journal (July 13, 1739), *Works* 19:79; Journal (February 20, 1745), *Works* 20:53; and Journal (August 26, 1752), *Works* 20:435; and on melancholy in Journal (April 22, 1766), *Works* 22:39.

55. Cf. Sermon 47, "Heaviness through Manifold Temptations," §III.1–2, *Works* 2:226–27.

56. For a more detailed survey of this balance, see Joe Gorman, "John Wesley and Depression in an Age of Melancholy," *Wesleyan Theological Journal* 34, no. 2 (1999): 196–221.

57. Sermon 47, "Heaviness through Manifold Temptation," §III.2, *Works* 2:227.

58. For more analysis of this distinction, focused on Wesley's setting, see Harold J. Cook, "Physick and Natural History in Seventeenth-Century England," in *Revolution and Continuity: Essays in the History and Philosophy of Early Modern Science*, ed. Peter Barker and Roger Ariew (Washington, D.C.: Catholic University of America Press, 1991), 63–80.

59. He was clearly applying "physick" to the therapies collected in the volume, rather than to the advice in the preface. See his comment: "There can be no doubt that your bodily disorder greatly affects your mind. Be careful to prevent the disease by diet rather than physick," in Letter to Alexander Knox (October 26, 1778), *Letters* (Telford) 6:328.

60. Cf. Antoinette Emch-Dériaz, "The Non-naturals Made Easy," in *The Popularization of Medicine, 1650–1850*, ed. Roy Porter (New York: Routledge, 1992), 134–59.

61. See also Philip Wesley Ott, "John Wesley and the Non-Naturals," *Preventive Medicine* 9 (1980): 578–84.

62. Cf. Ginnie [i.e., Virginia] Smith, "Prescribing the Rules of Health: Self-Help and Advice in the Late Eighteenth Century," in *Patients and Practitioners*, ed. Roy Porter (New York: Cambridge University Press, 1985), 249–82, esp. 259, 264–65; and Virginia Smith, "Physical Puritanism and Sanitary Science: Material and Immaterial Beliefs in Popular Physiology, 1650–1840," in *Medical Fringe and Medical Orthodoxy, 1750–1850*, ed. W. F. Bynum and Roy Porter (London: Croom Helm, 1987), 174–97, esp. 177–81.

63. Note as well his critique of a physician who persisted with the "hot regimen" in treating citizens of London when it was clearly ineffective, in Journal (August 16, 1748), *Works* 20:239; and his commendation of Tissot for avoiding this, in *Advices with Respect to Health*, Preface, §3, *Works* (Jackson) 14:255.

64. See Cheyne, *English Malady*, iv–v; and the analysis of Bryan Turner, "The Government of the Body: Medical Regimens and the Rationalization of Diet," *British Journal of Sociology* 33 (1982): 254–69, esp. 265–66.

65. See A Letter to the Right Reverend the Lord Bishop of London, §14, *Works* 11:344–45.

66. See especially "Thoughts on Nervous Disorders," §§6–7, *Works* (Jackson) 11:518; and the Preface to his "Extract from Cadogan's Dissertation on the Gout," *Works* (Jackson) 14:265–69. But note also that he suggests a vegetarian diet for weight loss (Appendix A, #330). William Stroup's helpful recent study overplays a little Wesley's encouragement of vegetarianism; see Stroup, "Meat, Ethics, and the Case of John Wesley," in *Orthodoxy and Heresy in Eighteenth-Century Society*, ed. Regina Hewitt and Pat Rogers (Lewisburg, PA: Bucknell University Press, 2002), 267–80. More balanced is Charles I. Wallace, Jr., "Eating and Drinking with John Wesley: The Logic of His Practice," *Bulletin of the John Rylands Library* 85, no. 2–3 (2003): 137–55.

67. See the advice for avoiding costiveness (i.e., constipation) in Appendix B, §V.1. The phrase "soft, cool, open diet" is Wesley's summary, not found in Cheyne's original.

68. For more on the broad conviction of the benefits of open country and fresh air in health manuals of the time, see Andrew Wear, "Making Sense of Health and the Environment in Early Modern England," in *Medicine in Society*, ed. Andrew Wear (New York: Cambridge University Press, 1992), 119–47.

69. Letter to Lady Maxwell (February 23, 1767), *Letters* (Telford) 5:42.

70. "Extract from Dr. Cadogan's Dissertation on the Gout," Preface, §10, *Works* (Jackson) 14:268.

71. "Thoughts on Nervous Disorders," §10, *Works* (Jackson) 11:520.

72. Letter to Miss Agnes Gibbes (May 1785), *Methodist History* 6, no. 3 (1968): 59.

73. Cf. Porter, "Eighteenth Century," 419–20; and Cheyne, *Essay of Health*, 95.

74. Letter to Mrs. Christian (July 17, 1785), *Letters* (Telford) 7:281.

75. Cf. Letter to Miss Agnes Gibbes (January 14, 1785), *Methodist History* 6, no. 3 (1968): 57.

76. See Letter to Sarah Wesley (August 18, 1790), *Letters* (Telford) 8:234.

77. Wesley may have learned of this device from a description in *The Gentleman's Magazine* 16 (1746): 478. John Fletcher also apparently used one regularly; see "The Life and Death of Mr. Fletcher," §3.13, *Works* (Jackson) 11:291. For a picture and discussion of one of the few remaining examples, see Conrad Volk, "The Dumb-Bell at Knole: A Seventeenth-Century Exercising Device," in *National Trust Studies 1981*, ed. Gervase Jackson-Stops (London: Sotheby Parke Bernet, 1981), 133–38. See also David Bryant, "The History of the Dumb Bell," *The Ringing World* 98 (2002): 260–61.

78. "Thoughts on Nervous Disorders," §7, *Works* (Jackson) 11:518.

79. Sermon 93, "On Redeeming the Time," §II.4, *Works* 3:326–27 (1782).

80. See, for example, Keith Thomas, "Cleanliness and Godliness in Early Modern England," in *Religion, Culture, and Society in Early Modern Britain*, ed. Anthony Fletcher (New York: Cambridge University Press, 1994), 56–83, esp. 65.

81. See especially "Large Minutes," Q. 44, *Works* (Jackson) 8:320; Sermon 88, "On Dress," §5, *Works* 3:249; and Sermon 98, "On Visiting the Sick," §II.6, *Works* 3:392.

82. The phrase "it prevents abundance of diseases" in §IV.10 of Wesley's abstract of Cheyne (Appendix B) is Wesley's addition, not found in Cheyne, *Essay of Health*, 108.

83. For individual examples, see remedies 3, 35, 41, and 138 in Appendix A. The appended list is found in every edition of *Primitive Physick* through Wesley's life (pp. 117–18 in 1791).

84. John Floyer, *The Ancient Psychrolousia Revived; or, an essay to prove cold bathing both safe and useful . . . also a letter of Dr. [Edward] Baynard's containing an account of many eminent cures done by the cold baths in England* (London: Smith & Walford, 1702). Note Wesley's reference to this work in *Desideratum*, Preface, §4, *Works* (Jackson), 14:242.

85. Cf. Smith, "Physical Puritanism," 180.

86. Eunice Bonow Bardell, "Primitive Physick: John Wesley's Receipts," *Pharmacy in History* 21 (1979):111–21.

87. *Primitive Physick*, Preface, §11, *Works* (Jackson) 14:311.

88. A good study of the contemporary practice of apothecaries, which can help in identifying many of Wesley's remedies as well as in discerning his distinctive preferences, is Juanita G. L. Burnby, *A Study of the English Apothecary, From 1660 to 1760* (London: Welcome Institute for the History of Medicine, 1983).

89. *Primitive Physick*, Preface, §14, *Works* (Jackson) 14:313. See as well his praise of Sydenham, Dover, and Cheyne in ibid., §12, 14:311–12; and of Tissot in *Advices with Respect to Health*, Preface, §2, *Works* (Jackson) 14:255.

90. Wesley's Oxford diary records that he read Boyle's *Specific Medicines* (see note 7) on July 9, 1725. Pages 137–225 of this work are devoted to Boyle's defense of simple medicines.

91. See Barbara Beigun Kaplan, "Divulging of Useful Truths in Physick," *The Medical Agenda of Robert Boyle* (Baltimore: John Hopkins University Press, 1993); and Michael Hunter, "The Reluctant Philanthropist: Robert Boyle and the 'Communication of Secrets and Receits in Physick,'" in *Religio Medici: Medicine and Religion in Seventeenth-Century England*, ed. Ole Peter Grell and Andrew Cunningham (Hants, England: Scolar Press, 1996), 247–72.

92. *Primitive Physick*, Preface, Postscript, §2, *Works* (Jackson) 14:316.

93. Cf. Andrew Wear, "Medicine in Early Modern Europe, 1500–1700," in *The Western Medical Tradition*, ed. Lawrence Conrad et al. (Cambridge University Press, 1995), 215–360, esp. 309–10.

94. Peruvian bark (or Cinchona) is the natural source of quinine. It was discovered by Jesuits in Peru but is native to other hot climates as well. It is definitely not native to England. For an example of Wesley criticizing certain prescriptions of the bark, see *Advices with Respect to Health*, Preface, §7, *Works* (Jackson) 14:257.

95. Wesley emphasizes the problem of lack of familiarity with exotics in *Primitive Physick*, Preface, §10, *Works* (Jackson) 14:311.

96. Ibid., §4, 14:308–9.

97. Ibid., §6, 14:308–9. See also §3, 14:308.

98. Cf. Sermon 59, "God's Love to Fallen Man," *Works* 2:423–35; and Sermon 63, "The General Spread of the Gospel," §27, *Works* 2:499.

99. The most helpful essay on this topic is H. Newton Malony, "John Wesley and the Eighteenth Century Therapeutic Uses of Electricity," *Perspectives on Science and Christian Faith* 47 (1995): 244–54.

100. In the Preface to *Desideratum*, §1 (*Works* [Jackson] 14:241) he refers to the following in particular: Benjamin Franklin, *Experiments and Observations on Electricity* (London: E. Cave, 1751); John Freke, *An Essay to Show the Cause of Electricity* (London: William Innys, 1746); Dr. Hoadly and Benjamin Wilson, *Observations on a Series of Electrical Experiments*, 2nd ed. (London: Payne, 1759); Richard Lovett, *The Subtil Medium Proved* (London: J. Hinton et al., 1756); Benjamin Martin, *An Essay on Electricity* (Bath: for the author, 1746); William Watson, *Experiments and Observations Tending to Illustrate the Nature and Properties of Electricity*, 3rd ed. (London: C. Davis, 1746); and Benjamin Wilson, *A Treatise on Electricity* (London: Davis et al., 1750).

101. See Journal (November 9, 1756), *Works* 21:8; *Desideratum*, Preface, §5, *Works* (Jackson) 14:243; and Willem D. Hackman, *John Wesley and His Electrical Machine* (London: John Wesley's House and The Museum of Methodism, 2003).

102. See *Desideratum*, Preface, §3, *Works* (Jackson) 14:242. As Wesley admits, the work was almost entirely abridged from others, particularly from Lovett's *Subtil Medium*.

103. Wesley, *Desideratum* (London: Strahan, 1760), §I.1, p. 9.

104. *Desideratum*, Preface, §8, *Works* (Jackson) 14:243.

105. *Primitive Physick*, Preface, §10, *Works* (Jackson) 14:310–11.

106. In this consideration it may help to note that such attacks upon learned medicine for its cost and exclusivity had become a standard item in works popularizing medical knowledge by the middle of the seventeenth century; see Andrew Wear, "Medicine in Early Modern Europe, 1500–1700," 215–360, esp. 324.

107. Some sense of these dynamics can be gained from Mary Fissell, *Patients, Power, and the Poor in Eighteenth Century Bristol* (New York: Cambridge University Press, 1991); and Anne Digby, *Making a Medical Living: Doctors and Patients in the English Market for Medicine, 1720–1911* (New York: Cambridge University Press, 1994).

108. "Plain Account of the People Called Methodists," §XII.1–3, *Works* 9:275–76.

109. Ibid, §XII.6, *Works* 9:276.

110. Note how this specific point is made in one of the first admirable contextual studies of Wesley's interest in medicine: George Sebastian Rousseau, "John Wesley's Primitive Physic (1747)," *Harvard Library Bulletin* 16 (1968): 242–56; here, 247.

111. See in this regard his criticism of Tissot's fondness for bleeding and enemas [glysters], in *Advices with Respect to Health*, Preface, §4 *Works* (Jackson) 14:255–56; and another fine contextual study of Wesley: Clifford Wayne Callaway, "John Wesley's Primitive Physick: An Essay in Appreciation," *Proceedings of the Mayo Clinic* 49 (1974): 318–24, esp. 323.

112. John Wesley, *Primitive Physic* (London: Epworth Press, 1960), §467, 86.

113. Cf. *Primitive Physick*, Preface, Postscript, §3, *Works* (Jackson) 14:317.

114. Letter to Alexander Knox (August 16, 1778), *Letters* (Telford) 6:317–18.
115. Readers may find of interest at this point my subsequent study: "Reclaiming the Eccentric Parent: Methodist Reception of John Wesley's Interest in Medicine," in *"Inward and Outward Health": John Wesley's Holistic Concept of Medical Science, the Environment, and Holy Living*, ed. Deborah Madden (London: Epworth, 2008), 15–50.

8. HOLY HEART, HOLY LIFE, HOLY WORK

1. I dedicate this article to the bishops of The United Methodist Church, many of whom represent the best and worst of Wesleyan work habits. May they continue to learn to work in ways that are good for the health and holiness of themselves, their families, and the church.
2. Russell Richey, "An Invitation," *Celebrating and Revisioning the Wesleyan Movements: John Wesley, 1703–2003*. This brochure was for the Emory University conference at which this chapter was first presented.
3. My interest in work and vocation stems from an interdisciplinary book I am writing on the ways that workplace changes in the United States have altered our vocations as family members, citizens, and Christians. Because the current chapter is part of my larger research project, the editors of *The United Methodist Circuit Rider* have granted me permission to include here several sections of my earlier brief essay "Wesley's Legacy of Work: Living in the Splendor and the Shadow," *The Circuit Rider* 29, no. 3 (May/June 2003): 34–36. See also my article "The Arts of Holy Living," *Quarterly Review* (Summer 2005): 141–57.
4. Richard Heitzenrater, "The Wesleyan Tradition and the Myths We Love," *A Living Tradition: Critical Recovery and Reconstruction of Wesleyan Traditions*, ed. Mary Elizabeth Moore (Nashville: Kingswood Books, Abingdon, 2006).
5. Letter to His Brother Samuel (without date), *Works* (Jackson) 12:20.
6. Sermon 4, "Scriptural Christianity," IV.9, *Works* 1:178.
7. Sermon 29, "Upon our Lord's Sermon on the Mount, Discourse the Ninth," §16, *Works* 1:639.
8. These statistics are cited in many popular books and articles on Wesley, as well as on several official United Methodist websites. See, for example, http://gbgm-umc.org/umw/wesley/order.stm. Even George Will, columnist for *The Washington Post*, quoted these statistics in his column on January 10, 2000. See also Burnis Bushong, "An 18th Century Preacher with 21st Century Vision," in *Wesleyan Life* (Noblesville, Ind.: Wesleyan Pub. House, Spring 2005), 6.
9. Letter to Thomas Greathead (January 22, 1791), *Letters* 8:257.
10. Umphrey Lee, *The Lord's Horseman: John Wesley the Man* (Nashville: Abingdon Press, 1954), 211.
11. David Baines-Griffiths, *Wesley the Anglican* (London: MacMillan and Co., Limited, 1919), 72.
12. *The Book of Discipline of The United Methodist Church*, ¶327.19a (Nashville: United Methodist Publishing House, 2000), 214. Earlier Methodist Books of Discipline carried "The Rules for Preachers" that bore the stamp of Wesley's own rule of life: "We advise you, 1. As often as possible to rise at four. 2. From four to five in the morning and from five to six in the evening

to meditate, pray, and read the Scriptures with notes . . . ." For example, *The Discipline of the Methodist Church*, ¶124 (New York: Eaton & Mains, 1896), 82.

13. J. B. Sykes, ed., *The Concise Oxford Dictionary of Current English*, 6th ed. (Oxford: Oxford University Press, 1976).

14. See Gustaf Wingren, *Luther on Vocation* (Philadelphia: Muhlenberg, 1957).

15. Sermon 74, "Of the Church," II.20, *Works* 3:53.

16. Sermon 17, "The Circumcision of the Heart," II.10, *Works* 1:414.

17. Journal for December 14, 1775, *Works* 22:478. See also Journal for May 28, 1765, *Works* 22:3 and Journal for August 14, 1769, *Works* 22:199.

18. Journal for February 18, 1765, *Works* 21:500. See also Journal for May 7, 1756, *Works* 21:53.

19. Letter to Mary Bosanquet (June 13, 1771), *Letters* 5:257. There is debate as to whether this letter was actually written to Ms. Bosanquet or to another Methodist woman, Mrs. Sarah Crosby. See also "How shall we try those who think they are moved by the Holy Ghost to preach?" found in "Minutes of Several Conversations," Q. 50, *Works* (Jackson) 8:324–25.

20. "The Principles of a Methodist Farther Explained," V.8, *Works* 9:222.

21. Letter to His Brother Charles (June 23, 1739), *Works* 25:660.

22. See, for example, Journal for September 21, 1749, *Works* 20:299.

23. Letter to Mr. Francis Wolfe (September 15, 1773), Francis Wolfe (November 22, 1772), *Letters* 5:346. Wesley's next letter to Wolfe on a completely different subject contained only two lines and illustrated Wesley's sometimes abrupt tone: "Franky, are you out of your wits? Why are you not at Bristol?" *Letters* 6:41.

24. Sermon 89, "The More Excellent Way," III.1–3, *Works* 3:268–69.

25. Sermon 50, "The Use of Money," II.7, *Works* 2:273.

26. See, for example, Timothy Hall Breen, "The Non-existent Controversy: Puritan and Anglican Attitudes on Work and Wealth 1600-1640," *Church History* 35, no. 3 (1966): 277–79.

27. Sermon 50, "The Use of Money," I.1, *Works* 2:269. See also Sermon 79, "On Dissipation," *Works* 2:115–25.

28. Sermon 89, "The More Excellent Way," V.1, *Works* 3:272.

29. Sermon 93, "On Redeeming the Time," §1, *Works* 3:323.

30. "A Word to Sabbath Breakers," *Works* (Jackson) 11:166.

31. Sermon 79, "On Dissipation," §12, *Works* 3:120.

32. "Forms of Prayer for Every Day of the Week," *Works* (Jackson) 11:207.

33. "Thoughts upon Methodism," §1, in *Works* 9:527.

34. "Thoughts upon Methodism" §10, in *Works* 9:530.

35. Sermon 87, "The Danger of Riches," I.9, *Works* 3:233.

36. Sermon 68, "The Wisdom of God's Counsels," §16, *Works* 2:560.

37. Sermon 122, "Causes of the Inefficacy of Christianity," *Works* 4:85–96.

38. "Thoughts upon Methodism," §11, in *Works* 9:530.

39. Sermon 88, "On Dress," §15, in *Works* 3:254.

40. "Thoughts on the Present Scarcity of Provisions," §I.6, *Works* (Jackson) 11:56.

41. Journal for February 8, 1753, in *Works* 20:445.

42. "Thoughts on the Present Scarcity of Provisions," §II.1, *Works* (Jackson) 11:57.

43. Sermon 50, "The Use of Money," §2, *Works* 2:268.

44. Sermon 98, "On Visiting the Sick," III.3, *Works* 3:393.

45. Sermon 29, "Upon our Lord's Sermon on the Mount: Discourse the Ninth," §16, *Works* 1:640.

46. See, for example, Sermon 87, "On the Danger of Increasing Riches," *Works* 3:227–46; Sermon 50, "The Use of Money," III.3, *Works* 2:277; and Sermon 28, "Upon Our Lord's Sermon on the Mount: Discourse the Eighth," §11, *Works* 1:618–19.

47. Sermon 28, "Upon our Lord's Sermon on the Mount: Discourse the Eighth,"§11, *Works* 1:619.

48. Sermon 28, "Upon our Lord's Sermon on the Mount: Discourse the Eighth," §11, *Works* 1:619.

49. He pairs these two terms, "necessities" and "conveniences," almost two dozen times. See, for example, Sermon 51, "The Good Steward," §7, *Works* 2:286; and Sermon 80, "On Friendship with the World," §25, *Works* 3:139.

50. Sermon 87, "The Dangers of Riches," I.4, *Works* 3:231.

51. Sermon 98, "On Visiting the Sick," III.4, *Works* 3:393–94.

52. Sermon 93, "On Redeeming the Time," II.12-13, *Works* 3:329.

53. "A Letter to a Roman Catholic," §15, *Works* (Jackson) 10:85.

54. Sermon 37, "The Nature of Enthusiasm," §24, *Works* 2:55 (emphasis added).

55. Sermon 125, "On a Single Eye," III.2, *Works* 4:126.

56. Sermon 125, "On a Single Eye," III.7, *Works* 4:130.

57. Sermon 125, "On a Single Eye," III.5, *Works* 4:128.

58. See, for example: Gary Babcock, *The Way of Life: A Theology of Christian Vocation* (Grand Rapids: Eerdmans, 1998), 32–44.

59. "A Letter to a Roman Catholic," §15, *Works* (Jackson) 10:85.

60. "A Letter to the Rev. Mr. Downes," §6, in *Works* 9:355. This is in reaction to Mr. Downe's "Methodism Examined and Exposed."

61. Letter to Ebenezer Blackwell (August 14, 1748), in *Works* 26:322.

62. Sermon 79, "On Dissipation," §6, *Works* 3:118.

63. Charles Wesley, "For Believers Working," in *John and Charles Wesley: Selected Prayers, Hymns, Journal Notes, Sermons, Letters and Treatises*, ed. Frank Whaling (New York: Paulist Press, 1981), 212.

64. "Minutes of Some Late Conversations, Conversation II," Q. 5.A, *Works* (Jackson) 8:286.

65. Sermon 50, "The Use of Money," I.1, *Works* 2:269.

66. Sermon 50, "The Use of Money," I.1–8, *Works* 2:268–73.

67. "A Word to the Sabbath Breaker," *Works* (Jackson) 11:166.

68. "A Word to the Sabbath Breaker," *Works* (Jackson) 11:164.

69. See, for example, John Wesley, "An Earnest Appeal to Men of Reason and Religion," §40, in *The Appeals to Men of Reason and Religion and Certain Related Open Letters*, ed. Gerald R. Cragg, vol. 11 of *The Bicentennial Edition of the Works of John Wesley* (Nashville: Abingdon Press, 1976), 59, and Sermon 74, "Of the Church," §28, *Works* 3:56. Wesley used the terms whoremonger and whoremongers several dozen times in the Jackson edition, primarily in the lists of sinners described in the text.

70. See, for example, "The Principles of a Methodist Farther Explained," §VI.7, *Works* 9:231; Sermon 74, "Of the Church," III.28, *Works* 3:56; Journal

from February 6, 1740, *Works* 19:138; and Journal from February 18, 1747, *Works* 20:157.

71. "A Word to a Sabbath Breaker," *Works* (Jackson) 11:165.

72. Sermon 28, "Upon our Lord's Sermon on the Mount: Discourse the Eighth," §1, *Works* 1:613.

73. Sermon 50, "The Use of Money," I.1, *Works* 2:268–69.

74. Sermon 28, "Upon our Lord's Sermon on the Mount: Discourse the Eighth," §1, *Works* 1:613.

75. Sermon 39, "Catholic Spirit," §I.15, *Works* 2:88.

76. "The Character of a Methodist," §14, in *Works* 9:39–40.

77. See, for example, Breen, "The Non-existent Controversy," 273–86.

78. It is dangerous, for example, to rely on Wesley's references about other religions in his sermons and letters to determine what he actually thought about other religions! The primary point of these sermons is not to describe other faiths but to encourage Methodists to be more responsible in their own faith. In several reflections, he urged the Methodists to compare the lives of the righteous, virtuous "heathen" with the tepid lives of Methodists who have been given greater light than the heathen have, but fail to use it. Wesley's point in these sermons was not to set out a theology of non-Christian religions but to help Methodists become better Christians. See my article "John Wesley as Interreligious Resource: Would You Take This Man to An Interfaith Dialogue?," in *A Great Commission: Christian Hope and Religious Diversity*, ed. Martin Forward, Stephen Plant, and Susan White (Oxford: Peter Lang, 2000), 61–75.

79. He used this phrase (and variations of it) several dozen times to talk about the heart of Methodism, Christianity more generally, and even "all religion." See, for example, "A Farther Appeal to Men of Reason and Religion, Part III," §IV.9, *Works* 11:320; "Advice to the People Called Methodists," §2, *Works* 9:123; "Thoughts upon Methodism," §8, *Works* 9:529; "The Character of a Methodist," §4, *Works* 9:35; and Letter to Samuel Sparrow, Esq. (December 28, 1773), *Works* (Jackson) 12:477.

80. "Thoughts upon Methodism," §8, *Works* 9:529.

81. "Advice to the People Called Methodists," §2, *Works* 9:123–24.

82. "The Character of a Methodist," §5, *Works* 9:35.

83. See Randy Maddox's claim that salvation is holistic in Wesley. "John Wesley: A Heritage Reclaimed," *A Living Tradition: Critical Recovery and Reconstruction of Wesleyan Heritage*, ed. Mary Elizabeth Mullino Moore (Nashville: Kingswood Books, Abingdon, 2013).

84. Journal for February 8, 1753, *Works* 20:445.

85. Breen, "The Non-existent Controversy: Puritan and Anglican Attitudes on Work and Wealth 1600–1640," 280–83.

86. "A Farther Appeal to Men of Reason and Religion, Part III," §III.23, *Works* 11:306–7.

87. Sermon 37, "The Nature of Enthusiasm," §8–11, *Works* 2:48–49 (emphasis added).

88. For a more detailed account, see my article "That's All a Mule Can Do: The Ethics of Balancing Work at Home and on the Job," *Maguire Center Occasional Papers* (Dallas: Carey M. Maguire Center for Ethics and Public Responsibility, 2003), http://www.smu.edu/Provost/Ethics/Library/Publications/Occasional

Papers. See also Juliet B. Schor, *The Overworked American: The Unexpected Decline of Leisure* (New York: Basic Books, 1991); James T. Bond, Ellen Galinsky, and Jennifer E. Swanberg, *The 1997 National Study of the Changing Workforce, Executive Summary* (New York: The Families and Work Institute, 1998), http://familiesandwork.org/summary/nscw.pdf; and Ellen Galinsky, Stacy S. Kim, and James T. Bond, *Feeling Overworked: When Work Becomes Too Much, Executive Summary* (New York: The Families and Work Institute, 2001), http://familiesandwork.org/summary/overwork.pdf.

89. William Julius Wilson, *When Work Disappears: The World of the New Urban Poor* (New York: Alfred A. Knopf, 1996), especially 51–86.

90. For more on the spending habits of middle- and upper-income people in the United States, see Juliet Schor's *The Overspent American: Upscaling, Downshifting, and the New Consumer* (New York: Basic Books, 1998).

91. "Credit-card companies set sights on kids," *Fort Worth Star-Telegram* (May 22, 2005), 1(A).

92. This is not to argue that a conscious financial calculation is made, but that many people and institutions in the United States are formed by market forces and that these forces and institutions shape how people view the world. See, for example, Alan Wolfe, *Whose Keeper? Social Science and Moral Obligation* (Berkeley: University of California Press, 1989), especially 27–106.

93. Adam Gopnick, *Paris to the Moon* (New York, Random House, 2000), 71.

94. See my article "That's All a Mule Can Do."

95. Miles, "That's All a Mule Can Do."

96. See, for example, Reinhold Niebuhr, *The Nature and Destiny of Man: A Christian Interpretation*, vol. 1, *Human Nature* (New York: Charles Scribner's Sons, 1941), 185ff; Daphne Hampson, "Reinhold Niebuhr on Sin: A Critique," *Reinhold Niebuhr and the Issues of Our Time*, ed. Richard Harries (Oxford: A. R. Mowbray & Co., Ltd., 1986), 46–60; Valerie Saiving Goldstein, "The Human Situation: A Feminine View," *Journal of Religion* 40, no. 2 (April 1960): 108–10; Judith Plaskow, *Sex, Sin and Grace*; and Susan Nelson Dunfee, *Beyond Servanthood: Christianity and the Liberation of Women* (Lanham, MD: University Press of America, 1989). For an analysis of feminist and Niebuhrian understandings of sin, see Rebekah Miles, *The Bonds of Freedom: Feminist Theology and Christian Realism* (New York: Oxford University Press, 2001).

97. Sermon 125, "On a Single Eye," III.8, *Works* 4:130.

98. Sermon 87, "The Danger of Riches," II.9, *Works* 3:240.

99. Randy Maddox, "John Wesley: A Heritage Reclaimed."

100. Sermon 50, "The Use of Money," I.7, *Works* 2:273.

101. Sermon 29, "Upon our Lord's Sermon on the Mount: Discourse the Ninth," §16, *Work* 1:639.

102. Many popular news stories and articles have focused on the problem of sleep deprivation in the United States. See, for example, Barbara Kantrowitz and Karen Springen, "Why Sleep Matters," *Newsweek* 142, no. 12 (September 22, 2003): 75ff.; Karen Uhlenhuth, "To Sleep: The Impossible Dream," *The Fort Worth Star-Telegram*, September 22, 2003, 3(E); Schor, *The Overworked American*, 11–22; and Catherine Golub, "Sleep-Starved Americans: How to Keep Your Body Clock on Schedule," *Environmental Nutrition* 23, no. 10 (October 2000): 1–2.

103. Sermon 79, "On Dissipation," §12, *Works* 3:120.
104. Sermon 146, "The One Thing Needful," §1–2, *Works* 4:352.
105. Sermon 146, "The One Thing Needful," §1–2, *Works* 4:352.
106. Martha Mendelsohn, "Observing the Sabbath," *Tikkun* 11, no. 3 (May/June 1996): 44.

9. Recovering *Los Desaparecidos*

1. A version of this essay has been published in Spanish: "El Exilio de Metodismo Argentino," *Cuadernos de Teología* 26 (2007), a journal of ISEDET, Buenos Aires, Argentina.

2. "Identity" is a contested term and should not be viewed as a static, fixed reality, but as a dynamic process in which culture, politics, economics, language, religion, and other factors, including persons external to the national or ethnic group, interact in forming a collective, though evolving, social consciousness. See José Miguez Bonino, *Faces of Latin American Protestantism*, trans. Eugene L. Stockwell (Grand Rapids: Eerdmans, 1995), 99 fn. 34. For details of the military dictatorship, the response of Christian churches in Argentina, and the work of organizations that have been at the forefront of the struggle for human rights in the country, see Pablo R. Andiñach and Daniel Bruno, *Iglesias Evangélicas y Derechos Humanos en la Argentina* (Buenos Aires: Ediciones La Aurora, 1991).

3. The use of the word "overseas" to describe autonomous Methodist churches outside the United States reflects the historical roots of autonomy and the language of the Commission on the Structure of Methodism Overseas (COSMOS), which I will introduce later in this paper.

4. My metaphorical use of *los desaparecidos* is not intended to detract from or deny the deeply painful, unresolved reality with which Latin Americans continue to struggle, but to highlight how the church in the United States creates a situation in which whole nations have been virtually erased from our consciousness.

5. The English language has no form for identifying properly a person who is a citizen of the United States (in Spanish, for example, *estadounidense*), and the person is generally referred to as an "American." As discussed later in this paper, this language carries the connotation of the United States as "dominant" or the "center" of the continents of South and North America. As such, I suggest that scholars begin the use of "United Statesian" as a means of pushing back against this linguistic lacuna and introducing a decentered term into usage.

6. For a detailed analysis of these internal tensions, see Nicolas Shumway, *The Invention of Argentina* (Berkeley: University of California Press, 1991).

7. Ibid., xi.

8. Ibid., 214.

9. Jehlen uses the adjective "American" ironically, as she clearly recognizes the linguistic power it has wielded to render invisible the majority of the peoples of the American continents. Myra Jehlen, *American Incarnation: The Individual, the Nation, and the Continent* (Cambridge, MA: Harvard University Press, 1986), 23. I am indebted to my colleague Daisy Machado for introducing me to Jehlen's work.

10. Jehlen, *American Incarnation*, 3.
11. Ibid., 9ff.
12. Ibid., 15.
13. Ibid., 13.
14. The basic history of Methodism in Argentina is drawn and translated from *Constitución y Reglamento General*, Iglesia Evangélica Metodista Argentina (Buenos Aires: Methopress, 2000), 3–4.
15. Daniel A. Bruno, " 'Por una Iglesia con Alma Nacional': Nacimiento y Ocaso de un Sueño," *Revista Evangélica de Historia* 1 (2003): 109–53.
16. Bruno, 114.
17. Ibid., 129.
18. Bruno, 131.
19. Bishop Sante Uberto Barbieri and Rev. José Merlo, Letter to Bishop Richard C. Raines, Chairman of the Commission on the Structure of Methodism Overseas (March 18, 1968). An identical letter was forwarded to Raines by Bishop Barbieri and Rev. Aldo M. Etchegoyen, Executive Secretary, of the Patagonia Provisional Annual Conference. Records on the Committee on the Structure of Methodism Overseas (COSMOS). United Methodist Church Archives 1335-1:1:01 (Madison, NJ).
20. Carlos T. Gattinoni, "The Genius of the Autonomous Churches in Latin America," *Methodist History* (January 10, 1972): 6–10.
21. Ibid., 13.
22. With regard to the theological justification for autonomy, cf. Miguez Bonino, *Doing Theology*, and his report, written as the president of Comision Para el Estudio de la Estructura de la Iglesia Metodista en la Argentina, "Renovacion y Reforma" (May 2, 1967), COSMOS, UMC Archives 1335-1-8:09 (Madison, NJ).
23. Commission on Public Relations and Methodist Information, The General News Service of The Methodist Church (February 6, 1969), 2. COSMOS, UMC Archives 1335-1-8:07 (Madison, NJ).
24. I wish to emphasize here that I have great respect for the work that Dr. Robbins facilitated and accomplished as the general secretary of the GCCUIC. My intention is not to demean or belittle his ministry, but rather to demonstrate that as a product of US Methodism, he reflects its underlying ideology, even as he wishes to move beyond it.
25. I do not intend to imply in any way that the Argentine Methodists have disappeared in reality, but to suggest that the UMC has rendered them invisible within our own "guiding fictions" or ways of thinking and acting. It is, thus, the church in the United States that must begin to hear and see those whom it has marginalized or exiled, but who also have much to contribute to both the UMC and the church's larger mission.
26. Bruce W. Robbins, *A World Parish? Hopes and Challenges of The United Methodist Church in a Global Setting* (Nashville: Abingdon, 2004), 31.
27. Ibid., 116–17.
28. Jehlen, *American Incarnation*, 23.
29. Edward W. Said, "Afterword," in *Orientalism* (New York: Vintage Books, 1994), 331.

30. Bishop Ralph Dodge, "Needs and Problems in the Central Conferences" (April 1965), 3. COSMOS, UMC Archives 1335-1-5:04 (Madison, NJ). His use of "American" to represent the United States should be noted as well.
31. Harry C. Spencer, "Statement to the Committee on the Structure of the Board of Missions" (undated, ca. 1963), 4. COSMOS, UMC Archives, 1336-1-5:02 (Madison, NJ).
32. Robbins, 11.
33. Ibid., 12.
34. José Miguez Bonino, *Doing Theology in a Revolutionary Situation* (Philadelphia: Fortress Press, 1975), xxv.
35. Miguez Bonino, *Doing Theology*, xxvi-xxvii.
36. Miguez Bonino uses this phrase as the title of his third chapter in *Doing Theology*.
37. Leela Gandhi, *Postcolonial Theory* (New York: Columbia University Press, 1998), 4.
38. Ibid., 7.
39. Edward Said, "Orientalism Reconsidered," in *Reflections on Exile* (Cambridge, MA: Harvard University Press, 2000), 214.
40. Quoted in Ron Suskind, "Without a Doubt," *The New York Times Magazine*, October 17, 2004, 51.
41. Edward Said, "Representing the Colonized," *Reflections on Exile*, 305.
42. José Miguez Bonino, *Faces of Latin American Protestantism* (Grand Rapids: Eerdmans, 1997), 109. His usage predates *Empire*, the important work by Michael Hardt and Antonio Negri (Cambridge, MA: Harvard University Press, 2000).
43. Miguez Bonino, *Doing Theology*, 40.
44. José Miguez Bonino, "For Life and against Death: A Theology That Takes Sides," *The Christian Century* 97, no. 26 (November 26, 1980).
45. Of course, imbalances persist *within* the United States church as well.
46. Miguez Bonino, *Doing Theology*, 15.
47. Fernando F. Segovia, "In the World but Not of It: Exile as Locus for Theology of the Diaspora," *Hispanic/Latino Theology: Challenge and Promise*, ed. Ada María Isasi-Díaz and Fernando F. Segovia (Minneapolis: Fortress, 1996), 199.
48. Ibid.
49. Ibid., 200.
50. Miguez Bonino, *Doing Theology*, 15.
51. Although beyond the scope of this paper, diaspora theology could also be applied in relationship to the dynamics of center and periphery that exist within US Methodism (both within the UMC and in Pan-Methodist discussions). The ongoing power imbalances between the dominant segment of the church and ethnic-minority churches demonstrate similar dynamics, even as the Church seeks to repent of its racism.
52. Segovia, 203.
53. Ibid., 203.
54. Final Report of the World Division Latin America Task Force, 7. COSMOS, UMC Archives 1336-1-5:05 (Madison, NJ).
55. As of the writing of this essay, when "Latin America" is entered into the UM News Service search engine, 200 "hits" appear; if one types in

"Africa," 1,463 "hits" are listed. Even if the listings for "South America" (34) and "Central America" (57) are included, the attention given to the region is minimal by comparison to Africa. Other raw numbers that might suggest an imbalance include "Argentina" (69), "Bolivia" (41), and "Guatemala" (47) versus Congo (276), "Liberia" (334), "Angola" (185), and "Ivory Coast"—which seeks to become a central conference—(34). Although these raw numbers are unscientific and unsophisticated, they nonetheless seem to imply a trend deserving further study.

56. In fact, Robbins's suggestion is very similar to that offered by J. Robert Martin, in his memo to the Council of Bishops on "Restructuring the Methodist Church," dated February 27, 1967. COSMOS, UMC Archives 1335-1-5:36 (Madison, NJ).

57. See Elaine A. Robinson, "Restructuring The United Methodist Church in an Age of Empire," occasional paper, General Board of Higher Education and Ministry of The United Methodist Church (2008).

58. Michael Wacht, "A Letter Written Oct. 20 by Methodist Bishops," United Methodist News Service (November 28, 2001).

59. Ibid.

60. Final Report of the World Division Latin America Task Force, 2. COSMOS, UMC Archives 1336-1-5:05 (Madison, NJ).

61. Ibid., 19.

62. Miguez Bonino, *Doing Theology*, 17.

63. Edward Said, "Reflections on Exile," *Reflections on Exile*, 185.

64. On the rise of Southern Christianity, see Philip Jenkins, *The Next Christendom* (Oxford: Oxford University Press, 2002).

65. Joerg Rieger and John Vincent, *Methodist and Radical*. See also Catherine Keller et al., eds., *Postcolonial Theologies: Empire and Divinity* (Chalice Press, 2004).

10. Prophetic Grace

1. I dedicate this chapter to Russell Richey, whose vision inspired this book and whose lifelong commitment to living in and researching the Methodist theological traditions has influenced multiple generations.

2. Randy L. Maddox, *Responsible Grace*. Many have affirmed Maddox's rubric of "responsible grace" for Wesley's theological core. One example of work built upon this interpretive frame is John B. Cobb, Jr., *Grace and Responsibility: Wesleyan Theology for Today* (Nashville: Abingdon, 1995).

3. For the biblical concepts of grace, see "Gnade" I. Altes Testament (H. G. Reventlow), II. Judentum (R. Goldenberg), III. Neues Testament (E. Ruckstuhl), IV. Dogmengeschichtlich (W.-D. Hauschild), and V. Neuezeit/Systematisch-Theologie (K. Otte) in Gerhard Müller, Horst Balz, Gerhard Krause, eds., *Theologische Realenzyklopädie*, 13 (Berlin: De Gruyter, 1984), 459–511.

4. A similar communal emphasis is found in many monastic movements and early Protestant communities, such as Calvin's Geneva or European Anabaptist communities. The sense of mutual support and accountability in the early Methodist movement points to dimensions of prophecy and ways of being prophetic people that have not been fully highlighted in the Wesleyan studies but are suggestive for Christian practice in the present, especially in the face of rapid global change.

5. We are aware of the complexity in definitions and claims about prophecy. Walter Brueggemann explains that "the general phenomenon of prophecy is enormously diverse in its many manifestations," and thus "extreme caution should be used when attempting any generalization on biblical prophecy." See Brueggemann, *Theology of the Old Testament: Testimony, Dispute, Advocacy* (Minneapolis: Fortress, 1997), 622; cf. Lester L. Grabbe, *Priests, Prophets, Diviners, and Sages: A Socio-historical Study of Religious Specialists in Ancient Israel* (Valley Forge, PA: Trinity Press International, 1995), 66–118.

6. David B. Wyrtzen, "The Theological Center of the Book of Hosea," *Bibliotheca Sacra* 141 (1984): 325.

7. Abraham J. Heschel, *The Prophets: An Introduction* (New York: Harper Colophon Books, 1962), 12.

8. Susannah Heschel, introduction to the Perennial Classics Edition, *The Prophets*, by Abraham Joshua Heschel (New York: HarperCollins, 2001), xviii.

9. Alexander Rofé, *Introduction to the Prophetic Literature* (Sheffield, England: Sheffield Academic Press, 1997), 56–73. Rofé notes that descriptions of God's ways of communicating with prophets are quite varied, and many of the prophetic texts omit any reference to enthusiasm, or communication via God's Spirit. This complexity bears some resonance with the Wesleyan trust of prophecy, alongside suspicion or hesitation regarding enthusiasm (discussed later in this chapter).

10. One example of Wesley's willingness to stand apart is his defense of the second- and third-century Montanists, whom leaders of the early church had condemned for their enthusiasm, ecstatic prophecy, and apocalyptic, ascetic tendencies. Wesley also gave credence to a controversial book about the Montanists, written in his day. See Wesley's Journal (August 15, 1750), in *Journals and Diaries*, ed. W. Reginald Ward and Richard P. Heitzenrater, vols. 18–24 of *The Bicentennial Edition of the Works of John Wesley* (Nashville: Abingdon Press, 1988–2006), 20:356–57; hereafter *Works*. Similarly, Wesley defended the fifteenth-century "heretic" Savonarola, who was excommunicated for his apocalyptic and prophetic ways. See "A Letter to the Lord Bishop of Gloucester," in *The Appeals to Men of Reason and Religion and Certain Related Open Letters*, ed. Gerald R. Cragg, vol. 11 of *The Oxford [now Bicentennial] Edition of the Works of John Wesley* (Oxford: Clarendon Press, 1975), 11:505; hereafter *Works*. On the other hand, Wesley did not hesitate to critique political figures from time to time, as in his critique of the late King of Prussia. See Journal (May 3, 1789), *Works*, 24:132–33. In addition, Wesley spoke and wrote freely on such public issues as the revolution of the American colonies, the horrors of slavery, and so forth. See "A Calm Address to Our American Colonies," 11:80–90, *Works* (Jackson). See also "A Calm Address to the Inhabitants of England," *Works* (Jackson), 11:129–40; "Thoughts upon Liberty" (February 24, 1772), *Works* (Jackson), 11:34–46; "Some Observations on Liberty," *Works* (Jackson), 11:91–118; and "Thoughts upon Slavery," *Works* (Jackson), 11:59–79. A quite different example of Wesley's willingness to stand against the community comes in his occasional comments on his preaching or writing. Rather than dodge controversy, he finds disagreement to be inevitable if one is to be faithful to Scripture; at times, it may even be a good sign of a person's faithfulness. See Journal (February 26, 1738), *Works*, 18:226–27, and Sermon 40, "Christian Perfection," in *Works*, 2:99–121, esp. 120–21. In the 1738 journal entry, Wesley draws an explicit connection among

truth-telling, pleasing God, and giving offense: "I believe it pleased God to bless that first sermon most, because it gave most offence."

11. One introduction to this problem is found in David L. Petersen, *The Prophetic Literature: An Introduction* (Louisville: Westminster John Knox, 2002), 1–4. See also Petersen, *The Roles of Israel's Prophets* (Sheffield: Journal for the Study of the Old Testament Supplement Series, 17, 1981); Gerhard von Rad, *The Message of the Prophets* (New York: Harper & Row, 1965); Walter Brueggemann, *The Prophetic Imagination* (Philadelphia: Fortress, 1978); John F. A. Sawyer, *Prophecy and the Biblical Prophets* (New York: Oxford University Press, 1993); O. Streck, *The Prophetic Books and Their Theological Witness* (St. Louis: Chalice, 2000); Walter Brueggemann, *Texts That Linger, Words That Explode: Listening to Prophetic Voices*, ed. Patrick D. Miller (Minnesota: Fortress, 2000).

12. Petersen, *The Prophetic Literature*, 5; David L. Petersen, *The Role of Israel's Prophets*, 35–69; Walter Brueggemann, *The Prophetic Imagination*; John F. A. Sawyer, *Prophecy and the Biblical Prophets*.

13. Jacobus A. Naudé, "חָזָה (ḥāzā)," in *New International Dictionary of Old Testament Theology & Exegesis*, 2:60.

14. Jacobus A. Naudé, "רָאָה (rā'â)," in *NIDOTTE*, 3:1109.

15. John Wesley, "An Earnest Appeal to Men of Reason and Religion," in *John Wesley*, ed. Albert C. Outler, 386.

16. Ibid., 387, emphasis added.

17. Cf. 1 Sam. 2:27; 1 Kgs. 12:22; 13:1; 2 Kgs. 4:1-7, where the "man of God" brings a prophetic word to individuals or the people. See N. P. Bratsiotis in "אִישׁ 'îs'" in G. Johannes Botterweck and Helmer Ringgren, *Theological Dictionary of the Old Testament* (Grand Rapids: Eerdmans, 1974), 1:235.

18. J. Lindblom, *Prophecy in Ancient Israel* (Oxford: Oxford University Press, 1962), 60; quoted by N. P. Bratsiotis in "אִישׁ (îs')" in *TDOT*, 1:234.

19. Frédéric Gangloff, "L'homme d'Elohim ('ish ha-Elohim)," *Biblische Notizen* 100 (1999): 70.

20. Ibid.

21. See "נָבִיא," in Ludwig Koehler and Walter Baumgartner, *The Hebrew and Aramaic Lexicon of the Old Testament* II (Leiden: Brill, 2000), 661–62, and H.-P. Müller, "נָבִיא," in *TDOT*, 9:129–50.

22. Wesley, "The Doctrine of Salvation, Faith and Good Works, Extracted from the Homilies of the Church of England," in Outler, *John Wesley*, 130; cf. 128–33.

23. Bruce C. Birch, *Let Justice Roll Down: The Old Testament, Ethics, and Christian Life* (Louisville, KY: Westminster/John Knox, 1991), 218–21, 176–84; *What Does the Lord Require? The Old Testament Call to Social Witness* (Philadelphia: Westminster, 1985), 68–79.

24. Wesley, Sermon 15, "The Great Assize," §III.5, *Works*, 1:370–71; Sermon 16, "The Means of Grace," §III.9–10, *Works*, 1:388–89; Sermon 33, "Upon Our Lord's Sermon on the Mount—Discourse 13," §Intro. 1–2, *Works*, 1:687–88; "Christian Perfection," §2.29–30, *Works*, 2:120–21; Sermon 66, "The Signs of the Time," §I.2–4, *Works*, 2:523–24; Sermon 104, "On Attending the Church Service," §11, *Works*, 3:468; "Minutes of Some Late Conversations Between the Rev. Mr. Wesleys and Others," Conversation V (June 17, 1747), Q.4, *Works* (Jackson), 8:294; *A Plain Account of Christian Perfection*, *Works* (Jackson),

11:388–89. In "Christian Perfection," one sees characteristic themes of Wesley regarding the fulfilling of prophetic utterance, the call to holiness, God's making these things possible, and love being at the center. Wesley says: "Thus hath the Lord fulfilled the things he spake by his holy Prophets, which have been since the world began; by Moses in particular, saying, 'I will circumcise thine heart, and the heart of thy seed, to love the Lord thy God with all thy heart, and with all thy soul;' by David, crying out, 'Create in me a clean heart, and renew a right spirit within me' " (120–21).

25. John Wesley, Journal (September 6, 1745), *Works*, 20:88–89; "The Life of the Reverend John Wesley," *Works* (Jackson), 5:544; "The Principles of a Methodist," §29–31, *Works*, 9:64–65. Wesley did place more emphasis and confidence in the inward witness of God's Spirit than the more visible and dramatic witness, although he did not exclude the latter from view. See, for example, Letter to Mr. John Smith, *Works*, 26:291–92.

26. A Second Letter to the Author of *The Enthusiasm of Methodists and Papists Compared*, (November 27, 1750?), §7, *Works*, 11:390; A Letter to the Right Reverend the Lord Bishop of Gloucester, §I, *Works*, 11:467–73.

27. "A Farther Appeal to Men of Reason and Religion, Part 1," §V.4, *Works*, 11:141–46. In speaking of Jesus's promise of the Spirit, for example, Wesley says, "And who will assert that this is to be 'interpreted chiefly, if not only, of the apostolical Church?' " (11:142). Wesley was insistent that people recognize the ongoing work of God's Spirit in their age and into the future. He was able to emphasize the extraordinary gifts of the Spirit in apostolic times, but he drew upon patristic sources to support the continuing gifts of the Spirit during ancient times. See A Letter to the Reverend Dr. Conyers Middleton: Occasioned by His Late "Free Inquiry," *Works* (Jackson), 10:8–9, 17–33, 46–57. In making his case, Wesley pointed out to Middleton that the experiences and testimonies of the early fathers were consistent with Matthew, Mark, Joel, Peter, and Paul (10:43, 47, 50, 54). Further, Wesley could argue the continuing need for extraordinary gifts by making the case to the Lord Bishop of Gloucester that, though " 'the Apostles and first Christians were but infants' " (quoting from Gloucester) and that miracles would cease when Christian life arrived " 'to its full vigour and maturity' " (Gloucester), "that time is not yet come" (Wesley's argument). Wesley added, "I doubt, none that are now alive enjoy more of the vigour and maturity of the Christian life than the very first Christians did" (A Letter to the Lord Bishop of Gloucester, §II, 11:506; cf: 507–8). Thus, Wesley could accept Gloucester's vision of maturity, but could also refute his claim that the church had reached a maturity that rendered extraordinary gifts of the Spirit no longer needed. See also A Letter to the Reverend Dr. Conyers Middleton, *Works* (Jackson), 10:4–6.

28. Journal (January 7, 1763 and February 21, 1763), *Works*, 21:402, 407; "An Answer to the Reverend Mr. Church's Remarks," §III.7, in *The Methodist Societies: History, Nature, and Design*, ed. Rupert E. Davies, *Works*, 9:117; "The Principles of a Methodist Farther Explained," §II.5, *Works*, 9:182. In responding to accusations of the Reverend Mr. Church regarding a woman's enthusiasm, Wesley attributed the woman's strange powers to "the power of the devil," crediting the Spirit of God with "enabling her to strive against the power of the devil and at length restoring peace to her soul" (117).

29. Journal (April 23, 1763), *Works*, 21:408–11; *A Plain Account of Christian Perfection*, 11:406–7. Wesley was disturbed by the ways in which people in

London's Foundery were stirred up by such revelations, and he was critical of those who claimed, permitted, and encouraged them.

30. Journal (March 3, 1788), *Works*, 24:70; Sermon 91, "On Charity," §III.3–4, *Works*, 3:301–3; A Second Letter to the Author of *The Enthusiasm of Methodists and Papists Compared*, *Works*, 11:390; A Letter to the Lord Bishop of Gloucester, §I, 11:468–71. In Wesley's sermon "On Charity," he tells the story of a contemporary prophecy foretold by a member of the society in Flanders. The prophecy (or foretelling) was validated by the military events that followed in Flanders. The man's prediction of an engagement with the French and an injury to himself by "a musket-ball in the calf of his left leg" proved to be totally true. Wesley notes, however, that the person who had foretold the incident, though vindicated by the unfolding of events, allowed the honor to turn his brain: "In a little time he ran stark mad" (3:303). Again, we see Wesley subordinating prophecy to love and worrying about the dangers of prophecy. In another incident, Wesley himself had a future vision. He foretold that Satan would separate him from continued visitation with a soldier awaiting execution. Regarding this incident, Wesley later claims that his foretelling was real, as is the work of God "over all the earth," but he does not claim that sensing the future or seeing the movements of God represents a spirit or gift of prophecy (11:390).

31. A Letter to the Lord Bishop of Gloucester, §II, 11:503–4. Wesley agrees with the Lord Bishop of Gloucester that, in antiquity, the Holy Spirit wrought dramatic changes in people; however, he goes beyond Gloucester, not willing to discredit some that the Bishop has discredited, such as Savonarola (505). Most radically, Wesley argues that the Holy Spirit continues to work in his day, for the Church is not yet fully mature or established (506–8).

32. Sermon 17, "The Circumcision of the Heart," §2.9–10, *Works*, 1:413–14; Sermon 22, "Sermon on the Mount—Discourse 2," §III.1–17, *Works*, 1:499–507; Sermon 91, "On Charity," §II.6, §III.1–11, *Works*, 3:300–306; Journal (April 29, 1789), *Works*, 24:131. In "On Charity," Wesley quotes Dr. Nunes, who commended Paul of Tarsus as "one of the finest writers I have ever read," adding that Paul's single chapter of 1 Cor. 13 "contained the whole of true religion" (3:293).

33. See, for example, "A Farther Appeal to Men of Reason and Religion, Part 1," §IV.1, 11:132–33. In this work, Wesley refers to "sons of God," though his more common language is "children of God."

34. Ibid., 11: 133–34. Here Wesley makes a connection between "faith" in his description of Job's experience and "prophecy" in the description of his dialogue partner. He says, "My words were, 'Hear believing Job declaring his faith: 'I know that my Redeemer liveth.' . . . And all I affirm, you allow. Your own words are, 'God was pleased to bestow upon him a strong assurance of his favour; to inspire him with a prophecy of the resurrection, and that he should have a share in it.'"

35. Wesley, "Earnest Appeal," §9, *Works*, 11:48.

36. Sermon 64, "The New Creation," § 4, *Works*, 2:501–2. See also Sermon 15, "The Great Assize, §III.5–IV.5, 1:370–75.

37. Petersen, *The Prophetic Literature*, 7, 13.

38. Ibid., 39, cf. 37–41.

39. John Wesley spent much energy articulating the qualities of life among the people called Methodist. See especially Wesley, "The Character of a Methodist," *Works* 9:32–46. Likewise, Wesley attended to the nature of Christian life for all Christians and the oneness of the church. See Wesley, "A Plain Account of Genuine Christianity," *John Wesley*, ed. Albert C. Outler, 181–96; Wesley, Sermon 45, "Of the Church," § 3–14, *Works*, 3:47–50; Wesley, "Ought We to Separate from the Church of England?" § II.1–III.2, *Works*, 9:568–73. In recent years, more attention is given to John Wesley's accents on the cosmic dimensions of God's concerns and God's future. See John Wesley, Sermon 60, "The General Deliverance," § I.2–6, *Works* 2:439–42; Wesley, Sermon 62, "The End of Christ's Coming," § I.3, 5, *Works* 2:474–75; Wesley, Sermon 18, "The Marks of the New Birth," *Works* 1:417-430; Wesley, Sermon 45, "The New Birth," *Works* 2:187–201; Wesley, Sermon 4, "Scriptural Christianity," *Works* 1:159–80; Wesley, Sermon 26, "Sermon on the Mount, VI," *Works* 1:572–89; Wesley, Sermon 63, "The General Spread of the Gospel," *Works* 2:485–99.

40. Petersen, *The Prophetic Literature*, 39–41.

41. Ibid., 41–42; Marvin Sweeney, *Isaiah 1-39, with an Introduction to Prophetic Literature*, FOTL 16 (Grand Rapids: Eerdmans, 1996), 17; Alexander Rofé, *Introduction to Prophetic Literature*, 74–80; Y. Gitay, ed., *Prophets and Prophecy*, Semeia Studies (Atlanta: Scholars Press, 1997); Petersen, *The Role of Israel's Prophets*.

42. Wesley, "Justification by Faith," in Outler, *John Wesley*, 201.

43. See, for example, John Wesley, Sermon 60, "The General Deliverance," § I.2–5, *Works* 2:439–41; Wesley, Sermon 62, "The End of Christ's Coming," § III.5–6, *Works* 2:482–84; Wesley, Sermon 18, "The Marks of the New Birth," *Works* 1:417–30; Wesley, Sermon 45, "The New Birth," *Works* 2:187–201; Wesley, Sermon 4, "Scriptural Christianity," *Works* 1:159–80; Wesley, Sermon 26, "Sermon on the Mount, VI," *Works* 1:572–89; Wesley, Sermon 63, "The General Spread of the Gospel," *Works* 2:485–99.

44. "The Doctrine of Original Sin, Part VII," *Works* (Jackson), 9:449–50, 453–55. Wesley actually sees the human enmity toward God as being manifest against "Christ in his prophetic office" (9:453, 454). People continually resist Christ's teaching, both inwardly by the Spirit and outwardly by the word.

45. See one analysis in Edwin M. Schur, *The Awareness Trap: Self-Absorption Instead of Social Change* (New York: McGraw-Hill, 1977, 1976). See an analysis of narcissism and spirituality in S. J. Sandage and S. P. Moe, "Narcissism and Spirituality," in *The Handbook of Narcissism and Narcissistic Personality Disorder: Theoretical Approaches, Empirical Findings, and Treatment*, ed. W. K. Campbell and J. Miller (New York: John Wiley & Sons, 2011), 410–20.

46. Anne Marie Cox, "Phoenix Ascending," *In These Times*, May 13, 2002, 10. These phenomena are described in more detail in Christian Smith's analysis of therapeutic individualism and mass-consumer capitalism in young lives (Smith, with Melinda Lundquist-Denton, *Soul Searching: The Religious and Spiritual Lives of American Teenagers* (Oxford: Oxford University Press, 2005). See also Christian Smith and Michael O. Emerson, with Patricia Snell, *Passing the Plate: Why American Christians Do Not Give Away More Money* (Oxford: Oxford University Press, 2008); Katherine Turpin, *Branded: Adolescents Converting from Consumer Faith* (Cleveland, OH: Pilgrim, 2006).

47. Samuel Oliner and Pearl Oliner, *Embracing the Other* (New York: New York University, 1995), 375–76, 386.

48. See one analysis in Leonard William Doob, *Inevitability: Determinism, Fatalism, and Destiny* (New York: Greenwood, 1988), 5–6, 33–38. In social theories of primordialism, the determinism is defined as a weighty influence of early cultures on present ones, thus ascribing permanence to certain ethnic or national differences. The deterministic influence may be defined as biological, social, or geographic, but always in a primordial sense, or as a reality given in creation.

49. Chitra Golestani, "Teaching for Social Justice and Global Citizenship" (PhD diss., University of California at Los Angeles, 2006), 7–9. Dr. Golestani's dissertation presents the full range of her research with teachers.

50. Robert Jay Lifton, *The Protean Self: Human Resilience in an Age of Fragmentation* (New York: Basic Books, 1993), 160–77, 187–89.

51. Viktor E. Frankl, *Man's Search for Meaning* (New York: Washington Square Press/Pocket Books, 1984, 1959), 55–56.

52. See, for example, Shmuel Noah Eisenstadt, *Fundamentalism, Sectarianism, and Revolution: The Jacobin Dimension of Modernity* (New York: Cambridge University, 1999), 82–103.

53. Ibid., 101.

54. Rene Girard, *Violence and the Sacred*, trans. Patrick Gregory (Baltimore: The Johns Hopkins University Press, 1977); *The Scapegoat*, trans. Yvonne Frecerro (Baltimore: The Johns Hopkins University Press, 1986); *Things Hidden Since the Foundation of the World*, with Jean-Michel Ourgoulian and Guy Lefort, trans. Stephen Bann and Michael Metteer (Stanford: Stanford University Press, 1987); *Job: The Victim of His People*, trans. Yvonne Frecerro (Stanford: Stanford University Press, 1987).

55. Mark I. Wallace and Theophus H. Smith, eds., *Curing Violence* (Sonoma, CA: Polebridge Press, 1994); Gil Bailie, *Violence Unveiled: Humanity at the Crossroads* (New York: Crossroad, 1995); R. Scott Appleby, *The Ambivalence of the Sacred: Religion, Violence, and Reconciliation* (Lanham, MD: Rowman and Littlefield, 2000); Mary Elizabeth Moore, "Beyond Poverty and Violence: An Eschatological Vision," *International Journal of Practical Theology* 7, no. 1 (Summer 2003): 39–59.

56. Steven Levy, *Starting from Scratch: One Classroom Builds Its Own Curriculum* (Heinemann, 1996), 184–85; Levy, "The Power of Audience," *ASCD Educational Leadership* 66, no. 3 (November 2008): 75–79.

57. See, for example, Jay Newman, *Competition in Religious Life* (Waterloo, Ontario: Canadian Corporation for Studies in Religion, Wifrid Laurier University, 1989).

58. Robert Jay Lifton, *Destroying the World to Save It: Aum Shinrikyo, Apocalyptic Violence, and the New Global Terrorism* (New York: Henry Holt and Company, Metropolitan Books, 1999). This is one example of psycho-historical work on this phenomenon, tracing the internal and external dynamics that contribute to a violent escalation of competitive behavior.

59. Eisler, *Tomorrow's Children* (Boulder, CO: Westview, 2000), 25. See also David W. Johnson, *Cooperation and Competition: Theory and Research* (Edina, MN: Interaction Book Co., 1989).

60. Lifton, *The Protean Self*, 213–32.

61. Isabel Carter Heyward, *The Redemption of God: A Theology of Mutual Relation* (Washington, D.C.: University Press of America, 1982).

62. Frankl, *Man's Search for Meaning*, 170.

63. Viktor E. Frankl, *The Unheard Cry for Meaning* (New York: Washington Square Press/Pocket Books, 1985, 1978), 58.

64. Interpretations of these texts vary, as in the interpretation of Eph. 5:21-33, in which Paul follows the instruction for wives to be obedient to their husbands with an injunction for husbands to love their wives. Similarly, the instruction for servants to be obedient to their masters is followed by an injunction for masters to be good to their servants (Eph. 6:9). Even allowing for complexity in the texts and their interpretations, one cannot escape Paul's advocacy for unequal and submissive relationships. Such texts reveal the ambiguity of the radicality in early church teachings and practice. To the texts, we could add Col. 3 with its mixed messages, though the authorship of Colossians is contested and the context of the sayings is somewhat different.

65. See, for example, Elisabeth Schussler-Fiorenza, *Jesus: Miriam's Child Sophia's Prophet—Critical Issues in Feminist Christology* (New York: Continuum, 1994), 93–94; Dominic Crossan, *Historical Jesus: The Life of a Mediterranean Jewish Peasant* (San Francisco: HarperSanFrancisco, 1991), 261–64, 293–95.

66. Elisabeth Schussler-Fiorenza, *In Memory of Her: A Feminist Theological Reconstruction of Christian Origins* (New York: Crossroad, 1994, 1983), xlv–liv, xxvi–xxxv, 3–40; Kathleen E. Corley, *Women and the Historical Jesus: Feminist Myths of Christian Origins* (Santa Rosa, CA: Polebridge, 2002); Corley, "Slaves, Servants and Prostitutes: Gender and Social Class in Mark," in *A Feminist Companion to Mark*, ed. Amy-Jill Levine, with Marianne Blickenstaff (Sheffield: Sheffield Academic Press, 201), 191–221; Vincent Wimbush, *The Bible and African Americans: A Brief History* (Minneapolis, MN: Fortress, 2003).

67. Schussler-Fiorenza, *In Memory of Her*, xxvi–xxxv. Schussler-Fiorenza introduces these themes in the original edition of her book, but she engages in an explicit dialogue with those who have raised questions about her method in this "Introduction to the Tenth Anniversary Edition." In her view, the study of Christian origins requires the critical recovery of anti-patriarchal alternates to kyriarchy, both for adequate reading of the texts and for heuristic reasons.

68. Schussler-Fiorenza, *Jesus: Miriam's Child Sophia's Prophet*, 27.

69. Schussler-Fiorenza, *The Book of Revelation: Justice and Judgment* (Minneapolis: Augsburg/Fortress, 1998), 182–99; cf. 25–26.

70. Fiorenza, *Discipleship of Equals: A Critical Feminist Ekklesia-ology of Liberation* (New York: Crossroad, 1993).

71. One finds similar emphases in Tex Sample, *The Future of John Wesley's Theology: Back to the Future with the Apostle Paul* (Eugene, OR: Cascade Books, 2012); Kenneth J. Collins, *The Theology of John Wesley: Holy Love and the Shape of Grace* (Nashville: Abingdon, 2007); Theodore R. Weber, *Politics in the Order of Salvation: Transforming Wesleyan Political Ethics* (Nashville: Kingswood Books, Abingdon, 2001); Manfred Marquardt, *John Wesley's Social Ethics* (Nashville: Abingdon, 1992); Theodore W. Jennings, Jr., *Good News to the Poor: John Wesley's Evangelical Economics* (Nashville: Abingdon, 1990); José Miguez Bonino, "Wesley's Doctrine of Sanctification from a Liberationist Perspective," *Salvation and Liberation: Liberation Theologies in Light of the Wesleyan Tradition*, ed. Theodore Runyon (Nashville: Abingdon, 1981), 49–63.

72. Peter Grassow, "John Wesley and Revolution: A South African Perspective," *Rethinking Wesley's Theology*, ed. Randy L. Maddox (Nashville: Kingswood Books, Abingdon, 1998), 188–93; cf. 183–95.
73. Ibid., 194.
74. Ibid., 194–95.
75. Ibid., 195.
76. Theodore H. Runyon, *The New Creation*.
77. Mary Elizabeth Moore, "God's Spirit and the Renewal of Creation: Living in Committed, Ambiguous Hope," *Quarterly Review* 21, no. 2 (Summer 2001): 169–81; "New Creation: Repentance, Reparation, and Reconciliation," in *Wesleyan Perspectives on the New Creation*, ed. M. Douglas Meeks, 93–117.
78. Oduyoye, "Christianity and African Culture," *International Review of Mission* 84, no. 332–33 (Jan.-Apr. 1995): 77–90.
79. Keith Hunte, "Protestantism and Slavery in the British Caribbean," in *Christianity in the Caribbean: Essays on Church History*, ed. Armando Lampe (Barbados: University of the West Indies Press, 2001), 101–2.
80. Ibid.
81. Ibid., 114–15.
82. *The Book of Discipline of The United Methodist Church, 2008*, §161F, 304.3, 341.6 (Nashville: The United Methodist Publishing House, 2008), 103–4, 206, 253. One does find some attempt at respect in the same volume, with a focus on equal rights. I would argue, however, that the church's basic discriminatory language and policies are themselves violations of human rights, or at least invitations for violations in other settings. See *The Book of Discipline*, §162J, 111–12.
83. José Míguez Bonino, "Wesley in Latin America: A Theological and Historical Reflection," in Maddox, *Rethinking Wesley's Theology*, 177; cf. 169–82.
84. Ibid., 178.
85. A fuller analysis of repentance is found in Mary Elizabeth Moore, "New Creation: Repentance, Reparation, and Reconciliation."
86. Wesley, *A Plain Account of Christian Perfection*, *Works* (Jackson) 11:394; cf. "Brief Thoughts on Christian Perfection," ibid., 446; 1763 Letter to Mrs. Maitland, *Works* (Jackson) 12:257.
87. Míguez Bonino, 179.

www.ingramcontent.com/pod-product-compliance
Lightning Source LLC
Chambersburg PA
CBHW011744290426
44113CB00017BA/2643